Case Studies on the Labor Process

Case Studies on the Labor Process

edited by Andrew Zimbalist

Monthly Review Press
New York and London

Copyright © 1979 by Andrew Zimbalist
All rights reserved

Library of Congress Cataloging in Publication Data

Main entry under title:
Case studies on the labor process.
  Bibliography: p. 299
  1. Labor and laboring classes—United States—
Case studies. 2. Machinery in industry—United
States—Case studies. 3. Division of labor—
Case studies. 4. Industrial sociology—Case
studies. I. Zimbalist, Andrew S.
HD8072.C29   301.44'42'0973   79-22728
ISBN 0-85345-518-X
ISBN 0-85345-519-8 pbk.

Monthly Review Press
62 West 14th Street, New York, N.Y. 10011
47 Red Lion Street, London WC1R 4PF

Manufactured in the United States of America

10 9 8 7 6 5 4 3 2 1

Contents

Introduction
   Andrew Zimbalist   xi

The Industrialization of Computer Programming:
From Programming to "Software Production"
   Philip Kraft   1

Social Choice in Machine Design:
The Case of Automatically Controlled
Machine Tools
   David F. Noble   18

Proletarianizing Clerical Work:
Technology and Organizational Control
in the Office
   Evelyn Nakano Glenn and Roslyn L. Feldberg   51

Carpentry: The Craft and Trade
   Bob Reckman   73

Technology and the Labor Process
in the Printing Industry
   Andrew Zimbalist   103

The San Francisco Waterfront:
The Social Consequences of Industrial
Modernization
   Herb Mills   127

Work Relations in the Coal Industry:
The Handloading Era, 1880–1930
   Keith Dix   156

The Labor Process in Coal Mining:
Struggle for Control
   Michael Yarrow   170

Origins of the Assembly Line and Capitalist Control
of Work at Ford
David Gartman 193

Roots of Power: Employers and Workers
in the Electrical Products Industry
Jeremy Brecher 206

Person and Machine in a New England Factory
Susan DiGiacomo Mulcahy and Robert R. Faulkner 228

Insurance: A Clerical Work Factory
Maarten de Kadt 242

Fighting the Piece-Rate System: New Dimensions
of an Old Struggle in the Apparel Industry
Louise Lamphere 257

The Piece Rate: Class Struggle on the Shop Floor.
Evidence from the Costume Jewelry Industry
in Providence, Rhode Island
Nina Shapiro-Perl 277

Bibliography 299

Notes on the Contributors

Jeremy Brecher is the author of *Strike* and co-author of *Common Sense for Hard Times*. He is currently preparing an anthology of materials on work relations, for use in labor education programs, for the Institute for Labor Education and Research in New York.

Maarten de Kadt lives and works in New York City where he teaches economics at Wagner College. He has published articles on the degradation of work and on the prevalence of unsafe working conditions in the United States. A careful analysis of work and production processes, he hopes, will help develop strategies for achieving a better world.

Keith Dix works at the Institute for Labor Studies at the University of West Virginia in Morgantown. He is the author of numerous articles and monographs on the labor process.

Robert R. Faulkner lives in Amherst, Massachusetts, and Los Angeles. At present he is working on a book dealing with occupational careers and social networks among Hollywood film composers.

Roslyn L. Feldberg teaches sociology at Boston University, where she has been active in developing and teaching the Women's Studies Program. As a member of the Women's Research Center of Boston, she has been conducting a study of single parent families, and has written several articles about family life and divorced motherhood.

David Gartman is a graduate student in sociology at the University of California at San Diego. He is currently writing a dissertation on the development of the labor process in the U.S. auto industry, from which this paper is drawn. The theoretical basis of his continuing research on the labor process is found in his paper "Marx and the Labor Process: An Interpretation," *Insurgent Sociologist*, Fall 1978.

Evelyn Nakano Glenn teaches sociology at Boston University. Her main interest is the area of women and work, and she is currently collaborating with Roslyn Feldberg under a National Institute of Mental Health grant. They are studying clerical work, exploring such facets as work consciousness and links between work and family life.

Philip Kraft teaches sociology at the State University of New York at Binghamton. He is the author of *Programmers and Managers: The Routinization of Computer Programming in the United States* (New York: Springer-Verlag, 1977) and is currently working on a study of women and minority men in the computer industry.

Louise Lamphere teaches anthropology at the University of New Mexico in Albuquerque. She is the co-editor of *Women, Culture, and Society* (Stanford: Stanford University Press, 1974).

Herb Mills is presently secretary-treasurer of Local 10 of the International Longshoremen's and Warehousemen's Union. That office, like that of the local's president and business agents, is a full-time, elected position with a one-year term. During his previous fifteen years on the San Francisco waterfront, he served as a business agent in the office he now holds, and in many other capacities. He has a B.A. from the University of Michigan and a Ph.D. from the University of California.

Susan DiGiacomo Mulcahy is a Ph.D. candidate in the Department of Anthropology, University of Massachusetts, Amherst. Her current research examines the problems of class and ethnicity in the changing political context of Catalonia (Spain).

David Noble teaches history at MIT. He is the author of *America by Design: Science, Technology, and the Rise of Corporate Capitalism* (New York: Alfred A. Knopf, 1977), and is a graduate of the course on machine-tool fundamentals at the Lowell Institute School. He is currently engaged in activities with machinists in the UE, IUE, and UAW in an effort to place the issues involving choice in the design and deployment of technology on the agenda of the labor movement.

Bob Reckman earns his living as an itinerant carpenter and builder. His other pastimes include extensive travel, self-directed study, and idle speculation on the relationship between technology, culture, and power. He currently lives in Northampton, Massachusetts.

Nina Shapiro-Perl has taught anthropology and sociology in community colleges for several years. She is presently writing her doctoral thesis for the University of Connecticut on consciousness among women jewelry workers in Providence, where she now lives.

Michael Yarrow is completing a dissertation on the structure of class consciousness of miners in the sociology department at Rutgers. While conducting research for his dissertation he covered the 1977/1978 coal strike for *The Nation, Seven Days*, and WBAI-FM Radio in New York City.

Andrew Zimbalist teaches economics at Smith College and is a research associate at the Labor Relations and Research Center at The University of Massachusetts, Amherst. He is the author of numerous articles on the labor process and is co-author of *Economic Democracy: Workers' Participation in Chilean Industry, 1970–1973* (New York: Academic Press, 1978).

Acknowledgments

The following individuals were extremely helpful to me in the preparation of this collection: Phil Kraft, Stanley Aronowitz, Susan Eckstein, Dave Noble, and Bob Reckman. Lydia Nettler made useful comments on many manuscripts, helping me to decipher the sensible and the pedantic, and provided me with much needed emotional support throughout the project. Susan Lowes skillfully edited the entire collection; much of the essays' readability is attributable to her efforts. My newborn son, Jeffrey, sensed the importance of the project from the beginning and required my attention only twenty hours a day.

Introduction

The essays in this volume derive much of their inspiration from Harry Braverman's by now classic *Labor and Monopoly Capital*. In the foreword, Paul Sweezy wrote:

> In important respects the function of this work is to pose rather than answer questions, to open (or re-open) lines of inquiry which have been neglected and which cry out for research and elaboration. There is hardly an occupation or other aspect of the labor process which would not repay a great deal more detailed historical and analytical investigation than are accorded to it in this broad survey.

The present collection represents an initial effort to meet this challenge.

In *Labor and Monopoly Capital* Braverman provides both a theoretical and empirical basis for undermining the claim that new technology washes away boring, routinized, and dirty jobs and erects in their place interesting, challenging, and clean ones. At the same time, Braverman demonstrates the social bias of technology in capitalist society. The great value of Braverman's contribution is attested to by the abundance of intellectual activity (articles, books, new courses, conferences, study groups, etc.) it has generated.*

To be sure, other factors have contributed to this surge of interest in the labor process. The study of the workplace was largely neglected during the 1960s after a series of important studies in the previous decade (e.g., Baritz, Bell, Bendix, Bright, Chinoy, Gouldner, Mills, Swados, Walker, Walker and Guest). During the 1960s the focus on civil rights and Vietnam consumed the energy of progressive and intellectual forces, while

---

* An ambitious survey of much of the growing body of literature on the labor process is provided by Jeremy Brecher and the Work Relations Group in their essay "Uncovering the Hidden History of the American Workplace" (1978).

economic prosperity reinforced the elusive "American dream" of the working class. The most prominent academic treatment of the labor process was Robert Blauner's *Alienation and Freedom,* which erroneously declared alienation and tedious work to be gradually disappearing with the advent of automated technology.

Material conditions have changed drastically during the 1970s, however, with the loss of international hegemony, slow productivity growth, high unemployment, stagnation of real wages, etc. Vietnam prompted a reevaluation of internal forces, while racism and sexism have been found to be integrally connected to fundamental characteristics of the labor market and the workplace. The continuing growth in levels of educational attainment, along with other factors, has encouraged rising expectations for fulfilling work. The new generation of Ph.D.s, M.A.s, and B.A.s increasingly face the prospect of low wages, routine work, and job instability. Little wonder, then, that the workplace has caught on on the campus.

Theoretical Approaches to the Labor Process

The timeliness as well as the substantive depth of *Labor and Monopoly Capital* has made it the seminal study for current work in the field. As such, it has been the focus of criticism as well as praise. The most common Marxist criticism has been that Braverman ignored or minimized the role of class struggle in forming the labor process. It is contended that as a result capital is portrayed as having uncontested, unilateral control over the labor process; Taylorism and technology are juggernauts introduced at will to subjugate the workforce, etc. The issues must be sorted out. Braverman's book is about the class struggle. Indeed, a central argument of the book is that the antagonism between classes gives rise to the problem of management and the degradation of labor. However, having posed the problem as resulting from class antagonism, Braverman depicts, according to his critics, one class as omnipotent in its effort to resolve the problem. His critics cite the works of Davis, Mathewson, Montgomery (1974), Palmer, Roy, Watson, Whyte, and others that represent the workers in vigorous struggle against Taylorism and rationalization, or they cite the activities of Taylor's disciples or the emergence of the human relations school to show that Taylorism itself was an impractical method of control.*

Braverman was well aware of worker resistance on the shop floor as well as the various modifications of Taylor's basic system, and, in general, the limitations to the capitalist project of controlling the labor process. A close reading of the text or a glance at his references makes this clear. For instance, on page 172 he writes: "The displacement of labor as the subjective element of the process, and its subordination as an objective element in a productive process now conducted by management, is an *ideal realized by capital only within definite limits, and unevenly among industries*" (emphasis mine). It is also clear that Braverman did not place much importance on the fine details or accoutrements of Taylor's system (see, for example, his arguments on pages 26, 87–88, 135–37, and 180n), but rather was concerned with Taylorism as the expression of capitalist management ideology, as well as the reflection of a new division of labor and basic reorganization within the workplace. The fact that management commissions time and motion studies is of interest not because the detailed control of each worker's motions is actually possible, but because it reflects the prevailing ideology in its treatment of the worker as a mechanical machine part. Braverman stresses again and again that the central lesson of Taylorism is the separation of skill and knowledge from the worker in the production process. This ideology is conveniently perpetuated and put into practice by the disguised technical ideology of engineering which emphasizes the importance of continually reducing the scope for human error in the design of production processes (see Noble in this volume).

While it is a relatively simple matter to defy time and motion technicians (see Shapiro-Perl and Lamphere in this volume), it is much more difficult to resist the introduction of new technology. The time and motion study person stands before the worker as a blatant symbol of worker oppression by capital. The machine, however, is a mystified oppressor, often taken to be a neutral artifact of technological society. Although there have been occasional incidents of workers sabotaging machinery in this country, there has never been an effective, self-conscious worker

* Excellent extensions of the discussion of scientific management found in Braverman are available in Nelson (1975:55–78) and Noble (1977:268–77).

struggle to preserve an old, or install a new, technology. Indeed, it is often the case that worker militance hastens the day of the new machinery, as appears to be the case today where machines are displacing organizing and striking migrant farmworkers in picking tough-skinned (and tasteless) tomatoes. The most successful trade union efforts have sometimes delayed new technology and obtained job protection, with attractive buy-out clauses for existing members, but nothing more (see the articles by Mills and Zimbalist in this volume).* Indeed, given the pressures of domestic and international competitive markets, localized worker struggles resisting new technology are more likely to lead to union busting or plant closings than they are to the preservation of worker skills or modified job control.†

The historical wedding of science to industry (at the service of capital) requires a much more fundamental approach to the design and deployment of new technologies (see Noble 1977). Workers must recapture the resources and institutions of technological research. Once designed, of course, workers must have the power to impose new methods of production. No easy matter. It at least implies an entirely different decision-making process, with goals that go beyond simple profit maximization. An intermediate situation is related in David Noble's present essay where the technology retaining worker job skills was available but had been suppressed by capital. However, after extensive internal education and political organizing, and in a society where there is much more of a power parity between labor and capital, Norwegian machinists succeeded in forcing capital to accept the technology which favored workers' control.‡

---

* The prototype of such contracts in this country are the mechanization and modernization (M & M) agreements reached by the longshoremen and stevedore companies in the 1960s. A useful and detailed account of the first M & M agreement can be found in Swados (1962).

The experience of productivity bargaining in England reveals much the same pattern (see Brown 1977). An excellent historical study on the role of labor relations, market structure, and other variables in the slow transition from mule spinning to ring-frame spinning in Great Britain has recently been published by Lazonick (1979).

† Of course, a given technology might allow for various divisions of labor. Here, too, the extent of alteration is constrained by both market forces and the capitalist drive to control the labor process.

‡ It is also interesting to note that over 90 percent of organized workers in

Braverman's theory suggests the generalization that in the long run capital has succeeded in imposing its techniques of control (rationalization and mechanization) over the work process. This position needs no apology. The political implication is not that workers should give up on struggle, but that they should take it more seriously. Short-run, localized, spontaneous, syndicalist responses to the initiatives of capital are ultimately inadequate.

The argument in *Labor and Monopoly Capital* regarding worker skills has also been a source of misunderstanding and a basis for criticism. Kusterer (1976), for instance, has interpreted Braverman to be making a static assertion that the modern worker is deskilled. He purports to undermine Braverman's position by describing how workers in a paper cone factory apply ingenuity and dexterity in carrying out their tasks. Braverman's analysis, however, is historical and dynamic. Briefly, its central thesis regarding skill might be put as follows: There is a long-run tendency through fragmentation, rationalization, and mechanization for workers and their jobs to become deskilled, both in an absolute sense (they lose craft and traditional abilities) and in a relative one (scientific knowledge progressively accumulates in the production process).* Even where the individual worker retains certain traditional skills, the degraded job he or she performs does not demand the exercise of these abilities. Thus, the worker, regardless of his or her personal talents, may be

---

Norway are currently covered by what is known as "the data [processing] agreement." It stipulates that prior to introducing new computer-related technology management must, among other things: give advance notice of its intentions to the workers; describe the new technology and its impact on work in understandable terms to the workers; and include a worker representative in the project group planning the technology. Formal agreements and legislation regarding worker rights to participation in decision making of course assure nothing, as the West European experience with works' councils and co-determination amply demonstrates. It seems, however, that the educational and ideological basis for an effective struggle around the "data agreement" is being built in Norway. See Noble in this volume; also Nygaard (1977).

* Regarding this relative loss of skills, Braverman writes (p. 425): "The more science is incorporated into the labor process, the less the worker understands of this process." The knowledge is removed from the shop floor and concentrated in the production planning offices.

more easily and cheaply substituted for in the production process.

To be sure, mechanization and deskilling of work in one economic sector imply that new processes and techniques are evolving in another (backwardly linked) sector. These new processes and techniques bring with them the demand for workers with new or initially scarce skills. It is not until a later stage of their development that these new processes and techniques become themselves subjected to rationalization, job fragmentation, and mechanization. The tendency to mold all processes according to the principles of mass production "is itself restrained in its application by the nature of the various specific and determinate processes of production" (Braverman 1974:172, 208–11). At any given historical moment, therefore, we would expect to find a distribution of production processes at various levels of rationalization and mechanization. Several of the essays in the present collection illustrate this uneven development. Lamphere makes the point that the highly competitive, small-scale nature of garment production, with its frequent style changes, has made further standardization and mechanization problematic. Shapiro-Perl proposes a similar explanation for the low level of rationalization in jewelry production and the essays by Dix and Yarrow point to a variety of economic, technical, and social features that have retarded the rationalization/mechanization process in coal mining. Although restricted until now, these essays show the direction of technological change in each of these industries is toward deskilling the labor process.

Various detractors have also criticized *Labor and Monopoly Capital* for not adequately dealing with sexism, racism, bureaucratic controls, internal labor markets, systems of pay differentials, runaway shops, etc. That is, Braverman did not present a thorough and comprehensive treatment of all the levers of capitalist control in the workplace. This, of course, is true and Braverman explicitly acknowledged these self-imposed limitations on his study. He chose rather to focus directly upon what has perhaps been the most neglected, misunderstood, and mystified aspect of the labor process: the control over the design and organization of production. Whereas few would maintain that racism, sexism, byzantine bureaucratic controls, and so on, are nature-given features of the workplace, most workers and intellectuals accept the march of technology as inevitable and immutable. Braverman, along with Marglin (1974), Noble (1977), and others, set out to explode this mythology about technology and the design of production.*

Job Degradation or Work Humanization?

The general story told by Braverman, as well as by the present essays, is one of progressive job fragmentation, degradation, and deskilling. This ongoing tendency toward job impoverishment and "worker alienation" is confronted by another tendency—a labor force with higher educational levels and higher expectations for rewarding work. The outcome of this confrontation is often high labor turnover, high absenteeism, and lackadaisical work which, in turn, imply low productivity and low quality. In recent years the job impoverishers have responded to this dilemma with programs of "job enrichment" and "work humanization." Although there is no overall coherence to these programs, and although they still affect only a small portion of workplaces, collectively they have been dubbed the "work humanization movement." What implications does this "movement" have for the thesis of increasing degradation?

In the hands of corporate public relations departments, practically anything passes for work humanization. We shall group this amorphous array of change into four categories: better working conditions, relaxation of work rules, job enlargement, and work teams. The first includes the physical amelioration of the working environment (e.g., new lockers, more vending machines, improved ventilation), sometimes provoked by OSHA standards, sometimes by concern for rising workmen's compensation premiums, sometimes by high absenteeism or turnover. Relaxation of rigid work rules can have varying degrees of significance to the lives of the workers involved. For instance, Eli Chinoy quotes an auto worker who benefitted from more flexible work rules introduced in her factory:

> In last year's auto negotiations, the fuss about what was euphemistically called "time to perform natural functions" struck most people as funny. But for an auto worker nothing could be so grimly serious, so brutally basic, as the guaranteed relief time to go to the toilet. (Cited in Chinoy 1964:64)

* See Schrank (1978:225–27) for a pertinent anecdote on how deeply ingrained, yet artificial, this mythology is, based on his experience with UAW shop stewards and committeemen.

Another, and somewhat more innovative, example of this form of humanization is flextime. Flextime, which to date has mainly affected office workers, allows workers to pick their own starting and finishing times within two-hour limits as long as they do a full day's work. These forms of work humanization unquestionably make work marginally more tolerable for those affected (and, in the process, often serve to also lower absenteeism and turnover), but they do nothing to alter the job itself.

The third type of reform is job enlargement and rotation. Although it may amount to more, job rotation was described by a packer at a British chemical company as follows:

> You move from one boring, dirty, monotonous job to another boring, dirty, monotonous job. And then to another boring, dirty, monotonous job. And somehow you're supposed to come out of it all "enriched." But I never feel enriched—I just feel knackered.
> (Quoted in Nichols and Beynon 1977:16)

Indeed, sometimes workers perceive job enlargement or rotation as a form of speed-up. They would rather perform one routine operation than several routine operations; in the former case at least they can daydream (see Brecher in this volume; also Friedmann 1961:16–17; Garson 1975).

Braverman assessed job enlargement in this way: in many cases the division of labor "has been pursued with such fanaticism that various jobs have been broken into fragments of fragments and can be partially reassembled without injury to the present mode of organizing the work process" (1974:38). This appears to be the case, for instance, at Traveller's Insurance Company, where keypunchers initially punched data as it was given to them even if they detected errors. The errors would come back from the computer and be sent to a second set of workers who did the corrections. Then came enrichment. The keypunchers were allowed to spot and correct errors themselves (Rinehart 1978:16).

Rinehart (1978) notes that "doubling-up," i.e., auto assembly-line workers doing two jobs while one partner rests and then resting while the other partner works, is also a form of job enlargement. But in this case there is the crucial difference that it is job enlargement initiated by the workers, not management. Job enlargement and rotation are not inherently good or bad. It depends on where, why, and how they are introduced.

Another variant of work humanization is the practice of forming work teams. This seems to be one of the main strategies of the Big Three auto companies in their current humanization blitz (see, for instance, McDonald et al. 1977). Despite considerable rank-and-file uneasiness about the co-optive nature of these programs, the Big Three have been able to count on the cooperation of the international leadership of the UAW. However, even the UAW leadership is becoming ambivalent. It seems, as a *quid pro quo* for their continued support of work humanization efforts, the union demanded management's pledge to end their "Southern strategy" of resisting unionization drives in the South.

The Big Three, nevertheless, continue what might be termed their "Southern strategy" inside Detroit. This strategy is guided by the principle: if you can't deskill them, isolate and divide them. This has been effectively applied by the car companies to Detroit's 23,000 tool-and-die makers. Tool-and-die makers, who make the jigs, fixtures, gauges, and dies used by semiskilled machinists to mass-produce metal parts, represent the most skilled group within the increasingly fragmented machinist occupations. The car companies subcontract well over half of their tool-and-die work to small "back alley" shops of ten to twelve workers. The consequence is twofold: first, rather than having to worry about directly managing these highly skilled workers in a few large shops, the marketplace competition disciplines these numerous small shops for the Big Three; second, less than one-quarter of Detroit's tool-and-die shops are unionized. To the extent that these small shops begin to create problems, it is now a relatively mundane procedure to transfer the information on computer tapes (which guide numerically controlled machine tools) from one shop to another in a different city, state, or country.*

---

* The introduction of integrated data-processing systems poses a potentially larger problem to skilled machinists. These systems, *inter alia* allow for: close monitoring of the work performed by each worker through sensing devices which record data on the use and output of each machine; computer simulations to test for the practicability of new designs, bypassing the current practice of engineer/machinist cooperation; direct tape production from engineers' drafts; self-compensating machines with automatic maintenance signaling, etc. These changes represent a major threat of job loss and loss of job control to the skilled machinist. The threat has been identified by rank-and-filers of the Independent Skilled Trades Council within the UAW and a campaign to achieve a Norway-type "data agreement" (see above) is underway. (Much of this analysis on the

Perhaps the most heralded effort at using work team methods is the one at Volvo's plant at Kalmar, Sweden, where the traditional assembly line has been replaced with a system of subassembly stations. Computer-controlled dollies move the car from work station to work station. At each station a team of fifteen to twenty workers assemble a "natural unit" (e.g., electrical system, steering mechanism) onto a stationary car body. The team is said to decide upon its internal job assignments each day. The company expects, based on time and motion studies, 12.6 cars to be produced per hour, which means that on the average the dollies stay at each work station just over 4 minutes. Although this pacing is controlled by the computer, the workers have some discretion. They can, for instance, let several car dollies accumulate in a waiting area, which means that they will have to work faster later on. The system has what appear to be two advantages to the workers involved: increased control over and flexibility in the work assignments, and some increased control over the pace of their work. Management expects to benefit from lower absenteeism, lower turnover, and higher quality work (Gyllenhammer 1977). The absenteeism which persists will be more easily absorbed, since each work team is responsible for adjusting work assignments. Management is also counting on happier and more cooperative workers. And just in case workers are less than delighted with the new arrangements, management has constructed the hexagonal Kalmar plant so that each work team has its own plant entrance, locker room, cafeteria, and work area (Rinehart 1978). This, of course, precludes communication between work teams during the day. It is a safe assumption that the plant's designers were not oblivious to the control implications of this physical layout.

The long-run economic and social viability of the Kalmar experiment does not concern us here. Whether or not the Kalmar design survives and is reproduced elsewhere has as much to do with the antagonistic class relations in Sweden as it does with

---

auto industry was suggested in conversations with Harley Shaiken, a Detroit machinist, and David Noble.)

For an interesting glimpse at the future of job loss, job rationalization, and deskilling through the use of microprocessors, see the March 1979 report of the Center For Policy Alternatives at MIT entitled *Microprocessor Applications: Cases and Observations,* prepared for the office of the Chief Scientist, Department of Industry, United Kingdom.

the technical characteristics of the plant. What is interesting about Kalmar for our purposes is that it is a clear illustration that the assembly line is not a technical inevitability.

Although incremental improvements for the workers are sometimes involved, work teams and worker participation schemes have the intention of rechanneling worker militance and providing a false sense of worker identification with the enterprise. In nonunionized plants, their goal is to keep the unions out (T. Mills 1975:126). Job enrichment programs are invariably introduced top-down and all stimuli are management controlled. No change in power relations within the company is ever contemplated. However, in a dozen or so cases the initial modification of the experiment unleashed a degree of worker involvement and enthusiasm that could not be contained. Power relations began to change and, despite their economic success, the experiments were quickly terminated by management (see Noble in this volume; also Espinosa and Zimbalist 1978:21–24; K. Friedan 1978:36–38; R. Schrank 1978:219–21).

Andrew Friedman, in his book *Industry and Labor* (1977), offers a theoretical revision of Marx and Braverman. He argues that there are two basic and opposed types of management strategies for dealing with labor: "direct control" (basically Taylorism) and "responsible autonomy" (the opposite, e.g., work teams or gangs with more decision-making autonomy). He thus differs from Braverman, who argues that Taylor's basic principles define the fundamentals of organization of the labor process and that the human relations and work humanization schools (which correspond to Friedman's "responsible autonomy") simply deal with "worker adaptation to the ongoing production process as that process was designed by the industrial engineer" (Braverman, 1974:86). The difference, then, is in their interpretation of the relative significance of work humanization strategies. Braverman subsumes work humanization to the basic strategy of control, seeing it as only a short-run and often cosmetic variation. Friedman reifies it as an entirely different approach to organizing the labor process. Although it often seems that certain experiments with work teams have progressed far enough in generating team autonomy to warrant being labeled a different strategy, it is precisely these "significant" examples that have been terminated due to their threat to management control. Whereas work humanization experiments often derive from worker dissatisfaction and resistance, they can also reinforce them, causing management to revert to the basic strategy with a vengeance. This was in fact the case at Standard Car Company in Coventry, Friedman's major example of "responsible autonomy." Friedman is more on the mark at another point when he writes: "[The] ideal [of the responsible autonomy strategy] is to have workers behave as though they were participating in a process which reflected their own needs, abilities and wills . . ." (1977:101).

If management were genuinely interested in job enrichment, it could begin by ending its vehement opposition to labor law reform in this country. Neither the U. S. Constitution, nor any existing labor statute, grants workers the right of free speech in the private sector. If a worker, for instance, were to tell the press about an unsafe product being made in his or her factory, the employer could legally dismiss him or her. Nor are workers innocent until proven guilty. When an employer discharges a worker, he or she doesn't stay on the job until the grievance is arbitrated. He or she is off work and loses pay in the interim (Lynd 1978:11). In most companies, even where there is a strong union, the chances of worker success in grievance arbitration are very low (see, for example, Spencer 1977). Work humanization, then, should begin at the beginning with new labor laws which give the worker inside the workplace the same rights as he or she has outside the workplace.*

The papers in this collection cover a broad spectrum of industries and trades in the U. S. economy. Taken together, they highlight some important differences and similarities in the labor process and in its transformation. We begin, somewhat arbitrarily, with Philip Kraft's essay on the industrialization of computer programming because the computer is at the center of

---

* The repeal of certain existing labor laws is equally vital. Section 301 of Taft-Hartley, for instance, makes a collective bargaining agreement legally enforceable. An employer can thereby sue the union for contract violation, providing a strong incentive to the union leadership to restrain and discipline its rank and file. There is nothing inevitable about this. In Great Britain, collective bargaining contracts are not legally enforceable (Lynd 1978:22).

Recent Supreme Court decisions have further weakened legal protection for U. S. workers in this era of job enrichment (see Lynd 1976). One flagrant example is the Court's decision of May 23, 1978, ruling that OSHA inspectors must obtain search warrants before conducting safety inspections.

most modern-day workplace reorganization. The essay details how this industry, which has contributed to the deskilling of work throughout the economy, is itself being affected by occupational fragmentation and deskilling. Kraft uncovers an interesting, but not surprising, relationship between women's work and the deskilling process in computer programming, a theme that reappears in other essays (Glenn and Feldberg, Brecher, Mulcahy and Faulkner, Lamphere, de Kadt, Shapiro-Perl).

In the next essay, David Noble discusses technological change in the machine-tool industry. He argues that automatically controlled machine tools were developed in a certain mold in part to assert greater management control over the labor process, an effort fraught with impediments. He concludes with a discussion of an alternative automatically controlled machine-tool system which would preserve the skills of the operator.

Evelyn Glenn and Roslyn Feldberg examine the changing condition of clerical work in several types of small and large organizations. They observe a general, although uneven, trend toward proletarianization of clerical work and argue that certain efficiency-oriented work reorganization engenders new inefficiencies.

Bob Reckman traces the gradual diminution of the craft and trade of the carpenter. These developments are shown to be integrally related to technological change and the changing market environment. My own essay depicts the traditional craft nature of work and job control in the printing trades and sketches the process of craft destruction over time. Herb Mills discusses the transformation and degradation of the labor process, labor relations, and social relations in longshoring work that have been wrought by containerization.

Keith Dix's essay deals with the labor process in coal mining up to 1930, and Michael Yarrow's updates the analysis to the present. Dix relates early coal operator (owner) efforts to rationalize and mechanize, emphasizing handloading as the major constraint to further rationalization and deskilling. Yarrow shows how many subsequent constraints stood in the way of the coal operators' attempts to dominate the labor process.*

David Gartman tells the story of the prototype of mass pro-

---

* Dix and Yarrow actually differ somewhat in their interpretation of the skill levels necessary for certain tasks, a difference left for future research to clarify.

duction, the Ford assembly line at Highland Park, Michigan. Jeremy Brecher gives an overview of the labor process and labor relations in the electrical products industry.

The final four essays are all firsthand, ethnographic accounts of the labor process in various workplaces. Susan Mulcahy and Robert Faulkner present a theory of worker "individuation" as management's strategy for obtaining control over production in a major brush factory. Maarten de Kadt describes the deskilling of the insurance worker and other mechanisms for controlling clerical work in the insurance industry. Finally, Louise Lamphere and Nina Shapiro-Perl offer historical and ethnographic evidence of the struggle around the piece rate in the apparel and jewelry industries.

These papers provide concrete examples of the interaction of workers, managers, and technology in a wide variety of work settings and offer a grounding for the broad generalizations and theoretical discussions that have emerged in response to Braverman's book. Ultimately, a better understanding of the issues involved will help to promote a broad-based recognition of the need and possibilities for overhauling the progressively degrading and dehumanizing conditions of the modern workplace.

Case Studies on the Labor Process

The Industrialization of Computer Programming: From Programming to "Software Production"

Philip Kraft

Introduction

Nothing is a more fitting symbol of smoothly running modern capitalism than the computer. Like the market, it appears to operate independently of the people who made it, and has taken on a life of its own. It is the Invisible Hand become corporeal.

In spite of their supernatural image, computers are only machines, if impressively complex ones. Like other machines, they are used in the production process and therefore in the reproduction of social relations. Computers can do nothing—and this must be stressed because of the science-fiction aura surrounding them—unless they are told what to do and how to do it by human beings. Some of the most important of these people are computer programmers. Along with machine operators, who oversee the physical operation of the "hardware," programmers are responsible for a computer's day-to-day operation. In particular, they provide the computer with a detailed sequence of operating instructions, which can be in any one of a large and growing number of program "languages." Without these human-entered instructions—the "programs"—the most advanced computers would sit dumb and idle and useless. Programming work is exact and exacting: a single design (logic) error, a single clerical error, will cause an otherwise perfectly constructed program to malfunction. Programming, in short, is simultaneously meticulous, tedious, and demands a wide if not easily defined grasp of logic, mathematics, electronics, and usually a substantive field as well.

The nature of the work places programmers at the center of an on-going debate about the effects of technology on jobs and

---

I have received a great deal of help from Ronald Anderson, John Harris, Jeylen Mortimer, Joseph Weitzenbaum, Andrew Zimbalist, and Nancy Zimmet. I have also benehted in a very special way from ongoing conversations, some continuing for several years, with Ken Fox, David Noble, and Richard Sharpe.

work. Management writers, including various species of "futurologists," always herald the development of the latest labor-saving technology as a boon for the working class as well as for the capitalists who use it. The argument can invariably be reduced to this: new, more complex technology will benefit workers because it displaces unskilled and tedious labor. In its place, such technology provides new jobs, often related to the production of the new technology itself, jobs that are more skilled, less tedious, and offer greater occupational ("mobility") opportunities. Perhaps the most well-known statement of this position was made by Robert Blauner in his *Alienation and Freedom* (1964).

Sanguine assessment of technology's impact on work and jobs has always been challenged, but never with more effect than in Harry Braverman's remarkable *Labor and Monopoly Capital* (1974). Braverman's conclusions are too well known to require discussion, but it is useful to summarize a few of the most important: a basic *social* function of the most skilled members of the work force—engineers, scientists, technicians, managers, and so on—is to design machines, technologies, and work processes to deskill other workers; deskilling has been accomplished through the routinization and simplification of the work tasks themselves; and, contrary to the claims of the technology boosters, deskilling and degradation have been the goal in introducing new technology, not merely an unfortunate and minor by-product. In short, technology has been used to destroy skilled work and replace it with unskilled work, rather than the other way around.

Under these circumstances, programmers are in the belly of the beast. They are both the creations and the agents of the most spectacular technology yet, which in a generation has launched a transformation of the entire production process. The industry itself, in fact, is fully aware of its center-stage role and systematically exploits the propaganda opportunities—an excellent example is International Business Machines' advertising slogan: "Machines should work, people should think."

Programmers, then, can be considered a litmus-paper test of the skill-upgrading claims made for the new technologies. To what extent is their work challenging, rewarding, skilled and, perhaps most important of all, more secure than the jobs that computer technology has displaced?

Early Programming

Computing as a whole is still relatively young, and there is an understandable tendency to exaggerate its newness and ignore its immediate predecessors. Such historical nearsightedness in turn reinforces popular notions of computers and the people who make them work. The result has been an image, inside as well as outside the industry, of modern-day wizards who have materialized out of the future, charting unknown paths rather than following old ones.

The reality is considerably different. Computer programmers, along with most other computer workers, have a very real history, even a relatively long one, reaching as far back as some eighteenth-century artisans. Modern computer programming, however, was the accidental and largely unloved offspring of electrical engineering. Electrical engineers under contract to the United States Army built the first operational computer, the ENIAC, during World War II. Originally proposed to calculate shell trajectories, it was actually first used to perform some of the complex calculations required by the Manhattan Project.

The making of the ENIAC was possibly electrical engineering's most spectacular triumph. While the project was squarely within the purview of the occupation, nothing of its scope had ever been undertaken before. The wartime context added an urgency to the technical adventure associated with designing and building the machine. Herman Goldstine, the mathematician who oversaw the project for the Army, recalls that project leaders as well as engineers were convinced that the most important task was to build the ENIAC and get it to work properly. Providing it with operating instructions was considered hardly more than a clerical detail that would take care of itself at the last minute (Herman Goldstine, interview). Others involved in the ENIAC project confirm Goldstine's recollections.* The preoccupation with the "hardware" more or less guaranteed that programming the machine would be an afterthought.

An indication of just how unimportant programming was

---

* In conjunction with a current study of women in computing, I have interviewed several of the original ENIAC engineers and programmers. Readers who know of any of these individuals are asked to send me their names and addresses, or to send mine to them.

considered to be can be gotten from the people selected to be the programmers. They were a group of about one hundred young women, most of whom had in fact been hired to perform the shell trajectory calculations using mechanical calculating machines. Most were just out of college, and they had had no training but displayed a general aptitude for mathematics. The shell trajectory calculations were considered clerical and therefore "women's work," as the clerical-like task of programming the ENIAC was expected to be.* And so the "ENIAC girls" became the world's first computer programmers largely as a result of a serious miscalculation as to the skills involved and the traditional sexism in the engineering workplace.

What took place in 1944–1945 undoubtedly surprised the engineers. Programming the computer required familiarity with the machine's electrical logic, its physical structure, and its mechanical operation. The women learned by crawling around the ENIAC's massive frame, locating burnt-out vacuum tubes, shorted connections, and other nonclerical "bugs." In a matter of months they devised the programs required to perform the atom bomb calculations; they then turned their efforts to the shell trajectory calculations—all before the machine was officially unveiled in 1946.

The ENIAC experience changed the engineers' attitudes toward programming. "Software"—the overall design and detailed sequence of program instructions—was now viewed as the inseparable complement of hardware. The machine could do nothing without appropriate instructions in a format the hardware could accept. In a primitive machine like the ENIAC, which was essentially a collection of electronic switches, instructions had to be prepared in "machine language," which specified the state of every switch (i.e., whether the switch was "on" or "off") used in a given calculation or machine operation. To be a machine-language programmer, then, meant to be comfortable with abstract logic, mathematics, electrical circuits, and machines, as well as some substantive field, such as aerodynamics or cost accounting. When this was realized, programming was transformed into something akin to black magic, or at least into work which was considered intellectually demanding and even "artistic"; it also stopped being women's work. It is one of the ironies of programming that women pioneered in the occupa-

* Ironically, their official job classification was "computer."

tion, largely by accident, only to make it attractive to men once the work was redefined as creative and important.* The further irony, however, as we shall see, is that the men who followed the women pioneers—and effectively eased them out of the industry—eventually had their work reduced into something that was genuinely like clerical labor. It was at this point that women were allowed to reenter the occupation they had created.

Engineering and the Routinization of Computer Programming

Early "programmer-artists" approached programming as a whole task. They started with a desired outcome—for example, a program to calculate square roots on a particular machine—and the approach and program design, instruction sequence, instruction entry, testing correction ("debugging"), and on-site fixing ("maintenance") were done by the same group of programmers, or even by the same individual. The imprecise and integrated nature of the work was reflected in the terminology that characterized the occupation until about 1960. "Programmer" was an all-inclusive term applied to those responsible for the entire range of activities required to instruct a computer. The lack of more refined and specific titles or qualifiers indicated the absence of a clear-cut division of labor in the programming workplace: every programmer did more or less the same thing as every other programmer.

Computer vendors and buyers looked upon the integrated and highly skilled nature of early programming work, particularly that associated with machine-language programming, as a hindrance to the cheap use of the new machines. While the first computers were, by today's standards, clumsy, slow, and prone to frequent breakdowns, their improved performance and reliability were considered straightforward engineering problems. The "software," on the other hand, was more than an engineering problem: "human error" and "human inefficiency" hindered even the slowest machines.

---

* It is important to stress that programming's transformation from "clerical" work suitable for women into "intellectually demanding" work appropriate for men was merely a definitional change, and which came about when the new computer industry belatedly recognized programming's importance.

From the perspective of the manufacturers, the computer's potential could be realized only to the extent that the "inefficiency" associated with human programming was eliminated. Leaders of the rapidly growing electronic data-processing (EDP) industry believed that easy use of the machine, and thus its marketability to skeptical potential customers, hinged on making the programming workplace more like a traditional engineering "shop." In other words, improved programming was defined as a problem of management as much as a problem of technical refinement and hardware improvement.

At this point programming's origins in electrical engineering played a critical role in the development of programming as an occupation, for it was to the parent occupation that the new industry turned for ways of inserting these new workers into established relations of managerial control. It did so for good reason: not only was electrical engineering the immediate predecessor of programming, but it was the oldest and most organizationally developed of the modern technical-industrial occupations. Along with chemical engineering, electrical engineering was created in the second half of the nineteenth century by the new science-based industries to "wed the sciences to the useful arts." In less archaic if also less graphic language, modern electrical engineering was invented by the science-based industries to provide specialists who could apply the advances of science to the production process. Its chief task was to standardize and routinize the organization of the production process as a whole, as well as the work of particular individuals. Electrical engineers, in short, were skilled workers whose job was to use science to render the skills of other workers unnecessary.* These were thus extensions of management as well as technical experts, offering techniques of control as well as control of techniques.

There is little disagreement about the extent to which engineers succeeded in transforming the workplace and work process. Indeed, it may be said of electrical engineers in particular that they have succeeded only too well. The techniques of

---

* In both social and technical terms, modern engineers are to be distinguished from the classical civil and military engineers who preceded them. These were, by and large, not directly involved in an industrial production process or in work design. Civil engineers, moreover, were usually independent entrepreneurs rather than employees. For a complete discussion of the emergence of modern engineering, see Noble (1977); see also Layton (1973).

standardization and control they pioneered were quickly applied to electrical engineering itself, an ironic example of the deskiller being deskilled.

The most important early efforts to divide and distribute programmers in ways similar to electrical engineering "shops" took place during the Korean War. The SAGE (Semi-Automatic Ground Environment) project, sponsored by the air force to centralize the North American radar system, was the first project after the atom bomb to use computers on a large scale, and it was massive indeed: two thousand programmers were required, more than the estimated total number of programmers in the United States in 1950.

Partly in response to personnel demands which could not be met, SAGE programming work was subjected to a systematic, if also ad hoc, division of labor in an attempt to monitor and evaluate worker performance (for specifics, see Kraft 1977). In particular, SAGE was largely responsible for the creation of a new suboccupation in programming, the systems analyst. Although the systems analysts, or simply analysts, had precursors, it was not until the demands of the Korean War provided the needed inducement that software managers seriously tried to separate the conceptual tasks of designing a program from the more mechanical tasks of writing down the detailed instructions or code. "Coding" could be given to a relatively less-skilled specialist, freeing the "analyst" for the more intellectual work of designing the "system."

The creation of two software occupations, programming/coding and systems analysis, was to be the first of a long series of such subdivisions. If the analyst/programmer distinction was, and to a large extent remains, crude, tentative, and porous, it proved that programming could be divided into two main categories of more-thoughtful and less-thoughtful work. "Creative" software specialists—for example, those whose work involved relatively little mechanical detail—could then have much of their work routinized, and the fragments thus created parceled out to less-skilled workers. Managers could begin to replicate the finer divisions long established in electrical engineering and in other more conventional engineering occupations.

By the end of the 1960s, programming had been fragmented into three major subdivisions—systems analysis, programming, and coding—which are concerned, respectively, with the overall design of large-scale software, i.e., systems of programs, with program design and construction, and with the clerical work of putting down the "code" that constitutes the program. There are two qualifications to this, however. First, the substantive work done by programmers—business programming, scientific programming, and so on—will affect the actual division of labor in a given software workplace. Second, no matter what the workplace, the boundaries between, say, an analyst and a programmer will overlap in practice and be crossed as a matter of (seldom conscious) routine.

Techniques of Routinization

The routinization of programming and its transformation into appropriately named "software production" has been marked by a number of social and technical milestones. In addition to the initial and relatively crude head/hand divisions already described, these include the development of (1) "high-level" software languages; (2) so-called canned, i.e., standard, programs; and (3) structured programming and its corollaries.

High-level languages. Machine-language programming, which characterized most computers through the 1950s, required not only much logical and mathematical skill, but also some familiarity with the mechanics of the machine being programmed. A machine-language programmer was thus in many respects an electrical engineer. The so-called high-level languages, which began to be developed during the 1950s, made such quasi-engineering skills less important, and often completely unnecessary. While machine languages required that the programs take into account the circuitry and physical operation of the machine, high-level languages allowed programmers to concentrate on the logic of the problem to be solved. This saved the programmer time and tedium, and reduced, while not completely eliminating, the chances of clerical error. Programming languages such as FORTRAN (an acronym for Formula Translator) and COBOL (Common Business Oriented Language) make use of permanently entered "translators" that trigger multiple machine operations with a single instruction from the programmer. These specialized high-level languages (FORTRAN is used primarily for scientific and engineering applications, COBOL for commercial applications) allow programmers who have little or no knowledge of the machine or of machine languages to write complex and extensive programs. High-level languages and appropriate "translators" require advanced skill levels and knowledge on the part of those who design them, but once that slow and expensive task is completed, the products can be used by anyone who has mastered the "alphabet" and "syntax" of the high-level language.* Computer programmers no longer need to know anything about the computer they program, and "software people" are further subdivided from "hardware people" (see Greenbaum 1976).

Canned programs. "Canned" or "packaged" programs are off-the-shelf programs designed to handle common data-processing applications, e.g., payrolls, statements of account, inventories, regression analyses, etc. Effectively, they are extensions of the high-level language principle, although narrowly defined. Standard packages, like the high-level languages in which they are written, often require great skill in their design and making, but once debugged and in use, they can be watched over and even modified by programmers with much less skill and training.

The introduction of canned programs on a wide scale, beginning in the 1960s, gave rise to still another suboccupation in programming, the so-called applications programmer. The applications programmer is a specialist with substantially lower software skill than the older undifferentiated "programmer." In typical assignments, applications programmers do little more than adapt standard programs or collections of programs to specific EDP jobs. Their ability to "maintain" existing programs, however, is usually limited to a few preapproved modifications, which are likely to be miniprograms ("subroutines") written by someone else.

The creation of the applications programmer became possible once a number of important developments had taken place in both hardware and software technologies. Machines were becoming cheaper to use and "smarter." Hardware miniaturization allowed computer manufacturers to make machines with larger (and cheaper) storage capacities, which greatly expanded the

---

* Some of the high-level languages are remarkably close to English and are surprisingly easy to learn. They are often appropriately named, e.g., BASIC. You get what you pay for, however, and the uses of a language like BASIC are, well, basic.

machines' "memories." Increased memory capacity in turn made possible the use of more translators—even larger numbers of frequently used machine commands. The newer "smart machines" thus widened the application of high-level languages and canned programs, and therefore encouraged more extensive employment of the applications programmers, who used both.

In combination, these advances in hardware and software design allowed people with relatively less skill to "program" increasingly sophisticated and powerful computers. It became possible to operate computers with employees who were cheaper and less difficult to train, or replace, than old-style programmers.*

Structured programming. Although high-level languages and packaged programs expanded the use of comparatively low-skilled specialists, they did so only to the extent that the consumption of software had become standardized. What was still lacking from the perspective of the industry was a way to standardize the *production* of programs as well. Computer makers and computer users wanted to transform programming from a craft activity into something that resembled a conventional industrial production process. For corporate users, the ideal way to "generate" programs and code would be to have the computers design and write their own programs—a science-fiction fantasy of self-programming machines that has not yet proved possible. Another route was chosen instead. If hardware makers could not yet have machines that wrote programs, the making of programs could be engineered to require that human programmers act in a standard, routine, and machine-like way. Management journals during this period were preoccupied with ways of establishing programming "standards," that is, management-set modes of work behavior, production quotas, quality control, work flow, and so on.

By 1970 the computer industry had developed its chief instrument in the industrialization of computer programming: structured programming. Briefly, structured programming stresses orderliness, simplicity, and the economical use of

---

* Virtually any large-circulation newspaper or magazine now carries regular advertisements by hardware makers which promote the new minicomputers. Their major attraction, according to a typical ad, is that they can be "programmed by your secretary"!

standard languages and code. In its application, structured programming limits the range of choices available to programmers in designing and writing a program. Instruction sequences are specified, limited, or prohibited altogether. Some structured techniques even limit the number of instructions a programmer may use in a program or subroutine. Subroutines, which are commonly called "modules"—discrete components of a larger program or system—in turn allow further fragmentation of software tasks. Modules can be assigned to low-level programmers who must follow rigid coding guidelines in order to write the program fragment "correctly," i.e., according to management-set guidelines. They do not need to know anything about the overall system of which the module is a part, or even how the module fits into ("interfaces" with) other modules.*

Structured programming, in short, is the software manager's answer to the assembly line, minus the conveyor belt but with all the other essential features of a mass-production workplace: a standardized product made in a standardized way by people who do the same thing over and over without knowing—or needing to know—how what they do fits into the larger undertaking.

Structured programming and modularization simultaneously achieved two long-cherished managerial goals. They freed managers from a dependence on highly skilled software workers in the design and writing of programs and they made possible a genuine task-based fragmentation of labor in programming. Before the widespread use of structured programming techniques, the industry-wide divisions between analyst, programmer, and coder were little more than arbitrary divisions of authority and control, and actual work tasks inevitably overlapped at all levels. Structured programming, on the other hand, organized not only the formal relations of the workplace, but the content of the work itself and its allocation to different kinds of workers. A hierarchy of authority could be established for the first time by arranging substantively different job fragments in a rank-order on the basis of either skill, an understanding of the task as a whole, or both. *Managers* defined EDP problems and gave them to high-level *analysts* or similar specialists whose job it was to design the software system. Each component was then

---

* A detailed description of structured programming and its managerial uses is available in Kraft (1977), Ch. 3 and Appendix.

given to a separate and independent *project group*. These groups in turn were hierarchically arranged, and included managers, experienced specialists, entry-level workers, etc. If the project fragment was trivial enough, the group might consist of only one *programmer/coder*, but even in complex systems, fragments could be made so routine, narrow, and restricted that they were essentially coding exercises, making no sense to the people doing the work.

Canned programs, structured programming techniques, and modularization of programs are designed to make the supervision of software workers easier and more like the supervision of other workers. By carefully designing and structuring the work so that workers are forced to regulate their actions according to the demands of the work process, the organization of the work and of the workplace are turned against them. For all practical purposes, regulation and supervision become automatic.

Training and Careers

The transformation of programming into "software production," well underway by 1970, had proceeded far enough for employers to be able to create a structure of training and a system of career patterns to suit their needs. Once again it is necessary to refer briefly to the history of electrical engineering, if only because the computer industry has relied on its parent occupation for a model of employee training. In a recent study, Noble (1977) has carefully documented the development of electrical engineering training institutions in the United States between 1860 and 1920. By the end of World War I, such training institutions formed the structure which still characterizes the occupation today.

The training of electrical engineers takes place in a three-tiered system which differs in the content of instruction, the social origins of the students, and the institutional destinations of the graduates. The first tier is composed of science institutions which conduct state-of-the-art research. These are the elite schools and there are a handful of them: MIT, the California Institute of Technology, the Department of Applied Science at Harvard, and so on. The second level is made up of four-year engineering colleges which train practitioners to apply the discoveries of science to the production process. The third and last consists of two-year institutions producing "technicians" whose work is the least skilled and most fragmented of the three.

The EDP industry turned to electrical engineering schools for its initial supply of adequately trained software employees. In fact, apart from an early period of in-house training by hardware makers and in-government projects such as SAGE, formal programmer training was begun as a specialization within preexisting departments of electrical engineering in science and engineering schools. Today programmer training, although for the most part institutionally separate from electrical engineering departments, almost exactly parallels the structure and organization of its model. The lowest-level specialists—coders and applications programmers—are trained in junior and community college programs designed to prepare them for technician jobs in local industry. More skilled programmers—those who work on complete programs rather than on program fragments—are trained in traditional engineering colleges, or occasionally in liberal arts colleges, in which case they may receive degrees in applied mathematics, applied science, or computer science. Finally, systems analysts and high-level technical specialists—people who design whole systems, languages, or other large-scale software—are typically trained in the elite science institutions, universities such as MIT (Gilchrist and Weber 1972a and 1972b; Hamblen 1972; Kraft 1977: Ch. 2; on engineering, see Noble 1977).

These neat divisions are no more fixed than is the actual process of writing a program or designing a software system, but a well-defined institutional structure nevertheless exists. Its impact on the career patterns of software workers remains to be determined, but here too the experiences of the older engineering occupations give us our idea of what to expect. By and large, graduates of the elite science institutions become research specialists or entrepreneurs. The second group, the graduates of engineering schools, may remain technical specialists or may end their careers as middle-level managers (including nonengineering managers): long-term surveys indicate that this has been a consistent trend since the turn of the century (Rothstein 1969). Finally, the least-skilled engineering specialists—the technicians—are the intellectual equivalent of industrial detail workers, and there is evidence that these institutional and career divisions are parallel and largely exclusive career "ladders," rather than successive steps on the same ladder (Fischer and Lesser 1973; Goldner and Ritti 1962). In programming, social class origin seems to play an important role in the emerging divisions, although no conclusive studies have yet been made of the social origins of the workers in the various programming suboccupations.* Any such study would be confounded by the newness of the occupation as a whole, not only because many of the first generation of programmers and analysts are still occupationally active, but also because any pioneering generation is by definition atypical. In the case of software workers rapid expansion has created mobility opportunties for first entrants such as are found in few other fields. The question is: Can this relative openness be sustained?

The Industrialization of Computer Programming

To make sense of programming's present and to make reasonable predictions about its future requires taking to heart one of the major insights in Braverman's *Labor and Monopoly Capital*: changes within an occupation are as important as changes between occupations. In particular, Braverman pointed to the pressures on capitalists to simplify the work process in order to cheapen labor costs. He labeled this the "Babbage Principle," after the nineteenth-century English entrepreneur and ideologue of "rational capitalism," Charles Babbage. The Babbage Principle applies no less to the computer age than it did to the age of steam-driven mills; indeed, it was Charles Babbage who designed and built the prototype for the modern computer, the "difference engine," 150 years ago.

Keeping the consequences of the Babbage Principle in mind, let us look at employment in the computer industry. Programming's recent growth rate would seem to lend support to the

---

* Studies of the social class origins of scientists and engineers are not unanimous. Kornhauser, for example, claims that there were no significant differences in the social origins of the scientists and engineers in his sample, but his definitions of class are questionable. Other studies find sharper class differences between engineers and scientists, and between the various scientific and engineering suboccupations (see Krohn 1971; Meir 1951; Perrucci 1969 as examples).

claims made by the proponents of the skill-upgrading theory. As the table below shows, such growth rates have been impressive. Between 1970 and 1976, while total employment for all occupations in the United States increased by 11.3 percent, the number of computer specialists (computer programmers, analysts, and the inevitable "other") increased by a dramatic 41.1 percent. Not only does this seem to demonstrate the growth the technology boosters have been talking about, but the demand for software workers has always exceeded the supply, and more programmers and analysts would have been hired if they had been available.

The percentages are less impressive, however, if we remember the *size* of the work force we are talking about. The increase in the absolute number of computer programmers of all types was from approximately 279,000 to 394,000, or from *one-third of 1 percent to one-half of 1 percent of the total number of employed*. This is hardly a figure to take comfort from if programming is expected to take up the slack caused by technology-induced unemployment, particularly since many computer-related occupational categories have actually been reduced in size. For instance, during the same period the number of keypunch operators, which swelled in the early days of computers, declined from about 300,000 to 276,000, in part because of advances in data-processing technology, including programming advances, which made it possible to eliminate mechanical keypunching operations in an increasing number of data-processing workplaces. And this is only one of many such affected operations.

Another indication that programming as an occupation will not make much of a contribution toward filling the employment

Table 1
Growth of Employment of Computer Specialists

	1970		1976		% increase
	No. employed	% of total U.S. employment	No. employed	% of total U.S. employment	
Computer specialists	279,211	0.36	393,995	0.45	+41.11

Source: National Science Foundation, *Women and Minorities in Science and Engineering* (NSF 77–304 [1977]:5).

gap it has created is the programmer/computer ratio (the ratio of employed programmers to the number of mainframe computers in use). Between 1970 and 1976 there was a 41 percent increase in the number of programmers but over a 100 percent increase in the number of mainframe (large-scale) computers. The number of minicomputers, which require fewer programmers, and "micros"—the miniature computers in everything from hand-held calculators to automotive ignition and combustion systems to navigational guidance instruments—have increased even more dramatically. Even so, programming as an occupation cannot be expected to have much of an impact on the society's need for jobs.*

The growth in programming jobs does not, then, offer much support to the skill-upgrading argument made on behalf of technological development under capitalism. The changes *within* programming itself suggest an even grimmer future employment picture. The development of structured programming and similar forms of work simplification indicate that the period of relative openness and high levels of occupational mobility is about to come to an end. The reappearance of large numbers of women in programming, largely at the lowest skill levels—as applications programmers or coders—is an indication of the rapid routinization and deskilling of programming as a whole. Women have traditionally been used as a pool of cheap labor, allowed into skilled occupations only during acute labor shortages or when an occupation has been drained of skill through technological and social innovation. Their rapid introduction into any previously male-dominated occupation is almost always a guarantee that either a war has depleted the traditional (male) labor pool or the work itself has been sufficiently degraded to make it unattractive to male workers.

By 1970 women had entered—or, more accurately, reentered—programming in substantial numbers. In 1970 about 20 percent of computer programmers were women—while they made up only 0.5 percent of those employed in all en-

---

* While occupational projections are at best informed guesses and therefore must be regarded with appropriate caution, it is interesting that the Bureau of Labor Statistics anticipates that the percentage increase in the employment of software specialists for the nine-year period 1976–1985 will be significantly lower than it was for the six-year period 1970–1976: 27.3 percent vs. 41.1 percent.

gineering occupations in 1974 (National Science Foundation 1977:5). Although it could be argued that the reappearance of women in programming means that the computing industry had responded to a commendable degree to the affirmative action and equal opportunity regulations enacted over the last few years, and while to some extent this may be true, the *kind* of work that women software workers do indicates that something else is happening. The NSF survey offers compelling evidence that the software occupations are polarizing, and that the most skilled suboccupations are still thoroughly male-dominated. For example, of the 2900 computer specialists with Ph.D.s in 1973, only 100, or 3.5 percent, were women (ibid.:4).*

Programming is still very much an occupation in process, and generalizations must therefore be both tentative and subject to careful examination. It is clear, however, that programming has experienced a steady process of fragmentation and routinization while programmers as a group have experienced a rapid deskilling. These trends call into question the major claim of technology advocates, that increasingly sophisticated technology in the workplace creates jobs that are better than those it displaces. If this were so, surely computer programming would exemplify the process better than any other occupation created by the new technologies; yet computer programming itself has been subjected to the same processes of routinization and deskilling as the older and less technologically advanced occupations, and for exactly the same reasons. Programming's transformation into "software production" shows that even the most complex work can be trivialized, and underscores the self-serving nature of the larger claims made for technological development in general—that improved machines automatically mean better jobs. On the contrary, the extent to which this is true depends on who has designed the machines and why they are used.

---

* Probably as significant as the NSF figures is the habit of *Datamation* (the computing industry's largest-circulation monthly) of referring to applications programmers and coders in the feminine.

Social Choice in Machine Design: The Case of Automatically Controlled Machine Tools

David F. Noble

Introduction

Almost everyone would agree that the technology of production and the social relations of production are somehow related. The explanation of this relationship often takes the form of a more or less "hard" technological determinism: Technology is the independent variable which effects changes in social relations; it has its own immanent dynamic and unilinear path of development. Further, it is an irreducible first cause from which social effects automatically follow. These effects are commonly called its "social impact."

Social analysts have recently begun to acknowledge that the technology and the social changes it seems to bring about are in reality interdependent, and it has become fashionable to talk about the dialectic between the forces of production and social relations. Nevertheless, most studies of production continue to focus primarily on the ways in which technology affects social relations and there is precious little effort made to show precisely how technology reflects them. That is, although grantsmanship now demands that people refer to the mutual dependence of technology and society, and although socialists and other radicals now take it for granted that technological development is socially determined, there remains very little concrete, historical analysis that demonstrates the validity of the position. The present essay, a case history of the design, deployment, and actual use of automatically controlled machine tools, is meant to be a step in that direction.

Elsewhere I have tried to show that technology is not an autonomous force impinging upon human affairs from the "outside," but is the product of a social process, a historically specific activity carried on by some people, and not others, for particular purposes (Noble 1977). Technology thus does not develop in a unilinear fashion; there is always a range of possibilities or alternatives that are delimited over time—as some are selected and others denied—by the social choices of those with the power to choose, choices which reflect their intentions, ideology, social position, and relations with other people in society. In short, technology bears the social "imprint" of its authors. It follows that "social impacts" issue not so much from the technology of production as from the social choices that technology embodies. Technology, then, is not an irreducible first cause; its social effects follow from the social causes that brought it into being: behind the technology that affects social relations lie the very same social relations. Little wonder, then, that the technology usually tends to reinforce rather than subvert those relations.

Here I want to render this abstract argument concrete by examining a particular technology. Moreover, I want to go a step further and show that the relationship between cause and effect is never automatic—whether the cause is the technology or the social choices that lie behind it—but is always mediated by a complex process whose outcome depends, in the last analysis, upon the relative strengths of the parties involved. As a result, actual effects are often not consonant with the expectations implicit in the original designs. The technology of production is thus twice determined by the social relations of production: first, it is designed and deployed according to the ideology and social power of those who make such decisions; and second, its actual use in production is determined by the realities of the shop-floor struggles between classes.

This essay is divided into six parts. A description and brief history of the technology involved is followed by a two-part section on social choice in design that discusses both the horizontal relations of production (between firms) and the vertical relations of production (between capital and labor). The fourth part examines social choice in the deployment of technology and the fifth looks at shop-floor realities where this technology is being used in the United States today. In the last part some alternative realities, with different social relations, are described.

The Technology: Automatically Controlled Machine Tools

The focus here is numerically controlled machine tools, a particular production technology of relatively recent vintage.

According to many observers, the advent of this new technology has produced something of a revolution in manufacturing, a revolution which, among other things, is leading to increased concentration in the metalworking industry and to a reorganization of the production process in the direction of greater managerial control. These changes in the horizontal and vertical relations of production are seen to follow logically and inevitably from the introduction of the new technology. "We will see some companies die, but I think we will see other companies grow very rapidly," a sanguine president of Data Systems Corporation opined (Stephanz 1971). Less sanguine are the owners of the vast majority of the smaller metalworking firms which, in 1971, constituted 83 percent of the industry; they have been less able to adopt the new technology because of the very high initial expense of the hardware, and the overhead and difficulties associated with the software (ibid). In addition, within the larger, better endowed shops, where the technology has been introduced, another change in social relations has been taking place. Earl Lundgren, a sociologist who surveyed these shops in the late 1960s, observed a dramatic transfer of planning and control from the shop floor to the office (1969).

For the technological determinist, the story is pretty much told: numerical control leads to industrial concentration and greater managerial control over the production process. The social analyst, having identified the cause, has only to describe the inevitable effects. For the critical observer, however, the problem has merely been defined. This new technology was developed under the auspices of management within the large metalworking firms. Is it just a coincidence that the technology tends to strengthen the market position of these firms and enhance managerial authority in the shop? Why did this new technology take the form that it did, a form which seems to have rendered it accessible only to some firms, and why only this technology? Is there any other way to automate machine tools, a technology, for example, which would lend itself less to managerial control? To answer these questions, let us take a closer look at the technology.

A machine tool (for instance, a lathe or milling machine) is a machine used to cut away surplus material from a piece of metal in order to produce a part with the desired shape, size, and finish. Machine tools are really the guts of machine-based industry because they are the means whereby all machinery, including the machine tools themselves, are made. The machine tool has traditionally been operated by a machinist who transmits his skill and purpose to the machine by means of cranks, levers, and handles. Feedback is achieved through hands, ears, and eyes. Throughout the nineteenth century, technical advances in machining developed by innovative machinists built some intelligence into the machine tools themselves—automatic feeds, stops, throw-out dogs, mechanical cams—making them partially "self-acting." These mechanical devices relieved the machinist of certain manual tasks, but he retained control over the operation of the machine. Together with elaborate tooling—fixtures for holding the workpiece in the proper cutting position and jigs for guiding the path of the cutting tool—these design innovations made it possible for less skilled operators to use the machines to cut parts after they had been properly "set up" by more skilled men;* but the source of the intelligence was still the skilled machinist on the floor.

The 1930s and 1940s saw the development of tracer technology. Here patterns, or templates, were traced by a hydraulic or electronic sensing device which then conveyed the information to a cutting tool which reproduced the pattern in the workpiece. Tracer technology made possible elaborate contour cutting, but

---

* The use of jigs and fixtures in metalworking dates back to the early nineteenth century and was the heart of interchangeable parts manufacture, as Merritt Roe Smith has shown (1976). Eventually, in the closing decades of the century, the "toolmaker" as such became a specialized trade, distinguished from the machinist. The new function was a product of modern management, which aimed to shift the locus of skill and control from the production floor, and the operators, to the toolroom. But however much the new tools allowed management to employ less skilled, and thus cheaper, machine operators, they were nevertheless very expensive to manufacture and store and they lent to manufacture a heavy burden of inflexibility, shortcomings which one Taylorite, Sterling Bunnell, warned about as early as 1914 (cited in David Montgomery, unpublished ms.). The cost-savings that resulted from the use of cheaper labor were thus partially offset by the expense of tooling. Numerical control, as we will see, was developed in part to eliminate the cost and inflexibility of jigs and fixtures and, equally important, to take skill, and the control of it, off the floor altogether. Here again, however, the expense of the solution was equal to or greater than the problem. It is interesting to note that in both cases expensive new technologies were introduced to make it possible to hire cheaper labor, and the tab for the conversion was picked up by the state—the Ordnance Department in the early nineteenth century, the departments of the army and navy in World War I, and the air force in the second half of the twentieth century.

it was only a partial form of automation: for instance, different templates were needed for different surfaces on the same workpiece. With the war-spurred development of a whole host of new sensing and measuring devices, as well as precision servomotors which made possible the accurate control of mechanical motion, people began to think about the possibility of completely automating contour machining.

Automating a machine tool is different from automating, say, automotive manufacturing equipment, which is single-purpose, fixed automation, and cost-effective only if high demand makes possible a high product volume. Machine tools are general purpose, versatile machines, used primarily for small batch, low volume production of parts. The challenge of automating machine tools, then, was to render them self-acting while retaining their versatility. The solution was to develop a mechanism that translated electrical signals into machine motion and a medium (film, lines on paper, magnetic or punched paper tape, punched cards) on which the information could be stored and from which the signals could be reproduced.

The automating of machine tools, then, involves two separate processes. You need tape-reading and machine controls, a means of transmitting information from the medium to the machine to make the tables and cutting tool move as desired, and you need a means of getting the information on the medium, the tape, in the first place. The real challenge was the latter. Machine controls were just another step in a known direction, an extension of gunfire control technology developed during the war. The tape preparation was something new. The first viable solution was "record-playback," a system developed in 1946–1947 by General Electric, Gisholt, and a few smaller firms.* It involved having a machinist make a part while the motions of the machine under his command were recorded on magnetic tape. After the first piece was made, identical parts could be made automatically by playing back the tape and reproducing the machine motions. John Diebold, a management

---

* The discussion of the record-playback technology is based upon extensive interviews and correspondence with the engineers who participated in the projects at General Electric (Schenectady) and Gisholt (Madison, Wisconsin), and the trade journal and technical literature.

consultant and one of the first people to write about "flexible automation," heralded record-playback as "no small achievement . . . it means that automatic operation of machine tools is possible for the job shop—normally the last place in which anyone would expect even partial automation" (1952:88). But record-playback enjoyed only a brief existence, for reasons we shall explore. (It was nevertheless immortalized as the inspiration for Kurt Vonnegut's *Player Piano*. Vonnegut was a publicist at GE at the time and saw the record-playback lathe which he describes in the novel.)

The second solution to the medium-preparation problem was "numerical control" (N/C), a name coined by MIT engineers William Pease and James McDonough. Although some trace its history back to the Jacquard loom of 1804, N/C was in fact of more recent vintage; the brainchild of John Parsons, an air force subcontractor in Michigan who manufactured rotor blades for Sikorski and Bell helicopters. In 1949 Parsons successfully sold the air force on his ideas, and then contracted out most of the research work to the Servomechanisms Laboratory at MIT; three years later the first numerically controlled machine tool, a vertical milling machine, was demonstrated and widely publicized.

Record-playback was, in reality, a multiplier of skill, simply a means of obtaining repeatability. The intelligence of production still came from the machinist who made the tape by producing the first part. Numerical control, however, was based upon an entirely different philosophy of manufacturing. The specifications for a part—the information contained in an engineering blueprint—are first broken down into a mathematical representation of the part, then into a mathematical description of the desired path of the cutting tool along up to five axes, and finally into hundreds or thousands of discrete instructions, translated for economy into a numerical code, which is read and translated into electrical signals for the machine controls. The N/C tape, in short, is a means of formally circumventing the role of the machinist as the source of the intelligence of production. This new approach to machining was heralded by the National Commission on Technology, Automation, and Economic Progress as "probably the most significant development in manufacturing since the introduction of the moving assembly line" (Lynn et al. 1966:89).

Choice in Design: Horizontal Relations of Production

This short history of the automation of machine tools describes the evolution of new technology as if it were simply a technical, and thus logical, development. Hence it tells us very little about why the technology took the form that it did, why N/C was developed while record-playback was not, or why N/C as it was designed proved difficult for the metalworking industry as a whole to absorb. Answers to questions such as these require a closer look at the social context in which the N/C technology was developed. In this section we will look at the ways in which the design of the N/C technology reflected the horizontal relations of production, those between firms. In the following section, we will explore why N/C was chosen over record-playback by looking at the vertical relations of production, those between labor and management.

To begin with, we must examine the nature of the machine-tool industry itself. This tiny industry which produces capital goods for the nation's manufacturers is a boom or bust industry that is very sensitive to fluctuations in the business cycle, experiencing an exaggerated impact of good times—when everybody buys new equipment—and bad times—when nobody buys. Moreover, there is an emphasis on the production of "special" machines, essentially custom-made for users. These two factors explain much of the cost of machine tools: manufacturers devote their attention to the requirements of the larger users so that they can cash in on the demand for high-performance specialized machinery, which is very expensive due to high labor costs and the relatively inefficient low-volume production methods (see Rosenberg 1963; Wagoner 1968; Brown and Rosenberg 1961; Melman 1959). The development of N/C exaggerated these tendencies. John Parsons conceived of the new technology while trying to figure out a way of cutting the difficult contours of helicopter rotor blade templates to close tolerances; since he was using a computer to calculate the points for drilling holes (which were then filed together to make the contour) he began to think of having the computer control the actual positioning of the drill itself. He extended this idea to three-axis milling when he examined the specification for a wing panel for a new combat fighter. The new high-performance, high-speed aircraft demanded a great deal of difficult and expensive machining to produce airfoils (wing surfaces, jet engine blades), integrally stiffened wing sections for greater tensile strength and less weight, and variable thickness skins. Parsons took his idea, christened "Cardomatic" after the IBM cards he used, to Wright Patterson Air Force Base and convinced people at the Air Material Command that the air force should underwrite the development of this potent new technology. When Parsons got the contract, he subcontracted with MIT's Servomechanism Laboratory, which had experience in gunfire control systems.* Between the signing of the initial contract in 1949 and 1959, when the air force ceased its formal support for the development of software, the military spent at least $62 million on the research, development, and transfer of N/C. Up until 1953, the air force and MIT mounted a large campaign to interest machine-tool builders and the aircraft industry in the new technology, but only one company, Giddings and Lewis, was sufficiently interested to put their own money into it. Then, in 1955, N/C promoters succeeded in having the specifications in the Air Material Command budget allocation for the stockpiling of machine tools changed from tracer-controlled machines to N/C machines. At that time, the only fully N/C machine in existence was in the Servomechanism Lab. The air force undertook to pay for the purchase, installation, and maintenance of over 100 N/C machines in factories of prime subcontractors; the contractors, aircraft manufacturers, and their suppliers would also be paid to learn to use the new technology. In short, the air force created a market for N/C. Not surprisingly, machine-tool builders got into action, and research and development expenditure in the industry multiplied eightfold between 1951 and 1957.

The point is that what made N/C possible—massive air force support—also helped determine the shape the technology would take. While criteria for the design of machinery normally includes cost to the user, here this was not a major consideration; machine-tool builders were simply competing to meet performance and "competence" specifications for government-funded

---

* This brief history of the origins of N/C is based upon interviews with Parsons and MIT personnel, as well as the use of Parsons' personal files and the project records of the Servomechanism Laboratory.

users in the aircraft industry. They had little concern with cost effectiveness and absolutely no incentive to produce less expensive machinery for the commercial market.

But the development of the machinery itself is only part of the story; there was also the separate evolution of the software. Here, too, air force requirements dictated the shape of the technology. At the outset, no one fully appreciated the difficulty of getting the intelligence of production on tape, least of all the MIT engineers on the N/C project, few of whom had had any machining experience before becoming involved in the project. Although they were primarily control engineers and mathematicians, they had sufficient hubris to believe that they could readily synthesize the skill of a machinist. It did not take them long to discover their error. Once it was clear that tape preparation was the stumbling block to N/C's economic viability, programming became the major focus of the project. The first programs were prepared manually, a tedious, time-consuming operation performed by graduate students, but thereafter efforts were made to enlist the aid of Whirlwind, MIT's first digital computer. The earliest programs were essentially subroutines for particular geometric surfaces which were compiled by an executive program. In 1956, after MIT had received another air force contract for software development, a young engineer and mathematician named Douglas Ross came up with a new approach to programming. Rather than treating each separate problem with a separate subroutine, the new system, called APT (Automatically Programmed Tools), was essentially a skeleton program—a "systematized solution," as it was called—for moving a cutting tool through space; this skeleton was to be "fleshed out" for every particular application. The APT system was flexible and fundamental; equally important, it met air force specifications that the language must have a capacity for up to five-axis control. The air force loved APT because of its flexibility; it seemed to allow for rapid mobilization, for rapid design change, and for interchangeability between machines within a plant, between users and vendors, and between contractors and subcontractors throughout the country (presumably of "strategic importance" in case of enemy attack). With these ends in mind, the air force pushed for standardization of the APT system and the Air Material Command cooperated with the Aircraft Industries Association Committee on Numerical Control to make APT the industry standard, the machine tool and control manufacturers followed suit, developing "postprocessors" to adapt each particular system for use with APT.

Before long the APT computer language had become the industry standard, despite initial resistance within aircraft company plants. Many of these companies had developed their own languages to program their N/C equipment, and these in-house languages, while less flexible than APT, were nevertheless proven, relatively simple to use, and suited to the needs of the company. APT was something else entirely. For all its advantages—indeed, because of them—the APT system had decided disadvantages. The more fundamental a system is, the more cumbersome it is, and the more complex it is, the more skilled a programmer must be, and the bigger a computer must be to handle the larger amount of information. In addition, the greater the amount of information, the greater the chance for error. But initial resistance was overcome by higher level management, who had come to believe it necessary to learn how to use the new system "for business reasons" (cost-plus contracts with the air force). The exclusive use of APT was enforced. Thus began what Douglas Ross himself has described as "the tremendous turmoil of practicalities of the APT system development"; the system remained "erratic and unreliable," and a major headache for the aircraft industry for a long time.

The standardization of APT, at the behest of the air force, had two other interrelated consequences. First, it inhibited for a decade the development of alternative, simpler languages, such as the strictly numerical language NUFORM (created by A. S. Thomas, Inc.), which might have rendered contour programming more accessible to smaller shops. Second, it forced those who ventured into N/C into a dependence on those who controlled the development of APT,* on large computers and

---

* The air force funded development of APT was centered initially at MIT. In 1961 the effort was shifted to the Illinois Institute of Technology Research Institute (IITRI) where it has been carried on under the direction of a consortium composed of the air force, the Aircraft Industries Association (AIA), and major manufacturers of machine tools and electronic controls. Membership in the consortium has always been expensive, beyond the financial means of the vast majority of firms in the metalworking industry. APT system use, therefore, has tended to be restricted to those who enjoyed privileged access to information about the system's development. Moreover, the APT system has been treated as proprietary information within user plants; programmers have had to sign out

mathematically sophisticated programmers. The aircraft companies, for all their headaches, could afford to grapple with APT because of the air force subsidy, but commercial users were not so lucky. Companies that wanted military contracts were compelled to adopt the APT system, and those who could not afford the system, with its training requirements, its computer demands, and its headaches, were thus deprived of government jobs. The point here is that the software system which became the de facto standard in industry had been designed with a user, the air force, in mind. As Ross explained, "the universal factor throughout the design process is the economics involved. The advantage to be derived from a given aspect of the language must be balanced against the difficulties in incorporating that aspect into a complete and working system" (Ross 1978:13). APT served the air force and the aircraft industry well, but at the expense of less endowed competitors.

Choice in Design: Vertical Relations of Production

Thus far we have talked only about the form of N/C, its hardware and software, and how these reflected the horizontal relations of production. But what about the precursor to N/C, record-playback? Here was a technology that was apparently perfectly suited to the small shop: tapes could be prepared by recording the motions of a machine tool, guided by a machinist or a tracer template, without programmers, mathematics, languages, or computers.* Yet this technology was abandoned in favor of N/C by the aircraft industry and by the control man-

---

for manuals and have been forbidden from taking them home or talking about their contents with people outside the company.

* Technically, record-playback was as reliable as N/C, if not more so—since all the programming was done at the machine, errors could be eliminated during the programming process, before production began. Moreover, it could be used to reproduce parts to within a tolerance of a thousandth of an inch, just like N/C. (It is a common mistake to assume that if an N/C control system generates discrete pulses corresponding to increments of half a thousandth, the machine can produce parts to within the same tolerances. In reality, the limits of accuracy are set by the machine itself—not to mention the weather—rather than by the electrical signals.)

ufacturers. Small firms never saw it. The Gisholt system, designed by Hans Trechsel to be fully accessible to machinists on the floor, was shelved once that company was bought by Giddings and Lewis, one of the major N/C manufacturers. The GE record-playback system was never really marketed since demonstrations of the system for potential customers in the machine-tool and aircraft companies elicited little enthusiasm. Giddings and Lewis did in fact purchase a record-playback control for a large profile "skin mill" at Lockheed but switched over to a modified N/C System before regular production got underway. GE's magnetic tape control system, the most popular system in the 1950s and 1960s, was initially described in sales literature as having a "record-playback option," but mention of this feature soon disappeared from the manuals, even though the system retained the record-playback capacity.*

Why was there so little interest in this technology? The answer to this question is complicated. First, air force performance specifications for four- and five-axis machining of complex parts, often out of difficult materials, were simply beyond the capacity of either record-playback or manual methods. In terms of expected cost reductions, moreover, neither of these methods appeared to make possible as much of a reduction in the manufacturing and storage costs of jigs, fixtures, and templates as did N/C. Along the same lines, N/C also promised to reduce more significantly the labor costs for toolmakers, machinists, and patternmakers. And, of course, the very large air force subsidization of N/C technology lured most manufacturers and users to where the action was. Yet there were still other, less practical, reasons for the adoption of N/C and the abandonment of record-playback, reasons that have more to do with the ideology of engineering than with economic calculations. However useful as a production technology, record-playback was considered quaint from the start, especially with the advent of N/C. N/C was always more than a technology for cutting metals, especially in the eyes of its MIT designers, who knew little about metalcutting: it was a symbol of the computer age, of mathematical elegance, of power, order, and predictability, of continuous

---

* This history is based upon interviews with Hans Trechsel, designer of Gisholt's "Factrol" system, and interviews and correspondence with participating engineering and sales personnel at GE (Schenectady), as well as articles in various engineering and trade journals.

flow, of remote control, of the automatic factory. Record-playback, on the other hand, however much it represented a significant advance on manual methods, retained a vestige of traditional human skills; as such, in the eyes of the future (and engineers always confuse the present and the future) it was obsolete.

The drive for total automation which N/C represented, like the drive to substitute capital for labor, is not always altogether rational. This is not to say that the profit motive is insignificant—hardly. But economic explanations are not the whole story, especially in cases where ample government financing renders cost-minimization less of an imperative. Here the ideology of control emerges most clearly as a motivating force, an ideology in which the distrust of the human agency is paramount, in which human judgment is construed as "human error." But this ideology is itself a reflection of something else: the reality of the capitalist mode of production. The distrust of human beings by engineers is a manifestation of capital's distrust of labor. The elimination of human error and uncertainty is the engineering expression of capital's attempt to minimize its dependence upon labor by increasing its control over production. The ideology of engineering, in short, mirrors the antagonistic social relations of capitalist production. Insofar as the design of machinery, like machine tools, is informed by this ideology, it reflects the social relations of production.* Here we will emphasize this aspect of the explanation—why N/C was developed and record-playback was not—primarily because it is the aspect most often left out of such stories.

---

* It could be argued that control in the capitalist mode of production is not an independent factor (a manifestation of class conflict), but merely a means to an economic end (the accumulation of capital). Technology introduced to increase managerial control over the work force and eliminate pacing is, in this view, introduced simply to increase profits. Such reductionism, which collapses control and class questions into economistic ones, renders impossible any explanation of technological development in terms of social relations or any careful distinction between productive technology which directly increases output per person-hour and technology which does so only indirectly by reducing worker resistance or restriction of output. Finally, it makes it hard to distinguish a technology that reduces pacing from a gun in the service of union-busting company agents; both investments ultimately have the same effect and the economic results look the same on the balance sheet. As Jeremy Brecher reminds us, "The critical historian must go behind the economic category of cost-minimization to discover the social relations that it embodies (and conceals)" (1978).

Ever since the nineteenth century, labor-intensive machine shops have been a bastion of skilled labor and the locus of considerable shop-floor struggle. Frederick Taylor introduced his system of scientific management in part to try to put a stop to what he called "systematic soldiering" (now called "pacing"). Workers practiced pacing for many reasons: to keep some time for themselves, to exercise authority over their own work, to avoid killing "gravy" piece-rate jobs by overproducing and risking a rate cut, to stretch out available work for fear of layoffs, to exercise their creativity and ingenuity in order to "make out" on "stinkers" (poorly rated jobs), and, of course, to express hostility to management (see articles by Roy; Mathewson 1969). Aside from collective cooperation and labor-prescribed norms of behavior, the chief vehicle available to machinists for achieving shop-floor control over production was their control over the machines. Machining is not a handicraft skill but a machine-based skill; the possession of this skill, together with control over the speeds, feeds, and motions of the machines, enables machinists alone to produce finished parts to tolerance (Montgomery 1976b). But the very same skills and shop-floor control that made production possible also make pacing possible. Taylor therefore tried to eliminate soldiering by changing the process of production itself, transferring skills from the hands of machinists to the handbooks of management; this, he thought, would enable management, not labor, to prescribe the details of production tasks. He was not altogether successful. For one thing, there is still no absolute science of metalcutting and methods engineers, time-study people, and Method Time Measurement (MTM) specialists—however much they may have changed the formal processes of machine-shop practice—have not succeeded in putting a stop to shop-floor control over production.*

Thus, when sociologist Donald Roy went to work in a machine shop in the 1940s, he found pacing alive and well. He recounts an incident that demonstrates how traditional patterns of authority rather than scientific management still reigned supreme:

* The setting of rates on jobs in machine shops is still more of a guess than a scientific determination. This fact is not lost on machinists, as their typical descriptions of the methods-men suggests: "They ask their wives, they don't know; they ask their children, they don't know; so they ask their friends." Of course, this apparent and acknowledged lack of scientific certainty comes into play during bargaining sessions over rates, when "fairness" and power, not science, determine the outcome.

"I want 25 or 30 of those by 11 o'clock," Steve the superintendent said sharply, a couple of minutes after the 7:15 whistle blew. I [Roy] smiled at him agreeably. "I mean it," said Steve, half smiling himself, as McCann and Smith, who were standing near us, laughed aloud. Steve had to grin in spite of himself and walked away. "What he wants and what he is going to get are two different things," said McCann. (1953:513)

Thirty years later, sociologist Michael Burawoy returned to the same shop and concluded, in his own study of shop-floor relations, that "in a machine shop, the nature of the relationship of workers to their machines rules out coercion as a means of extracting surplus" (1976).

This was the larger context in which the automation of machine tools took place; it should be seen, therefore, as a further managerial attempt to wrest control over production from the shop-floor work force. As Peter Drucker once observed, "What is today called automation is conceptually a logical extension of Taylor's scientific management" (1967:26). Thus it is not surprising that when Parsons began to develop his N/C "Cardomatic" system, he took care not to tell the union (the UAW) in his shop in Traverse City about his exciting new venture. At GE (Schenectady), a decade of work-stoppages over layoffs, rate cuts, speed-ups, and the replacement of machinists with less skilled apprentices and women during the war, culminated in 1946 in the biggest strike in the company's history, led by machinists in the United Electrical Workers (UE) and bitterly opposed by the GE Engineers' Association. GE's machine-tool automation project, launched by these engineers soon afterward, was secret, and although the project had strong management support, publicist Vonnegut recalled, with characteristic understatement, that "they wanted no publicity this time."*

During the first decade of machine-tool automation development, the aircraft industry—the major user of automatic machine tools—also experienced serious labor trouble as the machinists and auto workers competed to organize the plants. The postwar depression had created discontent among workers faced with layoffs, company claims of inability to pay, and massive downward reclassifications (Allen and Schneider 1956). Major strikes took place at Boeing, Bell Aircraft (Parsons' prime contractor), McDonnell Douglas, Wright Aeronautical, GE (Evandale) (jet engines), North American Aviation, and Republic Air-

* Kurt Vonnegut, letter to author, February 1977.

craft. It is not difficult, then, to explain the popularity among management and technical men of a November 1946 *Fortune* article entitled "Machines Without Men." Surveying the technological fruits of the war (sensing and measuring devices, servomechanisms, computers, etc.), two Canadian physicists promised that "these devices are not subject to any human limitations. They do not mind working around the clock. They never feel hunger or fatigue. They are always satisfied with working conditions, and never demand higher wages based on the company's ability to pay." In short, "they cause much less trouble than humans doing comparable work" (Leaver and Brown 1946:203).

One of the people who was inspired by this article was Lowell Holmes, the young electrical engineer who directed the GE automation project. However, in record-playback, he developed a system for replacing machinists that ultimately retained machinist and shop-floor control over production because of the method of tape preparation.* This "defect" was recognized immediately by those who attended the demonstration of the system; they showed little interest in the technology. "Give us something that will do what we say, not what we do," one of them said. The defects of record-playback were conceptual, not technical; the system simply did not meet the needs of the larger firms for managerial control over production. N/C did. "Managers like N/C because it means they can sit in their offices, write down what they want, and give it to someone and say, 'do it,'" the chief GE consulting engineer on both the record-playback and N/C projects explained. "With N/C there is no need to get your hands dirty, or argue" (personal interview). Another consulting engineer, head of the Industrial Applications Group which served as intermediary between the research department and sales department at GE (Schenectady) and a key figure in the development of both technologies, explained the shift from record-

---

* The fact that record-playback lends itself to shop-floor control of production more readily than N/C is borne out by a study of N/C in the United Kingdom done by Erik Christiansen in 1968. Only in those cases where record-playback or plugboard controls were in use (he found six British-made record-playback jig borers) did the machinist keep the same pay scale as with conventional equipment and retain control over the entire machining process. In Christiansen's words, record-playback (and plugboard programming) "mean that the shop floor retains control of the work cycle through the skill of the man who first programmed the machine" (1968:27, 31).

playback to N/C: "Look, with record-playback the control of the machine remains with the machinist—control of feeds, speeds, number of cuts, output; with N/C there is a shift of control to management. Management is no longer dependent upon the operator and can thus optimize the use of their machines. With N/C, control over the process is placed firmly in the hands of management—and why shouldn't we have it?" (personal interview). It is no wonder that at GE, N/C was often referred to as a management system, not as a technology of cutting metals.*

Numerical control dovetailed nicely with larger efforts to computerize company operations, which also entailed concentrating the intelligence of manufacturing in a centralized office. In the intensely anti-Communist 1950s, moreover, as one former machine-tool design engineer has suggested, N/C looked like a solution to security problems, enabling management to remove blueprints from the floor so that subversives and spies couldn't get their hands on them. N/C also appeared to minimize the need for costly tooling and it made possible the cutting of complex shapes that defied manual and tracer methods, and reduced actual chip-cutting time. Equally important, however, N/C replaced problematic time-study methods with "tape time"—using the time it takes to run a cycle as the base for calculating rates—replaced troublesome skilled machinists with more tractable "button-pushers," and eliminated once and for all the problem of pacing. If, with hindsight, N/C seems to have led to organizational changes in the factory, changes which enhanced managerial control over production, it is because the technology was chosen, in part, for just that purpose. This becomes even clearer when we look at how the chosen technology was deployed.

Choice in Deployment: Managerial Intentions

There is no question but that management saw in N/C the potential to enhance their authority over production and seized upon it, despite questionable cost effectiveness.† Machine-tool

---

* GE Company 1958. See also Forrester *et al.* 1955.

† The cost effectiveness of N/C depends upon many factors, including training costs, programming costs, computer costs, and the like, beyond mere time saved in actual chip-cutting or reduction in direct labor costs. The MIT staff who

conducted the early studies on the economics of N/C focused on the savings in cutting time and waxed eloquent about the new revolution. At the same time, however, they warned that the key to the economic viability of N/C was a reduction in programming (software) costs. Machine-tool company salesmen were not disposed to emphasize these potential drawbacks, though, and numerous users went bankrupt because they believed what they were told. In the early days, however, most users were buffered against such tragedy by state subsidy. Today, potential users are somewhat more cautious, and machine-tool builders are more restrained in their advertising, tempering their promise of economic success with qualifiers about proper use, the right lot and batch size, sufficient training, etc.

For the independent investigator, it is extremely difficult to assess the economic viability of such a technology. There are many reasons for this. First, the data is rarely available or accessible. Whatever the motivation—technical fascination, keeping up with competitors, etc.—the purchase of new capital equipment must be justified in economic terms. But justifications are not too difficult to come by if the item is desired enough by the right people. They are self-interested anticipations and thus usually optimistic ones. More important, firms rarely conduct postaudits on their purchases, to see if their justifications were warranted. Nobody wants to document his errors and if the machinery is fixed in its foundation, that is where it will stay, whatever a postaudit reveals; you learn to live with it. The point here is that the economics of capital equipment is not nearly so tidy as economists would sometimes have us believe. The invisible hand has to do quite a bit of sweeping up after the fact.

If the data does exist, it is very difficult to get a hold of. Companies have a proprietary interest in the information and are wary about disclosing it for fear of revealing (and thus jeopardizing) their position vis à vis labor unions (wages), competitors (prices), and government (regulations and taxes). Moreover, the data, if it were accessible, is not all tabulated and in a drawer somewhere. It is distributed among departments, with separate budgets, and the costs to one are the hidden costs to the others. Also, there is every reason to believe that the data that does exist is self-serving information provided by each operating unit to enhance its position in the firm. And, finally, there is the tricky question of how "viability" is defined in the first place. Sometimes, machines make money for a company whether they were used productively or not.

The purpose of this aside is to emphasize the fact that "bottom-line" explanations for complex historical developments, like the introduction of new capital equipment, are never in themselves sufficient, nor necessarily to be trusted. If a company wants to introduce something new, it must justify it in terms of making a profit. This is not to say, however, that profit making was its real (or, if so, its only) motive or that a profit was ever made. In the case of automation, steps are taken less out of careful calculation than on the faith that it is always good to replace capital with labor, a faith kindled deep in the soul of manufacturing engineers and managers (as economist Michael Piore, among others, has shown. See, for example, Piore 1968). Thus, automation is driven forward, not simply by the profit motive, but by the ideology of automation itself, which reflects the social relations of production.

builders and control manufacturers, of course, also promoted their wares along these lines; well attuned to the needs of their customers, they promised an end to traditional managerial problems. Thus the president of the Landis Machine Company, in a trade journal article entitled "How Can New Machines Cut Costs?" stressed the fact that "with modern automatic controls, the production pace is set by the machine, not by the operator" (Stickell 1960:61). The advertising copy of the MOOG Machine Company of Buffalo, New York, similarly described how their new machining center "has allowed management to plan and schedule jobs more effectively," while pointing out, benevolently, that "operators are no longer faced with making critical production decisions" (MOOG Hydra-Point News 1975).

Machine-tool and control system manufacturers peddled their wares and the trade journals, forever in search of advertisements, echoed their pitch. Initially, potential customers believed the hype; they very much wanted to. Earl Lundgren, the sociologist who surveyed N/C user plants in the 1960s concluded that the "prime interest in each subject company was the transfer of as much planning and control from the shop to the office as possible" and that management believed that "under numerical control the operator is no longer required to take part in planning activities" (Lundgren 1969).

In my own survey (1977–1978) of twenty-five plants in the Midwest and New England—including manufacturers of machine tools, farm implements, heavy construction equipment, jet engines and aircraft parts, and specialized industrial machinery—I observed the same phenomenon. Everywhere, management initially believed in the promises of N/C promoters and attempted to remove all decision making from the floor and assign unskilled people to N/C machines; to substitute "tape time" for problematic time studies to set base rates for piecework and measure output quotas; and to tighten up authority by concentrating all mental activity in the office and otherwise to extend detail control over all aspects of the production process.

This is not to say, however, that I drew the same conclusions that Lundgren did in his earlier survey. Characteristically, for an industrial sociologist, he viewed such changes as requirements of the new technology whereas, in reality, they reflected simply the possibilities of the technology which were "seized upon" (to use Harry Braverman's phrase) by management to realize particular objectives, social as well as technical. There is nothing inherent in N/C technology, however, that makes it necessary to assign programming and machine tending to different people (that is, to management and workers, respectively); the technology merely makes it possible (Braverman 1974:199). Management philosophy and motives—reflecting the social relations of the capitalist mode of production in general and a historically specific economic and political context in particular—make it necessary that the technology be deployed in this way.

One illustration of managerial choice in machine deployment is provided by the experience of a large manufacturing firm near Boston. In 1968, owing to low worker morale, turnover, absenteeism, and the general unreliability of programming and machinery, the company faced what it termed a "bottleneck" in its N/C lathe section. Plant managers were frantic to figure out a way to achieve the expected output from this expensive equipment. In that prosperous and reform-minded period, they decided upon a job enlargement/enrichment experiment wherein machine operators would be organized into groups and their individual tasks extended. Although it was the hope of the company that such a reorganization would boost the morale of the men on the floor and motivate them to "optimize the utilization" of the machinery, the union was at first reluctant to cooperate, fearing a speed-up. The company was thus hard pressed to secure union support for their program and instituted a bonus for all participants. At one of the earliest management-union meetings on the new program, the company spokesman began his discussion of the job-enlargement issue with the question (and thinly/veiled threat), "Should we make the hourly people button-pushers or responsible people?" Given the new technology, management believed they now had the choice, and, given the pressure of unusual circumstances, they were prepared to exercise it in what they understood to be an atypical way.*

---

* This experiment was relatively successful, but short-lived. Attracted to the program by the bonus, the reorganized work groups soon grew accustomed to the new conditions: no foremen or punch clock, their own tool crib, their own scheduling of parts through the shop, and even some training in programming. Morale improved and turnover, absenteeism, and the scrap-rate declined accordingly. However, managerial enthusiasm for the experiment soon waned, and, after only a few half-hearted years, it was unilaterally called off. The company claimed that the union's desire to extend the experiment to other areas of the shop and to other plants within the same corporation threatened to make

A second illustration of the managerial imperative behind technological determinism is provided in an interview I had with two shop managers in a plant in Connecticut. Here, as elsewhere, much of the N/C programming is relatively simple, and I asked the men why the operators couldn't do their own programming. At first they dismissed the suggestion as ridiculous, arguing that the operators would have to know how to set feeds and speeds, that is, be industrial engineers. I pointed out that the same people probably set the feeds and speeds on conventional machinery, routinely making adjustments on the process sheet provided by the methods engineers in order to make out. They nodded. They then said that the operators couldn't understand the programming language. This time I pointed out that the operators could often be seen reading the mylar tape—twice-removed information describing the machining being done—in order to know what was coming (for instance, to anticipate programming errors that could mess things up). Again, they nodded. Finally they looked at each other, smiled, and one of them leaned over and confided, "We don't want them to." Here is the reality behind technological determinism in deployment.

Reality on the Shop Floor

Although the evolution of a technology follows from the social choices that inform it, choices which mirror the social relations of production, it would be an error to assume that in having exposed the choices, we can simply deduce the rest of reality from them. Reality cannot be extrapolated from the intentions that underlie the technology any more than from the technology itself.* Desire is not identical to satisfaction.

"In the conflict between the employer and employed," John G. Brooks observed in 1903, "the 'storm centre' is largely at this point where science and invention are applied to industry."† It is

---

the program too expensive since an extension of the experiment meant also an extension of the bonus. The union business agent, formerly a shop steward in the experimental program and one of its stauchest supporters, explained the termination in another way: the company was losing control over the work force.

* This is an error that Braverman tended to make in discussing N/C.

† Cited in D. Montgomery (unpublished: Ch. 4, p. 1).

here that the reality of N/C was hammered out, where those who chose the technology finally came face-to-face with those who did not.

The introduction of N/C was not uneventful, especially in plants where the machinists' unions had a long history. Work stoppages and strikes over rates for the new machines were common in the 1960s, as they still are today. At GE, for example, there were strikes at several large plants and the entire Lynn, Massachusetts plant was shut down for a month during the winter of 1965. There are also less overt indications that management dreams of automatic machinery and a docile, disciplined work force but they have tended to remain just that.†

---

† Perhaps the single most important, and difficult, task confronting the critical student of such rapidly evolving technologies as N/C is to try to disentangle dreams from realities, a hoped-for future from an actual present. The two realms are probably nowhere more confused than in the work of technologists. Thus, criticism of existing, or past, realities are typically countered with allusions to a less problematic future; the present is always the "debugging phase," the transition, at the beginning of the "learning curve"—merely a prelude to the future. As such, it is immune from scrutiny and criticism. To argue, as we do here, that N/C machinery does not run by itself or that mere "button-pushers" cannot produce good parts consistently on N/C, invites the rebuffs of those in the know, who refer to the automatic loading of N/C machines by the Unimate robots, to Flexible Manufacturing Systems (FMS) that tie any number of machines together with an automatic transfer line, to adaptive controls with sensors that automatically correct for tool wear and rough castings and the like, or to Direct Numerical Control systems (DNC) which centralize control over a whole plant of N/C equipment through one computer. Three important things must be kept in mind when dealing with such counterarguments.

First, technical people, it must be remembered, always have their eyes on the future—it is their job; they live in the state-of-the-art world which often has very little connection with industrial reality. Thus, it is hardly surprising that technical forecasters of the late 1950s predicted that by now at least 75 percent of machine tools in this country would be N/C (it is less than 2 percent), and that we would be seeing fully automatic metalworking factories (there are none). There is no better reason to believe the engineering and trade journals today, much less the self-serving forecasts of manufacturing engineers. All too often, social analysts merely echo these prophets, extrapolating wonderful or woeful consequences of projected technological changes without paying the slightest attention to the mundane vicissitudes of historical experience, or industrial practice. To them, the critic must respond: look again.

Second, judging from past experience, there is little reason simply to assume that the new experimental or demonstration systems will actually function on the shop floor as intended, much less perform economically. This author has visited

Here we will examine briefly three of management's expectations: the use of "tape time" to set rates; the deskilling of machine operators; and the elimination of pacing.

Early dreams of using tape time to set base rates and measure performance and output proved fanciful. As one N/C operator observed, while rates on manual machines were sometimes too high, they were usually within a reasonable range, whereas the rates on N/C were "out of all relation to reality—ridiculously high; N/C's were supposed to be like magic but all you can do automatically on them is produce scrap." The machines, contrary to their advertisements, could not be used to produce parts

---

four plants in the United States with FMS systems and found their economic justifications suspect, their down time excessive, and their reliability heavily dependent upon a highly skilled force of computer operators, system attendants, and maintenance men; there was also little sign of further development. Adaptive systems, under development at Cincinnati Milacron, are still in an experimental stage; when placed on the shop floor, these even more complex and sensitive pieces of machinery are bound to produce more maintenance problems than they solve. DNC is simply another name for the automatic factory, the supreme fantasy of the industrial technocrats, now heralded by self-serving computer jocks, supported by beleaguered corporate managers (whose farsightedness is more rhetorical than real), and, as usual, funded by the military (in this case, the air force ICAM program).

Third, the ultimate viability of these technologies under the present mode of production depends, in the final analysis, upon the political and economic conditions that prevail and upon the relative strengths of the classes in their struggle over the control of production. To assume simply that the future will be what the designers and/or promoters of these technologies think it will be, would be to beg all of the questions being raised here, to ratify, out-of-hand, a form of technological determinism. Further, it would be to deny the realm of freedom that is being described, a freedom which could result not only in the delaying or subverting of these technologies (and thus the purposes they embody)—allowing for more time to struggle for greater freedom—but also in the fundamental reshaping of their design and use to meet ends other than simple capital accumulation and the extension of managerial and corporate power. See, for example, the discussion of Computer Numerical Control (CNC) in the final section on "alternative realities."

In short, a facile reference to the future is the educated habit of technical people in our society, people who are quite often seriously (and sometimes dangerously) ignorant of the past and mistaken about the present. To adopt their habit would be to suspend judgment (or, rather, yield to their judgment), to forego the critical, concrete, historical examination and assessment of the present situation, which alone can guide us intelligently into the still clouded future.

to tolerance without the repeated manual intervention of the operator in order to make tool offset adjustments, correct for tool wear and rough castings, and correct programming errors (not to mention machine malfunctions, such as "random holes" in drills and "plunges" in milling machines, often attributable to overheating). As the N/C operator just quoted explained, in a response to a *New York Times* article on the wonders of computer-based metalworking:

> Cutting metals to critical tolerances means maintaining constant control of a continually changing set of stubborn, elusive details. Drills run. End mills walk. Machines creep. Seemingly rigid metal castings become elastic when clamped to be cut, and spring back when released so that a flat cut becomes curved, and holes bored precisely on location move somewhere else. Tungsten carbide cutters imperceptibly wear down, making the size of a critical slot half a thousandth too small. Any change in any one of many variables can turn the perfect part you're making into a candidate for a modern sculpture garden, in seconds. Out of generations of dealing with the persistent, ornery problems of metal cutting comes the First Law of Machining: "Don't mess with success." (Tulin 1978:16)

In reality, N/C machines do not run by themselves—as the United Electrical Workers argued in its 1960 *Guide to Automation*, the new equipment, like the old, requires a spectrum of manual intervention and careful attention to detail, depending upon the machine, the product, and so on. The fiction that the time necessary to do a job could be determined by simply adding a standard factor or two (for setup, breaks, etc.) to the tape (cycle) time, was exploded early on, and with it hope of using the tape to measure performance (although some methods people still try).

The deskilling of machine operators has also, on the whole, not taken place as expected, for two reasons. First, as mentioned earlier, the assigning of labor grades and thus rates to the new machinery was, and is, a hotly contested and unresolved issue in union shops. Second, in union and nonunion shops alike, the determination of skill requirements for N/C must take into account the actual degree of automation and reliability of the machinery. Management has thus had to have people on the machines who know what they are doing simply because the machines (and programming) are not totally reliable; they do not run by themselves and produce good finished parts. Also, the machinery is still very expensive (even without microprocessors) and thus so is a machine smash-up. Hence, while it is true that many manufacturers initially tried to put unskilled people on the new equipment, they rather quickly saw their error and upgraded the classification. (In some places the most skilled people were put on the N/C machines and given a premium but the lower formal classifications were retained, presumably in the hope that someday the skill requirements would actually drop to match the classification—and the union would be decertified.) The point is that the intelligence of production has neither been built entirely into the machinery nor been taken off the shop floor. It remains in the possession of the work force.*

This brings us, once again, to the question of shop-floor control. In theory, the programmer prepares the tape (and thus sets feeds and speeds, thereby determining the rate of production), proofs it out on the machine, and then turns the show over to the operator, who from then on simply presses start and stop buttons and loads and unloads the machine (using standard fixtures). This rarely happens in reality, as was pointed out above. Machining to tolerances generally requires close attention

* The shortage of skilled manpower has always been cited by managers and technical people as a justification for the introduction of labor-saving technologies like N/C. Rarely, however, is the shortage actually demonstrated or explained in any compelling way; it remains a necessary and unquestioned ideological prop. For a manpower shortage is a relative thing; relative to new air force and aircraft industry requirements in the cold war, there was a perceived shortage. But, given that shortages are only perceived in relation to a present or future need, they are predictable; they are not natural phenomena but socially created ones, remediable through training programs and sufficient monetary and other incentives. (This author remembers, for example, that not so long ago he went to college on loan programs created to deal with a recognized shortage of college teachers, relative to a vastly expanding educational system.) Thus, when managers introduce N/C because of the impending retirement of the last generation of skilled machinists, we must ask, where are their replacements? Why have apprenticeship programs been eliminated or shortened? Why do vocational courses habituate young people to "semiskilled" work in the name of training for a craft? The answer is that the shortage is, in reality, created to complement the new technology, not the other way around. Fortunately for capital, however, the skill is not entirely eliminated, however "unskilled" the classification; passed on informally and on the job, it remains on the shop floor. If it wasn't there, finished parts would never make it out the door.

to the details of the operation and frequent manual intervention through manual feed and speed overrides. This aspect of the technology, of course, reintroduces the control problem for management. Just as in the conventional shop, where operators are able to modify the settings specified on the worksheet (prepared by the methods engineer) in order to restrict output or otherwise "make out" (by running the machine harder), so in the N/C shop the operators are able to adjust feeds and speeds for similar purposes.

Thus, if you walk into a shop you will often find feed-rate override dials set uniformly at, say, 70 or 80 percent of tape-determined feed rate. In some places this is called the "70 percent syndrome"; everywhere it is known as pacing. To combat it, management sometimes programs the machines at 130 percent, and sometimes actually locks the overrides altogether to keep the operators out of the "planning process." This in turn gets management into serious trouble since the interventions are required to get the parts out the front door.

It is difficult to assess to what extent the considerable amount of intervention is attributable to the inherent unreliability of the complex equipment itself, but it is certainly true that the technology develops shortcomings once it is placed on the shop floor, whether or not they were there in the original designs. Machines often do not do what they are supposed to do and down time is still excessive. Technical defects, human errors, and negligence are acknowledged problems, and so is sabotage. "I don't care how many computers you have, they'll still have a thousand ways to beat you," lamented one manager of N/C equipment in a Connecticut plant. "When you put a guy on an N/C machine, he gets temperamental," another manager in Rhode Island complained. "And then, through a process of osmosis, the machine gets temperamental."

On the shop floor, it is not only the choices of management that have an effect. The same antagonistic social relations that, in their reflection in the minds of designers, gave issue to the new technology, now subvert it. This contradiction of capitalist production presents itself to management as a problem of "worker motivation," and management's acceptance of the challenge is its own tacit acknowledgment that it does not have shop-floor control over production, that it is still dependent upon the work force to turn a profit.

Thus, in evaluating the work of those whose intentions to wrest control over production from the work force informed the design and deployment of N/C, we must take into account an article written by two industrial engineers in 1971 entitled "A Case for Wage Incentives in the N.C. Age." It makes it quite clear that the contradiction of capitalist production has not been eclipsed—computers or no computers:

> Under automation, it is argued, the machine basically controls the manufacturing cycle, and therefore the worker's role diminishes in importance. The fallacy in this reasoning is that if the operator malingers or fails to service the machine for a variety of reasons, both utilization and subsequent return on investment suffer drastically.
>
> Basic premises underlying the design and development of N.C. machines aim at providing the capability of machining configurations beyond the scope of conventional machines. Additionally, they "de-skill" the operator. Surprisingly, however, the human element continues to be a major factor in the realization of optimum utilization or yield of these machines. This poses a continuing problem for management, because a maximum level of utilization is necessary to assure a satisfactory return on investment. (Doring and Saling 1971:31)

The motivation problem boils down to this: What will a machine operator, "skilled" or "unskilled," do when he sees a $250,000 milling machine heading for a smash-up? He could rush to the machine and press the panic button, retracting the workpiece from the cutter or shutting the whole thing down, or he could remain seated and think to himself, "Oh, look, no work tomorrow." For management, the situation poses the dilemma faced by every capitalist, a contradiction succinctly, if inadvertently, expressed by another plant manager in Connecticut. With a colleague chiming in, he proudly described the elaborate procedure they had developed whereby every production change, even the most minor, had to be okayed by an industrial engineer. "We want absolutely no decision made on the floor," he insisted; no operator was to make any change from the process sheets without the written authorization of a supervisor. A moment later, however, looking out onto the floor from his glass-enclosed office, he reflected upon the reliability of the machinery, and the expense of parts and equipment, and emphasized, with equal conviction, that "We need guys out there who can think."

Alternative Realities

Shop-floor realities are determined by the social relations, as well as the technology, of production and, as we have seen, the latter is shaped by the former no less than the reverse. But thus far we have examined only the ways in which managerial intentions, introduced in the form of new technology, are subverted in practice; this is only part of the story, the part defined, in a restricted way, by social relations which assign to labor a "negative" role. Having had to adopt a defensive posture against a far more powerful adversary, the American trade union movement opted out of certain struggles (for instance, for the right to make production decisions, now an exclusive "management prerogative") in order to concentrate on and gain advantage in others (for example, job security, wages, benefits). Accordingly, when confronted with changing technology labor has generally limited its response to post-hoc resistance. This has meant, of course, that labor's choices have not been registered in the actual design and deployment stages and that, therefore, the technology does not reflect its interest. A more forward-looking and sophisticated labor movement, however, facing an intensified management drive toward rationalization and automation, could transcend this passive role and begin to act positively, demanding, and preparing itself for, a voice in design and deployment decisions. As one American N/C machine operator has argued:

> The introduction of automation means that our skills are being downgraded, and instead of having the prospect of moving up to a more interesting job, we now have the prospect of either unemployment or a dead-end job. [But] there are alternatives that the union can explore. We have to establish the position that the fruits of technological change can be divided up—some to the workers, not all to the management, as is the case today. We must demand that the machinist rise with the complexity of the machine. Thus, rather than dividing his job up, the machinist should be trained to program and repair his new equipment—a task well within the grasp of most people in the industry.
>
> Demands such as these strike at the heart of most management prerogative clauses which are in many collective-bargaining contracts. Thus, to deal with automation effectively, one has to strike another prime ingredient of business unionism: the idea of "let the management run the business." The introduction of N.C. equipment makes it imperative that we fight such ideas. (Emspak, unpublished)

The real potential of this challenge can perhaps best be illustrated by the existing variations in deployment of the latest generation of N/C machines, called Computer Numerical Control (CNC) systems. CNC machines come equipped with a small minicomputer control unit. With this addition, made feasible by the advent of microprocessors, it becomes possible to store the information from a dozen or so tapes right on the machine itself and then simply retrieve the right program to make a part. More important, the information from the tape can be manipulated and edited: the sequence of operations can be changed, and operations can be added or subtracted. After the changes are made and the parts are run, the machine can produce a "corrected" tape for permanent storage in the company library. With this technology, it becomes possible not only to edit tapes on the shop floor but to create them from scratch; in some systems, programs for even rather complex contours can be made right at the machine by either punching in the required information at a keyboard on the console (so-called manual data input—MDI) or by moving the machine itself to make the first part and entering the information after each operation. (This feature, of course, reintroduces the record-playback concept in an updated digitized form.)

Made possible by the revolution in microelectronics and introduced by machine-tool manufacturers in order to penetrate the vast job market (because it eliminates the overhead requirements of software preparation—the major obstacle for the job shop) and by large metalworking plants in order to get around insurmountable software programming problems (because it allows for easy tape correcting and editing), the new CNC technology lends N/C as never before to total shop-floor control.

Although the large metalworking plants in the United States are steadily introducing CNC equipment, the potential for shop-floor control is far from being realized. The GE plant in Lynn, Massachusetts, is a typical example. Here machine operators are not permitted to edit programs—much less to make their own—on the new CNC machines; quite often the controls are locked. Only supervisory staff and programmers are allowed to edit the programs. Managers are afraid of losing shop-floor control or confusing their tidy labor classification and wage system; programmers are afraid that operators lack the training and experience required for programming—an argument that has convinced at least some operators that these functions are beyond their intellectual grasp. The shortcomings of this system for the operators are obvious. Less obvious are the shortcomings for management: lower quality production and excessive machine down time. If the programs are faulty and the operator cannot (or is not allowed to) make the necessary adjustments, the parts produced will be faulty. If a machine goes down because of programming problems on the second and third shifts, when the programmers are not around, it is likely to be down for the night, with a corresponding loss in productivity.

The situation is quite different in the state-owned weapons factory in Kongsberg, Norway, a plant with roughly the same number of employees, a similar line of products (aircraft parts and turbines), a similar mix of commercial and military customers, and, most important, the same types of CNC machinery (although here they tend to be European-made rather than Japanese) as at GE.* But in Norway the operators routinely do all of the editing, according to their own criteria of safety, efficiency, quality, and convenience; they change the sequence of operations, add or subtract operations, and sometimes alter the entire structure of the program to suit themselves. When they are satisfied with a program and have finished producing a batch of parts, they press a button to generate a corrected tape which, after being approved by a programmer, is put into the library for permanent storage.

All operators are trained in N/C programming and, as a consequence, their conflicts with the programmers are reduced. One programmer—who, like most of his colleagues, had received his training in programming while still a machine operator—justified having any programmers at all by the fact that the programmer was a specialist and was thus more proficient (he also dealt directly with customers and did most of the APT programming of highly complex aircraft parts). Yet when asked if it bothered him to have his well-worked programs tampered with by the operators, he replied, without hesitation, that "the operator knows best; he's the one who has to actually

---

* The following discussion of the situation in Kongsberg, Norway, is based upon correspondence and personal contact with participants in the trade union participation project and a recent research visit to Scandinavia (October 1978).

make the part and is more intimately familiar with the particular safety and convenience factors; also, he usually best knows how to optimize the program for his machine."

This situation, it should be pointed out, is unusual even for Norway. It is the result of many factors. The Iron and Metalworkers' Union in Norway is the most powerful industrial union in the country and the local "club" in Kongsberg is a potent force in the industrial, political, and social life of Kongsberg, representing a cohesive and rather homogeneous working-class community. The factory is important in state policy, as a holding company in electronics, and is an important center of high technology engineering. Also, social democratic legislation in Norway has encouraged worker participation in matters pertaining to working conditions and has given unions the right to information. Most important, however, the local "club" has been involved for the last seven years in what has been called the "trade union participation project," an important development in workers' control which focuses upon the introduction of computer-based manufacturing technology.

In 1971, the Iron and Metalworkers' Union, faced with an unprecedented challenge of new computer-based information and control systems (for production, scheduling, inventory, etc., as well as machining), took steps to learn how to meet it. They succeeded in hiring, on a single-party basis (that is, without management collaboration), the government-run Norwegian Computing Center to research the new technology for them. As the direct result of this unprecedented effort, computer technology was demystified for the union, and the union—and labor in general—was demystified for the computer scientists at the Center; the union became more sophisticated about the technology and the technical people became more attuned to the needs and disciplines of trade unionists. In practical terms, the study resulted in the production of a number of textbooks on the new technology, written by and for shop stewards, the creation of a new union position, the "data shop steward," and, in time, the establishment of formal "data agreements" (between individual companies and their local "clubs" and between the national union and the employers' federation) which outlined the union's right to participate in decisions about technology.

The Kongsberg plant was the first site of such trade union participation. Here the data shop steward, a former assembly worker, is responsible for keeping abreast of and critically scrutinizing all new systems; another man is assigned the job of supervising the activity of the data shop steward to ensure that he doesn't become a "technical man," that is, captive either of the technology or of management and out of touch with the interests of the people on the shop floor. The responsibilities are enormous: this is not a situation in which union and management cooperate harmoniously, nor is it a management-devised job-enlargement scheme to motivate workers. The task of the data shop steward, and the union in general, is to engage, as effectively as possible, in a struggle over information and control, a struggle engaged in, with equal sophistication and earnestness, by the other side.

When management plans to introduce a new computer-based production system, for example, the union must assume as a matter of course (based upon long experience) that the proposed design reflects purposes that are not necessarily consonant with the interests of the workers. The data shop steward and his colleagues must learn about the system early enough, and investigate it thoroughly enough, to ensure that it contains no features that make possible, for example, the measurement of individual performance or any monitoring of shop-floor activities that would restrict worker freedom or control. As it turns out, all new systems invariably contain such features (since they are often camouflaged attempts to introduce control mechanisms that have been successfully resisted by the workers in other forms), and it is up to the union to identify them and demand that they be eliminated. It is the union's responsibility to its members, in short, to struggle to "recondition" the system so that it meets their own, as well as management's, specifications. At Kongsberg, for example, after a long battle, the union has succeeded in securing for all of the people on the shop floor complete access to the computer-based production and inventory systems. Just as CNC has made automatic machining more accessible to shop-floor control, so computer-integrated production systems have made it possible to eliminate certain managerial functions by simply extending the reach of the people on the shop floor. How this technology will actually be employed in a plant depends less upon any inherent nature of the technology than upon the particular manufacturing processes involved, the political and economic setting, and the relative power and sophistication of the parties engaged in the struggle over control of production.

The social relations of production shape the technology of production as much as the other way around. Given different social relations, one sees different designs, different deployment. Of course, these relations are themselves shaped by larger conditions—the political, economic, and cultural climate, the labor market, trade union traditions and strengths, international competition and the flow of investment capital. These factors always influence the conditions for struggle, define its constraints. But whatever the constraints, whatever the social conditions, the technological possibilities remain.

Proletarianizing Clerical Work: Technology and Organizational Control in the Office

Evelyn Nakano Glenn and Roslyn L. Feldberg

Introduction

As the American dream of upward mobility through hard work dissolves in the face of limited opportunity, analysts have turned their attention to the meaning of routine work. The pioneer studies of the 1950s and 1960s examined blue-collar work in large, highly mechanized factories (Blauner 1964; Chinoy 1955; Gouldner 1954). Recently, it has become fashionable to say that white-collar work, particularly clerical work, is becoming factory-like. A federal task force acknowledges changes in the office:

> Secretaries, clerks and bureaucrats were once grateful for having been spared the dehumanization of the factory . . . they had higher status than blue collar [workers]. But today the clerk . . . is the typical American worker . . . and such positions offer little in the way of prestige . . . imparting to the clerical worker the same impersonality that blue-collar workers experience in the factory. (HEW 1973:38)

In addition, some authors have written personal accounts of their own or other women's experience in routinized office work, for example, Tepperman (1976), Howe (1977), and Garson (1975). On the whole, however, we lack detailed studies of the overall conditions in clerical work and the implications of these conditions for over 12.7 million female clerical workers (Glenn and Feldberg 1978). The research reported in this paper

---

This paper is a revised, expanded, and up-dated version of "Degraded and Deskilled: the Proletarianization of Clerical Work," *Social Problems,* 25 (October 1977):52–64. Research for the revisions was supported in part by an NIMH grant from the Center for Studies of Metropolitan Problems. We would like to thank Andy Zimbalist for suggestions for revision, as well as Carol Brown, Susan Eckstein, Helen Hughes, and Ruth Jacobs for their comments on various drafts. We especially appreciated the cooperation of the clerical workers who told us what their work involved and how they felt about doing it.

is the first, exploratory stage of such a study. We analyze the changing conditions of clerical work, examining the extent to which they can be understood by the concept of proletarianization.

Proletarianization can be defined as a "shift in middle-class occupations toward wage workers, in terms of: income, property, skill, prestige or power, irrespective of whether or not the people involved are aware of these changes" (Mills 1956:295). Following Mills, we use the term proletarianization to refer to objective conditions rather than to the workers' subjective feelings and identities.

The features that distinguish clerical work, justifying its inclusion among "middle-class" occupations, are its clean physical surroundings, an emphasis on mental as opposed to manual activities, reliance on workers' judgment in executing tasks, and direct personal contact among workers and between workers and managers. *Proletarianization occurs as clerical work loses these special characteristics, i.e., as work is organized around manual rather than mental activities, as tasks become externally structured and controlled, and as relationships become depersonalized.* We therefore examine changes in three areas: the organization of clerical activities, the control of the work process, and the social relationships in the office. We argue that the increased size of organizations, the application of machine technology, and prevailing organizational goals have had a proletarianizing effect in all three areas. However, we will also argue that proletarianization has progressed at different rates for workers in different specialties and in different types of organizational settings.*

Organization and Technological Changes in the Office

Clerical work is, above all, work in organizations. It does not and cannot exist as an independent occupation. In turn, the characteristics of the organization define the nature of clerical

* The materials for this paper are drawn from several sources, the most important of which are data we collected through informal observations of clerical arrangements in five large organizations; discussions with managers about the organization and functions of clerical work; and intensive interviews with thirty clerical workers. See the *Social Problems* article cited above for further details on the sample interviews and analysis.

work within it. The easiest way to appreciate the way organizational structures shape clerical work is to compare the small office of the nineteenth century with the large one of today.

The Nineteenth-Century Office

In the older offices the clerical staffs were small. Clerks were "all-around" workers: they handled all phases of an assignment, both organizing and executing it, and they did a wide variety of tasks. In 1905, Dorothy Richardson was "entrusted with the revision of the least important manuscripts" in the office of a publishing company where she also took dictation and typed (Richardson 1972:272). Clerks often had extended responsibilities that today would be classified as managerial or administrative (Lockwood 1958). A bookkeeper, intimately familiar with all of the financial details of a firm, might be readily consulted on financial decisions. In the 1920s, for example, one secretary ran a business for most of the year while the head of the firm lived in the southwest for his health (Bureau of Vocational Information 1929). The organization of the work allowed the worker to develop skills and to identify as a skilled craftsman, a professional, or a part of management (Lockwood 1958).

The Growth of Organizations

The rise of large national companies in the latter part of the nineteenth and early twentieth centuries profoundly changed the office (Stinchcombe 1965). The demand for clerical services soared, not only absolutely, but also disproportionately to the growth of production (Melman 1951; Rushing 1967). National companies established central administrative offices with huge clerical staffs (Mills 1956). Industries such as banking, insurance, and brokerage, whose primary work force was clerical, accounted for an increasingly large share of the economy (Braverman 1974).

The demand for clerical services was met by hiring more workers, by introducing machines, and by bringing "scientific management" into the office. The numerical growth of clerical workers between 1870 and 1970 is documented in the table below. At first, simple machines such as typewriters were introduced; after World War I, multiple-function machines—for example, bookkeeping machines which performed a sequence of tasks—were used to speed up operations (Baker 1964). Scientific management was used to break jobs into a series of steps, which were then reordered to save time, and/or divided among different groups of workers. Physical rearrangements eliminated wasted motion.

These changes in office routine transformed the office hierarchy. A new, male managerial stratum took over the quasi-managerial activities of the clerks, leaving the detail work to the now predominantly female office staffs (Crozier 1964; Mills 1956). Two distinct occupational hierarchies evolved: a male one, made up of many layers of managers, and a female one of file clerks, typists, stenographers, clerical supervisors, and secretaries (Coyle 1929; Davies 1973; Mills 1956; Rotella 1974). Thus began an increasing distinction between those conceptualizing a task (mental work) and those doing it (manual work).

The Modern Office

To appreciate and evaluate the effects of these as well as more recent organizational and technological changes, we now look at the large contemporary office. Here workers are organized into functional subunits (e.g., sales, accounting, inventory control). Within units, clerks are further subdivided according to task. In fact, the most striking features of "paper work" in large organizations are the elaborate subdivision of tasks and the extreme specialization of workers. One large insurance company, for example, had over 350 separate job titles for its 2,000 clerical employees.

Two current developments furthering these trends are the application of new office technology and the increased use of pooling arrangements for clerical functions. Office technology involves several elements: the use of computers to capture, process, and store large quantities of information; the use of electronic communications to transmit information between two points instantaneously; and the application of systems and behavioral sciences to analyze and simulate office procedures in order to automate them. With accelerating developments in each of these areas, the term "office automation" has taken on a new meaning. Originally, the use of computers to perform routine clerical tasks, such as processing payrolls, keeping inventories, and maintaining insurance policy records, was viewed as the culmination of technical developments that began with the

Table 1
Growth of the Clerical Force, 1870–1977
(in thousands)

	1870	1880	1890	1900	1910	1920	1930	1940	1950	1960	1970	1977
Total clerical workers	91	186	490	770	1,885	3,311	4,274	4,847	7,635	9,783	13,714	16,106
As % of employed persons	.7	1.1	2.1	2.6	5.1	8.0	9.0	9.1	12.8	14.7	17.4	17.8
Female clerical workers	2	8	83	204	677	1,601	2,223	2,549	4,597	6,629	10,233	12,715
As % of all clericals workers	2.4	4.3	16.9	26.5	35.9	48.4	52.0	52.6	60.2	67.8	74.6	78.9

Note: Figures are not strictly comparable due to minor reclassifications of occupational categories.
Sources: For 1870–1940: Total Clerical Workers, Female Clerical Workers, compiled from Janet M. Hooks, *Women's Occupations Through Seven Decades*, U.S. Department of Labor, Women's Bureau, Bulletin #218 (Washington, D.C.: Government Printing Office, 1947). Table 11A: Occupations of Women Workers, 1870–1940; Table 11B: Occupations of All Workers, 1870–1940.
For 1870–1940: Employed Persons, from U.S. Bureau of the Census, *Historical Statistics, Abstracts of the United States*, Series D57–71.
For 1950–1970: U.S. Bureau of the Census, *Statistical Abstract of the United States* (1972), Table 366: Employed Persons, by Major Occupation Group and Sex: 1950–1972.
For 1977: U.S. Department of Labor, Bureau of Labor Statistics, *Employment and Earnings*, 25 (January 1978), Table 21: Employed Persons by Occupation, Sex, and Age.

typewriter, the adding machine, and other simple machines. Now, however, the use of computers for routine tasks is looked upon as merely laying the groundwork for true office automation. Since the 1960s, the wedding of computers to electronic communications systems has made possible the replacement of "paper flow" with "electronic information flow" (Zisman 1978). Systems and behavioral analysis of nonroutine office processes is still in its infancy but the goal of researchers committed to office automation is to build programs which automatically make decisions and initiate sequences of actions, functions which were formerly reserved for human judgment (Conference on Office Technology 1978).

While the impact of early computer technology has been studied (e.g., Shepard 1972; Rico 1967; "Effects of mechanization and automation in offices" 1960), the effect of the newer technology on the conditons of clerical work have not been systematically assessed. Computers were originally introduced as labor-saving devices, and today's sophisticated computers and communications equipment are expected to increase productivity even more. Interestingly, the literature advertising the new equipment emphasizes the improved quality of the output and greater speed in producing it, rather than the reduction in the work force per se. Nevertheless, there is some evidence that fewer workers are needed to do the same amount of work: for instance, an insurance company that switched from entering data by keypunching cards to direct disc entry reduced the number of data-entry operators from 110 to 85.* The net reduction would have been even greater if the amount of information entered had stayed the same.

There is, however, a countervailing trend. The capacity to store and process huge amounts of information appears to con-

---

* In disc entry, operators type characters from written documents on an electronic keyboard. The characters are transmitted electronically to central magnetic discs. These discs, which resemble stacks of phonograph records, rotate rapidly and a reading and writing mechanism enters data wherever there is available space on them. The discs act as an intermediate storage medium and data can be edited, corrected, augmented, and organized into specific formats as desired. Once this is done, the data are transferred to magnetic tapes for computer processing. The main advantages of disc entry for speed of entering data are that many operators can enter onto a set of discs simultaneously, and that they can type the data in the order they are written in a document because they can be reordered later into a format acceptable to the computer.

tribute to a demand for even more information, which eventually means more clerical workers.* Managers demand more data in order to make more "rational" decisions, internal and external record keeping becomes more complex, and new services are added on to previous ones. In the company mentioned above, although the basic information on the claim could be entered more quickly, the number of pieces of information that had to be entered on each claim expanded enormously, thus maintaining the need for a large number of operators.

In the debate about the impact of technology on the organization of work, the most common hypothesis has been that mechanization brings about fragmentation while automation makes possible reintegration of previously separated tasks (Shepard 1972; Rico 1967). If the current state of office technology is viewed as automation, the hypothesis appears to be disproved. On the other hand, there are those who argue that the present level of technology is laying the groundwork for automation and argue that reintegration will occur in the future (Zisman 1978).

At the present time, even with the most advanced office systems now in use, we have found that most clerical workers connected to these systems have experienced neither increased autonomy nor decreased fragmentation. Regardless of technical differences among automated systems, all require that "information be handled in standardized and regularized form, which, in turn, implies that previous steps have been taken to put the information in such form" (Hall 1975:319). Moreover, when a system covers an entire firm, all activities must be translated into the same format (Rico 1967:31). As a result, work throughout the organization is structured by the requirements of the computer. Although the clerks may be less directly supervised, they do not gain autonomy; the requirements of the machine replace the directives of an immediate supervisor. Their mental choices are limited to predetermined categories. They have little discretion to do the work as they see fit and they are under pressure to

---

*There is historical evidence for this pattern. Typewriters, bookkeeping machines, adding machines, etc., were also hailed as labor-saving devices in the early days of their use (Coyle 1928:17–18). While they, too, reduced the number of person hours required to do a given volume of work, their use did not mark the beginning of a general reduction in the size of office staffs—although additional clerks often had different functions.

work quickly, since their work has to feed into subsequent stages. In some offices, each worker must meet base levels for output and accuracy; greater speed is encouraged by offering incentive pay to those who surpass these levels. In other offices, the individual rating of workers has been replaced by a group rating in order to encourage teamwork, reduce the paperwork involved in supervision, and maintain morale. In both cases, the worker is proletarianized by our definition.

Although many routine clerical jobs, such as tabulating, are eliminated, other equally routine jobs are created—such as transporting tapes and typing in data at a terminal. New skilled jobs, such as programming, are also created, but clerks are rarely upgraded to fill these new positions ("Effects of mechanization" 1960; Hall 1975). In any case, these new jobs are themselves becoming subdivided and deskilled, leaving the bulk of skilled work to systems analysts (Greenbaum 1976; Kraft 1977; and in this volume), who are part of the group of professional and technical workers, recruited from outside the organization, who form a new higher status category within the office hierarchy. The proportion of low-level clerical jobs remains roughly the same.

The trend toward subdivision and specialization has been furthered by clerical pooling arrangements. Pools have long been used for such routine tasks as typing and tabulating, but the new arrangements extend the use of pools to secretarial functions, with automatic machinery downgrading the skills required. These features are evident at Public Utility (a pseudonym for one of our research sites) where IBM's Work Processing/Administrative Support System has been introduced. While managers (called "clients" in the new system) were previously serviced by one-to-one secretaries, supplemented by a typing pool, now secretarial work is divided among three pools. The first is the Word Processing Unit, made up of eight "general service clerks" who do the typing on "automated typing equipment" (Hilaael 1975). Two "clerical assistants" type and help to supervise the work. Recording equipment, accessible through ordinary telephone lines, automatically accepts dictation phoned in by "clients" and other members of the organization at any time of the day or night, even from distant cities. A supervisor receives assignments and instructions from "clients" and parcels it out. In the second pool, the Administrative Support Center, between ten and twelve women handle all the nontyping clerical tasks: they answer telephones, schedule appointments, order supplies, and keep records and charts. This unit, which handles thirty to forty "clients," also has a head supervisor and two working assistants. The third pool, consisting of four or five men and women, does all the reproduction work.

Dividing up secretarial work in this way makes it easier to identify the elements of each task and to set up standard procedures for carrying them out. For example, Public Utility has developed rules for transferring phone calls received by an administrative support clerk. Proper routing thus does not depend on the clerk's special knowledge of her "clients" duties, and the clerk's job no longer requires the general knowledge that characterized the all-around secretary.

Current Patterns and Trends

Clerical work is still undergoing change and its conditions vary. Although we interviewed women from many companies and organizations, including Technical Research, Techtronics, and Municipal Offices (pseudonyms), we studied five in greater detail. Of these Big City Insurance and Public Utility—a major insurance firm and a utility company—have subdivided clerical work to the greatest degree, using extensive electronic equipment and pooling. Progressive Products, a large manufacturer of sophisticated technical equipment, provides a contrast. It retains all-around clerical and secretarial arrangements, with finely graded steps for upward mobility. Rationalization has been resisted because the founder's belief in "meaningful" work still molds company policies. Proponents of rationalization argue, however, that this company's creed can be adhered to only because the company is financially successful. Brand Name Foods, a medium-sized regional distributor, and Personal Manufacturing, the corporate headquarters of a national manufacturing giant, fall somewhere between these extremes. They retain middle-level, all-around secretaries, but also rely on a separate staff which uses the new office technology to perform highly routinized clerical chores.

Many managers believe that Public Utility and Big City Insurance are establishing the pattern for the future. Every manager we talked to was interested in upgrading equipment or in expanding the use of equipment already installed. In addition, the volume of sales and intensity of use of computers and communications systems has grown sufficiently for costs to be actually declining. According to a recent article, communications costs are falling at 11 percent, computer logic at 25 percent, and computer memory at 40 percent per year (Burns 1977). The costs of conversion and reorganization necessary to install these systems thus becomes more attractive. A Stanford Research Institute study predicted that the investment in equipment per office employee will rise to $10,000 by 1985, indicating that the "total market for office systems technology could reach $85 billion" by that time (Zisman 1978). Acting on these predicted trends, a number of major manufacturers, including Xerox, IBM, Digital, A. B. Dick, Honeywell, and Wang, have developed complete lines of office equipment and are battling for a share of the market. Over three hundred representatives of large corporations recently attended a two-day conference devoted to describing current trends, as well as research efforts to develop such new systems as electronic mail (Conference on Office Technology 1978).

Although we did not conduct a systematic survey, our impression is that the leaders in using new office technology are large organizations, either private profit-making or public and semipublic monopolies, whose basic activities are to process information on large numbers of accounts. These organizations, principally insurance companies, public utilities, and large banks, began introducing new office systems as soon as they were available, as early as 1966. A 1972–1973 Bureau of Labor Statistics wage survey of office workers who work with computer technology found that the banking and insurance industries combined accounted for roughly one out of every four workers surveyed (Taylor 1978:11). These industries have continually changed equipment and reorganized their information processing as new systems have been introduced, but the federal government, which supported the development and use of computers from the earliest period (Kraft 1977), has been slow to install the new systems. Educational institutions and human service organizations, which traditionally invest little capital in office equipment, appear to be the slowest to convert, but as the competition among sellers "shakes down" to a few compatible systems, as the application of equipment becomes more sophisticated, and as unit costs fall, vendors of the new systems expect to attract even these conservative customers.

In those organizations with the most advanced technology, we observed that almost the entire clerical staff, and much of the managerial and professional staff, is affected in one way or another. All information has to be put into a form compatible with the system. Thus, for instance, managers must learn to dictate letters according to a standard format so they can be transcribed correctly in a Word Processing Center. Different departments are required to use the same symbols to record information. The degree of change in the organization of jobs varies, but change is widespread. Specific jobs for capturing, processing, and storing data are created and expanded: in one large insurance company almost one hundred people, approximately 5 percent of the work force, were employed solely to enter data into the computer by typing at terminals. Other jobs are reorganized around the information capability of the computer. Each office had at least one computer terminal, and several customer service units were consolidated so that one terminal could be installed for every two representatives. Telephone inquiries were answered by immediately calling up the computer to retrieve stored information. The representatives no longer had to leave their desks to look up information or to consult with specialists familiar with specific types of policies.

Although the exact details may change as systems are tested and "debugged," the general outline is clear. New office systems will use a technology based on subdivision and standardization. Choices among different work structures now available to workers will be considerably narrowed for those working in large organizations.

Impact of Changes on Clerical Activities

As a result of the changes described above, old skills have been made trivial and opportunities to develop new skills have been reduced. Such traditional specialities as stenography and bookkeeping, which required extensive training, have been displaced or simplified beyond recognition. The skills now required are more *mechanical,* as in operating a xerox machine, *lower level,* as in typing addresses on automatically typed correspondence, and/or *more technical and narrow,* as in the administrative support center.

An example of this change in skills is seen in the job of "approval clerk" in one insurance company. Formerly, this clerk received telephone questions about claims from field representatives, tentatively approved the claims, and explained to the field representative which kinds of claims were routinely accepted and how much money was normally allowed. For this job, the clerk specialized in one type of policy and had a fairly full knowledge of the contract and of usual practices in processing claims. Once the approval system was computerized, the field representative could type questions onto a computer terminal and receive answers directly. The approval clerk is called only if the computer rejects the question, and then the clerk's job is to examine the format of the question and decide why it was rejected: the knowledge required is technical and almost completely standardized. The necessary formats, collected in notebooks, can often be taught in a few days.

Many clerical workers still acquire a full range of traditional office skills in high school or commercial colleges. When they enter organizations that use the new office technology, they find that their more specialized jobs preclude using and maintaining these skills. A thirty-seven-year-old clerk at Public Utility wanted to keep up her typing, but all of the typing was done in a separate pool. She did not want to type full time; as a result, she never types at all. While articles on the impact of office technology emphasize opportunities for women to develop new skills (e.g., *Word Processing* 1976), some clerical workers keenly feel the loss of the old ones.

The simplification of jobs and the absence of mental activity makes many jobs more demanding. The worker experiences great pressure to work quickly, accurately, and to maintain the pace set by the machines. The strain of routine jobs is demonstrated by workers' emphasis on their need for temperamental qualities rather than skills. "Patience" was mentioned by fourteen of thirty workers. As a twenty-one-year-old typist in Word Processing stated; "You need a lot of patience. You need to be more or less good-natured, easy going. Sometimes the tension gets really bad. Some people look on it as boring. If you go on saying, 'Oh God, another day!' you wouldn't last too long."

Since the reorganization of clerical work first began, managers have looked for "clerks who are satisfied to remain clerks" (Coyle 1929:186). Opportunities for upward mobility, never very extensive, have been further curtailed by the collapse of meaningful skill differentials. The more energetic and ambitious workers reach the top of their job ladders in a few years, then find themselves blocked. And while routine computer jobs such as keypunching have long been "universally regarded as dead-end occupation(s)" (Hoos 1962:75), even the newer, "better" computer jobs offer few opportunities for learning and experimentation. A young woman, promoted and trained in computer operation at Brand Name Foods, repeats the same operations day after day. "At first there was a lot to learn, but now that I've mastered it, there's nothing new. I know the work backwards and forwards." The next step up for her was "nowhere"; the company would be reluctant to move her, for not only would she have to be trained for a different position but someone else would have to be trained to replace her.

The main avenues of mobility for clerical workers are either horizontal or downward. A woman working for Big City Insurance said; "I thought about changing my job, but it took ten years of seniority to get a month's vacation. If I left and went to another job, I'd have to start up the levels again and I don't know how long it would take." Clericals have become similar to blue-collar workers, and unlike professionals, in that the skills they develop on the job rarely qualify them for better positions in new settings.

Control of the Work Process

Subdivision and standardization of the work process have been accompanied by changes toward more "rational" and impersonal methods of control. This close association has led some observers to argue that subdivision and specialization were not instituted primarily for the often-stated reasons of efficiency (Gorz 1973; Marglin 1974), but were designed to increase the company's control over the work, as shown in recent studies of steel manufacturing (Stone 1975) and computer programming (Kraft 1977 and this volume). However, it is important to note the managerial ideology that rationalization of work and formal control ensure profitability.* Managers consider the work pro-

---

* Nonprofit and governmental organizations are not exceptions, since they are typically accountable to outsiders for maintaining the appearance of "productivity." Standards can be nonmonetary (e.g., number of clients served) as well as monetary (e.g., the cost of servicing each client). Because of the lack of a profit measure, large nonprofit organizations often develop elaborate bureaucratic standards to assess efficiency.

cess and the worker the means—and sometimes the obstacles—to realization of this goal. Both need to be controlled.

To appreciate the changes in control mechanisms, it is useful to look again at the early office. Workers then were no less closely controlled than workers today, but the control was more personal and dependent on internal motivation. Clerks were few and worked in close physical proximity to, and under the visible eye of, the employer. Moreover, the work of clerk and employer were inseparable: the activities of the owner generated the work of the clerk, while the clerk's activities made it possible for the owner to carry on his or her business. Relationships typically involved mutual loyalty and obligation. The clerk performed a variety of both official and personal functions; in return, he was afforded a measure of leniency and protection. In short, the organization of the office and the conditions of work created direct bonds between boss and clerk, encouraging the latter to identify with the former.*

Formal Controls

As businesses grew, the sheer number of clerical workers made face-to-face controls impossible. More formal, administrative controls were introduced, beginning the process of bureaucratization (Gerth and Mills 1958). An increasingly fine hierarchy, headed by an office manager and staffed by unit supervisors and assistants, supervised the clerks according to rules. In addition, subdivision and standardization made impersonal control easier and more necessary.

Personal forms of control imply a certain degree of flexibility in the pace and organization of work. However, subdivided work requires inflexible routines to insure that the subparts fit together. Subdivision prevents workers from gaining an overview of the total work process, thus necessitating external coordination, which is supplied by managers. Managers devise a work plan to be implemented by the supervisors, who divide the work load and see that production requirements are fulfilled.

---

* It is important not to romanticize clerical jobs in the old office. Workers were frequently overworked and underpaid, and the personal controls could be oppressive and arbitrary. Some of these problems have been eliminated through standardization and formal controls. However, the workers we interviewed generally prefer personal control, even with its potential abuses.

External coordination requires standardization, introducing new opportunities for control. As the work becomes standardized, the supervisors can regulate workers simply by observing their movements. A supervisor at Big City Insurance reported that she can tell at a glance whether workers are doing their assigned tasks.

These external controls over the work process increase the worker's vulnerability. The worker is open to constant inspection (similar to the "listening-in" method of monitoring customer service representatives and telephone operators; see Langer 1972). Errors can't be hidden. The more clearly bounded the job is, the easier it is to assess output—how many forms are checked or the number of pages that are typed. It becomes a simple matter to rate a clerk on numerical production, and it can be argued that as a job is reduced to quantifiable elements it loses status, thus contributing to its proletarianization.

The workers' hold over their position becomes precarious: their services are interchangeable and replaceable. Speed and dexterity, rather than finely honed skills, are required. The older and more experienced workers do the same work as younger, less experienced ones. A forty-nine-year-old clerk-typist for Municipal Offices says, "If I left tomorrow, they'd get someone else. Sometimes they'll give me [forms to type] and say I can do it better. I'm not flattered when I know someone else could do it as well." An experienced worker who complains or becomes expensive through raises can easily be replaced.

Processes that depend on particular individuals with specialized skills and knowledge can be disrupted by absences and turnover, and large organizations can avoid such disruption through standardization. Public Utility requires each clerk to write a desk manual detailing duties and daily routine, including instructions on how to answer the telephone, how to deliver mail, etc. As one clerk said, "If I'm out, my fill-in should be able to do what I do. It took two weeks to do it [write the desk manual], one or two hours a day. . . . It's writing yourself out of a job. Everything is written in logs and on paper."

Once formal controls are instituted, they become increasingly necessary because they undermine a worker's internal motivation. Personal control provides incentives to do a good job or to complete tasks before the end of the day; impersonal control leads to work by "rule"—to put in the required number of hours and to do only a defined task, regardless of the organization's needs. A secretary transferred to supervising a pool says, "I used to work until 7 or 8 P.M. to get things done. Now, as soon as it's 4:30, I'm out the door." A vicious cycle arises. As Gorz (1973) describes it: the less management is willing to rely on the worker's motivation, the more extraneous, regimented, and idiotic work has to become, while the more extraneous, regimented, and idiotic work becomes, the less management *can* rely upon the worker's motivation.

In this transitional period, some workers act as though the older conditions of work still existed. A nineteen-year-old typist says, "When I type, I don't like to make mistakes. When I finish, it gives me a feeling of satisfaction." A thirty-two-year-old staff secretary says, "When I clear up everything on my desk, then it's been a good day. I don't like to leave stuff hanging over until the next day." Employers benefit even while the changes they have introduced are undermining the basis of these internal standards.

Sex as a Basis for Control

Managerial responses to issues of control in the United States have been shaped by the belief that workers are irrational, individualistic, and lack a long-term perspective (Kanter 1974). Thus, managers rely on external controls to ensure that workers do what they are supposed to do. In the case of clerical workers, managers are also influenced by prevailing stereotypes about women: that they are oriented toward pleasing others, are more sensitive than men to the quality of their surroundings, and are more honest and less mercenary. Acker and Van Houten suggest that "unique mechanisms [may be] employed in organizations to control women" (1974:153). Thus while clerical workers are sometimes thought to be treated "better" than production workers, on closer inspection this "better" treatment may disguise closer, more restrictive controls. Elinor Langer (1972) showed how the New York Telephone Company "rewards" workers while maintaining both control and low wages. The women are "treated" to candy on holidays, jewelry on their anniversaries with the company, and appliances for recruiting new employees. "Niceness" is stressed throughout the company, to create a pleasant atmosphere. The "niceness," which extends to sharing work loads, helps the women cope with the strains of constant supervision and rigid formats; it also enables the company to continue imposing "unreasonable" demands. Similarly, in an ostensibly more enlightened setting, clerks in a college business office are allowed to cover for each other, thereby ensuring that work gets done at no extra cost (Garson 1973).

Orders are cloaked in the guise of personal requests, which women often find difficult to refuse. A typist for Technical Research reports, "One doesn't have time to go to the bathroom when typing a proposal to meet a deadline." The president of the company always sends her a memo of appreciation for extraordinary effort when such a proposal is completed. Sometimes changes in routine, designed to formalize control, are presented as moves to improve personal relationships, presumably because women would welcome such changes. A clerk at Public Utility reports, "When they set up the Administrative Services Center, they said it was more democratic. We wouldn't have 'bosses' anymore, just clients. But they were just trying to save money. A clerk gets $150 a week while a secretary gets $185, for serving just one person." Even when management is aware that its employees see through its rationale, they rely on them to act like ladies and to continue to be loyal, dependable, and polite.

Extending Control: Why Secretaries Are "Out"

How far control over the worker has been extended can be appreciated by looking at the one group that has seemingly escaped control—the private secretaries. Within the office structure, the secretary is both a personal assistant and a company employee, but her principle tie and loyalty is to her boss rather than to the company. The secretary to the president of Techtronics describes her duties in this way: "Basically, I try to help my boss succeed. If he succeeds, I succeed." The company rarely measures a private secretary's performance directly. Her status and pay reflect her boss' position—they rise as he or she moves up.

Researchers have long recognized that a secretary's status is tied to that of her boss (Moore 1951; Mills 1956; Benet 1972), but they have rarely explored the implications of that tie on organizational control. The secretary is accountable to her boss;

in return, the boss protects her from company scrutiny.* A secretary at Progressive Products, for instance, reported that her boss screened out unpleasant assignments and safeguarded her free time. The company has little control over the secretary's activities, and management complains about "under-utilization" of the secretary's time (Hilaael 1975). Replacing private secretaries with pools is, therefore, another way to extend company control over employees.

Relationships Among Workers

Changes in the work process and in the control structures have transformed relationships in the office. We will look at two sets of relationships: those between supervisors and those they supervise, and those among lower level workers.

Again it is useful to compare these relationships with those in the offices of an earlier period. Relationships then were face-to-face. The experienced specialists, such as bookkeepers and chief clerks, occupied positions analogous to those of "master craftsmen" in the trades. They took charge of the whole work process, aided by junior bookkeepers, copiers, and office boys. Like apprentices, these assistants learned the rudiments and then the refinements of their specialties by working alongside the senior clerks (Braverman 1974). Since each individual made a unique contribution, the interdependence among workers was immediately obviously. At the same time, the paternalistic structure of the office encouraged them to identify with those above (Mills 1956).

Supervisors, Secretaries, and Clerks

In the large, modern office with specialized clerical units, the relationships between higher and lower levels are impersonal. Contact with managers is limited and filtered through several

---

* It is also well known that secretaries "cover up" for their bosses' absences from the office and serve as excuses for their errors, as in the phrase, "My secretary must have forgotten to send it out . . .". This consequence of the boss-secretary tie also reduces control and limits accountability of lower level managers to higher level ones.

layers of supervisors. Because of the separation between planning and doing, supervisors do not directly generate the work for those under them. Their authority stems more from their formal position than from their expertise as a skilled craftsperson. Like the factory foreman, supervisors oversee routines and enforce rules set up by others. They stand in for management, sheltering it from direct confrontations with workers. An assistant supervisor at Big City Insurance complained that she had to do all the "dirty work." "If there's any disciplining, I have to do that," as well as "correcting our children's mistakes" (see Hughes 1959).

Supervisors are defined as first-level management and are paid entry-level managerial salaries. However, since the position does not lead to higher grades, the supervisor occupies a no-man's land. By defining supervisors as "management," companies remove them from the worker category, creating barriers to personal relationships. They also enforce informal rules to forestall face-to-face relationships that might undermine impersonal control. As a recently promoted supervisor at Public Utility reported: "They don't like management people socializing with non-management. They think it hinders work. I don't think it does. I used to have lunch with one girl and I had to stop, and I couldn't even tell her [why]. My supervisor told me I couldn't have lunch with her any more."

It is *not* that managers have lost sight of the importance of "human relations" or are no longer interested in having "loyal" employees. Quite the contrary. Extensive employee benefit programs are the rule in large organizations and managers are proud of such new services as career counseling and personnel training for supervisors (which includes methods such as transactional analysis). Unlike earlier practices, current programs are designed to create loyalty to the organization without fostering personal ties between individuals that could introduce "irrational" elements into supervisor decisions. In effect, an *impersonal* paternalism is being substituted for the *personal* paternalism of the earlier period.

Under these conditions, many workers shy away from promotion to supervisor, recognizing the conflicts inherent in the position. A typical remark was made by a twenty-six-year-old clerk at Giant Investment, who said, "I wouldn't want to be responsible for more people, but I would want to be responsible for more work." This remark illustrates an underlying problem: since workers don't aspire to supervisors' positions, there is little basis for identifying with them. This is quite unlike the close identification assistant bookkeepers could form with head bookkeepers, the people they could see themselves becoming.

The other high-status clerical position, the secretary, is also isolated from the lower levels. Unlike the supervisor, the top-level secretary rarely begins in the clerical ranks, and so lacks a common base of experience with other clerical workers. The top-level secretaries we studied entered at, or near, the top, like the nineteen-year-old secretary to the president of Technical Research. She came directly from a secretarial school which taught not only technical skills, but also poise, grooming habits, and general polish. A secretary for a high level executive has to protect her reflected authority by keeping her distance, by not mixing too much with others in the office. The secretary to the vice-president of Techtronics said she was well suited to her job because she was a "loner."

Relations among Lower Level Workers

If workers no longer identify with higher level supervisors and secretaries, what happens to relationships among workers at lower levels? Individuals within a work group are no longer interdependent, since everyone does the same job; the interdependence is instead between clerical units, a much more abstract concept. As a result, it is difficult for individual workers to know what those in different units do, and whether they share common conditions and occupy comparable positions in the hierarchy.

Divisions are reinforced by physical separation. At Public Utility and Big City Insurance, different clerical units are located in separate parts of the building. An administrative assistant in Giant Investments, which employs hundreds of clerks, claimed that after five years she only knew the two other women working in her own unit. Clerks rarely move around or observe workers in other parts of the building. Messengers deliver and pick up communications. At Big City Insurance, clerks must stay at their desks except during designated break periods. While these arrangements are defended on the grounds of efficiency, they limit workers' opportunities to form face-to-face relationships with other workers.

Within units, external supervision and standardization of activities create contradictory forces. On the one hand, workers are tempted to ease the strains through cooperation and solidarity. On the other hand, they feel vulnerable, which decreases their desire for personal ties. Some are fearful of being too open. A typist at Technical Research says, "They [the company] are aware of what's going on, sometimes too aware." When asked whether she had close friends at work, a clerk at Public Utility replied: "To me a close friend is someone you can divulge anything to. But here, you are reluctant to talk about personal things. . . . In a large company there is a lot of gossip and things spread."

Traditionally, lower level clerical workers were said to lack worker identity because they identified with their superiors. With impersonal control, this tendency has been reduced. Now other structural factors make worker-worker identification problematic.

Conclusion

Proletarianization is the outcome of changes in the organization of work designed to increase managers' control of the work process. It affects workers psychologically, economically, and politically—as individuals and as members of a class. In an earlier paper we explored the effects of proletarianization on worker consciousness (Feldberg and Glenn 1977). Here we turn our attention to two other interrelated outcomes: first, the down-grading of the work itself and consequent changes in the worker's relationship to it; and second, the resulting inefficiencies in carrying out of clerical work and, therefore, in coordinating operations throughout organizations.

The transformation of clerical work itself has been analyzed in the body of the paper: the changes remove the very features that once made clerical work interesting, attractive, and of higher status. At a more abstract level, the changes alter the relationship of the workers to their work, to each other, and to management (Ollman 1971). As managerial decisions are substituted for workers' decisions, the work force becomes an "inert" collection of bodies mechanically related to a set of materials and sustained in motion by external force. Managers' greater control is control over a transformed work force: less knowledgeable, less involved, less committed, and therefore less able and willing to respond to variation.

If the process is carried far enough, the very efficiency managers claim to seek is sacrificed (Marglin 1974).* This is illustrated in a recent evaluation of a Work Processing/Administrative Support System (Hilaael 1975): managers found that their telephones were answered quickly under the new system and were pleased with the "good coverage," but once the phones were answered, problems arose. Some unimportant calls reached managers directly, while more important ones were transformed into messages. With subdivided tasks and standardized procedures, the workers who answered the telephones had neither the information nor the authority to handle routine matters or even to sort routine from important information.

When clerical work cannot be performed efficiently, the control structure it services is similarly hampered (Giddens 1975). Clerical units have been described as the "arteries through which the life blood flows." Activities such as record keeping, scheduling, and copying link the various internal departments of an organization and connect it to "other businesses and to the rest of the people" (Mills 1956:190). These connections are essential for maintaining control of the various departments in an organization and for coordinating their activities. Changes which rigidify or interfere with these connections can result in organizational paralysis. The paradox is that as managers gain greater control over clerical activities, they may become less able to manage their organizations.

---

* Researchers developing new office systems readily acknowledge these problems. However, they seek the solution not in expanding workers' training and restoring to them control of the new technology, but in more sophisticated technical systems, capable of responding to more complex situations.

Carpentry: The Craft and Trade

Bob Reckman

Introduction

This paper traces the historical evolution of carpentry in the United States. It examines both the technologies and the web of social relations within which the carpenter worked—what he built, how he was paid, whom he worked for, and what he was responsible for—as they developed from colonial times through industrialization and the elaboration of monopoly capitalism.* It is based on my personal work, conversation, and observation as a carpenter specializing in remodeling and restoration, as well as on more formal research on various buildings, documents, and academic/historical analyses.

The academic/historical sources reveal an interesting pattern. There are many books on related topics: the technologies of building, the architectural aesthetics of various historical periods, the history and documents of carpenters' organizations and contractors' associations, etc. But no one has focused on the central figure around whose labor all of these separate questions turn—the working carpenter. The roles and problems of the actual mechanic—the person who does the work and is most responsible for or affected by changes in each of the other areas—has somehow been overlooked in the grand sweep of engineering, art, or labor history as written "from above."

The author wishes to thank the following people for their help: George Danko, Tom Tully, and Rodres Roth of the Smithsonian for discussions on early bridge builders, hand tools, union carpentry, and the balloon frame; Wilman Spahn of the American Philosophical Society for arranging access to the documents of the Carpenters Company and the building records of the Philadelphia Society of Friends; a host of librarians; and most importantly my friends, especially Donald Bell, Joan Braderman, Mark Ehrlich, and Andy Zimbalist for their comments and encouragement on earlier drafts.

* In this article I have sometimes used the male noun and pronoun for reasons of historical accuracy. I trust that the women carpenters and cabinetmakers with whom I have worked, learned, and shared much will accept this in that light.

Building is a highly characteristic human activity. Very few cultural groups have the bodily fortitude or climactic opportunity to live without shelter. Highly industrialized cultures in temperate zones devote an especially large proportion of their economic and psychological energies to altering their natural environment and to building structures. Because it is so pervasive, this activity tends to be taken for granted. Because it is so scattered geographically, its bulk is hard to see. A few statistics, however, easily demonstrate the economic importance of construction.*

"Construction" is the second largest contributor to U.S. Gross National Product, surpassed only by the multidimensional "food" category. In 1975 new construction accounted for 9 percent of GNP, while construction maintainance expenditures added another 4 percent making this "industry" responsible for fully one-eighth of total economic activity. Further, construction is the only goods-producing industry whose share of total employment has not dropped markedly in the last quarter century.

Construction activity is distributed among all sectors of the economy. In 1976 approximately 75 percent was private and 25 percent public. Forty-one percent of all construction was residential, 13 percent was for public utilities, 9 percent commercial, and 5 percent industrial. Institutional, health, private educational, and nonresidential farm construction account for the rest of the private sector share. Similarly, organizational settings are widely varied. The industry is characterized by a very large number of companies—920,000 in 1972—so that there are many small firms and self-employed persons, especially in residential construction. The 20 percent of all companies which are organized as corporations, however, receive 77 percent of total construction receipts and dominate large-scale building. Unions are strong in some types of construction: approximately 75 percent of industrial and 60 percent of commercial construction is unionized. Residential construction, however, is 80 to 90 percent nonunion. With highway and heavy construction (dams, airports, etc.) falling between the two groups, the total construction workforce is about evenly divided between the union and nonunion shops (Northrup and Foster 1975:349).

Apart from its sheer size and economic importance, the pecul-

---

* All statistics, unless otherwise indicated, are taken from the various census sources listed in the bibliography.

iar composition of the construction labor force makes its study particularly relevant to any analysis of the evolution of the labor process. The construction labor force contains a far higher proportion of skilled manual workers than any other major type of economic activity. Almost half of all construction workers are "craftsmen, foremen, and kindred workers," compared to less than 20 percent in manufacturing. In fact, approximately 30 percent of *all* "craftsmen and kindred workers" are employed in construction. Within this unique concentration of skilled workers, the largest single group are carpenters: in 1970, there were 910,000 carpenters, representing almost one-third of the total construction craftsmen. It is to the evolution and prospects of their skills and roles that I will now turn.

The problem of defining "carpentry" prefigures many of the historical developments we shall see. Traditionally, a carpenter was a person who worked with wood and the colonial carpenter's products may have included buildings, windows and doors, bridges, furniture, tools, and even clocks. Yet a contemporary definition of carpentry includes only the first item—the use of wood in building. Windows and doors are now the product of the millwork industry and the machine woodworker, bridges are built by the engineer and structural steelworker, furniture is assembled by a factory operative, tools come from the forge or stamping plant, and digital plastic clocks increasingly come from Japan. The definition of carpentry has changed over time, revealing a main stem—the design, construction, and repair of a building—increasingly diminished and isolated by the branching off of related activities or products into the factory or into other materials. In focusing on the development of this main stem, I will attempt to note when and why certain areas have moved outside of the carpenter's province, but I will not follow their further separate evolution except when these wayward tendrils loop back to menace those carpenters who continue to try to find gratifying and decently paid work in the actual "building trades." It must be recognized, however, that each of these diminutions—even if they occur only because plastic is better for clocks than wood—represents a real loss of skill and independence for carpenters as a whole. Finally, I find it helpful to think of the carpenter's activities as involving two dimensions: (1) *craft*—the actual skills, tools, technologies, and logic of the work, and (2) *trade*—control over the processes and products toward which that craft is applied. The two dimensions are not perfectly separate, of course: technical knowledge or skill can give a person real power and control in the work setting. It may or may not, however, give independence or positive, directive control, which are key elements of autonomy as a "tradesman."

I will first present some brief observations on the nature of building construction as an activity and of wood as a material—technical considerations which bear on the possibilities and constraints to change. The second section presents a historical synopsis of the carpenter's actual work activities and position in the network of work-related social relations. The final section organizes and analyzes the broad patterns of change which emerge from the intersection of technical possibilities/necessities and historical facts.

The Nature of the Material, the Process, and the Product

The art of building with wood in the material world of time, weather, and people has several objective characteristics that are important for this analysis.

(1) The people I work for often say to me: "I want it done right!" While this is a reasonable and valuable statement in a specific setting and relationship, it is important to realize that there is no absolute dividing line between right and wrong when it actually comes to building. Or, more correctly, while there are clearly wrong solutions (the floor board that breaks when you step on it), building is a set of continuous marginal choices beyond this minimum (the floor board that sags but doesn't break, the floor board that creaks but doesn't sag, and the floor board that is firm, silent, and beautiful). The working carpenter must decide a thousand times a day what is good enough—where to place himself and his work among the almost infinite possibilities of perfection or compromise. A door can be hung so it closes, or so it closes tight. A board is never perfectly straight, only straight enough for this use or not for that. Another nail is probably better, but is it necessary?

(2) The dilemma of "what's good enough" is compounded by the fact that buildings are usually intended to last a long time. The carpenter's ongoing battle is to make his work last: to keep that floor from sagging even after three pianos or to keep his

mortal enemy, water, from eventually seeping in above the window and slowly rotting away the foundation. What looks good new may not have the bead of caulking it needs against that once-a-year driving southwest rain. Thus the possibilities of compromise vs. lasting quality are even greater over time and are often initially invisible to the inexperienced eye.

(3) Building even the simplest structure is a complex, sequential process. This has several implications. First, there is the need to organize and integrate a wide variety of materials, skills, and amounts of labor over a period of weeks or months. Foresight, organization, and flexibility are indispensible. Second, since each stage literally builds upon earlier stages, a decision taken at one moment often determines necessities and possibilities at a later time. "Sure, I can move that window over—but I'll have to pull off the outside sheathing, reframe the wall, and move that electrical outlet. Plus, we'll probably have an additional sheetrock joint to tape and bed when we get to that." Third, steps must proceed in order. Failure to be ready with the right nail, board, or screw puts everything on coffee-break hold. And, finally, the complex, sequential nature of the building process means that the related stages of design and layout are especially crucial. To actually cut the studs or fashion the joints requires manual skill but relatively little understanding of the total process and purpose. To determine the length and spacing of the studs or the design of the joints, however, requires full understanding of both structural and aesthetic principles, and their practical interrelation. Design and layout require conceptual, process skill and understanding, after which steps the rest is comparatively simple, though skilled, manual execution.*

(4) Although the causes are complexly rooted in both the natural world and the varieties of human society, one needs little theory to note that the buildings all around us have basic common features (roofs, doors) which are combined in a multitude of ways depending on the local site and climate, the needs and wealth of the owner, etc. Buildings are basically all the same, and at the same time tremendously, deliciously different.

* In volume I of *Capital*, Marx distinguishes between two fundamental forms of manufacture: heterogeneous and serial. The origin of his distinction is in the physical nature of the product itself. By my reading, traditional construction is a case of the "occasional blending" of the two forms when independently made parts (studs cut to length, window sashes) are mechanically fitted together in a series of connected processes and reciprocal manipulations.

Historical Synopsis

The Colonial Period

Basic carpentry, woodworking, and building skills were widely distributed among the colonial populace. Even the first colonial governor of Massachusetts tried his hand at designing a shelter based on materials and structural principles borrowed from the Indians. More significantly, farmers usually built their own barns and made simple repairs on their tools and furniture. The construction of public buildings and homes, however, was usually handled by the professional "house carpenter."

Professional carpenters were divided into masters, journeymen, and apprentices. Urban master carpenters often formed associations such as The Carpenters Company of the City and County of Philadelphia, organized in 1724 "for the purpose of obtaining instruction in the science of architecture and assisting such of their members as should by accident be in need of support, or the widows and minor children of members."* The master carpenters performed the actual work, with the assistance of a journeyman or apprentice, who could reasonably aspire to independent status in time.

The master carpenter was usually responsible for the design of the building as well, for which he referred to various European traditions and to local practice. It is possible, for instance, to trace both the structural models and fine-finish details of buildings in colonial Connecticut towns to the particular part of England from which that town's nucleus of early carpenters emigrated (Kelly 1924:22). These techniques and traditions were carried in the carpenter's head, along with the particular plane needed to make a favorite distinctive molding in his small toolbox. To keep up with the times, local carpenters' associations maintained libraries of newly arrived British and European treatises on building, each new volume describing the latest structural innovation or fancy trim, along with the complex plane geometry necessary for its reproduction.

Educational and mutual insurance purposes aside, these professional organizations served another important function: to fix

* The records and documents of the Carpenters Company of Philadelphia are deposited in the library of the American Philosophical Society. All quotes or comments in this paper concerning the Carpenters Company are from this collection.

prices and restrain competition between members. They were organizations of carpenters as tradesmen as well as craftsmen. The Philadelphia Carpenters Company maintained "a book of prices for the valuation of carpenters' work . . . so that workmen should have a fair recompense for their labor." Members agreed to work only at these prices and not to take up work left undone by another member.

The method of translating these listed prices (specified for standard component tasks and work of the first or regular quality) into a final price for a complete job deserves special note. The price of the total job was not fixed in advance. Client and carpenter simply agreed to abide by the listed prices, the work was done, and then a "measurer" (another master carpenter) was called in to total the various elements and calculate the value of the work. Like the master/journeyman/apprentice hierarchy and the system of structural/aesthetic design, the arcane formula used for this calculation (involving a cube of the amount of wood used) was derived from the European guild tradition.

Rural areas saw less fine distinctions between master and journeyman. Indeed, moving to the country was often the journeyman's first step toward professional independence and responsibility. Carpenters were often itinerant, traveling from town to village with only a few tools, the knowledge in their heads, and maybe a letter of reference. The rural client might hire a carpenter to construct the basic frame of a new house, the farmer himself cutting and hauling the timber, perhaps arranging for its rough sawing or hewing into square beams, and often providing bed and board for the carpenter as well. The skilled carpenter would cut, shape, and number the complex joints and pieces on the ground. The farmer and his family or neighbors would then lift the heavy posts, girts, summer beams, and rafters into place under the guidance of the professional. Doors and windows might be made by the carpenter himself on the job, or supplied by a local woodworker to avoid delay during the short building season. Completion of the house might be in the hands of the hired carpenter, who would sometimes leave a token tool or initial in a hidden spot. Or the professional might simply make the house weather-tight outside, finish the front stairs and panel the parlor, and leave the rest of the work to be done by the farmer during the winter.

Although complete and formal in most respects, colonial building contracts usually specified nothing more about the actual house than perhaps its size and that "the whole job be finished in a workmanlike manner." This was possible because the system of "measuration"—determining the final value and price by the total work done—meant that both client and carpenter were assured of a "fair" settlement, and because expectations of appearance and quality were established by tradition, collectively understood, and easily communicated between the carpenter and his relatively knowledgable client. A client's typical contractual obligation to "furnish and supply all the materials for said building so that the carpenter work be not hindered or delayed for want of materials or mason work" clearly reflects this high level of shared understanding, competence, and responsibility.

From the Revolution to the Civil War

The 1830s saw a significant structural breakthrough in house carpentry: the invention of the balloon frame. Colonial "post-and-beam" framing used a structural skeleton of massive posts spaced 8 to 14 feet apart. These posts supported heavy horizontal oak or chestnut beams called girts, which carried the floors and roof or walls above. Small vertical members (studs) set between the posts served only to hold the windows and exterior covering (usually clapboards) in place and did not bear any of the structural weight. The balloon frame, apparently originated by an itinerant Connecticut carpenter named Augustine Deodat Taylor in Chicago in 1833, replaced these massive posts and beams with a larger number of smaller pieces—the 2" by 4" studs still used today—spaced 16 inches apart, each one carrying a portion of the wall, floor, or roof load directly above it.

The balloon frame was made possible by two earlier developments. First, the invention of machines to cut nails from rolled iron plates dramatically lowered the price of nails, many more of which are necessary to fasten the larger number of bearing members in the balloon frame. Second, improvements in the application of steam and water power to sawing logs and the development of the circular saw meant that the cutting of many smaller uniform pieces was no longer the expensive, difficult, and backbreaking labor it had been in colonial times.

The balloon frame had two significant advantages. First, it used wood much more efficiently. Heavy timber post-and-beam framing is a "brute force" structural technology, relying on massive horizontal pieces to carry great weight (much of it their own) to relatively distant corner posts. The balloon frame takes advantage of the geometrically greater strength of deeper structural members which are, in turn, placed directly above the vertical stud which carries their load to the ground. This reduction in the weight of the material used had the secondary effect of reducing still further the amount of lumber (and weight) needed to support the "dead weight" of the house itself. The combined result was to reduce the total amount of wood needed to frame an equivalently strong house by about one-half.

The second advantage of the balloon frame was that it used labor more efficiently. The smaller structural members could easily be handled by one or two people. More importantly, their assembly simply required far less total labor, which led to its rapid adoption in an expanding country with a shortage of skilled labor.

Architectural and economic historians have mistakenly assumed, however, that the balloon frame solved the problem of a shortage of skilled labor by enabling the use of less-skilled workmen. Apparently seduced by the rhapsodic account of the day, Sigfried Giedeon wrote: "The balloon frame led to the replacement of the skilled carpenter by the unskilled laborer" (Giedeon 1941:271).* A careful reading of these nineteenth-century accounts makes it clear, however, that the balloon frame served, if anything, to eliminate slightly more of the unskilled "bullwork" needed to move and place the massive timbers of a traditionally framed building.

Historical evidence aside, the point is clearly demonstrated by a comparison of the two systems. A typical post-and-beam house contained perhaps sixty complex mortise and tenon joints which had to be accurately cut and fitted in order to bear weight or stress. A simple balloon-frame house of equal size might contain five hundred simpler but no less structurally important cuts and joints. There are also a correspondingly greater number of structural members, such as floor joists and rafters, which must be placed and leveled at least as truly as those in the post and beam house, whose bearing members are farther apart and can

---

* Others arguing the same point are Daniel Boorstin, Walker Field, and Nathan Rosenberg, as well as an impressive new exhibit at the National Museum of Science and Technology which proclaims the skill-saving advantages of the balloon frame but curiously lacks any explanation of their specific sources.

therefore disguise greater discrepancies. Thus the layout stages of a balloon-frame house are even more complex and exacting. After the layout of a particular section, cutting and assembling the balloon frame can be accomplished much more quickly and easily, but less skilled execution has the same effects in either house: sagging floors, wavy walls, and sticking windows. Having worked in both techniques with hand and power tools, I must argue that building well in either requires skill and care—one with the chisel and mortise gauge, the other with cross-cut saw and framing square. Similarly, building poorly in either—which was often done, despite the myth of the sturdy colonial house—requires neither. The balloon frame clearly saved total labor, but not by changing skill inputs. It was, in fact, a surprisingly simple case of technical change with essentially fixed factor proportions.*

House carpentry also became more elaborate as the upper classes grew in size, wealth, and pretension. The colonial "book of prices" of the Philadelphia Carpenters Company needed only a dozen or so pages to list the various classes of work. The 1805 edition, however, explicitly noted how much more complex and ornate work had become, was much longer, and included drawings of the classical orders as well as fancy window and door treatments. The 1852 edition, reflecting the expanded structural possibilities of the balloon frame, contained 184 pages of prices, listed alphabetically under headings from architraves, awnings, arched ceilings, to venetian shutters and verandas. Such frills were obviously not part of most homes, but nonetheless required a high degree of craft ingenuity and skill on the part of carpenters who worked in such settings, and this undoubtedly filtered down to simpler houses and the mass of carpenters as well.

The most important change of this period, however, was not in house carpentry. It was the rise of a whole new type of job: the large-scale commercial or industrial building. Until roughly

---

* I have also been conducting an informal "blind" poll which now includes six experienced carpenters. They all think that the balloon frame is at least as complex and skill demanding as the post-and-beam method. The source of the academicians' error lies, I suspect, in a change in expectations and quality of construction in a young, booming Middle West. Houses built with the speed reported by nineteenth-century observers could not have been more than crudely finished, inside or out. While this would have clearly saved on skilled carpenter labor, it has nothing to do with the balloon frame directly.

1800 all carpentry and building in wood was house carpentry.*
The geographical expansion of the young republic and the
beginnings of industrialization presented new and more difficult
construction tasks. There were multistory mills, warehouses,
and office blocks to be built, wide rivers to be bridged permanently and strongly, and railroads, canals, and roads leading
everywhere. The problem of mills and commercial buildings was
solved by the iron reinforcement and repetitive multiplication of
the traditional braced post-and-beam wood framework, as far as
necessary in whatever direction. The problems of bridge and
railroad construction, however, spurred development of a completely new form, the timber truss.†

The development of the timber truss affected the carpenter in
two contradictory ways. Laying out and building a timber truss
bridge requires very precise and careful workmanship with large
and awkward members. Since the entire structure derives its
strength from the compound interaction of its geometric lattice,
accurate placement and secure fastening in every joint is crucial.
In addition, the work was often performed, or at least installed,
under difficult conditions, fifty feet above the ground or from
the middle of a frozen river. Thus the carpenter's working skill
and ingenuity were challenged and expanded.

On the other hand, the design of these masterpieces became
increasingly the product of a single, theoretically knowledgable
person. Scientific testing of materials and complex mathematical
models for predicting the properties of a proposed design developed rapidly in the first years of the nineteenth century.
Although many of the earliest bridge designers were self-taught
men with carpentry experience, they were soon replaced by the
scientifically trained structural engineer. Design became a
specialized elite profession.

* I have ignored ship carpentry, a highly developed but traditionally and
practically distinct form of woodworking. Shipwrights will undoubtedly claim
the reason is that we house carpenters cannot stand a comparison between our
respective skills. They are probably right.

† A truss is a lattice or web of short pieces able to span a great distance. All
older trusses relied on the only inherently rigid geometrical form—the
triangle—to create a structural member of great depth without the dead weight
of a solid piece. Almost all old iron railroad and highway bridges still in existence
are truss types, often based on the timber forms perfected in the first half of the
nineteenth century.

Whether they were warehouses, bridges, or railroad stations, the new commercial, industrial, and public works projects were also radically larger and more complex. Logistics and organization passed accordingly into the hands of professional organizers and master builders. The carpenter, while faced with more complex tasks of craft execution, began to lose his role of planner and organizer.

These nonresidential projects also required large amounts of money. The 1806 Permanent Bridge across the Schuykill, for instance, was built by a private joint-stock company that charged tolls. The financing of such projects, as well as their design and organization, far surpassed the means and abilities of the traditional master carpenter. The results were not surprising:

> Building became more costly, and the small master carpenter could no longer finance the cost of an entire structure. Consequently, speculators with large reserves of idle capital or access to it stepped in as middlemen, between the master and consumer, and the whole scheme of market and trade regulation pursued by the masters' organizations collapsed for want of direct access to the consumers market. (Christie 1956:21)

This change in the position of the master carpenters, from independent merchant producer to small labor contractor, resulted in the first trade unions of journeymen carpenters trying to protect their traditional status and prerogatives. Although journeymen in Philadelphia had organized and struck in 1791 for a twelve-hour day, the traditional structure of the trade was still sufficiently intact for the masters to respond that the strike "must eventually operate to their [the journeymen's] prejudice" when they became masters themselves and expected compensation (roughly 20 percent over the journeyman's wage), for "the trouble of procuring materials, superintending the workmen, and giving directions and likewise procuring the tools for the different kinds of work and shops in which it may be conveniently performed." Yet the traditional structure was beginning to break down. The masters cited the problem of competition among themselves as being at the root of the wage issue, and the journeymen took the unprecedented step of publicly offering to contract directly for work during the strike (Commons et. al. 1910:vol. V).

By the 1820s and 1830s the pattern was increasingly clear. The idea of a journeymen's unions catalyzed under the growing pressure of large-scale types of work and forms of organization. Carpenters struck for a ten-hour day in Boston in 1825, 1832, and 1835, in Philadelphia in 1827 and 1836, and in New York, Baltimore, and Washington in 1833. These strikes were marked by a growing understanding of the contradictory position of the masters:

> We would not be too severe on our employers . . . they are slaves to the capitalists as we are to them. "The power behind" their "throne is greater than the throne itself." But we cannot bear to be servants of servants and slaves to oppression, let the source be where it may. (Commons 1918:388)

The masters for their part were quite clear about the necessities of their changing position. They demanded complete control of wages, hours, and hiring under the guise of championing "individual bargaining." The "power behind the throne" also showed itself: resolutions by Boston capitalist clients, calling themselves "Gentlemen Engaged in Building in the Present Season," appeared in the papers supporting the masters and pledging extensions of contractual deadlines to those who held out. Anonymous notices also appeared in newspapers in other cities advertising a shortage of carpenters in Boston, intended to draw carpenters from elsewhere to break the ultimately successful strikes (Commons et al. 1910:vol. VI).

From the Civil War to the Turn of the Century

The last half of the nineteenth century saw continuing change on both technological and organizational fronts. While earlier technological and aesthetic changes increased the carpenter's skill and knowledge, the widespread introduction of power woodworking machinery and factories after the Civil War constituted a direct frontal assault on the carpenter's craft.

The invention of woodworking machinery began in the 1790s with Sir Samuel Bentham's development of a number of hand-powered machines for use by the Royal Navy in their shipbuilding yards. A royal commission empowered to compensate Bentham for his inventions described "a system of machinery for the employment of men without skill and particularly with a view towards utilizing convict labor" (Richards 1872:5), Bentham's 1791 patent application for a planing machine elaborated its advantages:

> Machines may take the place of human skill in this operation to as perfect a degree as in any of the other manufactures. . . . Hence three capital advantages: First, the quantity of force used at one time can be increased at pleasure. Second, the force of men may in this way be exerted to a greater advantage than while confined, as in present practice . . . by the necessity of care and dexterity. Third, the labor of the awkward and unpracticed may be used. (Ibid.:7)

Despite these hopeful beginnings, machine woodworking technology (except for saws and planers) was slow to blossom. Its development was not a high priority in Britain, and leadership in the development of woodworking machines passed slowly to the timber-rich United States. During these formative, experimental years their development and construction was in the hands of scattered local carpenters, woodworkers, and sawyers who worked independently in their own towns and shops, tinkering with and improving machines for their own use. By the 1880s however, the mechanical engineer/designer, backed by widespread demand for such machines, had stepped in. New technologies of high-speed power supply and the metallurgical skills needed to produce strong, flat frames and durable, standardized cutting edges made the production of such machines a factory affair. The *Report of the 10th Census on Power and Machinery Used in Manufacturing* concluded in 1888:

> It is difficult to leave this class of woodworking machinery without referring to two points, which are indicative of recent progress. The first is the change by which the manufacture of this class of machines has passed from the hands of woodworking operatives into those of mechanical engineers . . . the second point is the gradual increase in speed of feed and the capacity for enlarged output. (P. 290)

These three factors—(1) the lack of skill needed by machine operatives, (2) the large standardized output of the machines, and (3) the loss of control of the design and construction of the machines themselves—resulted in a profound challenge to the carpenters' craft position:

> Although prior to 1872 organizational and market changes had exercised hardship on the journeyman carpenter, technically he worked much the same as he had a century before, fashioning by hand all of the complicated detail work—doors, windows, newel posts and mantels—outside on the site of the building. In the winter he worked indoors, in the contractor's shop, laying in a

stock of such handwork for the building season. This intricate "finishing work" made the greatest demands upon the carpenter as an artisan and hence preserved the identity of his craft and protected it.

After 1871 a host of woodworking machine inventions rained down upon the unprotected craft. A sander which smoothed wood as fast as a dozen carpenters and a compound carver which turned out six wood duplicates and replaced three-score carpenters were but two of a series of such inventions which lured handicraft work into the factory and effected a major upheaval in the woodworking industry.

The first effect of machine inventions was to give birth to the "green hand"—a woman, immigrant or child—who displaced a score of carpenters at half the wages of one. One labor paper held in 1877 that "as improved machinery has advanced . . . hundreds of thousands have been . . . thrown in idleness on the pavement. In proof of this it is only necessary to refer to carpentry . . . thousands upon thousands of whose members have been reduced to want." (Christie 1956:25)*

On the organizational front, carpenters faced the growing wave of pressures that had begun in the first half of the century. First, the always present problem of fire became greater as cities became more crowded and the use of gas lighting spread. Chicago and New York suffered terrible fires which greatly increased the emphasis on masonry and spurred experiments with "fireproof" cast and wrought iron construction.

Second, the larger projects demanded a reliable system of mass labor supply and control. The increasingly dominant competitive capitalist economic system in turn offered the greatest possibility of profit to the labor contractor who could charge

---

* Three technical factors encouraged the mass production of doors, windows, trim, and simple moldings: (1) as components common to all buildings, they were readily standardizable and mass marketable; (2) the technical difficulty of their fabrication (they are solid objects made of a nondimensionally stable material which must move easily yet snugly in and out of a given opening) favored the use of specialized tools and joinery; and (3) the undeniable physical virtues of mechanical power—which existed only in the factory before the portable electric motor—in removing large amounts of stock and shaping small pieces. The centralizing of this production in factories marked by extensive division of labor and immigrant wages, however, was the "genius" of monopoly capitalism. Imperatives of social relations directed the concrete manifestation of technical possibilities. The carpenter, having fewer things to make and less work in the winter, lost both craft skill and trade security.

most, pay least, and run the biggest operation. These two pressures combined to destroy any remaining cooperative cohesion between the master carpenters themselves. Although the Committee on Prices of the Philadelphia Carpenters Company continued to meet into the 1890s, it often failed to draw a quorum and apparently did not issue a new "Book of Prices" after 1853. The final entries in the committee's minutes clearly document three of the trends we have noted. First, the committee recommended that customers be charged a 40 percent markup over journeymen's wages—double the markup of earlier years—although most carpenters now owned many of their own tools and high overhead shopwork had moved into the factories. The master carpenters were now clearly large labor contractors and profiteers. Second, the committee recommended a "10 percent surcharge for all labor and materials furnished by others when done under the supervision of the carpenter." The masters were pressed by competing trades and materials. Third, "millwork [is] to be measured as work prepared by another"—i.e., with the 10 percent surcharge. They were pressed by the factory and the machine.

If the master carpenter/contractor was hard pressed, he in turn pressed the journeyman. The boom and bust pattern of economic growth and the relative ease of railroad transportation made the itinerant carpenter a common figure. It also made the problem of local union organization and resistance increasingly complex. The struggle between contractor and journeyman took two forms. The first was the traditional battle over wages and hours. Despite, or perhaps because of, the problems of itinerancy, carpenters were relatively successful in organizing a coherent national union. Because of this, as well as their still central role in the building process, journeymen carpenters were chosen to lead the new American Federation of Labor's fight for the eight-hour day in 1890. Led by their socialist founder Peter J. McGuire, and buoyed by the wave of labor solidarity of those years, they were successful in Chicago, St. Louis, Denver, Indianapolis, San Francisco, New York, and Brooklyn in 1891.

The second form of struggle between contractor and journeyman was over the introduction of piece rates and the partially skilled "green hand" who specialized in one specific job, such as hanging factory-made doors or installing mill-built stairs. Thus, the loss of doors, windows, and trim to the factory came back to haunt the carpenter a second time. The standardization and specialization of the production of these items led easily to the standardization and specialization of their installation. Building speculators had previously dealt with a single contractor who oversaw the entire building process, but with the introduction of the pieceworking specialist the speculator was able to bypass the traditional contractor and carpenter entirely, hiring to have each small part done individually, as does a modern "general contractor." A nineteenth-century newspaper observed:

> Speculators . . . [started] putting up shoddy houses on ninety day builders' loans. . . . One of the curses in the carpentry work on these shoddy houses is the system of lumping and subletting or piecework. The lumper . . . takes a whole job at a certain figure; he then sublets it to another, who, in turn, parcels it out to others, who do the work in as rapid . . . a manner as possible . . . tearing and rushing to get it done. They all have to make a profit, at the expense of [both] the buyer and the laborer. (Quoted in Christie 1956:27)

The symbiotic emergence of the residential speculator and the general contractor (the lumper) as the moving forces in housing laid the organizational foundation for the residential construction industry as it exists today.

Finally the floor gave way beneath carpenters in the commercial and industrial sector as a result of the "industrial revolution in construction" which occurred in the last decade of the nineteenth century. Like most revolutions, this one had clear antecedents, especially from the carpenter's point of view. The new areas of commercial and industrial construction which had opened to the carpenter in the first half of the century kept expanding: trains got faster and heavier, factories and machines bigger, cities thirstier. The structural possibilities of wood, however, are finite, and it was slowly displaced by industrially produced materials: iron, steel, and concrete. These new materials first appeared in mills and factories about 1850, after which date only floors and roofs continued to be made of wood. The railroads provided jobs for carpenters a while longer, but then:

> the bridges of the Pacific railroads marked a climax in the history of the wooden truss. After 1870 its popularity declined rapidly as iron and steel took the place of wood to carry the ever increasing traffic load. (Condit 1960:100)

Even the balloon frame came back to threaten the carpenter's craft by making possible the sectional prefabrication of smaller buildings. Although the prefabrication industry died out temporarily about 1900 for reasons which are still not clear, in the 1880s:

> the manufacture of portable homes had become an important industry in the United States. . . . they were extensively used by builders of such public works as railroads and canals; by the army (as barracks, hospitals, etc.); and by miners, sportsmen, photographers and others. Railway stations, storehouses, bathing houses, pavilions, fruit stands, summer kitchens, and out buildings of every description were available, and one could buy substantial summer cottages "of many styles and as elaborately finished outside and inside as may be wished."(Kouwenhoven 1948:83)

Despite these early tremors, the final collapse still seemed to come all at once, ironically embodied in the towering urban "skyscraper." The commercial production of steel by the Bessemer process, the introduction of reinforced concrete, the invention of the electric elevator, and the pioneering of new techniques for digging deep foundations—the four key ingredients of the skyscraper—all occurred in the decade before 1900. Writing in the *New York Times* of October 25, 1925, George Otis Smith described the erection of a modern building:

> . . . take by weight sixty parts of gravel, sand and crushed stone; fifty-eight parts of tile and brick; twenty-seven parts of building stone; nineteen parts of cement; and sixteen parts of steel, with such other ingredients as copper and glass and asbestos and paint . . . to suit one's taste.

Wood had become only an accessory.

Major technological changes are usually accompanied by organizational regrouping as affected parties try to claim new territory and power or defend their traditional grounds and prerogatives. The first organizational result of the skyscraper was to solidify the grasp of the speculator, engineer, and general contractor on industrial and commercial construction. The financial, technical, and organizational skills needed were theirs alone.

Traditional organizations of builders responded by attempting to capture the second rung in the nonresidential hierarchy, that of the smaller subcontractor. They changed the names of their professional organizations and eliminated provisions requiring that members do much of the work themselves. This new alliance of general contractors and their subcontractors then launched an assault on the weakened journeymen carpenters and their union. The lines between capital and labor became increasingly sharply drawn. Members of professional contractors' and builders' associations were prohibited from belonging to unions. As a result of a lockout in Chicago in 1903, the Carpenters Union was forced to sign a working agreement based on eight principles:

(1) That there shall be no limitation as to the amount of work a man shall perform during the day.
(2) That there shall be no restriction in the use of machinery and tools.
(3) That there shall be no restriction on the use of any manufactured materials, except prison made.
(4) That no person shall have the right to interfere with the workmen during working hours [e.g., no union organizers or stewards].
(5) That the use of apprentices shall be limited.
(6) That the foreman shall be an agent of the employer.
(7) That the workmen are at liberty to work for whomever they see fit.
(8) That all employers are at liberty to employ and discharge whomever they see fit. (Wallin 1966:12; *The Carpenter,* August 1905)

The union resisted, of course. The 1901 *By-Laws of the Manhattan Borough District Council* of the United Brotherhood of Carpenters and Joiners, for instance, specified an eight-hour day and forty-four-hour week as well as that:

Sec. 34. Any member who does an unreasonable amount of work or acts as a leader for his employer for the purpose of getting all the work possible out of the men working in the same job or shop with him shall be fined for first offense $10, for second offense he shall be suspended or expelled.

Sec. 35. No member of any union . . . shall work for an employer known as a lumper.

Sec. 39. Any foreman hiring laborers to do carpenter work or permitting any other than a Union Carpenter to do any work involving the use of carpenter's tools, or allowing them to do any cutting, bracing, etc. on buildings or in shops shall for the first offense be fined $10, and for the second offense he shall not have the right to act as foreman for the term of one year, nor shall members of this District be allowed to work under a non-union foreman.

The struggles of the carpenters' unions is a familiar story—lockouts, strikes, support and solidarity, lack of organization, and the squeezing out of older, more political leaders. But unions or not and successful strikes or not, the effects of the revolution in building techniques on the working carpenter were much the same:

> (1) It changed his most important source of employment from small local contractors to large intercity construction firms. . . . In 1911 Gompers estimated that "probably a dozen or more great business contractors . . . do nearly all the construction of modern business buildings throughout the continent of America."
>
> (2) It created an even greater demand for the specialist carpenter. The modern skyscraper had ten, fourteen, even twenty stories of standardized rooms, each with the same door, floor, window and wall measurements.
>
> (3) It created new crafts such as sheet-metal workers, plumbers and electricians, many of whom worked on materials which replaced wood, and all of whom, while jurisdictional lines were fluid, usurped woodwork related to their job.
>
> (4) The revolution in building techniques intensified the effect of woodworking mills upon the outside carpenter. The floors upon floors of standardized fixtures in a large skyscraper were easily produced by machine. More and more of the carpenter's work disappeared into the planing mills. (Christie 1956:80)

The Twentieth Century

Increasing specialization is the distinctive feature of carpentry in the twentieth century. There are many lines along which carpenters have been divided into specialized subgroups. The first, which we have encountered before, is the line between commercial/industrial work and residential "house carpentry." Although these areas of construction were already distinct in scale and product in the nineteenth century, they did not involve significantly different or specialized skills. Post-and-beam warehouses, timber truss bridges, or railroad trestles involved the same materials, tools, and working principles that the house carpenter used. An experienced man could work on a wharf, a factory, or a residential roof. The tasks which a carpenter performs on a twentieth-century office tower or power plant, however, are very different from those of a residential carpenter. Carpentry work on large-scale jobs primarily involves concrete forms, the erection of complex scaffolding and staging, routinized hanging of sheetrock or doors, and cosmetic decoration with wood trim or panels in the executive offices or lobby. A residential carpenter is familiar with none but the last and most trivial of these tasks.

A second line along which carpenters may be distinguished is union vs. nonunion. While this does not ostensibly imply a distinction of skills or specialization, the fact is that most commercial/industrial jobs are unionized and most residential jobs are not. Thus union membership strongly implies a parallel specialization in certain types of construction.

Carpenters in the union/commercial-industrial group continue to be in the difficult strategic position they occupied at the beginning of the century. Unions are strongest in this type of construction because of the large size of the job site and the collective power of the various building trades assembled there. Similarly, the largest factories and mines have usually been the most easily organized, while widely scattered small businesses (or residential building sites) have been hard to organize. But while the union is formally strong in commercial/industrial construction, the work position of the carpenter is extremely marginal because wood is used only as an auxilliary or decorative material. Thus in the very area where carpenters have the most organized power to protect their jobs and skills, they are confronted with far less real need for those skills. The result has been the evolution of a maze of archaic work rules specifying trade jurisdictions, responsibilities, and prerogatives. With other trades also jealously guarding their perhaps more stable turf, lines of hierarchy and specialization have become very rigid, both between trades and within them. These rules undoubtedly frustrate the carpenter personally and impede the progress of the work, but they at least serve to guarantee jobs, although where there is a declining demand for real skills they can never be more than a holding action. The contradition between the carpenters' union strength and the realities of steel and concrete construction thus lead to a second contradiction between holding jobs and skillful participation in the progress of the work. As the battle is fought over whether there will be jobs or not, craft skills and their exercise become a secondary concern to workers who must feed families. Because of higher labor costs, archaic work roles, and the capitalist's natural desire for greater control, building trades unions are still under continuous attack. Nonunion contractors are slowly increasing their share of total construction activity as they challenge union control over the supply of labor power. The major reasons for the competitive advantage of nonunion contractors are that "employees are utilized out of craft concentrations, unnecessary personnel are not utilized, and skilled personnel are not utilized for unskilled and semi-skilled work" (Northrup and Foster 1975:35). At the same time, of course, both hourly and annual wages are less on nonunion jobs, and the size of the gap is increasing. In addition, some nonunion contractors hire unskilled workers whom they train to do only one or two very specialized tasks. Along with cheaper labor power, increasing the division of labor also gives the contractor a more secure grip on such employees, who do not have enough skills to look elsewhere for a job. Finally, sophisticated systems analysis techniques, such as PERT (Performance Evaluation Review Technique) and CPM (Critical Path Management), allow for greater control and subdivision of crucial skills and tasks.

Specialization in residential construction is also increasing. The mechanisms and settings are different, however, since house carpenters are not organized into unions and wood is still a primary ingredient in the building of new homes. When I leave the house in the morning my first stop is usually the local lumberyard. The retail lumberyard is a twentieth-century phenomenon. The local sawmill is logged out and obsolete, and has been replaced by a network of large lumber corporations and local retail yards. This network makes both supplies and prices dependent on national or even international fluctuations and speculation. Plywood prices may soar everywhere because of a surge in Japanese demand. There is even a futures market for speculation in high-demand items. The scale of the system also means that local yards no longer stock an item especially suited to one geographical or historic area. I often need a piece of new trim or flooring to match the rest of an old house, but when I go looking my man at the lumberyard says, "Sorry, we can't get that—the wholesalers don't stock it anymore."

Thus the local carpenter or builder is increasingly dependent on what sells nationally—or what is left over. A striking example of the results of this system is the theory versus the reality of the lumber grading system. The federal government and various manufacturer's organizations publish elaborate systems for lumber classification and grading which list ten or more different grades of either hardwood or softwood, distinguished by structural characteristics and appearance. Nonetheless, I have worked in ten states and have yet to trade at a lumberyard that stocks more than two grades of softwood and perhaps one of hardwood. The carpenter has less choice to make in supplying himself with materials; he needs to know less and is thereby partially deskilled.

When I leave the lumberyard I probably have some wood in the truck. I may also have some sheetrock, asphalt shingles, a roll of formica, or a vinyl-sheathed, insulated glass window unit, complete with precut exterior trim. Some of these materials, such as the sheetrock (also known as drywall or gypsum wallboard—a half-inch-thick sandwich of plaster and cardboard) or the asphalt shingles, have replaced such traditional wood products as wood lath and plaster grounds or cedar shingles. Fiberglass insulation and formica, on the other hand, are entirely the new products of chemical technology. Whether they are replacements or innovations, all these items are produced in mines and factories and shipped great distances. They have come to make up by far the largest portion of both materials and labor in the construction of a new house. By 1969, in fact, on-site labor accounted for only 38 percent of the total labor required to build a private, single family home (Bureau of Labor Statistics 1972:11).

Once these manufactured components arrive at the job site, their installation still requires a wide range of skill and tools. To build an entire modern house, even with all these manufactured components, would require a level of skill equal to that of any of our historical prototype carpenters. Unfortunately, however, few carpenters work regularly with all the different items and stages. Instead, they specialize in framing, roofing, sheetrock, or formica countertops, thus limiting their skill horizons and experience. The sources and implications of this specialization will be examined in detail in the next section.

The Patterns of Change

The preceding sections suggest the need to look in a variety of areas for the long-run determinants, constraints, and reflections of change in the carpenter's craft and trade. What emerges is not a simple historical sequence, but a series of simultaneously developing tendencies. Each of these may, at a given moment, motivate, block, or enable further developments in its own or related spheres. Their effect depends on a complex interaction of technical possibilities and the alignment and self-consciousness of social forces and relations. I will start with an examination of changes in technical areas, not because these are necessarily self-determining or exogenous, but because they provide the most obvious openings through which expanding capitalist/industrialized social relations and forces have destroyed parts of the carpenter's craft skill or trade autonomy.

The Technology the Carpenter Uses: Tools, Techniques, and Materials

There have been many ostensible changes in this most concrete dimension—from hand to power saw, from pine board to plywood. Contrary to appearances, however, these have meant little significant net change in what the carpenter must know and decide. Hand-held power tools, though certainly faster, louder, and physically easier to use, neither do different things nor act on the material via fundamentally different physical principles than the tools of the colonial carpenter. Similarly, the structural principles of wood construction have not changed so as to diminish the carpenter's skill. Though he might be amazed and I impatient, neither the colonial carpenter nor I would fail to recognize or understand the tools, materials, and methods of our trade were we transported to a residential job site two hundred years forward or back in time.

It is, rather, to related areas that we must look for deskilling influences. The factory production of doors, windows, and trim clearly had such an effect. The growing popularity of factory-cut and-assembled roof trusses leads in the same direction. The modern system of lumber production and building materials' supply is also marginally deskilling. Most important, however, has been the rise of completely new, noncarpentry technologies. These are of two types: complementary and competitive.

The Rise of Complementary or Allied Technologies and Trades

There are now at least half a dozen allied trades with whom the carpenter must share his once eminent domain. Neither the modern plumber nor electrician existed one hundred years ago. The central heating man, in turn, starts off from the chimney where the mason once finished his contribution.

These developments are statistically very clear. From 1900 to 1970 the "economically active population" increased from 29 to 79 million, or 2.75 times. The number of electricians, however, increased nine times and the number of plumbers and pipefitters over four times. The percentage of carpenters, by comparison, fell by one-third. Wood and carpenter's labor made up at least 80 percent of the cost of a colonial house (the other notable items being masonry work, glass, nails, and hauling). In 1860 lumber production was the second largest manufacturing industry in the United States (Rosenberg 1975:40) and in 1880 Chicago's master carpenters were still termed "kings of the contractors" (Wallin 1966:77). By 1969 lumber and wood products accounted for only 37.4 percent of the total materials and equipment required for the construction of a typical single-family home. Likewise, carpenters provided just 34 percent of on-site man hours, which represented only 7 percent of total building costs (Bureau of Labor Statistics 1972:12,15). The carpenter and his lumber pile are now but one of many sources of trucks and confusion on the residential job.

While these complementary trades do not threaten the carpenter directly, their existence has naturally increased the logistical and organizational complexity of the building process. The work of the various trades must be carefully coordinated. The carpenter must frame part of the bathroom wall extra deep for the plumber's plastic waste and vent pipes. Floors and walls must have clearance for heating ducts. Due to the sequential nature of the process, however, this coordination must occur at the earliest stages of planning and layout, rather than in the actual doing of the work. Thus it is now in the hands of the architect, engineer, or general contractor and out of the hands of any one of the trades. Certain recent innovations in materials, such as sheetrock and concrete block chimneys, have also served to eliminate the last few traditional occasions for real on-site cooperation. The plumber, carpenter, and mason often have little to talk about except last night's ball game.

The Rise of Competitive Substitute Technologies and Trades

In addition to trades with which the carpenter must share the job site, there have also arisen materials and trades that displace him completely. By the start of the twentieth century the vast new realms of commercial, industrial, and government construction had marched past the carpenter. He found himself down in the foundation hole with only plywood forms to assemble (though accurately and strongly to be sure) within which the ironworker and concrete truck did the "real" construction of the actual product. Or once the skeleton was built he found only endless, steel-studded sheetrock covering the curtain walls, with periodic openings to be filled by a carpenter-"installed" (note the word) factory-hung door–window installation by now being the province of the glazier. To walk through the great wooden wharf warehouses which still line the Hudson River opposite Manhatten is almost like a dream to me.

We have already noted the impact of factory-produced component parts. The threat of complete factory/industrial production of both houses and larger buildings is also real and growing. Residential prefabrication was tried, died, and is now born again in the mobile and modular home.* The structural and materials technologies for both are essentially the same as those for a conventionally constructed house, but assembly-line production allows the use of essentially unskilled, poorly paid operatives. Differential pay rates rather than greater technical efficiency are, in turn, the predominant reason such homes are less expensive. Although this industry has experienced major fluctuations in output and prospects, it has contributed an average of 25 percent of new single family dwelling units over the last ten years. Large industrial companies, building products manufacturers, and conglomerates are also actively experimenting with factory prefabrication and with industrially organized and paid "assembly" of large buildings (Lefkoe 1970:9–12).

Craft, Technology, and Social Relations

All these developments have collectively compounded the inherent complexity of the construction process, both organizationally/logistically and technically/structurally. In a hierarchical capitalist setting, this growing complexity was en-

---

* The modular home is the half-house with a plastic side which takes up a lane and a half on the interstate. It is built completely in a factory. The halves are then trucked to the site, set on a locally built foundation, and hooked up to the utilities. There are apparently about 150,000 such homes in use today. See Reidelbach for an interesting discussion of the technical, economic, and labor principles of their manufacture.

abled by, and has enabled, a change in the social mechanisms of knowledge, organization, and control. We see, then, the rise of the "supraconstruction" professions. These are divided, not surprisingly, into technical and financial/organizational specialities.

The technical realm is inhabited by the engineer and architect. While civil and mechanical engineers have taken over the job of analyzing and achieving given structural and functional ends, architects have usurped the somewhat broader role (in the residential and commercial areas at least) of aesthetically integrating process and function. Their task today is half "design" and half paging through manufacturers' catalogues of component parts—from siding to sinks—to come up with a workable, attractive "package." Thus the power of the colonial carpenter in design, both structural and aesthetic, has passed into the hands of elites with "broader" theoretical skills and access to information. The newness of these professions is clear from census data. Starting at the relatively late date of 1900, the number of architects increased twice as fast as the economically active population, while the number of civil engineers increased almost three times as fast.

Engineers and architects, however, do not possess the magic ingredient in the capitalist organization of construction: financial and organizational motive power. These are provided by the key figures of the developer and general contractor. The overall effect of the developer/general contractor system has been the "commoditization" of building. Buildings are not built for their use value to a particular family or storeowner who initiate their construction for their own specific, long-term needs and purposes. Buildings are now built for their potential value on the market—their exchange value. The office building, shopping mall, condominium, or tract of houses are all built speculatively to rent or sell to whomever has or can borrow the money. In residential construction, which is the remaining area of importance for the carpenter's craft, 65 percent of all building activity is explicitly speculative (U.S. Department of Housing and Urban Development 1976:284). Since most individuals who commission custom homes also have to be conscious of their eventual "market value," it is safe to say that all housing construction is deeply touched by such exchange considerations. This has several results.

(1) In all speculative building there is an inherent gap between the needs and wants of a specific user and design and

construction. Not only does a carpenter/builder no longer mediate between the user, his resources, etc. and the specific result; no one does. Mediation is instead between minimizing costs and maximizing the price received according to various trade-offs and probabilities. The speculative builder earns his money by his ability to manipulate and predict the size of the difference, rather than by producing an agreed-upon product by his own labor. Thus the possibilities of minimizing cost by compromising quality—especially in the almost invisible dimension of time—are exploited wherever possible. A perfect example is the asphalt shingle roof which covers the vast majority of new homes. The standard 240-pound asphalt shingle is good for about twenty years and costs about $55 per 100 square feet in place. A heavier 300-pound shingle costs about 20 percent more installed but is good for thirty years, yet it is almost never laid. Similarly, the new apartment building on my street has small balconies off each living room. Despite the availability of pressure-treated, chemically preserved lumber for only 20 percent more installed cost, they are built of everyday framing stock—guaranteed to rot in one-third the time. Examples of similar compromises of lasting quality for short-term economy are endless, as a quick walk through almost any new apartment complex or housing tract quickly demonstrates to the practiced eye, and often to the unpracticed but quickly enlightened buyer as well.

(2) The developer or general contractor, in order to control and minimize his costs, takes competitive bids from lumberyards, masons, framing crews, plumbers, sheetrock men, central heating contractors, ceramic tile installers, painters, etc. The effect of this system of competitively bid contracts and subcontracts is, of course, simply to spread the disease.* Although not piecework in the traditional small unit sense, this system has several of the same effects. First, it increasingly delineates spheres of individual or small group responsibility. A framing crew, sheetrock hanger, or roofer has one and only one specific job to do in the course of a given construction process. As we have seen, however, each step depends profoundly on those which have come before. The mason may or may not pour

---

* Actually, the spread of subcontracting appears more like a plague. In 1930 original contractors paid 21 percent of their gross receipts to subcontractors; in 1967 general contractors subcontracted fully 63 percent of their total receipts.

the foundation square and level—a matter of great importance to the framing crew. A member of the framing crew may absentmindedly put a stud on the wrong side of the line—leaving the sheetrock man grunting and swearing as his nail disappears into thin air. The finish carpenter, in his turn, depends upon the sheetrocked walls to be flat and square as he lays the baseboards, which the painter is supposed to paint neatly, be they scarred with hammer tracks or not. Yet none of these people ever sees the other, and their responsibility to one another is only what they choose to make it.

In addition, since payment for the job is a fixed amount (that is what the bid procedure is all about), the subcontractor's economic motivation is to do the job as quickly and cheaply as possible in order to maximize his earnings. He needs to do the job only well enough to secure his reputation and his next job. These, however, depend upon the general contractor, and therefore probably more on price than on quality; they do not in any way depend on the people who will actually live in the house, who will probably never even know his name. And since the subcontractor's help is generally paid by the hour, the more production he squeezes out of them the more his total profit. This is not to say that any of these people will work with no other motivation than the economic. But economic forces do motivate them strongly in one direction.

Finally and perhaps most importantly, to the extent that subcontractors must bid competitively against one another, there is a powerful tendency to specialize in whatever they are able to estimate most accurately, do quickly, and afford specialized tools for. Thus responsibility in and understanding of the overall procedure tend to diminish greatly. A crew may be very fast at this or that, but their general skills are usually unpracticed and often nonexistent. Similarly, their sense of meaningful contribution and participation is very low.

Speculative building requires the contract/subcontract system, and this, in turn, encourages specialization. Specialization, finally, has two effects. It works against quality by limiting responsibility to small, specific tasks. More importantly, the specialized small subcontractor or worker becomes only a part of what the carpenter used to be. The total carpentry of on-site residential building is at least as complex as ever. To do it all would require a carpenter who could easily hold his head up historically. The system of financial organization and social relations, however, works to ensure that few carpenters do, in fact, do it all. They do this part or that, thereby perhaps earning more in the short run but ironically locking themselves into relatively narrow, powerless, repetitive jobs.*

The roof of the Hartford Civic Center collapsed last winter under a heavy load of snow. Fortunately no one was inside. Preliminary reports indicate three contributing factors: faulty design, poor materials, and unsatisfactory workmanship. Everyone attempts to "get by," all participants slicing their margins thin, and a $20 million roof falls in.

Profoundly more distressing was the scaffolding collapse at Willow Island, West Virginia, in April 1978. Caught between weather delays, the high cost of capital, and possible deadline penalties, construction supervisors put production first and took a gamble on a layer of fresh concrete. Fifty-one men lost in that gamble, plunging 170 terrifying feet to their death. Neither of these events was an accident: they could have been forseen and they should have been avoided. They happened for the same reason that new dormitories at the University of Massachusetts leak water and the door on many a new house sticks. The solution is not better-trained engineers or more regulation/supervision/bonded guarantees on contractors, big or small. The solution is a system that gives each participant the best reason to care that the job be well done: because responsibility and the product belong to them and to us all.

---

*The independent house carpenter—the manually skilled craftsman/producer who understands and is responsible for a significant portion of the building process—has been progressively restricted to a smaller and smaller arena. In 1978 this arena consists basically of two types of work: the first is the custom, upper-class home, which accounted for roughly 20 percent of single family homes built in 1975, or 7 percent of total new construction expenditures. The custom character of such jobs, the small scale, and the fact that the small builder may have his origins or some skill in one of the actual trades gives the carpenter more room to move and think. The second area is residential remodeling, restoration, and improvements, which account for 12 percent of new construction. These projects usually involve the creative integration of new intentions into an existing set of aesthetic and physical constraints, which often cannot be completely forseen until the old plaster is torn out or the roof stripped. Though standardized windows or moldings may be used, they must be worked into an existing structure rather than built for from the ground up, thus necessitating a higher level of flexibility and decision making at the point of actual doing.

Technology and the Labor Process in the Printing Industry

Andrew Zimbalist

The printing trades were one of the last craft holdouts. Writing *Alienation and Freedom* in 1964, Robert Blauner chose the printing industry as the quintessence of remaining craft production in the United States: "Printers have a non-alienated relation to their work, which recalls the craftsmen of preindustrial times. . . . long apprenticeships of from four to six years are required to master these skills" (pp. 35, 37). Yet Blauner's lofty claims were out of date before the first edition left the bindery: apart from small-scale job printing, advancing technology has obliterated the traditional craft skills of the printing trades—typesetting, page makeup, photoengraving, stereotyping, and presswork. This development will be detailed in the first part of this paper.

Historically, through their craft skills printers were able to gain a strong control over the immediate job process. Indeed, many authors have asserted that printers exercised more control at the workplace than any other occupational group (Lipset et al. 1956:24; Blauner 1964:44; Perlman and Taft 1935:51; Kelber and Schlesinger 1967:11), and one scholar has argued that "Controls over jobs seem to have been more important in the history of the [printers'] union than the matter of the hourly wage rate" (Porter 1954:61). The printing industry, then, has combined rapid technological change with a reputation for effective worker control over the labor process, making it an appropriate subject for the study of the interdependence of class relations and technology. This will be our concern in part two.

In 1976, according to the Bureau of Labor Statistics, there were 390,000 printing craft workers in the United States: 152,000 compositors (typesetting and makeup); 149,000 press

---

The author wishes to thank Bob Critchlow, Henry Freedman, Joe Tarrar, John Werner, Abe Raskin, Charlie Whipple, William F. Martin, David Weinstein, and Danny Weinstein for their patient tutelage as well as Bill Lazonick, Lydia Nettler, Susan Lowes, Bob Reckman, Dave Noble, and Phil Kraft for commenting on an earlier draft of this paper.

operators and assistants; 39,000 lithographers and photoengravers; and 4,000 electrotypers and stereotypers (Bureau of Labor Statistics 1978:47–56).* The practice of craft unionism in the industry has made it commonplace for a single newspaper to bargain with ten separate unions. As technology has wiped out traditional crafts, unions struggling for survival have fought each other for jurisdiction over the new, deskilled jobs. This factionalism, as we shall see, has at times debilitated labor's bargaining strength and contributed to the breaking of strikes (Taft 1978; Kelber and Schlesinger 1967; Baker 1957; Dugan 1976).

The Printing Process and Its Evolution†

When the National Typographical Union was formed in 1852 it represented all the printing crafts, an indication of an integrated work process just beginning to be fragmented by the detailed division of labor. In the middle of the nineteenth century it was not at all untypical for a single craftsperson to set and edit the type by hand, make the necessary engravings, prepare and block the galleys, and run the platen or cylinder press.‡ One 1871 printer's manual declared that the prepared journeyman "should be a thorough workman . . . a good reader, as well as

* The term "printer" is used to refer generally to any of these groups.

† Due to space limitations, this discussion will concentrate primarily on newspaper printing. An interesting survey of the impact of the latest technology on the industrial structure and labor requirements outside of the newspaper section of the industry (e.g., job shops, book printing, in-house printing, etc.) can be found in Gottschall (1977a, 1977b).

‡ The actual production of the type was an extremely skilled process performed by the typefounder. One expert on industrial labor in mid-nineteenth-century England made the following comment on this work:

> This operation, when once understood, can scarcely fail of being deemed one of the most remarkable instances of manipulative dexterity. . . . That all this can be done in seven or eight seconds is a fact so astonishing that even ocular demonstration scarcely removes incredulity. (Dodd 1843, 1975:329)

Typefounding has also undergone a progressive subdivision of tasks and mechanization which will not be detailed here for lack of space. The linotype machine of the 1880s reduced the demand for type, effecting a gradual demise of the independent typefounder. Offset printing of this century obviates the production of metal type altogether.

job compositor, and book printer, should have a knowledge of prices, of presswork, of ruling, binding and kindred branches" (DeVinne 1871:415–16).

With the introduction of steam-powered cylinder presses in the 1830s and 1840s, of web-rotary presses in the 1860s, of semiautomatic typesetting machines in the 1880s, and of the halftone technique for newspaper reproduction of photographic images in the 1880s and 1890s, the small shop with an integrated work process gradually gave way to the printing factory with an increasing technical division of labor.* As a reflection of this change in the organization of production, the pressmen split off from the International Typographical Union (ITU)† to form their own union, soon to be followed by the bookbinders, photoengravers, and stereotypers.

The Setting of the Type

Prior to the 1880s, type (raised characters cast on a metal shaft) was always set by hand. The typesetter or hand compositor holds a metal stick in one hand, picks individual letters from boxes with the other hand, and arranges them upside down in the stick. Blank type separates words and leads separate lines; the blanks come in different sizes, so that lines can be justified (made all the same length). When the stick is full, the worker slides the type into a metal tray known as a galley; the completed galley is placed on a press and a proof is pulled. Any errors are identified and corrected. The type form is then slid off the galley onto a metal table, a metal frame is placed around it, and the type is blocked in with pieces of wood or metal. The

---

* Jacob Loft sketches an overview of the growing technical division of labor in the first decades of this century:

> By 1925, a survey of the printing trades found that two-thirds of the total number engaged in the printing industry were grouped in six distinct crafts—composition, stereotyping, electrotyping, photoengraving, presswork, and binding. Each of these was again divided into separate skills numbering over 50 in all. Printing had changed radically from the time when the hand compositor could edit the copy as he set type in his composing stick, make-up, feed the platen press, and run it if necessary. By 1939, if it occurred to the usual craftsman to perform all printing functions, he would find little opportunity to do so in most print shops and less basis to master those diverse functions in the light of his specialized training. (1944:39)

† Name changed to this from National Typographical Union in 1869.

form is then locked in the frame with wedges and clamped to the bed of the press.

To be completed effectively this job requires both manual and mental skill.* The compositor reads copy, often with proofreading notations, and selects type from one or more cases each containing one hundred-odd different characters. The position of each character in the case must be memorized. Titles must be set in different type and then centered above each article. Pages must be made up. And so on.†

This process was obviously very slow and labor-intensive and with the introduction of steam-powered and rotary presses increasingly became a bottleneck. By the 1880s, several companies were developing semiautomatic typecasting machines. Mark Twain invested $190,000 in the unsuccessful Paine Compositor and boasted: "It could work like six men and do everything but drink, swear and go out on strike" (Kelber and Schlesinger 1967:3). The Mergenthaler Company introduced a successful linotype machine in 1886 and by 1900 there were some 4,000 in use in the United States alone.

The linotype machine was the most widely used of several typecasters. Here the operator depresses a key which releases a matrix (a mold with a recessed letter impression) in the order required, together with the necessary spacebands. The matrices travel down a chute and assemble along two metal bars to form a line. When the line of matrices and spaces is approximately the required length, the operator presses a lever that brings the matrices into contact with molten metal. The metal cools almost immediately to form a continuous line, known as a slug. These slugs are then delivered to the galley at the front of the machine. When the galley is full it is proofed and printed in the same manner as handset type.

Over the years the linotype machine improved, becoming more reliable, versatile, and faster. The latest model was introduced in

---

* By the last decades of the nineteenth century in larger printing establishments a subdivision of the labor of hand composition had slowly begun. Specifically, in some shops preedited "straight"-matter composition (i.e., of a single font with uniform margins) requiring less skill was assigned to female and boy labor. The effect of this practice and other aspects of the sexual division of labor on industrial relations in the printing trades is discussed by Barnett (1909:309–20).

† An excellent description of the compositor's job in a large mid-nineteenth-century British printing factory can be found in Dodd (1873, 1975:331–342).

1966. Whereas the linotype machine preserved the operator's mental skill in arranging type and artwork in accordance with a layout, it required less manual dexterity.* In smaller shops, operators were often responsible for maintaining and repairing the machines. The basic apprenticeship program run by the International Typographical Union for linotypists was four to six years.

Signs of the printing industry's potential independence from the skills of the linotype operator began to appear in the early 1950s with the wide-scale use of teletypesetting (TTS) machines and the introduction of phototypesetters. A teletypesetting machine operator perforates a tape for wire transmission to other offices and and eventual entry into a linecasting machine. Although these machines first appeared in the 1930s, they were derivative of the cumbersome monotype machines and required highly skilled operators. By the 1950s, however, the keyboards of teletypesetting, tape-perforating machines were simplified to resemble those of a basic typewriter, substantially downgrading the requisite skills of the operator. Equipment manufacturers emphasized this point in their promotion. A typical advertisement of the Teletypesetter Corporation stated:

> Beginners should produce usable tape a day or two after instruction and surveys show that within six months a good typist can punch tapes at 400 or more lines an hour. (Quoted in Kelber and Schlesinger 1967:65)

This point is further developed by Kelber and Schlesinger in their authoritative history of technology bargaining by the International Typographical Union:

> Operating a teletypesetting keyboard was admittedly more confining and monotonous than working at a linotype machine. Job printers, in particular, would be bored by the lack of variety and the limitation on the use of their skills. In addition, TTS operators were under greater strain to increase their output because the number of lines they produced could be accurately clocked and recorded. It was quite understandable that a printer with pride in

---

* The linotype machine had another important advantage to the organizers of production which is clearly stated by Barnett: an "unfavorable effect of the machine from the standpoint of the workman is the increased intensity of labor. Linotype operators are universally agreed that machine work is far more exhausting than hand composition" (1909:202).

his craft would not aspire to become a teletypesetting keypuncher. (Ibid.:199)*

Publishers derived further advantages from teletypesetting. The Associated Press began using teletypesetting in November 1951 and United Press International in January 1952, allowing newspapers to receive news stories in the form of already perforated tape. In addition, it was now possible to separate editorial and composition work geographically. In the spring of 1951, *Billboard* perforated tape in New York and sent it by wire to its composing and press plant in Cincinnati. In 1963, the *Wall Street Journal* moved its composing room operation to Chicopee, Massachusetts. Thus, newspapers and magazines with a national distribution could relocate their production operations hundreds or thousands of miles away from their central offices, enabling them, among other things, to bypass troublesome unions. In the 1970s this facility has been further developed with the emergence of microwave— satellite-computer information systems.†

TTS tape perforation still relied on one important set of operator skills: word hyphenation and line justification. When the computer made its debut in the newspaper composing room in 1962, the eventual extinction of all craft vestiges became a certainty. An ordinary typist using a special electronic typewriter

---

* A supplement to July 1951 *Typographical Journal* reprinted a statement by an ITU international representative on the teletypesetter:

> We have contended that the teletypesetter . . . should prove its efficiency on merit. . . . But, if the machine merely takes away from a typesetting machine operator the opportunity to set type at the established wage and transfers the work to an office employee at a lower wage, then saving is not a result of the machine, but the machine instead of becoming a better method of producing proves to be efficient only in cutting wages. (Quoted in Porter 1954:59)

In a rather unique form of struggle against a new technology, in 1953 the ITU began publishing its own newspapers in several cities with standard linotype processes in an attempt to show them to be technically superior to teletypesetters (Porter 1954:60, 101).

† The Chicopee plant of the *Wall Street Journal* can send the computer-stored content of a typeset newspaper article to its Asian plant in Hong Kong via satellite in less than five seconds. The same system is used to transmit fully composed newspaper pages to its plants in Florida and New Jersey, taking approximately three minutes (personal interview with Chicopee production manager, Bill Reed).

with a perforator attachment could now produce tape for the computer. The computer processed this "raw" tape into justified, properly hyphenated tape at a rate of ten typewritten lines of copy per second. This processed tape could be stored in the computer or allotted to as many high-speed typesetting machines as were available for converting it onto hot metal or film. As Kelber and Schlesinger comment: "The computer downgraded the linotype operation by taking over most of the specialized skills. It left [the operator] the choice of preparing input tape as an ordinary typist, or monitoring the automatic linecasters which received the computer's input tape" (1967:170). In 1964 there were 98 computer typesetting installations; by 1968 their number had grown almost 600 percent to 663 (Bureau of Labor Statistics 1973:7).

A complementary development was the introduction of phototypesetting in the 1950s. In this process the operator, using a familiar typewriter-like keyboard, types in the text without regard to column width or hyphenation, and produces either perforated tape or magnetic tape. This tape is processed by the computer and inserted into a photocomposition machine which produces finished columns of type on paper (looking as it will in the newspaper). Because this process uses no metal type and image reproduction is photographic, it is referred to as a "cold-type" process.

The third generation of phototypesetting machines introduced word processing. Here reporters type their stories using keyboards with video display terminals (VDTs). These television-like screens display the typed story so that the reporter can erase, add, move, and otherwise edit it easily. The final version is then read by an optical scanner and stored by the computer. It can be recalled later for re-editing or to add late-breaking news. Here even the function of the ordinary typist is removed from the composing room.*

In the mid-1960s an estimated 1,000 phototypesetting machines performed 2 percent of all typesetting. In early 1973 some 15,000 did 35 percent of all typesetting. And, according to Bureau of Labor Statistics (BLS) projections, by 1983 all newspapers in the United States will be using phototypesetting equipment (Bureau of Labor Statistics 1973:9, 34).

---

* Although some typists will still be necessary to type the stories phoned in by on-the-spot reporters who do not have portable data-entry terminals.

Since with phototypesetting the traditional craft of typesetting is eliminated, we might expect the BLS to also project zero craft workers in the newspaper composing rooms by 1983.* Far from it. Whereas, according to official BLS figures, there were 48,694 craft compositors and typesetters working on U.S. newspapers in 1976, for 1985 they project there will be 41,080. The official reckoning clearly grossly overestimates the presence of skilled workers in newspaper composing rooms.

It is often alleged that as automation wipes out skilled production labor, it creates a commensurate number of highly skilled technicians (computer specialists and technical engineers). If we again use the BLS as our source (and if anything this seems to bias matters toward discovering skill where there is none), we find no statistical basis for this claim. The BLS projects that all U.S. newspapers together will employ only 399 electrical, industrial, mechanical, and other technical engineers in 1985 (compared to 331 in 1976) and only 96 computer systems analysts (compared to 136 in 1976).†

Makeup

Although the nineteenth-century typesetter also composed the page, the twentieth-century typesetter does not (except perhaps in the smallest of job shops). Until recently, an artistically skilled makeup person would lay out articles in slugs of metal type, and add headlines, engravings, captions, and advertisements to create the complete page in metal. Reporting on their switch to cold type on July 3, 1978, the *New York Times* described how the new system affects the makeup compositor:

> Now, strips of paper have replaced all the metal. A wax adhesive is placed on the back of these pieces and they are placed on a large

---

* The other composing room craft, makeup, will be discussed below.

† Bureau of Labor Statistics, *National Industry Occupational Matrix: 1970, 1976, projected 1985*, unpublished. Revised Bureau of Labor Statistics for 1985 will appear in *Tomorrow's Manpower Needs*, vol. 4, 1978.

The number of computer programming positions at U.S. newspapers is projected to increase slightly from 558 in 1976 to 609 in 1985. As Kraft points out in this volume, the occupation of computer programmer has itself been deskilled. Indeed, a 1973 BLS study reports that a large newspaper filled its four programming slots with journeymen typesetters who were retrained in just twelve weeks of programming classes (Bureau of Labor Statistics 1973:22).

sheet for which an editor's layout sketch has been prepared. (Winfrey 1978:21)

To drive the point home, the article continues by quoting Arthur George, a makeup person:

> To me it's no challenge anymore. Editors used to come up and work with you. "Does this fit? Can we make this work?" You had a sense of artistry. You were a craftsman. Now you paste it on the board. There's nothing to it.* (Winfrey 1978:38)

But matters promise to get worse, not better, for Mr. George and other makeup people. Pagination, or computer page makeup, is on the verge of making the entire composing room obsolete. The only thing holding it back is the difficulty in storing in the computer the millions of dots necessary to reproduce displays and pictures. However, new storage techniques promise to make full pagination economically viable for large newspapers within the next five years. It is already being used for word formatting at a handful of newspapers in this country, and in Japan a full program for computer page makeup currently exists at two newspapers (International Press Institute 1978:5; Raskin 1978:46).

George White, vice-president of the typesetting equipment corporation CAMEX Inc., describes the impact full computer pagination will have on the labor process of the makeup compositor:

---

* Although cold type perhaps facilitates this division of labor, which removes makeup skills from the composing room, it does not necessitate it. A given technology is compatible with more than one rigid division of labor. The same is true to a certain degree with the typesetter. Even with the latest phototypesetting equipment, depending on the computer program as well as the extent of font and style standardization, the typesetter might be called upon to exercise considerable judgment and coding skill. Although this tends not to happen in U. S. newspaper printing rooms, it does occur in some book and job shops in this country. It also occurs at *Dagens Nyheter,* Sweden's leading liberal daily newspaper, where, in an effort to combat the effects of the new technology, the workers last year abandoned their craft unions to form a single union. They have bargained for new work rules, including extensive job sharing, rotation, and enlargement. This struggle, however, took place in the context of a self-conscious worker movement to educate itself about, and defend itself from, the potential impact of new technology. The Swedish industrial relations environment is also very different than that of the United States, particularly since the adoption of many pieces of progressive labor legislation in the 1970s.

The next five years will see the development of terminals for interactive composition and makeup of type, live art, and photographs into complete pages on a display screen. As a visual page image is being put together on the screen, a digital page image will simultaneously be assembled in a computer.

As soon as complete page images can be produced in this way, *there will be a strong impetus to bring the whole process of page creation into the publisher's office where it has always logically (sic) belonged.* . . . Partial automation of the page production process has not radically altered traditional relationships between publishers, printers and their distribution channels. Complete automation will change these relationships completely and forever. (Quoted in Gottschall 1977b:63; emphasis mine)

Photoengraving

In the era of hot type and letterpress, photoengraving was an integral part of the production process. Photoengravers make metal plates of graphics, photographs, and other copy that cannot be set in type. Flat pictures must be reliefed before being added to the plate in letterpress processes.* To perform this operation the photoengraver must understand and be able to skillfully execute the chemical processes of photographic reproduction.† They must also be skillful in the use of hand tools for inspecting and touching up the plates. Most photoengravers learn their trade through a five-year apprenticeship program with a minimum of 800 hours of classroom instruction (Bureau of Labor Statistics 1978:52).

Over the last thirty years newspapers have rapidly converted to cold-type, offset processes. The BLS estimates that approximately 88 percent of all newspapers today use offset presses. These newspapers do not require the traditional craft of the photoengraver. As newspapers convert to offset systems, photoengravers are frequently assigned the task of simple photographic print developing. Automated film processors are even trivializing this simple task.

---

* In letterpress operations the image to be printed is raised above the press plate surface. In lithographic processes the image is flat and is transferred to paper either directly (dilitho) or indirectly (offset), based on the principle that oil and water will not mix.

† The introduction of etching machines, which splash or spray acid onto the plates, in the 1920s somewhat simplified the operator's job (see The Times, *Printing in the Twentieth Century*, p. 101).

Stereotyping

Stereotyping was an essential part of hot-metal, letterpress processes. The stereotyper makes press plates of metal or plastic from the original flat form of metal type and photoengravings.* The purpose of stereotyping (first introduced in the United States in 1861) is threefold: (1) It produces the curved plates required by rotary presses; it produces duplicate plates enabling (2) several presses to print the same page at the same time and (3) the replacement of worn-out plates in the middle of a long run.

The process involves making a papier-mâché mold of the original type and photoengravings, and using this mold to cast either metal or plastic letterpress plates. Since 1901, automatic stereotype casting machines have simplified the second stage of the process, but stereotyping remains a skilled trade, learned through a five-year apprenticeship program. However, like photoengravers, stereotypers are obviated by offset processes wherein duplicate plates can be made easily by automatic platemaking machines using photographic principles.†

Technology, then, has made the technical skills of the photoengraver and stereotyper obsolete. Their functions have been collapsed into tending automatic photo and plate reproduction machines. While many photoengravers and stereotypers have been "retrained" to operate this new machinery, many others are no longer needed; this has produced jurisdictional conflicts over the new jobs between the respective unions.‡

---

* Electrotyping, a more complex process, performs the same function but is not commonly found in newspaper production and hence is beyond the scope of the present essay.

† Some large newspapers, such as the *New York Times*, still use letterpresses. Their large capital investment in these presses would not justify the purchase of new offset presses for their city pressroom. However, on July 3, 1978, the *Times* converted from using a 43-pound metal plate to a 12-ounce plastic one, produced by automatic laser platemaking machines that bypass the skills of the stereotyper. To operate the laser mask and letterflex platemaking machine requires little more skill than operating a xerox machine and, according to John Werner, head of production research and development at the *New York Times*, the necessary operator skills can be obtained in a couple of weeks (personal interview).

‡ The International Photoengravers' Union was formed as a splinter from the International Typographical Union in 1904 and the International Stereotypers and Electrotypers Union, also an ITU splinter, in 1901. However, in an effort to

Presswork

Most presswork today is done on offset presses. In newspaper and large commercial pressrooms the paper usually comes off a very large roll of paper in a continuous web. In smaller shops the offset press uses individual, automatically fed, sheets of paper.

The pressroom is the only stage of the modern printing operation where some traditional craft skills have been preserved. Web presses have been in use since the Civil War and offset presses were introduced in 1909. By 1910, there were 500 offset presses in use. The overnight popularity of the offset press provoked a thirty-year jurisdictional battle between the lithographers' and pressmen's unions over who should operate offset presses (see Baker 1957: Ch. 19). The web-fed offset press came into use in the early 1940s and was gradually adopted by American newspapers. It was used by 47 percent of daily newspapers in 1970 and approximately 88 percent in 1978 (Bureau of Labor Statistics 1973:13, 34). The basic equipment of the modern pressroom, then, has been around for a long time. Modifications and improvements have, however, significantly simplified the necessary skills of presswork and the increasing application of a detailed division of labor on large presses with many units has narrowed the range of skills of an individual pressman. New techniques under development will further reduce the need for skilled presswork, if not eliminate it all together. It is to a brief consideration of these developments that we shall now turn.

The operation of all presses, old and new, letterpress or offset, requires the performance of certain procedures. The first step is called "makeready," and involves inserting and locking the letterpress or offset plate onto the plate cylinder and assuring that it is level and meets the printing surface flushly and with the proper force. This is an extremely complex job, and may require placing paper packing of exactly the right thickness under parts of the plate or under the blanket cylinder, mixing and applying a chemical compound, "blanket fix," to get parts of the blanket cylinder to puff out, etc. Makeready is a larger and more skill-

---

save unionism for those crafts being eliminated by technology, the International Photoengravers' Union merged with the lithographers in 1972 to form the Graphic Arts International Union and the stereotypers merged with the International Printing Pressmen and Assistants' Union in 1973 to form the International Printing and Graphic Communications Union.

demanding job in letterpress operations because of the greater likelihood of unevenness in the reliefed press plate.

The second step is to prepare the ink mixture and add drier or thinner as it is required by the particular job. Once prepared, the ink must be spread over the fountain rollers. Since 1915, keys have been used to control the distribution of the ink across the rollers. The operator adjusts these keys to assure that the ink is evenly distributed (a recent development allows for even ink distribution across the rollers with the adjustment of a single key), and must prepare the water mixture and assure that the correct amount is being applied to attain the proper ink/water balance. In modern presses, the ink is automatically pumped to the press and, in some cases, the water/ink balance can be controlled by turning a knob at a remote control panel.

While the press is running these elements must be continually checked (if controls are not automated). In addition, the operator must control the top, bottom, and side margins of the print on the paper. If the margins need changing or the register is off (as when printing one color on top of another), there are a number of delicate manipulations which can be made. In the latest control consoles these adjustments can be controlled automatically.

In nineteenth-century printing shops and in smaller job shops today these different functions were and are generally performed by one operator. This operator may also be in charge of feeding paper into the press, oiling and cleaning it, and in general maintaining and repairing it.* This integrated work process has changed gradually over time. William Martin, associate director of research for the International Printing and Graphic Communications Union, recalls a pressroom adage of his early craft days in the 1940s: "Give me the keys to the room and I'll run the presses."† A typical subdivision at a modern web press might be: flyboy, apprentice, journeyman, console

---

* Today's small job press operator is being threatened with extinction by the Xerox 9200, 9400, and 9600 machines. After warming up and ravenously consuming energy for twenty minutes these machines can, with no set-up, produce and collate up to 7,500 copies per hour. This is comparable to the printing speed of an average sheet-fed offset press, but the xerox machine has the added advantage of being able to reproduce different master sheets, automatically feed and collate them, and do it all with an unskilled laborer

† Personal interview.

operator, assistant man-in-charge, pressman-in-charge, floor man, foreman, and superintendent. Several nonunion and exunion newspapers have introduced more elaborate subdivisions. Since the *Washington Post* successfully busted its press union in 1975, they have employed one crew to do makeready and another crew to operate the presses. The scab training school, Southern Production Program, Inc. (SPPI), in Oklahoma City,* does not prepare rounded journeyman operators; rather, it trains paper handlers, reel tenders, plate inserters, ink setters, color setters, folder checkers, washers, etc. Most of these functions require little more than machine or remote-control console tending. In her history of the pressmen's union, economist Elizabeth F. Baker wrote:

> New inks, electronic devices, and precision instruments are constantly advancing these methods, reducing the need for continuous inspection and lowering production costs. More or less with success the uncanny photoelectric eye starts and stops some presses, detects and sets press vibrators, adjusts register, adjusts illumination intensity, and exercises various other controls. (1957:13)

In a 1973 report on the manpower implications of the new printing technology, the BLS found that:

> The increasing automation of printing press controls is changing the skill requirements of pressmen. Electronic monitors and controls can perform many press operations faster and more accurately than the press crew. This frees the crew from many machine operations . . . [and] in the process traditional craft skills become less important. (1973:23, 26)

And Sol Fishko, international president of the pressmen's union, bemoans the impact the new technology has had on worker skills and union bargaining power:

> Manning used to be sacred with our locals; now nothing is sacred anymore. Each new development makes the presses simpler to operate and our people easier to replace. When realism raises its

---

‡ SPPI is run by southern publishers and is blatantly antiunion. It offers interested publishers two classes of membership: full and associate. Full membership obligates members to mutually cooperate in strikebreaking at a member paper, including the loaning of scab workers. Associate membership carries no such obligation but offers the member a three-week training program for its strikebreakers. The *Washington Post* availed itself of an associate membership (Harvard Business School 1976:8).

awful head in that way, you do a lot of things out of necessity that you never thought you would do. (Raskin 1978:46)

The next new development, the most ominous yet to the press journeyperson, is anticipated by Henry Freedman of the Program of Policy Studies in Science and Technology at George Washington University:

For the next generation, just entering the market now, there is no plate—the images are transferred directly to a drumbelt, or to paper from the computer. Xerographic reproduction uses a laser for the transfer onto a belt or drum; sprayed ink systems form the image directly on the paper. (Freedman 1978:7)

That is, jet-sprayed ink systems replace the press.

Class Relations and Technology

The Case of the Pressmen at the Washington Post

Labor relations became particularly troublesome for *Washington Post* publisher Katherine Graham in the late 1960s when the craft unions began to use their partial control over the production process to obtain a fuller control. By long-standing practice, foremen in the printing industry were union members. In the union codes typographers and pressmen stipulated controls over the rights and responsibilities of their supervisors.* Prin-

---

* The role of foreman is central to understanding the extensive job controls attained by printers. First, printers bargained with their employers to have the sole power to hire and fire vested in the foreman, who in turn was required to be a union member. Thus, as Porter put it: "Disciplinary action by a foreman over an employee takes on the character of a dispute between two union members rather than between the union (representing the individual) and the employer" (1954:75). Second, since 1857 the union's Book of Laws has narrowly circumscribed the discretionary prerogatives of the foreman. For example, with regard to hiring, a printer absent from work has the right to designate his own substitute as long as the latter is judged to be competent. In the case of work force enlargement, hiring is done according to a union priority list and a lottery conducted by the president of the chapel (the union organization at a particular workplace). With regard to discharge, the foreman is again limited and proscribed from firing for personal reasons. The discharged worker in turn has the right to three levels of appeal (chapel, local, international) and a foreman judged guilty is subject to fine and replacement. The best single source for a discussion

ters came to expect decent treatment, respect, and cooperation from their supervisors. When they didn't get it, they responded. A Harvard Business School study described the late 1960s labor situation at the *Washington Post* as follows:

> Printers would curse their supervisors and had even thrown lead slugs at them. The stereotypers had responded to the arrival of a new production manager, whom they considered anti-union, by imposing a $10 fine on any member who talked to him. (The ban of silence was only removed eight months after the manager had significantly improved working conditions.) Pressmen had occasionally displayed their disapproval of certain executives by shutting down the presses when those individuals came into the pressroom. (P. 7)

Printers were able to successfully play their hand in the 1967, 1969, and 1971 contract negotiations by staging slowdowns and, in 1971, by disrupting operations for several weeks. Advertisers regularly complained of errors in the setting of their ads and distributors complained of often waiting for hours for their pick-ups. According to management, it took *Post* typesetters twice as long to set a page as typesetters in an average union shop (ibid:8). The press operators routinely forced rips in the rolls of paper feeding the presses, causing long delays and large amounts of overtime. With overtime paid at time and one-half or more, the *Post*'s 205 union pressmen boosted their average annual pay fully 50 percent above their base scale (Raskin 1978:45).

In November 1971 Katherine Graham hired a new general manager, John Prescott, and gave him a mandate to assert management control over the labor process. Prescott inaugurated "Project X," with the goal of countering the unions' ability to shut down production, thereby enabling management to successfully bargain with the unions. The strategy was to develop the capacity to print a newspaper without craft union labor and the tactic was to introduce new technology: "To Prescott the new developments in process technology looked to be a means of challenging the strength of these unions. Prescott believed that with cold-type composing as its centerpiece, Project X could be made to work" (Harvard Business School 1976:8). Employees

---

of the printers' job controls is Porter (1954); also Lipset et al. (1956), Executive Council of the ITU (1964), Loft (1944), and Barnett (1909).

were secretly sent to SPPI for pressroom training and to the *Post*'s own secret school in Virginia for composing-room training.

By the end of 1973, this new approach to labor relations provoked a confrontation. The typographers were negotiating a new contract, and again staging a slowdown. Management retaliated by firing a worker. In protest, the printers sat down in the composing room and eventually had to be removed by U. S. marshals. After missing two editions, Prescott and Graham called Project X into action. Without the aid of the typographers, a special forty-page edition was prepared and readied for press. As scab pressmen were doing makeready operations, 100 workers from the pressmen's union arrived. The following events ensued:

> Their [the pressmen's] local president, James Dugan, told Prescott that rather than let amateurs run the presses, the pressmen would run them. The pressmen were allowed into the pressroom, whereupon they promptly seized the room. The presses would run, Dugan stated, only after management settled with the printers by rehiring the fired employee. . . . Some hours later, *The Post* management agreed to reinstate the fired printer with only a reprimand. (Harvard Business School 1976:9)

A temporary victory, forged from craft unity. However, the 1974 settlement with the typographers, following a national trend, gave the *Post* a free hand in introducing new technology in exchange for lifetime job guarantees and a hefty buy-out provision. Cold-type facilities were subsequently installed in the *Post* composing room, giving the publishers more clout in their next confrontation with the pressmen.

The pressmen's contract was to expire on September 30, 1975. The *Post*'s labor relations chief, Larry Wallace, stressed that "the company had to regain control of the pressroom, which meant exempting all salaried supervisors from union discipline" (Harvard Business School 1976:11). The paper also demanded reduced manning and diminished union prerogatives with regard to scheduling. By October 1, no accord had been reached. At 4 A.M. the pressmen's union called a strike and most of the 115 pressmen working the night shift left. Many, however, stayed and damaged the presses, although the extent of the damage is disputed: the union claims $13,000, the *Post* claims over

$100,000.* The union also maintains that management had been harassing and threatening workers in the pressroom for months.

Three hours after the strike was called the *Post*'s public relations firm put out a twenty-four-page document on the union, the beginning of a sensationalist and very successful propaganda campaign directed against it.†

The *Post* began publishing scab editions on October 3. For this they made use of six printing plants from Pennsylvania to Virginia. By October 6, part of the pressroom was back in working order and, with the help of the employees trained at SPPI (plus sixty pressmen and several stereotypers on loan from SPPI), 100,000 papers were turned out that night. The *Post* continued publishing scab editions, each week moving closer to its normal size and advertising volume.

On December 3, a final offer was made to the union; it was rejected. On December 16, the *Post* began to place ads for pressmen and to commence rehiring. On December 22, labor unity began to crack when the paper handlers reached a separate accord with the publisher. In a retrospective appraisal, local president Dugan blamed the pressmen for this and not the paper handlers. The latter were primarily black and had been effectively kept out of the pressroom by racist union practices (Dugan 1976:4); according to Dugan, management took advantage of this divisiveness by offering pressroom jobs to the paper handlers (Harvard Business School 1976:2). In addition, Dugan claims that the ITU, which had lost the militancy of its earlier years and had passively accommodated itself to the new technology, "as early as in October [was] dealing behind our backs directly with *The Washington Post* . . . [and] screwed up these negotiations" (Dugan 1976:3).

Although other unions remained on strike for weeks, the *Post*

---

* The union's estimate is based on a television report (WTTG in Washington, D.C.) stating that $13,000 of replacement parts for the presses had been ordered from the Goss Company (the original supplier). The *Post,* on the other hand, says this estimate is misleading because it refers only to initial purchases, which were necessarily reduced due to a simultaneous strike at the Goss Company (personal interview with Jim Cooper, assistant vice-president for operations at the *Post*). It seems likely that some of the alleged $100,000 in equipment purchases represents press modernization and improvement rather than simply replacement.

† Among other things, this campaign was instrumental in inducing Newspaper Guild members to cross the picket line early on.

was able with automated processes to continue production. No further offers were made to the pressmen, who were eventually decertified. Following the lead of newspapers in Miami, Los Angeles, Portland, Oregon, New Haven, Dallas, and Kansas City, the *Post* had successfully used new technology and other tactics to break the pressmen's union.

The Case of the Typographers at the New York Times

In *Union Printers and Controlled Automation,* Kelber and Schlesinger argue that "Local Six [the New York City local of the ITU] earned the distinction of driving the hardest bargain on automation of any of the 60,000 or more local unions in the United States" (1967:267). From the time of the introduction of the linotype machine in New York City composing rooms in the 1890s, Local Six had aggressively sought to obtain jurisdiction over new processes and preserve jobs for its members. Their success in these endeavors had led to, among other things, excessive staffing in the composing rooms. A prominent example of this is "bogus" work, where it is required that display advertisements sent to the newspaper as ready-to-use electrotypes must, after publication, be set in type anew by the paper's own printers, proofread, corrected, and then discarded.

In August 1899, when the *New York Sun* hired nonunion printers to operate the newly installed linotype machines, Local Six went out on strike for thirty-one months. Their next major confrontation over automation came in 1962–1963 and was over the issue of the use of outside tape from news services. This provoked a 114-day strike. The ultimate agreement allowed the New York papers to use wire services only for the automatic typesetting of stock market tables, and guaranteed the printers no layoffs due to labor saving from the use of tapes. The biggest success for Local Six, however, came in the 1965 contract which brought the union not only higher wages but, more significantly, veto power over any new automation! The New York City newspapers had their hands tied and had to sit back while newspapers throughout the country introduced the second and third generations of cold-type phototypesetting equipment.

For some New York City typesetters, however, the victory was pyrrhic. When the merged paper *The World-Journal-Tribune* folded on May 5, 1967, it marked the death of four New York papers in as many years, resulting in the loss of 971 regular typesetting jobs and 140 substitute jobs.* The city's newspapers had been experiencing financial pressure from television's cut into media advertising, population migration to the suburbs with retail advertising following, and the increased price of newsprint, ink, and other items. Their failure to gain control over their own composing rooms and introduce labor-saving equipment may have provided the final nudge into bankruptcy. Thus, if the 1963 and 1965 collective bargaining contracts are considered alone, it appears that a strong and effective union stance to control automation in some plants resulted in failure for the New York City typographers as a whole. It is thus possible that due to competition among capitals (be it municipal, national, or international) the successful harnessing of technology by labor requires a focus that goes beyond the individual plant or bargaining unit.†

When cold-type automated typesetting facilities were being introduced throughout the newspaper industry in the late 1960s and early 1970s, the remaining New York City papers prepared themselves to battle the unions once again over the automation issue. The *New York Times*, for instance, in 1971 made itself the hub of a communications conglomerate, including book publishers, magazines, a TV station in Memphis, and newspapers in North Carolina and Florida—thereby providing itself with the resources necessary to withstand a prolonged strike (Raskin 1974:12). In addition, "*The Times* and *The News*

---

* Under ITU regulations, any member has the right to seek work in any union jurisdiction in the United States or Canada. When an ITU printer wants to move to another area, he gets a traveling card from his local and takes it to the local of the city where he is settling. This enables itinerant printers to find jobs around the country while retaining their rights and privileges as ITU members. If a regular position is not open, the itinerant printer becomes a substitute, filling in for absent printers, or working on heavy shifts (e.g., producing the Sunday paper). A printer can retain a regular position by working once every ninety days with a substitute, designated by the absent printer, filling in for the remaining eighty-nine days. This degree of worker control over scheduling is indicative of the general control printers maintained over their job situation.

† Indeed, the role of newspaper competition cannot be ignored when trying to understand the union's 1965 success in obtaining a veto over new technology. The *New York Times, Daily News,* and *Post* were, in effect, betting that they could survive using hot type for another five or ten years and that the *Mirror, Journal-American, World-Telegram & Sun,* and *Herald Tribune* could not. They won their bets.

had established a super-secret training center in West Orange, New Jersey, to train nonunion secretaries and other personnel in the operation of electronic typesetting devices" (ibid:12).

The showdown came in 1973. The old contract expired on March 31, and a new one was not signed until August 1, 1974. The printers bargained long and hard, but ultimately surrendered their veto over automation, giving the publishers a *carte blanche* for new composing-room technology. In exchange, they were given lifetime job guarantees for their regular and substitute members, a six-month paid "productivity leave" for all, a $2,500 bonus for printers retiring within six months, and a string of other benefits and emoluments.* Two events must have influenced the ITU's bargaining philosophy. In 1972, a printers' strike at the *Morning Telegraph,* a New York racing daily, resulted in the permanent closing of the paper and elimination of 260 jobs. In May 1974, the *Daily News,* with the printers on the picket line, continued to put out over 2 million copies a day with only thirty-five employees, most of them confidential secretaries and news executives (ibid:12).

Local Six of the ITU drove a hard bargain. Former *New York Times* labor reporter A. H. Raskin suggests why the material provisions of the contract were so alluring: "The New York publishers' willingness to be so generous in negotiating the 1974 contract with the printers stemmed from an awareness on both sides that the packet represented the last hurrah for the typographical union" (1978:42).

The 1974 contract, of course, provided the basis for the July 1978 conversion of the *New York Times* news composing room to cold type (the ad room had converted earlier). With the typographers' death warrant signed, the New York city publishers went after the pressmen in August 1978. Buttressed by a time and motion study it had commissioned, management sought to reduce the number of journeymen per six-unit press from 12 to 8 and to significantly cut back the number of junior pressmen or flyboys from 68 per shift. After an 88-day strike, the settlement

---

* The work force was to be reduced by attrition. At the *Times,* for example, there were 830 printers given lifetime job guarantees. Two hundred bit the bait of the retirement bonus and retired within the six months. It is estimated that the *Times* will need only 350 printers by 1980; others will retire at a rate of about 30 per year and will be given makework in the meantime (National Center for Productivity 1977:50).

provided for 11 journeymen operators per press and 18 to 38 flyboys per shift, the exact number to be set by a fact-finding commission. Regular pressmen were guaranteed job security for the duration of the six-year pact, but management was allowed to reduce the press force by attrition or incentive retirement schemes and substantially decrease overtime and manning for maintenance and cleanup operations. (Prior to the strike, overtime had accounted for over 50 percent of an average pressman's paycheck [Stetson 1978].)

The pressmen owe these modest and temporary constraints on full management control of pressroom staffing to the support of the truck drivers. So far, management has not found a way to automate the delivery of newspapers to their distributors and readers.* Referring to the truck drivers, publishers' spokesperson H. J. Kracke commented: "It's really up to them. If they come to work, we'll publish" (quoted in *The Guardian*, August 23, 1978:5).

Conclusion

This paper has outlined both the traditional forms of job control and the progressive deskilling of work in the newspaper printing trades over time. The interaction of technological forces with inter- and intraclass relations was illustrated through two case studies. Several analytical threads can be traced throughout.

Labor has been weakened by the historical experience of craft unionism in the printing industry. More energy has been devoted to delineating craft and union boundaries than to fashioning craft and union solidarity. While providing capital with an opportunity to play labor off against itself, craft divisions have created another arena for the flourishing of racism with the union movement, the latter reinforcing the former.

It is also true, however, that in bargaining over automation labor has been strengthened by disunity among the publishers. The publishers' willingness to accept labor's terms has been informed by an evaluation of how their competitors are likely to

---

* Experiments with news printout systems installed in the home are underway in England (with *New York Times* participation) and in Japan.

be affected. Financially strong publishers have been more amenable to postponing automation, expecting this to force some of their competitors under. Financially weak publishers have been tempted to pull out of united bargaining fronts and settle earlier, expecting gains in advertising revenue and readership, as the *New York Post* and Boston *Herald-American* did in 1978.

Intralabor and intracapital divisions, however, have had their primary effect on the labor process in the short run. Short-term gains or losses by one side or the other have always been neutralized in the long run by the sustained impact of technology. New printing technology has not only offered capital the ability to turn out a paper with lower labor costs, later deadlines, and fewer errors, but it has enabled capital to assert control over the labor process. A. H. Raskin's assessment drives the point home:

> Automation is inexorably weakening the American labor movement. Despite the considerable economic and political clout the unions maintain, the balance of power is shifting—and management knows it. In no industry is the future more visible than in the newspaper business, where the once mighty printers' union is being brought to its knees by computer technology. (1978:41)

Many have challenged Harry Braverman's theoretical formulation of the labor process in *Labor and Monopoly Capital* for omitting the role of class struggle. Technology, these detractors argue, is portrayed as a capitalist juggernaut, Braverman's worker as a helpless victim. These critics misrepresent both Braverman and reality. Theory must be rooted in concrete historical experience, not in wishful thinking, and worker activism must be informed by correct theory if it is to have positive results. Misinformed activism is often devastating.*

If worker resistance and struggle were to lead to a reshaping of technological development anywhere in the U. S. economy, the printing industry would a priori be the right place to look. Yet even the printers' militant unionism, with its long experience in and wide reputation for dealing aggressively with automation, ultimately capitulated to its force. Local Six of the typographers in New York City, historically the pacesetter and toughest bargainer in the ITU, succeeded in altering the timing of the new technology but not in altering its form. The latter task, it would

---

* This point is further developed in the Introduction to this volume.

seem, is beyond the reach of a union local. Indeed, given the competition among publishers (or among capitals in general), even a local's ability to successfully delay the introduction of new technology must be questioned.* In the case of Local Six, it is probable that their 1963 and 1965 contracts expedited, if they did not provoke, the demise of four newspapers and hundreds of jobs.

The actual reshaping of technology is the task of a broad political movement. Consciousness of the uses and purposes of different technological forms and the resources to plan and implement alternatives are necessary conditions for such a movement to be successful. The sufficient condition might be a entirely different mode of production.

---

* Although at this writing there has not been a final resolution to the automation conflict at the *London Times*, this incident suggests that the development of multinational newspaper conglomerates makes localized struggle against new technology even more problematic.

The San Francisco Waterfront: The Social Consequences of Industrial Modernization

Herb Mills

During the past fifteen years the maritime industry of the nation has undergone a major technological revolution. Change has been rapid and all-encompassing. Both the shoreside and the shipboard operations of the industry have been transformed by the changes which have occurred in its technical base. Indeed, the pace and dimensions of this revolution may be compared to those which distinguished the replacement of sail by steam.

While the economics of this industrial modernization have received a great deal of attention, its social consequences for seamen and longshoremen have been largely ignored. For example, the ways in which the new technology has changed the nature of longshore work and the social relations among those so employed have not been detailed. This essay will briefly explore such consequences by focusing on the San Francisco longshoremen. To that end, the baseline experience—what these men remember as "the good old days"—will be delineated first. Most men date the beginning of that period to the late 1930s because their union, the International Longshoremen's and Warehousemen's Union (ILWU), had by that time been effectively asserting its presence on the waterfront for several years. What is remembered as a "golden age" lasted into the 1960s, but from the mid-point of that decade the utilization of a new technology began increasingly to transform the nature and social setting of the work. By the early 1970s, that transformation had produced a universal and nostalgic remembrance of things passed or passing. These circumstances will be delineated in the concluding parts of the essay.

The present essay is based on a two-part paper which appeared in the July 1976 and April 1977 issues of *Urban Life* (Los Angeles: Sage Publications, Inc.). A second two-part paper dealing with the ways in which the utilization of a new technology has affected the on-the-job relations of the San Francisco longshoremen and their employers has been published by the Institute for the Study of Social Change (Berkeley: University of California, 1978).

"The Good Old Days"

The General Conditions of Work and Job Satisfaction

During the golden era, most San Francisco longshoremen liked their work and the terms of their employment. Most were proud to be longshoremen and members of the ILWU. The structural basis for their occupational satisfaction and their sense of self-esteem and fraternity was provided by the nature of their work, the structure and terms of their employment, and the social relationships thereby engendered among them.

There were several sets of work-related circumstances which made it possible for the average San Francisco longshoreman of an earlier day to like his occupation. To begin with, the men who worked from the hiring hall could often work in one of nearly twenty different job categories on a day-to-day basis, while the volume and diversity of ship traffic also offered them a variety of discharge or loading operations and cargoes. A wide range of work locales was routinely available because the piers of the Embarcadero were numerous. There was nothing routine, then, about the work which the hall man could perform on a day-to-day basis or about his place of work.

Because of the wide variety of cargoes which each vessel typically loaded and discharged, there was also a very considerable fluctuation in the pace of shipboard work and, for the most part, of dock work. The changing deck configuration of the vessel also meant that the cycle of work, the movement of the cargo hook back and forth between the ship and the dock, was subject to frequent interruption. By the same token, the work was only rarely distinguished by an unrelieved monotony.

Because of the differing cargoes and operational circumstances, there was also great variation in the difficulty of the work performed, particularly in the hold of the vessel.* This was another source of considerable satisfaction. Indeed, within the limits of the usual variety, pace, and cycle of the operations, the least attractive cargoes and most demanding work were for the

---

* The hold of a vessel is the area below the weather deck (or main deck) which is designed to accommodate cargo. The hold is divided into "hatches" by watertight bulkheads. On a general cargo vessel, cargo is hoisted to and from each hatch by ship's gear, i.e., an arrangement of booms and winches.

most part "gobbled up," at least by those who were not severely "taxed" by it. The common posture, which of course reflected a prevailing social view of longshoring as "man's work," was "I don't give a damn what the cargo is."

The variety of work options available to the men was greatly extended by quite exceptional opportunities for mobility within the industry and the final (if temporary) "safety valve" of not working as a longshoreman at all. To begin with, a hall man could at any time join one of the "gangs" which had an opening in his job category or, if he were willing, in a job category requiring less seniority than he possessed. By contract, a gang was a regularly constituted group of job categories, i.e., a "gang boss,"* two winch drivers, six hold men (later reduced to four), six dock men (later reduced to two), and a dock lift driver. The gang was dispatched as a unit, and since this was done by telephone, they saved an hour or more a day and a lot of driving by going directly from home to the job. Frequently, a man joined a gang so as to drive to work with a neighbor or to work regularly with one or more friends or relatives. On the other hand, a gang man did not have the opportunity of "shooting for" a particular job or pier, nor, as a rule, of working in a job category other than his own. Having joined a gang, he was obliged to remain in it for at least thirty days.

Men had the additional option of working the day or night shift. They could generally work in another port on a temporary visitor status. As a rule, a transfer to another port could also be arranged. A leave of absence could routinely be secured, but even without one a man maintained his contractual right to employment simply by working one day out of thirty.

In summary, then, the occupational satisfaction of the San Francisco longshoremen was partly a consequence of his options vis-à-vis the nature, time, and place of his labor. These options also quite generally underwrote a sense of individual worth and personal autonomy. It was with good reason that this most assuredly hard-working man could declare: "I really like the freedom of working on the front."

---

* The "boss" was a member of the local and elected to his station (as he is to this day) by the members of his gang. As a rule, he had spent many years with the gang prior to his election.

The Institutional and Social Roots of Community

The occupational satisfaction that the San Francisco longshoremen enjoyed was rooted, too, in the pride and sense of camaraderie they gained from their union with one another. By the late 1930s, most of them were fiercely proud of their membership in the ILWU. They were routinely proud (if not always satisfied) with the wages, hours, and conditions they had won. Most were proud of the union's lengthening history of progressive militancy on public issues and in community affairs.

This pride was more than justified. It sprang from a collective and vivid remembrance of what had gone before, a widely shared and deep appreciation of what was by then enjoyed, and a lively understanding of how things had been changed. For decades, life for a San Francisco longshoreman had been as difficult, as dangerous, as unrewarding, and as socially stigmatized as that of any waterfront worker in the world. The old Barbary Coast had richly deserved its worldwide reputation as a degrading social maelstrom within which brutal exploitation was enforced by violence and corruption. By the late 1930s, however, the waterfront had been transformed. It was now the domain of men who by long and bitter struggle had won a far better life for themselves. In that struggle, and as its social bedrock, they had forged a clean and democratic union through which they had also made important contributions to the struggle of many other workers. Thus, in what was truly a remarkable chapter in U. S. labor history, the men of the San Francisco waterfront had won a dignity which had long been sought and long denied.

Most American trade unions have at least upon occasion been distinguished by some sense of community, if only at an ideological level. However, the sense of community which began to surface among the San Francisco longshoremen during the early 1930s was destined for a unique longevity and elaboration. By the end of that decade, that sense of community had become extraordinarily rich, both in form and content, because it was rooted in the social relationships which had by then been produced among the men by (1) the manner in which their work was allocated among them, (2) the contact they routinely had with one another both on and off the job. Having delineated these two relationships, the discussion will then move to the third set of circumstances that underwrote the emergence, articulation, and stability of this community: the nature and structure of the work its members performed.

The central demand of the long and bitter West Coast longshore strike of 1934 focused on the "shape-up"—the practice of hiring men from among those who showed up each morning at one or another of the pierheads. The union sought and won a "hiring hall," jointly administered by the union and the employers through a "labor relations committee." The reasons for this demand were simple enough: the shape-up was riddled with favoritism, discrimination, corruption, and payoffs. Once on the job, its victims were relentlessly subjected to an exhausting and dangerous speed-up enforced by capricious and arbitrary firings. By contrast, the hiring hall meant the preferential dispatch of union members. While promoting membership directly, this also reduced the number of firings simply because anyone fired was almost always replaced by another union member. As an institution, the hiring hall incorporated a number of job categories, agreed to by the parties and jointly maintained on the basis of seniority promotions. Within this framework, the "low-man-out" system of job dispatch was fundamental. At each dispatch, the man in each category who had worked the least number of hours during the calendar quarter—the "low-man"—had first claim on any job available in his category. The sequence of dispatch then proceeded on the basis of the next "low-man" exercising his right to select a job from those remaining. As for the gangs, their dispatch was based on a similar "low-gang-out" system. This dispatch system not only precluded favoritism, discrimination, and payoffs, but it also tended to equalize the income of the men in each category and that of the gang men. An equalization of work opportunity and income between the categories was sought, too, by attending to the number of men in each category. On the other hand, an equalization between the hall men and gang men was largely maintained by the men exercising their option of working out of the hall or with a gang. With respect to the on-going equity of these systems, this was sought by an annual election by and from the rank and file of the union side of both the labor relations committee and the promotions committee. An annual election of dispatchers by and from the ranks also insured a day-to-day honesty and fairness in the dispatch itself.

This centralized and scheduled dispatch meant that over a period of time the hall men became very well acquainted, an acquaintance reinforced when they were dispatched to the same gang, ship, or dock. Since hall man were dispatched "to fill out the gangs" with needed men, acquaintances between them and the gang men again developed over time. Men of different gangs likewise became acquainted by being dispatched to the same ship and, not infrequently, were assigned to opposite ends of the same hatch. With the passage of time, then, the average man developed at least a nodding acquaintance with all of his union brothers, and had become very well acquainted with a substantial number of them. These acquaintances frequently became real and lasting friendships over breakfast at the many waterfront cafés, at the "coffee break," over a deck of cards at lunch, and when the men were "sent to supper" prior to finishing a vessel (a practice that continued until 1966). Then, too, there were those who were not adverse to having a drink or two following the completion of their shift.

Within this setting, endless conversation ensued. This often drifted to work and union matters, but there was a fondness for such diverse topics as "women," baseball and football, fishing and hunting, gambling and horse racing, "capitalistic exploitation" and the "profit motive," facism, and, of course, the Great Depression—that unforgettable fountain of experience from which all had been obliged to drink. Conversation continued on the job because there was little machine noise either on the dock or aboard ship and because the pace and cycle of the work permitted it. As a result, there emerged a quite extraordinary world of discussion, reflection, and debate and, by the same token, a sense of fraternity which was widely shared and frequently made manifest. It followed that there were two sets of circumstances in which a man would invariably terminate an on-the-job discussion or even refuse to begin one: when he felt a man he was working with was intentionally failing to do his part, or was refusing to work in a safe and sensible manner. To put the matter simply, one did not converse with a man who failed to reflect a sense of pride and community in accomplishing the work at hand. At this point, then, the discussion comes full circle: the nature and structure of the work was such that it could give rise to a community and brotherhood of men who took pride in its performance.

Pride and Community as the Social Product of Work

Conventional longshore work is distinguished by widely varying and ever changing operational circumstances. New and challenging problems and difficulties are constantly posed, especially for the hold men. Since such work cannot be subjected to direct and continuous supervision, the efficiency with which it is performed is essentially a function of the initiative the individual longshoreman is willing to assume and the willingness of the men to innovate cooperatively. Indeed, since it is in no way "routine," an efficient performance of such work requires a radical and broadly defined decentralization of initiative. Given a continuous demand for initiative, experience, innovative skill, and ingenuity, conventional longshore work allows the men simultaneously to take pride in their work and to express their sense of brotherhood with one another. Because of these circumstances and the social organization that distinguished the industry during the "good old days," it also followed that the community and union of the San Francisco longshoremen was made a concrete and vibrant social reality as their work proceeded.

Further, due to the nature of their work, each dock, winch, and hold man worked as partner with another man. Within the gangs, partnerships were typically maintained for years, and partnerships between hall man also had great stability. These relationships went a long way toward generating an unquestioned willingness to contribute to the performance of the work. Indeed, to work cooperatively with one's partner was an imperative embedded in the work and its social setting. It was simply axiomatic. By the same token, it was the partnership that constituted the basic sociopsychological unit through which the forces of pride and community were generated on the job.

A vessel which was to discharge and load general cargo was usually on berth for at least a week. Having arrived alongside the dock, its mooring lines were taken and secured by "linesmen." The crew secured the rat guards, the gangway, and a safety net beneath the gangway. Had they not already done so, they then unshipped and raised the cargo booms (from the boom rests to which they are secured while at sea) and let go the battens securing the hatch tarpaulins. The vessel was thus readied for a longshore operation.

The gang men began arriving at the pier sometime after 7:00 A.M. They went to a nearby café for coffee and often breakfast. Meanwhile, each gang boss got his hatch assignment from his operational supervisor, the ship "walking boss."* The walking boss, or "walker," then informed the gang bosses as to the nature of the cargo, its place of stow, any unusual circumstances, and the number of days the job was expected to last. The gang boss in turn passed this information on to his gang, usually over morning coffee or breakfast. The hall men, who had begun to be dispatched to the gangs and to the ship or dock walkers at 6:30 A.M., begin to drift in. Greetings were exchanged. Conversations were begun; others were resumed. There was a lot of catching up to do.

Toward 7:45 A.M., the men began to move toward the pierhead. The dock workers, who had been dispatched directly to the dock walker, now received their assignments, as did the late arrivals to the gangs or ship walker. The day began in earnest when at 8:00 A.M. the ship walker hollered, "O.K. men, let's go."

As the shipboard men streamed onto the vessel, the dock men for the gangs raised the doors of the cargo shed. They then proceeded to locate and ready the gear and dock equipment that would be required. Having cleared their work area of any debris and having constructed a suitable seat (or "house") for themselves, they stood ready to secure the "save-all."† Meanwhile, and on the basis of the information given them by the clerk with whom they worked, the other dockworkers "set up" for the palletizing and de-palletizing of cargo.

Having ascended the gangway, the shipboard men of each gang proceeded to rig the gear of their hatch. To facilitate this, half of the hold men rigged the inshore boom, while the other half rigged the one offshore. Except when operational circumstances might otherwise dictate, this inshore/offshore division of the hold men continued throughout the job. The hatch boards and strongbacks (or "pontoons") were then removed and safely stowed on the offshore weather deck or on the dock. Having

---

* The walking bosses "walk" the ships and docks to supervise the work. Up until 1948, the walkers were also members of the longshore local, but in that year they were separately chartered by the ILWU.

† This is a cargo net that is slung between the dock and a vessel so as to prevent either a worker or cargo from falling into the water.

thus "uncovered" the hatch, the hold men were ready to go below.

Frequently, the cargo to be discharged from the shelter deck (or upper 'tween) had been loaded up to the hatch covers. In that event, the hold men—having clambered over the edge of the hatch—began the discharge by building that cargo into loads (pallet, sling, or net) and sending them ashore. They continued to "dig down" until they reached the shelter deck itself. Next they cleared the "square," the deck area beneath the hatch covers. With that done, they began the discharge of cargo stowed in the "wings," the areas beneath the deck above. To do this, an important skill almost always came into play. This was the construction of a safe and suitable flooring over which the cargo could be moved from stow to the square and then hoisted ashore. The decision as to which of the available cargo-moving devices was best for this purpose was largely based on the nature of the cargo and its stow.

Once finished with the cargo to be discharged from the shelter deck, a loading operation might commence. As a rule, however, the men again uncovered to begin the discharge of cargoes from the lower 'tween deck. Frequently, this required re-rigging the gear. The operational circumstances encountered in the lower 'tween deck were a variation on those on the shelter deck, as was the subsequent uncovering and discharge of the "lower hold." On most vessels, the descent of the hold men into the hatches aft of the midship house (superstructure) continued beyond the lower hold into the "deep tanks." Since these tanks are separated from one another by the "shaft alley," i.e., by the "alley" of the propeller shaft, they always afforded very restricted access. For this reason, they also posed certain operational problems.

The work of the winch driver, who controlled the movement of the cargo hook and loads from his station above the hatch, became increasingly demanding as the hold men descended into the vessel. Considerable experience and skill was required because there were different types of winches, each with several designs. To a lesser degree, the same was true of the standing gear of the vessels. Then, too, the state of repair and general condition of the winches and gear varied tremendously. In any event, great responsibility always rested with the winch driver simply because each move of the cargo hook could endanger one or more of the men with whom he worked.

As a rule, a wide variety of cargoes occasioned a constantly changing set of operational circumstances. To begin with, there was usually a considerable amount of "general freight," i.e., all sorts of differently sized crates and packages of varying weights shipped by manufacturing firms, freight forwarders, or individuals. Larger crated shipments of such variously sized and weighted items as machines and machine parts, furniture, glassware, dishes and ceramics, sports equipment, clothing, and relatively exotic or "specialty" food products were frequently encountered. Still larger and variously packaged shipments of all sorts of food—from 25-pound boxes of Norwegian sardines to 100-pound cartons of New Zealand frozen meats to 750-pound barrels of Greek olives—were frequent, as were shipments of wine, beer, liquor, cheeses, teas, coconut and tapioca, tropical fruits, candy, cookies, speciality desserts, and a wide variety of canned goods. A host of industrial products—from ingots of copper, to sheet and bar steel, pipe and rails, steel pellets, corrugated metals, and fencing—were common, as were such baled goods as cotton, rubber, rags, gunnies, jute, pulp, and paper. The number of sacked or bagged goods was legion—cement, flour, wheat, barley, coffee, and all sorts of nuts and dried fruit—and there were deck-loads of lumber and/or logs, creosote pilings, utility poles, and railway ties, farm and construction equipment, and all sorts of commercial vehicles. Then there were the offensive sacks of cargo that were worked at penalty rates: animal bones and meat scraps, blood and bone meal, fish meal, coal, lime, phosphates and nitrates, lamp black, and soda ash.

While this is only a partial list, the task was always the same: to move the cargo to or from the dock and to or from its place of stow. To effect the first of these movements, a wide variety of pallet boards, scows, nets, slings, bridles, and hooks were used. For moving to and from stow, flooring of some sort was frequently necessary. To that end, the hold men might order a variety of heavily constructed skids, ramps, or "runways" from the dock. It was often necessary, however, to construct a floor from dunnage and plyboard. Once there was flooring, a four-wheeled hand truck, upon which pallet loads could be landed or built, was often used. On occasion a device called a gravity roller might be used instead. This is a rectangular steel frame (of approximately 1' by 12' dimensions) between whose longer sides are fixed a number of parallel steel rollers. Thus it can be rolled across flooring with a pallet of cargo atop it. In an area where the construction of flooring was especially difficult or impossible, a gravity roller could be turned "face-up" and elevated so as to span the area, secured in place, and then cargo rolled piece-by-piece across its face.

For many years, sacked goods were simply "belly-packed." When discharging, each hold man would in turn remove a sack from stow and carry it to where a load could be built and then sent ashore. The circle was reversed when loading.

When it came to moving heavy cargo, it was common to place a number of wooden rollers (some 6" in diameter by 3' long) beneath the cargo so that it could be "man-handled" to or from stow. For still heavier cargo, rollers and such block-and-tackle set-ups as might be required, together with the motive power of the ship's gear itself, were employed. When baled cargo, such as hemp or sisal, could be directly discharged from stow by the use of hooks, the ship's gear was again used for motive power. This was also true of the discharge of sacked goods such as coffee that might be built into sling loads near their place of stow, dragged to the square, and then hoisted to the dock.

In this connection, the longshoreman's basic hand-held tool, the cargo hook, must be mentioned. In the movement of most cargoes, this tool—of which there were many styles and designs—was frequently essential. This was true both on the dock and in the hold. As might be supposed, the crowbar was another hand tool which got a lot of use, especially in the hold.

In both loading and discharge, the manner in which the hold men proceeded was determined in part by the configuration of the deck being worked and in part by the presence of structural members and stanchions. The stowage plan of the vessel was equally important, i.e., the location of the particular areas to which or from which San Francisco cargoes, as distinct from those of other ports-of-call, were to be moved. Within these parameters, however, the loading of cargoes was typically the most challenging simply because a "tight stow" was necessary: for one thing, a tight stow and the utilization of all available space meant greater tonnage and greater profit. At the same time, a tight and proper stow of the cargo was essential to the safety of the vessel. A shifting of cargo while at sea could pose serious operational difficulties, if not, indeed, grave danger.

To effect a tight and economical stow, the hold men frequently had to work within the constraints of the sheer and declivity of the deck. When odd-sized and variously weighted cargo was being handled, "an eye for the work"—the ability to visually judge where a particular piece of cargo might best be fitted into the stow so as to safely and properly maintain its "face" while following the stowage plan—became particularly important. The use of dunnage as a means of preventing shifting was important, too, but became particularly so as the men proceeded "to go up with the cargo," i.e., to stack cargo atop cargo. As the final step, the men would request the lightest of the available cargoes for "topping off," the piece-by-piece, hand-handled stowing of cargo just beneath the decking above. The final end: "A proper stow. One you can take a picture of."

With the wings of the hatch fully loaded, heavy cargo was usually loaded to the square simply because the winch driver could generally land it pretty much in stow. Occasionally the two sets of gear standing at opposite ends of the hatch would be required to handle a lengthy and/or especially heavy piece. In that event, the cargo might be independently slung by each set of gear or the two sets might be "frisco'd" together into one hoisting unit. In either case, the men of the two gangs working the hatch worked together. Most vessels also had "jumbo" gear standing at the hatch just forward of the midship house, and occasionally this would have to be unshipped and rigged so as to load or discharge a still heavier item. As a rule, cargo was again placed atop cargo, frequently to the full height of the hatch. This accomplished, the men would climb to the deck above and proceed to "cover up."

Once the shelter deck had been covered up, the men went on to load and secure the deck cargoes, usually the largest, if not the heaviest, of cargoes simply because the weather deck and/or its hatch covers offered the largest area of open deck and because the cargoes could be directly landed in stow. This usually required either a re-rigging of gear or a rigging of the inshore boom into a "swinging boom."

Having finished with the deck cargoes, the men sent the watercan ashore, together with such tools as they had been using. They then let go the save-all, sent it ashore, and "winged in the gear," i.e., let go the guys and preventers and hauled in the booms until they were standing above the hatch. With that, they headed for the gangway.

Frequently as many as ten gangs (of some sixteen to twenty men each), plus the necessary dock workers, worked a general cargo vessel. With a proper allocation of the shipboard men, all of the hatches were generally finished at about the same time. As the last of the gangs finished up, tugs were positioned against the vessel. The pilot, who would take the vessel through the Golden Gate and into the open sea, appeared on the bridge. Linesmen stationed themselves abreast the bits to which the mooring lines had been secured.

As the gangs came down the gangway, the dock men would be closing the doors of the cargo shed. With the men ashore, the crew hauled in the gangway and slackened the mooring lines. As the vessel cleared the dock, the men poured onto the Embarcadero. By the time they reached their automobiles or the trolley stop, the vessel had moved into the "stream" and had headed for sea.

Modern Longshore Operations

Compared to the work just described, modern longshoring is utterly routine. As a result of the integration of standardized cargo units, a vessel designed for those units, and the hoisting gear and/or dock equipment necessary to move them to and from stow, there is little variation in operational circumstances. Since each unit can be loaded to a predetermined place of stow, or discharged to a predetermined place of dock storage, operations can be completely planned (and computer simulated) before the vessel arrives. With all subsequent shipboard and dock work then sequenced, the need for initiative, innovation, and ingenuity is eliminated, while the range of skills and experience which routinely come into play is dramatically narrowed. By the same token, circumstances that require a collective and truly cooperative approach on the part of the men are all but unknown. It follows too that the work can be closely and continuously supervised and subjected to an on-going audit and review.

Since the operational situation and the concrete tasks are essentially unchanging, modern longshore work is universally viewed by the men as dull and monotonous—at least as compared to conventional longshoring. It is neither as interesting nor as challenging. The new technology eliminates the variety of work and the problems to be solved. The cargo unit is always the same. The movement of those units to and from the vessel is always the same. The shipboard work is always the same. Thus the operational circumstances that for many years allowed the San Francisco longshoreman to enjoy his work, to take pride in its performance, and to thereby express his sense of community and union with his fellow workers have been virtually eliminated by a new technology.

As was suggested earlier, a very rich, day-to-day social contact underwrote the maintenance of community and union among the San Francisco longshoremen for many years. There were several main arenas for that social intercourse. The hiring hall had an extremely important social dimension. Hundreds of men were present for the early morning or late afternoon job dispatch. The hall was also a natural gathering place throughout the day and into early evening. Conversations which ensued were frequently "recessed" and thereafter "reconvened" at one of the many nearby cafés or bars. The Embarcadero piers were also surrounded by cafés and bars, missions and storefront churches, clothing and surplus stores. There were gun shops and pawn shops, recreation centers and locker rooms, corner groceries, inexpensive hotels and flop houses, boarding houses and rooming houses. There were movie houses that never closed. Liquor stores, smoke shops, pinball parlors, and pool halls abounded. One could always find a card game, a bookie, or a floating crap game. One could always find a companion, a new political tract or leaflet, a place to drop a crab pot or wet a line, or simply a place from which to watch the passing parade and the waters of the bay in solitude. In a word, the social setting of the work and union life of the San Francisco longshoreman was richly varied and exceptionally vibrant. The relationships they had with one another by reason of their work and union were necessarily strengthened and deepened by the experiences and activities that setting afforded them. Life along the Embarcadero also broadened their horizons: the seamen who were "on the beach" had sailed under every flag and to every corner of the earth.

On the ships and piers, as has been noted, men who were working as a unit could converse as the work proceeded. Then too, the distances between the men on a given ship and dock were never very great. Most vessels were 350 to 450 feet in length. The C-4 of World War II was "big"—some 550 feet. As for the piers and sheds, the average was perhaps 700 feet long. One would therefore know who was working a ship or pier within an hour or so of starting time. Since there was considerable fluctuation in the pace of work and a frequent shifting of men about the vessel and dock, those who were not working together could also seek each other out for at least a brief exchange. Because of this coming and going, brief salutations—which were almost invariably laced with good-natured banter—were frequent.

These social dimensions of the working and union life of the men have been eliminated by the new technology. To begin with, the modern facilities are scattered around the bay on previously vacant or landfill sites because the acreage required by the new technology is up to ten times as great as the five to ten acres afforded by the "finger piers" of the old waterfront. These facilities, which are ever more widely dispersed, are therefore not surrounded by the kind of neighborhood which distinguished the Embarcadero.* Indeed, unless one has packed a lunch or is willing to buy from either a coffee truck ("roach coach" or "ptomaine wagon") or a vending machine, a drive "into town" is necessary at lunch time. The opportunities for socializing that the men enjoyed for so long have been dramatically lessened. At the same time, those employed against a vessel at a modern facility are isolated from those who are otherwise employed there because the physical layout of these sprawling developments is dictated, of course, by the basic operational division of labor. Indeed, these men are also isolated from those who may be working a second vessel because at these facilities ships are moored "bow to stern" and because the modern vessels routinely exceed 850 feet in length.

While the new technology has thus effected a quite general "diaspora" of the San Francisco longshore community and an extraordinary routinization of its work, the work force on a modern operation is also "atomized." Thus, to begin with and as will presently be detailed, much of the work associated with a

* Due to this industrial dispersion and sprawl, most of the Embarcadero piers have fallen idle. By the same token, the neighborhoods which were supported by those abandoned piers have simply vanished. For the most part, the areas adjacent to the old waterfront are now dotted with high-cost apartment complexes, fashionable commercial and financial centers, and expensive hotels, restaurants, bars, boutiques, and shopping malls. Since the same is true of the area adjacent to the hiring hall and since the work is also increasingly distant from the hall, the question of "moving on" is presently being discussed by the men.

modern operation is performed in near isolation by individual men. At the same time, such groupings of men as are employed are much smaller than those required in a conventional operation. In brief, a modern division of longshore labor is distinguished by individual and small group tasks that can be performed in relative isolation and with a minimum of communication and cooperative activity.

The Unit of Cargo

The most widely publicized of the modern cargo units is the "container."* This is a rigid, steel-framed, oblong box which is

* In many respects, the most modern of cargo units is not the container, but the barge which is carried by the "lighter aboard ship" or "LASH" vessels. These barges have a tonnage capacity of 415 (short) tons. Cargo is loaded through watertight, folding hatch covers. The 54 barges which a LASH ship can carry are on- and off-loaded at the vessel's stern by an on-board crane that nearly spans the vessel rail to rail. This huge crane also travels between the stern of the vessel and a point just forward the midship so as to stow and unstow the barges. Most LASH barges are themselves loaded and discharged of cargo at the dock of a specially constructed "lighter station." This dock fronts on a sheltered channel which leads to the open waters of San Francisco Bay and the dock to which the LASH vessels are moored for loading and discharge.

The freight which can be carried by these barges extends from the largest of containers, through the smaller, odd-sized and expendable wooden "van-packs," to hand-handled and unitized cargoes, and to all manners of bulk and general cargoes (from buses to rails). Indeed, the LASH barge can accommodate a mix of cargoes similar to that which can be loaded to a hatch of a general cargo vessel. Much of the cargo handled at the lighter station is unitized. In that event, the operation can often be performed by a single man operating an overhead, cantilevered (and extremely versatile) crane which travels along the dock. As a rule, however, one or two men are aboard the barge so as to assist the crane operator even when unitized or some similarly standardized cargo is being worked. Naturally, a mix of cargoes is not at all uncommon, but this crane cannot handle containers or most van packs, or, of course, such things as buses or bulk cargoes. Such freight must be loaded and discharged by other dock equipment. When cargoes must be hand-handled in some manner, four men are assigned to the barge. Four men will also work a mix of cargo. As might then be supposed, the work of the barge men often approximates that which is performed by the hold men in a conventional operation. On the other hand, the box-like configuration of the barge means that few of the problems posed by a ship's hold will be encountered. Then, too, there are no structural members or stanchions to worry about, nor is the flooring anything but excellent. The versatility of the dock crane also precludes many of the problematic circumstances which are not between 20 and 40 feet in length. A wide variety of cargoes can be "stuffed" (as we say) into a container, secured against shifting, and sealed. In this way, nearly twenty-five tons of cargo can be moved as a unit through differing modes of transport. After being "unstuffed" at its destination, the container can be used again.

The container has had a revolutionary impact on the entire transportation industry because it can be stuffed and unstuffed at any location serviced by the trucking equipment and/or the hoisting and rail equipment that can move it when loaded. It thereby eliminates the otherwise recurrent need to "handle" the cargo as it is moved from shipper to consignee via the available modes of transport. Indeed, in a fully "intermodal" container system, a container can be moved in any sequence by truck, rail, plane, or ship, but the cargo itself will be handled by only the shipper and consignee. By eliminating the historic technological interfaces of the transport industry, this system essentially makes the work of freight handling, consolidation, and forwarding redundant.

Despite these circumstances, some containers are stuffed and unstuffed by San Francisco longshoremen. While this work is a functional equivalent to conventional hold work, it is much less challenging. As compared to shipboard areas of stow, any container is small. It is free of structural members and stanchions. It invariably offers something that is rare aboard ship—an excellent, even-surfaced, flooring. Its box-like configuration also eliminates the substantial problems posed by the molded curvature and sheer of the hold and sometimes its declivity. Because of the dimensions of that configuration, none of the skills and experience that routinely produce a tight and economic shipboard stow are required. Then, too, there is, of course, no hoisting of cargo or rigging of gear, and no uncovering: the cargo is simply moved to and from the container—if not, indeed, its place of stow—by lift truck. As compared, then, to a shipboard operation, the nature, "flow," and organization of such work is utterly routine. By the same token, its performance can also be much more closely supervised and monitored.

---

infrequently encountered in a conventional shipboard hoisting operation. While, then, a considerable variety of cargo is frequently handled in these operations, the challenge is never that of conventional shipboard work for either the men aboard the barge or the crane operator.

To and from Shipside

Once a container ship is ready to be worked, the operators of the dock equipment (e.g., tractors, straddle trucks, and fork lifts or "pickers") begin shuttling back and forth between the "hook" and the container yard with inbound and outbound containers.* The hook is a towering, cantilevered crane that can travel the length of the dock on an enormous, four-legged pedestal. In many operations as many as three such cranes are used simultaneously to hoist containers to and from stow. Four to six dock equipment operators usually work "against" each crane. Throughout the shift they are simply told by radio or computer printout where to pick up or place their next container. There is no occasion for initiative or innovation on their part; nor is there any on-going operational need for their employers to in any way consult with them. Since their work is performed in the isolation of an operator's cab, they also have no operational need and little opportunity to converse with one another or with anyone else.

The Hoisting Operation

A container operation begins with the crane operator positioning his gear abreast the first row of containers to be worked. The crane boom is extended over the width of the vessel and the final adjustments in positioning are made. As the operator proceeds to test the fail-safe devices and limit switches, the men who will be stationed on the dock ready such shipboard and dock gear as

* Another operation in which a variety of strads, pickers, lifts, and tractors may be used is the "roll-on/roll-off" or "RO/RO" type of operation. RO/RO vessels are loaded and discharged via one or more ramps (either ship or dock mounted) which span the distance between the vessel and the dock and a series of internal deck ramps like those of a multistoried parking lot. These ramps permit the operators of the dock equipment to move the cargo directly from the dock to its place of stow and vice versa. Since the decks of these vessels resemble the flight and hanger decks of an aircraft carrier, they can carry a unique variety of cargo. They are especially unique, however, in their flexible, below-deck capacity for heavy, lengthy, and large-volumed cargoes (e.g., prefabricated steel structures). Large-volumed cargoes which can be driven or rolled to and from their place of stow (e.g., self-propelled hauling equipment which is used in strip-mining operations) may also be uniquely accommodated. Because of the variety of equipment which may be used, the variety of cargo, and the changing configuration of the decks, such operations can challenge the skill and experience of the machine operator, but his physical and operational isolation is comparable to that experienced on a container operation.

will be needed. The dock equipment drivers begin to warm their engines. The lights, brakes, parking brake, air and hydraulic systems, horns, and warning devices are tested. Meanwhile, the men dispatched to the vessel go aboard and move to the first containers to be discharged, letting go such lashing and other fasteners as have secured the containers against shifting at sea. With that done, the hoisting operation and "merry-go-round" of dock equipment begins. As the work proceeds, the shipboard men move in preplanned sequences to the remaining containers, again for the purpose of letting-go lashings. Needless to say, the crane operators follow behind, but the details are necessarily communicated to them via "squawk box." The shipboard men then double back behind the cranes to lash the newly loaded containers.

As compared to the driving of conventional shipboard winches, the work of a crane driver in any modern operation is routine. There are no unusual circumstances. There is no rigging and re-rigging of the gear. The hoist is always the same. There is no need for initiative and innovation. The range of experience and skill is by comparison very narrow. There are no hold men endangered as the gear is activated, nor is there any need for a "lasher" or dock man to be in any way endangered during a hoist. That only happens when there is a speed-up and containers travel over the men. There is no need for the communication and cooperation that is essential in conventional operations. This work is performed essentially in total isolation, and for the most part without interruption. Indeed, and because of the climb involved, most crane drivers will not come down from their cabs at "coffee break," or even at lunch time, if they have packed a lunch from home and there are heavy rains.

Shipboard Work

The only longshore work aboard a containership is that of securing and letting-go the lashings and placing and removing the heavy steel "cones" which prevent shifting at sea. Twelve to eighteen lashers are usually dispatched to such a ship, but the men work in groups of two. Each two-man "gang" works in near isolation from the others, as well as from the crane operators and machine operators on the dock. Indeed, because of the beam and freeboard of the vessels in question and because they also work either in front of the crane or behind it, the lashers are even isolated from such dock men as may be employed.

Lashing is quite arduous. Heavy wire rope lashings and turnbuckles (or other fasteners) must be dragged about the deck. As a rule, the lashings must also be hoisted to and from the topmost deck-loaded containers, which are generally stacked at least three feet high. Often enough, they are four high. This means the men stationed atop them are working 27 to 35 feet above the weatherdeck, a dangerous spot, especially at night and in heavy winds and rain. In most operations, the cones must also be hoisted and lowered. Lashing is also completely routine. It presents no challenge to one's experience, skill, or innovative abilities. However, it may at least be intermittent simply because it is only rarely necessary to lash or unlash the containers stowed below decks.*

The Modernization of Employment

As a result of the West Coast longshore strike of 1934 and the cataclysmic San Francisco general strike that erupted out of it, the hiring hall became *the* central institution of the longshore industry; it was, indeed, *the* union, because it was the means

---

* The shipboard work of loading and discharging LASH barges is essentially the same as that just described, but the lashings and turnbuckles used are substantially heavier. Since the barges are stacked two high atop the hatch covers of the weather deck, the "top men" work 30 feet above the deck. However, there is no need to handle cones because the barges are themselves constructed with such fittings. As for the containers which are also carried by LASH vessels, they are worked as described in the text.

Lashings aboard a RO/RO vessel typically offers some variety and a fluctuating pace and cycle because of the differing cargoes and deck configurations. Since most of the cargo units cannot be stacked, it is also less arduous and dangerous than that performed against containers and barges. On the other hand, the men are constantly subjected to very high noise levels from the ship's ventilating system and the various machines which shuttle back and forth to the dock. Because of the noise and the amount of traffic, the men have typically likened the situation to that of working "in the middle of a god-damned Los Angeles freeway at rush hour." After a series of work stoppages and arbitrations resulting from these conditions, an arbitrator ruled that the employer had to provide earmuffs for the men. However, since a very substantial percentage of the accidents which occur result from "a breakdown in communication," many consider this "a remedy worse than the disease" and refuse to wear such "protective equipment."

whereby the reality of union could be fashioned and maintained by men who had sought to structure and divide their work on a fair and equal basis and who, through great strife and conflict, had won the right to do so. It was both the institutional and social bedrock of their profoundly egalitarian community and union with one another.

The social roots and bonds of that community and union have been very much weakened by the nature, structure, layout, and dispersion of modern longshore work. They were also rent asunder, however, once the employer secured the contractual right to remove men from the hiring hall by offering steady machine operator work (and a monthly pay guarantee) to those he chose. This occurred with the ratification of the industry's second five-year "Mechanization and Modernization" ("M & M") agreement (1966–1971). As the San Francisco employers began to exercise this right, a complex, bitter, and sometimes explosive division arose among the men. How this happened is a long and complex story that can only be touched on here.

The New Technology: Myths and Images

In the late 1950s, the employers began relentlessly to argue the following generality on behalf of technological change: "You can't hold back progress. You just can't fight the machine." In the absence of anything to the contrary from the union leadership, this view of things became common coin among San Francisco longshoremen. Indeed, by the time the first M & M agreement (1961–1966) was submitted to the membership for discussion and vote, it was championed by the international leadership of the union.

Following a very handy ratification of that contract, the employers began to argue that a stable group of operators was required for safe and efficient crane work. Within a year, that argument led to a "Crane Supplement" to the contract. A man who had been promoted to "crane driver" (i.e., jointly trained, certified, promoted, and dispatched) could henceforth be steadily employed by a single employer for the sole purpose of driving cranes. He would in return receive a monthly pay guarantee from that employer.

Having thus "modernized" the terms under which a crane driver might be employed, the employers turned their attention to securing a more inclusive right—that of employing "a stable core of key men as machine operators." To that end, they began to argue that "the equipment and machinery of the coming era of modern longshoring will be too sophisticated to be properly operated by hall men who might occasionally be dispatched to such work from a rotational skill board." An efficient and safe operation required steadily employed men. Overall efficiency, the argument continued, would be greatly increased by machine operators who were thoroughly familiar with the entire operation and its physical setting. Further, the cost of the new technology meant that the choice of operator "simply could not be left to chance."

After the barrage of argument laid down for the first M & M and its supplement, it appeared to many men that the employers had a good case. The new machines and ships—or at least the images that were studiously and tirelessly projected of them—did seem more "complex" and "complicated" than those of conventional longshoring. It also seemed to follow that the employers' interest in having a stable group of (what had to be billed as) very well trained, highly skilled, and extremely versatile machine operators was reasonable.

Since these views, too, came to be voiced by the leadership of the international, they became especially current among men who had been on the San Francisco waterfront since the 1930s. There was good reason for that "loyalty factor": the lives of these men had literally been transformed during the tenure of that leadership. Then too, the old timers, who up through the ratification of the second M & M constituted a full three-quarters of the membership of the San Francisco local, had a direct and lively interest in the basic quid pro quo of the industry's "mechanization and modernization" plan, an earlier and financially attractive retirement. It was primarily from that quarter that one could hear reference to the "unskilled work of old-style longshoring" and the "skilled work of modern operations."

The employer's campaign for this "modernization of employment" bore fruit in Section 9.43 of the second M & M:

> . . . the Employers shall be entitled to employ steady, skilled mechanical or powered equipment operators without limit as to numbers or length of time in steady employment. . . . The employer shall be entitled to assign and shift such steady men to all equipment for which, in the opinion of the employer, they are qualified.

While this provision occasioned a rather pervasive anxiety and some opposition, most San Francisco longshoremen were reassured when the negotiators explained that the employers had simply been afforded the right *to ask* men to "go steady." No one had to accept such an invitation; nor could the local be forced to provide such men. It was both possible and comforting to imagine that "maybe they'll never get their steady men."

As their vote was destined to indicate, a great majority of the men were on balance satisfied with the second M & M. There was a substantial wage hike, heavily "front-loaded" into the first year, and a substantial increase in pension benefits. Presumably retirements would counterbalance the loss of work opportunities that might result from new machines and operations. Indeed, the union negotiators had for this reason even agreed to drop the weekly pay guarantee that the first M & M had included as insurance against underemployment. As for the concern generated by the length of the contract, that was largely defused by a certain posturing: "If this contract doesn't work out, we've got the muscle to tear it up." In a word, there were some gains and many reassurances.

The New Technology: "It's No Big Thing"

The struggle against 9.43 was largely carried on by younger men who had recently entered the industry. Their struggle was rooted in a very fundamental circumstance—they were in no way intimidated by the new machinery. As compared to the "old timers," they had been socially conditioned to be comfortable with machinery. Their view was simply this: any piece of machinery obviously requires a competent and reliable operator, but the operation of modern equipment is "no big thing." This consciousness was concretely reinforced and made increasingly current by a particular operational circumstance. When the port was busy, employers were obliged to "supplement" their 9.43 men by hiring skilled hall men to drive the new machines. This simply contradicted the elitist rationale that had been manufactured on behalf of 9.43. While the struggle could therefore be broadened and deepened, it also became increasingly bitter— the operation of such equipment was reserved for 9.43 men when work was slack because they were receiving a monthly pay guarantee. The struggle was intensified, too, as hall men were promoted to the winch/crane categories to replace retirees. In time, these men also knew that driving conventional gear required greater experience, knowledge, and skill than did the operation of container cranes. That work was also much more demanding in that the on-going safety of the hold men, as well as those on deck and on the dock, was in the hands of the winch driver. Indeed, by 1968 a common view (which, perhaps for emphasis, was chauvinistic) had emerged: "Your grandmother could drive the biggest container crane in the world." Much the same thing happened as hall men were promoted to the lift categories and thereby gained experience with the dock equipment operated by 9.43 men. Most of these men had previously worked in the "skilled hold man" category, which frequently involved the operation of lift machines (of varying capacities) in the hold of the vessel. They invariably concluded that such work demanded much more skill, experience, and ingenuity than "simply running between a crane and the yard with one of these new pieces of equipment."

The employers' carefully sown and cultivated myth regarding the introduction of "highly sophisticated" equipment which required an elite corps of operators was thus eroded away. To put the matter briefly: the men were learning in concrete terms that there is no necessary correlation between the size, capacity, or cost of a piece of machinery and the skill and experience that are required to operate it efficiently and safely. Indeed, the mechanization and modernization of their industry was teaching them that the skills and experience required may in fact be inversely related to such factors. By the same token, the rationale for Section 9.43 was increasingly seen as simply a rationale for injustice.

As these things occurred, the employers increasingly rested their case on the notion that steady machine operators were necessary for a safe but productive operation. The 9.43 man was said to be more productive because he was intimately familiar with the overall operation and the facility within which it was carried on. The "productivity figures" to "prove" this point were of two kinds: (1) the average number of crane hoists the 9.43 men made each hour, as compared to the average of the hall crane operators, and (2) the average number of moves they made each hour to and from the hook, as compared to the hall lift drivers. As it happened, these figures were usually presented in a comprehensive and convincing manner, and many men came to believe them. On the other hand, most men also came to believe that "If the average 9.43 man can have a better showing than the hall man, that's because he's willing to go along with a speed-up and risk the safety of other guys." Thus, in the nation's second most hazardous industry, a new watchword emerged: "Keep your eyes open around that guy, he's nine point four three." As for the employers, they presently stopped citing such figures and shelved their arguments about needing steady men to insure efficiency and the safety of others.

Within this framework, the relationships between the men who had accepted an invitation "to go nine point four three" and those who had refused became particularly strained. That was especially true when the 9.43 man was younger and possessed less seniority. Older men who had never been asked to go steady faced another sort of circumstance. Some felt insulted or discriminated against because they were "just as good on those machines as anybody else." Most were quick to add, however, that the real insult was to be asked. That meant the employer thought you were the kind of man who would accept: "The employers know I'm just too good a union man to go steady." In any event, as the employers invited *real* men (and old acquaintances) to that station, few men felt that the abilities of those selected were in any way superior to many others. Indeed, since the skills of longshoring were so widely shared and since the men were so widely acquainted, *any* selection would have been viewed as arbitrary. There simply was nothing like a technological elite among them.

The Men and Their Union

As these views and understandings spread, the inflationary spiral which an escalating Vietnam war imposed upon the nation caught up with them. By 1968 their wage gains had been wiped out. By then, the "container revolution" was also there for all to see. Indeed, the greatly accelerated pace of that revolution was largely occasioned by the fueling of the tragic and immoral adventure of Vietnam. As work fell off, anxiety mounted. There were a full three years to go with a contract which in nearly 200 pages made no mention of a "container."*

* In an effort to get "at least some of the container work" there was a series of "wildcat" work stoppages in San Francisco and Los Angeles during the fall of

Given these developments, the functioning of Section 9.43 rapidly became the source of an all-pervasive instability within the San Francisco industry. By late 1967 there were over 150 such men; by 1968 their number had swelled to nearly 300, or about 10 percent of the work force. In the spring of 1968, the on-the-job struggle against "going nine point four three" had also been dramatically escalated and made visible through leaflets. Indeed, the men and local union officers had by then been occasionally warned by the industry arbitrator about the use of "coercion" against the steady men.

The community and union of San Francisco longshoremen were thus threatened with collapse. Section 9.43 and its adjudication through the grievance machinery negated the otherwise "sacred" contractual principles of rotational job dispatch, seniority, joint training and skill certification, and joint promotion. It also undercut the "one man, one job" principle of restricting a man's work to the job category in which he had been dispatched. Finally, and because the relevant contract language was not sufficiently precise, union efforts to use the grievance machinery for equalizing the work opportunity of the skilled hall men and the 9.43 men were unsuccessful. In short, this modernization of the terms of employment totally undermined the basic principles of the hiring hall. It therefore represented not merely a very broad and fundamental departure from the historically relevant contractual and institutional past, but a break with something still more fundamental—the profoundly egalitarian sense of justice which the hiring hall had concretely institutionalized.

With respect to the social relationships that came to exist among the San Francisco longshoremen by reason of Section 9.43, it is, of course, important to remember that the bonds of community and union were being quite generally atrophied by the use of the new technology. Within this evolving social framework, however, the circumstances of the 9.43 men were extreme. For the most part they avoided union meetings and activity. They seldom came to the hiring hall or the union

---

1968. These actions precipitated the negotiation of a "Container Freight Station Supplement" to the contract. For a variety of reasons, the most central of which was a court action which gutted the jurisdictional provisions of the supplement, little such work ever materialized.

offices. They lost touch with old friends and acquaintances. At best, they were only slightly acquainted with the newer men. Because of the nature of their work, they could not assist either shipboard or dock men. They could only "produce" for their employer and by so doing perhaps subject those men to a speed-up and/or an unsafe working condition.

Given these circumstances, and the collapse of any creditable rationale for 9.43, it was increasingly understood that after many years the San Francisco longshore industry was again distinguished by a shape-up. By the same token, 9.43 was increasingly viewed as having introduced a "cancer" into the local: "It's cancer. It's the cancer of wanting to make more money than anybody else. It's the cancer of looking to the employer for your future and not the union. It's a cancer because for every 9.43 man on the job, there's three or four other men trying to get that job. It's the cancer of a shape-up and with it the employers are out to destroy the hiring hall and break the union."

It followed that for most San Francisco longshoremen the slogan "No 9.43" largely underwrote what was destined to occur at the end of the contract—the longest maritime strike in the history of the nation. Indeed, the strike of 1971–1972 was widely viewed as essentially a replay of 1934 because the manner of assigning and distributing work was central. In their first major strike statement the men expressed themselves as follows:

> We are being asked to accept a set of demands which would destroy the system of job dispatch which has always prevented discrimination and favoritism, while insuring an equal work opportunity to all of us. Since these demands seriously jeopardize our immediate economic welfare and long-term job security while threatening *the very existence of our union,* they are in fact *a basic issue in our strike*!!!

While the very complex story of the strike cannot be entered into here, it must be noted that it ended with no modification of Section 9.43.

It was not until the present contract (1978–1981) that certain changes in that provision were negotiated. The San Francisco men who were working under 9.43 at the time of ratification were to periodically return to the hiring hall dispatch system for at least 30 days. During that period, they would be replaced by newly trained men, again on a steady basis. Unlike in the past, the new men would be trained, if not selected, on a seniority basis. In this way, the work in question would be rotated and more widely shared. Accordingly, those who supported this modification could argue that "a lot of new men will now get a crack at this work." They could also argue that "a lot of men who haven't been in the hall for years will come back to the fold." There was, however, a lot of skepticism: "All we've done here is double the number of steady men. We've just given the steady man a partner. We haven't done shit for the hall man or the hall, but that's where they've got us and that's where they've had us for a good long time." This quite typically elicited a response of the following order: "Well, maybe so, man, but at least this is something. After twelve long years, it's at least a step in the right direction."

The present contract, like all since 1934, is a coastwide contract. It was voted up by a coastwide majority of longshoremen (and ship clerks) in a secret referendum (5495 to 2474). But having noted this, it should also be noted that it contains separate provisions for steady machine operators in both Los Angeles and Seattle. As it happens, this represents a complete departure from over forty years of practice. For many San Francisco men, the cure of three "formulas" for the employment of steady machine operators was worse than the disease. To those men, the prospect of an emergent competition between locals of these ports and hence a further splitting of the union's coastwide unity was still another very good reason for voting against the contract.

Needless to say, the present author is in no position to discuss the experience which the Los Angeles or Seattle local has had in this connection. However, with respect to the San Francisco local, it may and should be noted that the employers have waged a very successful rearguard action against the implementation of the modification in question. They have raised a host of issues through the grievance machinery, i.e., through the local Labor Relations Committee, through arbitrations, and through referrals to the coastwide representatives of the industry. As a result, even those who voted for the contract and the modification do not yet know what it may come to mean. What they do know is that, despite the local's more recent success in implementing the modification, relatively few men have thus far been rotated into and/or out of the 9.43 status. At the same time, there is a growing consensus on two points: (1) the enormous impact which a new technology has had on their social relations—and hence on the unity, strength, and militancy of their union and community with one another—and (2) new technology cannot be successfully dealt with on an ad hoc, piecemeal basis and, since any local can be similarly victimized by a new technology and the way it is contractually utilized, such matters must be dealt with on a coastwide basis.

Work Relations in the Coal Industry: The Handloading Era, 1880–1930

Keith Dix

The single most striking feature of mining in the United States before the 1930s was that practically all bituminous coal—over one-half billion tons annually in the late 1920s—was loaded in the mine with a shovel, by hand. The details of the production process during this early period provide an important foundation on which to understand present-day coal mining systems and industrial relations.

Mine Entry

Underground bituminous mining may be classified according to the three approaches used to gain entry to the seam of coal. When coal reserves are found at some depth from the surface, the approach is to sink a shaft and erect a hoist for transporting workers, supplies, and coal. If the coal lies beneath the surface but not at a great depth, access to the seam is by a sloping entry and requires the movement of workers, supplies, and coal by rail. Finally, drift mining involves a direct approach to a seam of coal conveniently exposed on the side of a hill; the workers may walk to and from their workplaces while supplies and mined coal move by mule and an underground railway system.

Selecting one approach over another is largely a matter of geography and geology, of whether the coal seam outcrops on a hillside or lies buried at some distance below ground level. In the past, however, the mine entry decision was not neutral in its impact on overall economic conditions in the industry or on work relations inside the mine. Sinking shafts and developing a new mine required a much larger capital investment than did

---

This essay is an abridged version of a longer monograph with the same title that is available from the Institute for Labor Relations at the University of West Virginia.

drift mining. Ease of entry in a literal sense—as in drift mining—meant ease of entry in an economic sense, with the resulting problems of overexpansion during prosperous times and excess capacity and unemployment during depressed times. Since drift mining predominated in some coal regions, there was a differential impact among them during swings in the cyclical demand for coal.

Whether a coal mine was opened as a drift or shaft mine affected the ease with which the miners, who were paid by the number of tons produced each day, could enter and leave the mine. These pieceworkers, or "tonnage" men could walk out of the mine whenever they pleased. Before the 1920s, mine management had complained of this practice, but had been unable to stop it. Greater discipline was possible, however, in the shaft mines, where the mechanical means for entry and exit—the "cage" or the "man-trip"—was located on the surface, under management's supervision. Over the years, as coal output shifted to shaft and slope mines, it became increasingly difficult for the mine worker to leave the mine at will. This does not mean that one method of approaching the coal seam was preferred because of the discipline factor—nothing in the management literature of the period suggests this—but only that many decisions generally thought to be based solely on engineering or efficiency considerations have an impact on work relations and established patterns of human behavior on the job.

The extent of the mining operations also affected work relations. As coal removal proceeded further and further into a seam, the distance between the working "face" or "room" and the mine entrance grew longer. Older mines thus had, as they do today, workplaces which were literally miles from the drift mouth or mine shaft. This, of course, increased the length of time it took for a miner to begin earning an income since he was paid by the number of tons he produced; it also reduced communication among miners and between the miners and the outside, which had adverse safety implications. Further, deeper mine workings reduced the number of visits the mine foreman could make to each working place during the day. Mine haulage costs increased with distance, as did problems of coordinating the delivery of supplies and empty cars to the working miner and the removal of loaded cars from each room.

Mining Systems

Once the coal seam has been penetrated by shaft or drift, there are two basic systems of removing the coal: the "room-and-pillar" system and the "longwall" mining system. Both have endless modifications. While the room-and-pillar system predominated in the 1920s (as it does today), both systems will be considered briefly to show the physical context within which the miner works.

The room-and-pillar mining of the 1920s (Lubin 1924; Archibald 1922; U. S. Coal Commission 1925) involved opening tunnels, called main entries, which were driven forward horizontally into the solid coal seam from the bottom of the shaft or the drift opening. Side entries were then driven off the main entry, at intervals of approximately 400 feet, for a distance of 1200 to 1500 feet away from the main entry. Each thus "block out" a rectangular "panel" of coal. "Rooms" were driven off the side entries at right angles, and it was here that the principal coal mining activity occurred. A side entry 1200 feet long might have a row of twenty rooms, the sum of which constituted a "panel."

In the 1920s and earlier, a room would generally be 20 feet wide, with variations ranging from 12 to 40 feet. Depending on the distance between side entries, completed rooms would be from 250 to 400 feet long. The end wall in these rooms was where the miner and his helper were located, and was called the working "face." Dimensions of the face were determined, of course, by the width of the room (say 20 feet) and the thickness of the coal seam (which might vary from 2 or 3 feet up to 6 or 8 feet or more). The rooms, like the entries, are connected to one another by "breakthroughs" cut through the pillars of coal that come to serve as walls between the rooms. Breakthroughs permit the circulation of air and offer a means of communication from one room to the next. Coal is removed from the rooms on tracks which connect the rooms with the side entries and the main haulage ways.

Given this system, the mining process involves the following general procedure: the removal of the coal from the working face, loading it into cars which are pushed from the face to the room entrance, gathering the loaded cars by mule or locomotive, and transferring the coal to the outside. The quantity of coal mined, and the earnings of the miner, depended on such factors as the width of the room, the thickness of the seam, the presence of impurities in the coal, the suitability of the roof or "top," the availability and efficiency of the machinery, the availability of cars, and, of course, the skill and speed of the miner.

In a panel there would be fourteen or more rooms, enough places for fourteen or twenty-eight miners, depending on whether the rooms were considered single or double. The size of the mining property and the availability of customers largely determined the number of panels in operation at any one time. Work in the different rooms went ahead at different rates so that a diagonal advancement of the rooms could take place. When all the rooms in a panel were finished, the task of removing the pillars between the rooms—called "pillar drawing"—began. It involved retreating from the end of the room back toward the entrance and had to be done simultaneously for all rooms in the panel. Proper pillar drawing greatly reduced the amount of coal left in the mine and lost to production, but required careful management in advancing the workplaces and skilled workmen to "pull" the pillars.

Longwall mining has been described as

> the digging away of the entire seam of coal and filling of the open space either by allowing the earth overlying the coal to fall down and close in behind the miners as they advance or by packing in such waste rock as comes down with the coal. (Lubin 1924:15)

The cutting and removal of the coal may begin at the shaft and move toward the outer limits of the property—longwall "advancing"—or entries may be driven to the property limits and the coal removed backward toward the shaft—longwall "retreating." In some locations the panel system of mining was adapted to longwall mining.

Although longwall mining was used almost universally in Europe during this period, it was not popular in the United States, in part because of adverse physical conditions—for example, thin and irregular coal seams and poor roof conditions—in part because of labor force and capital investment considerations.

Longwall mining had the advantage of greater total recovery of coal reserves (up to 95 percent), potentially greater labor productivity, and improved haulage systems (e.g., conveyor belts). Men, machinery, and material could be used with the greatest efficiency: lower costs were, theoretically, obtainable because the system concentrates the men, and tends to bring the cost price for day laborers, as track men, drivers, etc. to a minimum. This cost in some mines is enormous, while by this system it will be comparatively small. It also makes easier supervision, and in every way tends to lessen the work of the mine superintendent. (Krebs 1911:135)

If longwall mining made supervision easier, it also gave the workers a strategic advantage not enjoyed in room-and-pillar mining. Successful longwall mining depended on uninterrupted production schedules "since irregularity in the removal of coal often causes the roof to shear at the face, resulting in the loss of some coal and mine equipment, and considerable additional cost to reestablish the working face" (U. S. Coal Commission 1925:1871). Although the availability of steady customers and regular delivery of empty railroad coal cars affected production schedules, so did strikes, and "even a short stoppage of operation may result in serious damage to the working area through the caving of the roof. In the pillar method this is less important" (Lubin 1924:16). The economic feasibility of longwall mining depended, therefore, not on physical and technological factors alone, but on market conditions and on the availability of a peaceful and disciplined work force.

The Miner's Job

A typical miner walked from his home to the mine entrance; in a drift mine, he walked from there to his "room" or "place." The first task facing him was the undercutting of the coal face. To do this, he would make a horizontal or wedge-shaped slit, usually three or four feet deep, with his pick at the bottom of the seam as deeply as he expected to be able to blast the coal loose. According to John Brophy:

> Most of this undercutting had to be done lying on your side and swinging the pick in a very confined space. There was always a danger of coal falling from the face onto a miner while he was undercutting. A man had to know the condition of the coal he was working on and judge his safety accordingly. (Brophy 1964:43)

Estimates for the length of time it took to make an undercut range from about three hours to five or six hours (Tams

1963:36; Parker 1910:678), depending on the width of the room, the hardness and purity of the coal, and the skill of the individual miner. It was this part of the job that was referred to as "mining." It was the most time-consuming task the miner had, taking a substantial part of his work day. It was arduous because the miner often had to lie on his side to swing his pick, and it was dangerous because of the ever present possibility of falling coal. If the mine was poorly drained, the miner had to work in wet clothing.

After the undercutting, it was necessary to drill a hole in the coal face. Using a five to five-and-a-half foot auger, turned by a U-crank like a common brace and bit, the miner drilled the hole to the proper depth and at the appropriate angle. The placement of the bore hole was quite important:

> If the miner judged his boring accurately, the explosion would not only break loose the coal below the hole, but it would also jolt the roof hard enough to dislodge any coal which might adhere to the roof—a prudent calculation, to get the most loose coal for the powder expended. (Brophy 1964:44)

Shooting down the coal with black powder of "permissible" explosives was the third task. Brophy explains how the powder was placed in the drilled hole and how the miner's needle, an iron rod five or six feet long, was left in the hole as dirt was tamped down on top of the powder. The needle was "very gently withdrawn, being rotated all the way, leaving a small channel under the dirt" for the placement of the fuse. His description of the blasting process is worth repeating to show the skill required to do the job safely and efficiently:

> A squib—a thin roll of waxed paper about the size of the needle, with a little powder in its upper part—was then inserted into the entrance of the channel, to act as a fuse. The lower few inches of the squib contained no powder, because the time it took the paper to burn up to the powder was the time the miner gave himself to get to safety in the main entry. The miner lighted the end of the squib with his lamp and then ran to his refuge. When the powder in the squib ignited, it flashed flame up the channel, the cartridge exploded and the coal was shattered away from the face, a ton or more by a single explosion. (Ibid:44)

The skill with which the miner undercut the coal, drilled, and blasted it determined the amount available for loading after each charge—an important consideration since the miner traditionally had to pay for his own powder—as well as the relative amount of "lump" coal the miner sent to the outside in each loaded car. Since lump coal sold at a higher price than fine coal, management expected miners to load as much of it as possible. "The amount of coal wasted depends largely on the skill and care of the miner in mining it," reported the U. S. Commissioner of Labor in 1905. "An unskilled or careless miner will make double the amount of fine and slack coal in mining out a cubic yard than a skillful and careful one will, thus practically destroying what is, and might otherwise continue to be, an item of economic value" (U. S. Commissioner of Labor 1905:412). Skill in the placement and firing of the shot was also required in order to prevent damage to the overhead strata of rock or slate, called the "roof." The use of too much powder could weaken the roof and increase the chance of an accident from falling rock.

Empty coal cars were pushed from the neck of the room and positioned near the coal so that they could be loaded with a minimum of effort. This was the fourth part of the miner's job. It was a straightforward task of shoveling, but in coal seams less than five feet high, "it was no simple matter . . . to throw it high enough to clear the sides of the car without hitting the roof and spilling over the far side" (Brophy 1964:44). Pieces of rock and slate had to be removed to avoid being "docked" for loading "dirty" coal. The loaded car was then pushed from the room by the miner and his helper, or "gathered" by a mule or locomotive.

The miner's job did not end when the loaded car was removed from the workplace. Brophy describes some of the miner's other tasks:

> Getting out the coal was not the whole job of the miner. He had to lay the track from the main entry into his work place. He had to timber his own place, and he often was required in thin seams to "take up bottom," as it was called, to enable the cars to get to the work face. The roadway had to be high enough to let the mine cars through loaded; perhaps four or five feet. If the coal seam was not that thick, and it frequently was not, rock or dirt had to be cut away to lower the floor. This was "company work" for which the company gave no pay unless forced to do so by the union. (Ibid:44)

The auxiliary work of timbering and track laying constituted a fifth category of tasks necessary to complete the mining cycle.

The miner's job clearly required a high level of knowledge, experience, and dexterity and these were acquired, as with most skilled jobs, by serving an apprenticeship of variable length, depending on law and custom. A 1920s Illinois mining law, for example, stated that "a man must have a certificate of two years' experience at the face before he can be left alone as a 'practical miner.'"

Once a miner was assigned a working place, the task of mining coal was left almost entirely up to him. The early coal miner was thus an independent craftsman who worked largely without supervision, and mining was a craft occupation with counterparts in other industries of the nineteenth century: iron molders, glass blowers, locomotive engineers, boiler makers, typographers, iron rollers, puddlers and heaters, certain shoe machinery operators, and some journeymen machinists all exercised broad discretion in the direction of their own work and that of their helpers. The knowledge of mining belonged to the body of miners at work in their respective rooms, and it was up to them to pass their knowledge and skills on to new workers. Goodrich observed that "the miner does in practice pick up his trade almost entirely from his buddy or his neighbors and hardly at all from his boss" (Goodrich 1925:37). He developed a proprietary interest in his room and was rarely transferred until it had been worked out. Even if he was absent for considerable time, his room was ordinarily held for him (Morris 1934:65).

The work force in each mine therefore consisted mostly of miners and their helpers. The mule drivers and helpers, who hauled the empties to the miners' rooms, removed loaded cars, and brought in supplies, constituted a second occupational category. There were also a small number of track layers, carpenters, and other inside "company" men.

The Pennsylvania *Reports of Inspectors of Coal Mines* shows the number of workers in each of these job classifications for the 79 bituminous mines in Allegheny County in 1890. The 7,905 miners and the 623 miners' helpers made up 90.4 percent of the underground force and 81.5 percent of the total mine work force. The underground work force—miners and nonminers—made up 90.1 percent of the total work force. There were only 83 foremen in these 79 mines, a ratio of foremen to underground workers of 1:114. This structure was typical of the industry before the introduction of mining machinery and the increased division of labor which accompanied it.

Early Mine Mechanization

With the introduction of a machine for undercutting the coal face, some customary tasks slipped away from the craft miner. The miner's job was divided into "mining" or undercutting, and drilling, blasting, and loading. The development of air-powered and electric drills, the employment of "shot-firers," the shifting of timbering and track laying duties to specialized workers further "deskilled" the pick miner's job. Yet even with all these changes, which were quite unevenly introduced between 1880 and 1930, coal was still loaded by hand and craft control remained characteristic of the mining process.

As long as coal was hand loaded management could not control production and work relations remained essentially unchanged: the miner worked in a room alone or with a partner, at his own pace and largely without supervision; he was paid on the basis of the amount of coal he loaded; and in many mines he was free to leave the mine whenever he wanted to.

We have shown how undercutting was a highly skilled, arduous, time-consuming, and dangerous task, and it is not surprising that management would seek cost-reducing, labor-saving machinery at this point in the production process. The first mining machines were virtually mechanical substitutes for manual undercutting. "The results of this introduction of machinery," reported the Illinois Bureau of Labor in 1888, "consist not only in the greater execution of the machine, but in the subdivision of labor which it involves." The advantage to the employer lay in the fact that machine mining

> relieves him for the most part of skilled labor and of all the restraints which that implies. It opens to him the whole labor market from which to recruit his force. (Quoted in U. S. Industrial Commission 1902:399)

Mining machines were also seen as "a weapon with which to meet organized skilled labor" and its "unreasonable demands." As West Virginia coal operator and mining engineer William M. Page wrote in 1894:

> Machine mining is coming into general use, not so much for its saving in direct cost as for the indirect economy in having to control a fewer number of men for the same output. . . . As the machine does the mining, the proportion of skilled labor is largely reduced, and the result is found in less belligerence and conflict; a sufficient inducement though the direct costs be the same. (P. 151)

And Dean C. R. Jones of West Virginia University's School of Mines commented critically:

> I found one reason why labor sometimes opposes the introduction of labor saving devices. I once worked for a firm that operated two machines and I asked why they did not operate four. I was pretty close to some of the members of management. They said the machines did not do quite as good work as the men could by hand but those machines were being used to keep the labor under subjection. But that is not a worthy motive and so long as operators install machines in mines just for the purpose of getting the upper hand of labor they are going to have trouble. I do not believe that motive is worthy.

Old Methods Versus New

Given these apparent advantages, the conversion from pick mining to mechanical undercutting was not as rapid as one might have expected it to be. The first cutting machines were introduced in 1876 and by 1900 only one-fourth of U. S. bituminous coal was machine mined; by 1915, the portion was over one-half, but it was not until 1930 that the industry had fully mechanized the undercutting operation.

The miners themselves resisted the use of the new technology, thus slowing down its introduction. In reviewing the history of the pick machine, Parker noted that there had been a great deal of opposition to undercutting by machine:

> This opposition has been, it is claimed, shown in a practical manner, and it is also claimed that much of the supposed imperfections and inefficiency of the earlier machines was due to the handling of the machine by the miner, who saw in it a supplanter of his labor, and therefore an enemy to be dealt with as harshly as possible. (Parker 1900:412)

Francis Lechner, father of the first cutting machine, warned that "the machine must be made so strong that it can't be broken with a sledge hammer" (*Mines and Minerals,* March 1903:377). And management apparently had difficulty in finding workers who were willing to run the machines.

Fear of job loss and concern over a weakening of craft control may have been the prime motivation for the resistance, but there were other reasons why mechanical undercutting was not looked upon as the miner's friend: it introduced new hazards to the workplace. First of all, the machines were noisy and created hearing disabilities for machine "runners" and their helpers. "One of the objections to [the machine's] use is its tendency to produce deafness in those operating it," admitted *Mines and Minerals,* an industry journal, in 1899 (December 1899:205). The noise factor also made it impossible for anyone working near the face to hear the life-saving signal that the roof was "working" and a slate fall was imminent (Ingalls 1907:164). Secondly, the machines vibrated so violently that they frequently caused internal injuries to the operators. And finally, they increased the amount of dust. Although it was not until recently that the relationship between dust levels and mine worker health was fully recognized, the explosive characteristics of coal dust were known at an early date. For example, it was acknowledged that there was an excessive amount of dust "as a result of mining machinery" in the Red Ash, West Virginia, mine explosion that killed forty-six workers in 1900.

In unionized districts, work rules were negotiated which discouraged the use of mechanical undercutters. Limitations on the number of "runs" a machine could make each shift and on the number of loaders a machine could cut for reduced the profitability of machine mining and undoubtedly slowed its rate of growth. These rules, common in labor agreements in Illinois and Indiana by the late 1890s, often virtually nullified the labor-saving advantage the employer hoped to realize from the use of the machinery.

An analysis of the output in West Virginia between 1897 and 1934 shows an interesting relationship between the old and new mining methods. Although undercutting by machine was faster than pick mining, the productivity of the workers (runners, helpers, and loaders) was not much greater than that of the pick miners. Up until 1920, the yearly output per man-day for West Virginia pick miners was often higher than for machine miners. The relative gains in the productivity of machine miners after the 1920s may have meant that the new technology had become superior, but it also may simply have reflected the shift in overall state output to larger and generally more efficient mines.

Part of the reason for the failure of the machine miners' productivity to increase at a greater rate is that the job of loading still had to be done by hand. It is thus not surprising that the 1923 U. S. Coal Commission placed great emphasis on mechanical loading as a primary means by which the industry could realize substantial gains in efficiency and profits.

In addition, any growth in productivity may have been the result of improvements that were being made away from the coal face, particularly in mine haulage systems. There was a rapid shift from animal to mechanical power in the first two decades of the century, making it possible to move larger quantities of coal to the surface and to return the empty cars at a faster rate. While less than 20 percent of all West Virginia mines used locomotives for underground haulage at the turn of the century, by the early 1920s nearly 75 percent had converted to mechanical transportation.

In the face of these conclusions, there would seem to have been another reason for introducing the new technology. Machine mining apparently sufficiently deskilled the labor process so that, in the face of a steady decrease in the number of skilled pick miners, inexperienced miners could be hired to meet the growing demand for West Virginia coal.

Early Division of Labor

The first and most obvious change in work relations brought about by the cutting machine was a division of the tasks of pick mining, sometimes including a further subdivision that assigned the tasks of drilling, shooting, loading, timbering, and tracklaying to the face to individual workers. The new technical division of labor developed gradually and unevenly across the industry. For example, by 1902, some mines in Pennsylvania were using full-time shot-firers and the employment of day men who did nothing but lay track became a common practice in some areas, notably in Ohio and Illinois. Drilling by specialized teams who carried power drills from room to room was introduced before World War I, and even the task of timbering was assigned to day men in some mines. Payment by the day (rather than by the ton) for these new jobs placed employees under the direct supervision of the mine foreman.

The 1923 U. S. Coal Commission study of the division of labor in a representative sample of bituminous mines indicates the extent of this process. In West Virginia, only nine of twenty-three mines sampled still had a hand loader performing all the basic job functions—drilling, shooting, loading, timbering, and track-laying. The division of labor in these mines was as follows:

Number of mines	Tasks performed by coal loaders
9	All tasks
6	All tasks except laying track
2	All tasks except shooting
1	All tasks except drilling and shooting
4	Only loading and shooting
1	Only loading

In other states, the process had progressed less far. Loaders did all tasks in twelve of thirteen Ohio mines studied; in one, timbering and track-laying were performed by company men. In Pennsylvania, the loaders continued to perform all the tasks in nine of eleven mines studied, but in the other two tonnage men were not required to drill and shoot their places. In the eight Illinois mines, coal leaders did everything but lay track (*Coal Age*, February 7, 1924).

It was widely believed that the introduction of machinery paved the way for the employment of inexperienced eastern and southern European immigrants and blacks from the rural South. This view was only partially correct, for while new machinery eliminated one of the skilled miner's tasks, the specialization process eliminated others. The experiences of Charles Elekes, who came to this country in 1911 from a farm in Hungary and found a job in a West Virginia coal mine within days after his arrival, were typical of the way the immigrant became a mine worker:

Dix: Tell me about what you were expected to do when you first took a job in the mines.

Elekes: Well, we drilled the hole, they shot it down, we loaded the coal and the track man came and fixed the track.

Dix: What about timbering?

Elekes: Company men did that.

Dix: Did the company undercut the coal for you?

Elekes: Yes, they cut it or punched it and we drilled the hole. We used to have a dynamite box, a wooden box, and that's what I used to stand on to drill my hole.

Dix: Who taught you to drill and tamp the powder?

Elekes: The good Lord. They showed me one time and that was all. Every once in a while somebody from my boarding house would sneak over to see how I was doing.

Dix: You were put in a place by yourself?

Elekes: Yes. The first day all three of us [he and his cousin and brother] was in one place. The second day my cousin and I worked one place, so the third day everybody was separated. We all had a place.

Dix: In other words, in three days, you were expected to learn the basics and take off on your own?

Elekes: I'll tell you, in six months' time, I load as much coal as any man.

The impact of the undercutting machine and the division of labor is reflected in changes in employee classifications for the mine work force. For example, total mine employment in Allegheny County, Pennsylvania, increased from 10,464 in 1890 to 15,189 in 1930, largely as a result of the increase in the number of mines (from 79 to 106), but the number of miners who still used the pick method declined dramatically from 7,905 to 1,401. By 1930, most of the work at the coal face was handled by machine runners and their helpers, who did the undercutting, and by machine miners who loaded the coal. The total number of face workers still being paid on a tonnage basis declined from 90.4 to 75.3 percent of the inside (i.e., underground) work force. The number of job categories inside the mine increased dramatically, from six in 1890 to eighteen in 1930. There was an increase in the number of workers involved in the mine haulage, and in the new category of shot-firers. The number of mine foremen increased in almost exact proportion to the increase in the number of mines, but the growing practice of hiring assistant mine foremen created additional supervision of workers. Furthermore, each mine had at least one fire boss whose job it was to test for gas in the mine.

These tendencies toward mechanization and task subdivision during the handloading era provided only incremental steps toward management control over the labor process in coal mining. Most of the segmented tasks still required significant craft skill and effective supervision was still impeded by the physical and spatial constraints of room-and-pillar mining.

Changes in work relations continued slowly and unevenly throughout the years until the late 1920s, when mechanical loading equipment began to eliminate the basic task of loading by hand. This second phase of mechanization made a more fundamental restructuring of the production process possible.

The Labor Process in Coal Mining: Struggle for Control

Michael Yarrow

Coal miners around the world are typically the "aristocracy of militant labor." The United States is no exception. Miners have a venerable tradition of fighting for their rights. In the past decade there has been a rising wave of wildcat strikes in the coal fields, many over working conditions but some over issues beyond the workplace, aimed at governors, legislatures, and judges. By 1977 miners were wildcatting almost 100 times more frequently than the average American worker (BCOA statement, October 6, 1977), while inside the mines miners disciplined management and retained considerable control of the labor process. Coal miners have not acted as the powerless robots that were expected to result from the capitalists' rationalization and mechanization of the labor process, making coal mining appear as a deviant case from Harry Braverman's (1974) depiction of the dominant development in the labor process in twentieth-century capitalism. By analyzing this deviant case, I will attempt to extend Braverman's assessment of the factors affecting the struggle for control of the labor process.*

This essay is part of a larger research project on the class consciousness of coal miners which I am conducting for my Ph.D. dissertation. It is based on observations of two deep mines and one surface mine, and interviews with forty miners, a section foreman, and a mining engineer. Comments on an earlier draft by the following miners and other thoughtful people have stimulated corrections and clarifications: Joe Mulloy, Keith Dix, Louie Nikolaidis, Maartin de Kadt, Rick Simon, and Andrew Zimbalist. Much of its readability results from the editing of Ruth Yarrow and Susan Lowes.

* I will *not* attempt a full explanation of why coal mining is a deviant case. That would require a broader focus, including macro political-economic factors, such as the state of competition in the industry, the structure of ownership, the level of demand, the rate of profit, the type of state involvement; regional sociocultural factors, such as the tradition of class conflict and working class solidarity, the amount of residential dispersion, and the penetration of bourgeois cultural forms and ideology; and also organizational factors, such as the structure and vitality of the three levels of union bureaucracy, the specifics of the contract, and the size and internal organization of coal companies.

Coal Mining: 1930 to 1978

Since 1930 coal mining technology, the ownership structure, and the miners' union have gone through several transformations that have affected the labor process. By 1930 the slow, fitful mechanization of underground coal mining had brought almost universal adoption of mechanical cutting machines, but mechanical loaders still accounted for only 10 percent of national production (Baratz 1955:41–43; and see Dix in this volume). The fall in demand during the depression prolonged the slow pace until 1935, after which mechanization proceeded rapidly, one major innovation closely following another. As a result, part of the industry has been continually converting to a mining system already obsolete. Many older miners have experienced two or even three revolutions in the mining labor process. By 1950, 70 percent of the industry had converted to mechanical loaders, but since the 1950s the industry has largely converted to the "continuous miner," a huge machine that gouges out the coal without blasting and loads it onto shuttle cars. In 1960 a mechanized longwall system was introduced from Europe. It shears coal from a 600 foot face onto a conveyor while the roof is held up by huge hydraulic jacks. By 1975 longwall produced only 4 percent of underground coal but there are indications that the rate is accelerating. Concomitantly, there has been an increase in highly mechanized surface mining, which in 1976 produced 56 percent of the total.

The fourfold increase in productivity between 1930 and 1969 combined with a postwar decline in coal consumption to produce a drastic reduction in employment. Two-thirds of those employed in 1948 were displaced by 1969 (Nyden 1974:470). This caused a terrific social and economic dislocation in one-industry Appalachia and profoundly affected the labor-management relationship within the mines. Miners who lived through this period remember being job scared while their bosses exploited this fear to the hilt. Younger miners believe that the operators used the massive layoffs to "weed out the good union men so all you had left was a bunch of company sucks." As in the 1920s when the union was nearly destroyed, the operators had a free hand and used it to discipline the unruly work force.

The transformation of the miners' union during these decades was, if anything, more pronounced than that of mining technology. The antiunion offensive of the 1920s had been particularly devastating to the United Mine Workers (UMW), and by 1930 effective union organization had been driven from all but the Illinois fields. Reunionization of miners did not come until federal protection was guaranteed under Section 7-A of the NRA, passed in 1933. John L. Lewis then launched an energetic organizing campaign, using the slogan "The President wants you to join" (Baratz 1955:49) and within two months over 300,000 miners, three-quarters of the total, had joined the UMW.

State intervention has continued to be significant, and not necessarily on the side of labor. During the 1940s union-operator relations were characterized by fierce struggles and repeated federal intervention in the collective bargaining process by means of federal mediators, mine seizures, and back-to-work orders. Although these interventions were often directed against the union, miners were able to win increases, portal-to-portal pay, full union-administered medical coverage, and a pension plan underwritten by operator royalties on production. The 1950s and 1960s witnessed an abrupt aboutface in labor relations. John L. Lewis, apparently convinced that the industry was in danger of total eclipse, came to an understanding with the large operators. While he attempted to guarantee labor peace (there were no contract strikes in two decades) and to encourage mechanization (the UMW went so far as to make loans through its bank to help the coal companies automate [Hume 1971:22]), the big companies finally agreed to royalty payments, to other bread-and-butter provisions, and to consolidate a "destructively" competitive industry. The consolidation involved the major producers dividing up market areas and acquiring or neutralizing their competition in those areas (Seltzer 1977:389–90).

This era of union-operator rapprochement ended in the late 1960s when the rank-and-file miners mobilized on the issues of mine safety and black lung compensation. A three-week wildcat in West Virginia persuaded a reluctant legislature to pass a black lung compensation bill while a threatened strike forced Nixon not to veto a tough new mine safety law (Nyden 1974:477). In the 1970s rank-and-file miners dislodged an encumbent union president, wildcatted at an increasing rate through 1977, and waged a protracted contract strike. One of the conditions fostering this upsurge has been the rapidly increasing demand for miners; employment has almost doubled since 1969.

The transformation to a more centralized ownership structure entered a new phase in the 1960s with the invasion of the giant conglomerates. The 1965 acquisition of Consolidation Coal Company, the largest operator at the time, by Continental Oil, spurred a flurry of acquisitions by other conglomerates, also predominantly oil companies (Seltzer 1977:796–97).* During the 1970s, in spite of the continued mechanization, productivity has fallen rapidly for the first time in this century—from 19.9 tons per man day in 1969 to 14 tons in 1976. The companies blame federal safety regulations, absenteeism, wildcat strikes, and a lack of control of the labor process. Miners point to poor equipment maintenance, the inefficiencies of opening new mines in thin seams, and thus see safety and productivity as contradictory goals.

Another important development has been the rapid expansion of surface mining in the Rocky Mountain states. Although this coal has a lower BTU rating, it often comes in very thick seams and can be mined at a much lower cost than Appalachian deep coal. Much of it is on government land that has been leased at extremely low rates, estimated at three cents a ton (Cannon 1974:6, 29). Western coal made up 17 percent of production of 1976 and is projected to increase to 30 percent by 1985. The union has had difficulty organizing surface miners, particularly in the west, and the percentage of all production under union contract has slipped rapidly to 50 percent.

These two developments—declining productivity and the competition of western surface mining—have motivated a drive by the BCOA (the eastern, chiefly deep mine producers' association) to increase its control of the labor process. The effectiveness of the miners' response will largely be determined by whether they can get effective leadership and whether the demand for their labor remains strong. The interplay of forces affecting the labor process in coal mining is volatile, and the following description should be viewed as a snapshot of dynamic reality.

* The eventual impact of this oil company domination of the coal industry is likely to be profound. Skyrocketting coal prices in the 1970s after twenty years of stability are attributed by Seltzer (1977) to the oil companies' desire to bring them in line with oil prices so that coal sales will not expand at oil's expense. Seltzer also suggests that the stagnation of the fastest growing, most profitable coal companies since their acquisition by oil companies results from the new owners' investment of coal profits elsewhere.

The Labor Process in Coal Mining Today

Underground Mining

Although modern coal mines are laid out much like the mines of the handloading era, there are differences. The room-and-pillar system is still dominant but working sections usually consist of only five entries. Intricate life support systems supply each section. A maze of airducts, created by building cement block walls (brattices) across breakthroughs and sucking air through them with huge fans, brings fresh air to the face and takes away some of the methane and coal dust freed in the mining process. Pipes bring fresh water to feed the nozzles on the mining equipment and take out the seepage, which in some mines continually threatens to submerge sections of tunnel. Six-inch 12,000-volt cables bring electricity to power the equipment. A conveyor belt usually brings in supplies and takes out the coal. Sometimes a side spur from the main line track allows supply and transportation to be handled by low electric rail cars. The modern mine is not only "as dark [and cramped] as a dungeon and damp as the dew"; it is also humming like a modern factory.

The shift to high technology mining has led to contradictory tendencies in the spatial dispersion of the work force. Where once miners were dispersed in many separate rooms, face crews are now often concentrated in two or three entries of a five-entry section. On the other hand, an army of support personnel—roughly 50 percent of the total underground work force, as compared to 10 percent in 1890 and 15 percent in 1930 (Seltzer 1977:109)—is dispersed throughout the miles of tunnels (some mines cover an area as large as Manhattan), laying or repairing tracks, doing brattice work, shoring up sagging roofs, maintaining and inspecting miles of belts, hoses, pipes, and cables, cleaning up after roof falls, maintaining pumps, running supplies, and rock dusting the entries to keep down the coal dust.

Planning and maintaining all these systems while taking a layer of coal out from under a mountain without having it fall on the miners requires more specialized engineers and technicians than were necessary in the handloading era. For example, one mine with 253 employees had 2 engineers charged with planning the development of the mine, 1 chief electrician, and 33 electrician/mechanics. In addition, there has been a dramatic increase in the ratio of bosses to workers. In 1890 it was 1:100, by 1930 it had doubled to 2:100, and by 1969 had reached 12:100 for underground operations (ibid.). The larger mines with 200 to 400 employees responsible for most of the tonnage are likely to have three levels of supervision above the section foreman and his crew of 8 to 12 miners. This means that not only are the miners more closely supervised, but so are their bosses.

On the other hand, the dispersion of the work force combined with the difficulty of movement and limited vision mitigate the effects of this increased boss/worker ratio. The basic sources of light are the miners' lamps and headlights on self-propelled equipment, which can spotlight objects up to 30 feet down a tunnel but leave the surroundings in darkness. Foremen can only observe their men at close range, and their lamps warn that they are coming and let the men know when they are being watched. Miners can turn off their lights and hide. The light beam dramatizes the act of surveillance and the foremen's superordinate position.

At the same time, limited vision affects the miners' ability to communicate among themselves. Since catching someone else's beam in the eyes is disagreeable, miners try to avoid shining lights in each other's faces. With their faces hidden in the shadow cast by the brim of their hard hats, their companions can't see their moods and reactions. Nevertheless, the miners' relations with their workmates tend to be intimate, perhaps because the work setting encourages this, or because the darkness creates a sense of privacy and hides embarrassment.

A mine's labor force is relatively small compared to that in a heavy industrial plant. The average underground mine in 1975 had 59 employees, but the 20 percent of the deep mines that had over 100 employees produced 75 percent of all production (*Coal Data* 1976:11–17). Mines can have from one to over twenty working sections. The work force is typically divided into three shifts, with the smaller midnight to eight A.M. shift (the "hoot owl") often being used for maintenance and supply. The typical underground miner on a production shift dresses in the bathhouse, rides underground, and returns for a shower with between 20 and 200 other miners. Transportation time to the work site can be anywhere from 20 minutes to an hour each way, often starting with an elevator or man-trip with miners from all parts of the mine and ending with a low trolley or conveyor-belt ride out to the section with the eight to twelve members of the crew.

While traveling on these noisy conveyances, miners can communicate without being overheard by their supervisors. According to my respondents, this combination of small numbers and ample time together enables many miners to know everyone on their shifts—in marked contrast to large industrial plants, where at the end of a shift thousands of workers explode out the doors in a headlong rush for their cars.

Once the crew gets to the section, they customarily eat a sandwich in the lunch hole while the foreman, as required by law, inspects the working face and checks the methane gas level. The foreman returns in 15 minutes, gives instructions to the crew, and they begin to work; this can be between 35 minutes and 1½ hours after starting time! The foreman's instructions vary according to the type of mining system employed, complications, the competence of the crew, and his personality. At the very least, he specifies the initial sequence of cuts; every member of the crew knows what that means in terms of his or her job.

From this point on, the work day and labor process differ depending on whether the mining system is conventional, continuous miner, or longwall: these systems were responsible for 32 percent, 64 percent, and 4 percent of underground production in 1975 (*Coal Data* 1976:11–14).

Conventional mining developed as a result of the first wave of mechanization when machines were designed to perform the tasks of the pick miner. Each of the five types of machine commonly in use is a large, low, electrically powered vehicle, 10' to 25' long by 6' to 8' wide, which moves on rubber tires or caterpillar treads. These machines make a lot of noise—up to 120 decibels—and considerable heat (Bobick and Giardino 1976:122); an average section has six of these large pieces of equipment rotating between 20-foot-wide entries through the connecting crosscuts, trailing their electric cables. Under normal conditions each operation takes roughly 30 minutes.

The first step in the process is undercutting. Cutting machines are low vehicles with a side cockpit and a long chainsaw blade that can cut in as far as 13 feet. The cutting machine is staffed by an operator and helper, who moves the cable and performs many other ancillary jobs on the whole section. Under optimal conditions the cutting machine makes a 13-foot undercut across the coal face, as well as additional cuts when the coal is hard, the face is irregular, or the seam is thick. "Bad top" may dictate a shallower cut so that less unsupported roof is exposed when the coal is shot down. An experienced cutting machine operator will make many of these decisions on his own, but some, such as how deep to cut, will typically be made by the section foreman or the mine engineer. After the cut the operator "trams" to the next face.

Next the drilling machine, usually mounted on a vehicle, drills holes in a predetermined pattern in the coal face. The driller does not have a helper. The shooter then enters the tunnel, tests for methane gas, sets the charges, and detonates them from behind a block of coal. After the coal is shot down, the loading machine with an operator and helper arrive to clean out the loose coal. The loading machine looks like a huge dust pan with mechanical appendages like crab claws that reach out and gather in the coal. A conveyor moves the coal backward from the pan and dumps it onto an 8' by 25' shuttle car or "buggy" that has moved up behind it. The operator of the loading machine sits 15 feet back so he can load the coal without going out from under the supported roof. Each shuttle car backs out of the entry and deposits its 4-ton load on the conveyor belt or rail car. The shuttle operator lies in a low cab on the side of the car, peering out over a rubber tire directly in front of him, and drives with levers at what appears to be breakneck speed around right angle corners with little clearance. When a section is running smoothly it will use two or more shuttles.

When the loading machine has cleaned up all the loose coal, the entry is ready for the final step, roof bolting. Roof bolts have rapidly replaced timbers as the permanent roof supports because they are more effective, do not deteriorate as quickly, and do not obstruct the entries, thus facilitating the movement of the equipment. They laminate the rock layers of the immediate roof together, preventing most crumbling. The roof-bolting machine, or "pinner," is a low vehicle up to 10' by 25' in size. Its operator and helper have the most dangerous job in the mines—to make the newly exposed top as safe as possible. The helper sets a row of temporary timbers about five feet in from the last bolts. Then the operator drills holes in the roof and inserts the bolts. He must know what length bolt to use to reach through the cracks. He operates the machine by levers four feet behind the drill arm while covered by a protective canopy but must continually move out from under the canopy to add pieces of steel to the bit. A skilled operator can divine the roof conditions by the look and sound of the top and the amount of pressure needed to drill the holes. The safety of the whole crew depends on his knowledge and care in adapting the engineer's roof-support plan to meet special conditions. Roof bolting is usually the most time-consuming task, so that if there are five faces, the cutting machine will be waiting to come back into this entry. For that reason the foreman tries to plan the mining process so that the section is also working on a few cross-cut faces.

The foreman makes periodic rounds, especially during place changing. At the end of lunch he often gives a new set of instructions, particularly to the general laborers, often called facemen, who do such tasks as hanging the plastic curtains to direct the air flow to the faces and spreading the new sections of tunnel with rock dust after they have been pinned to keep down the explosive coal dust. Their jobs are not as clearly defined as those of the machine operator and involve most of the manual work at the face. Their work needs to be synchronized with that of machine operators to avoid keeping machines waiting. Thus the facemen and the machine helpers receive the most supervision from the foreman. The 1969 federal mine safety law increases the foreman's safety inspection duties (one study of 115 mines found the new duties took an average of 116 minutes a shift out of 390 minutes available face time [Straton 1977]). This substantially reduces the time the foreman is able to supervise the production process.

If the conventional mining system works smoothly, a crew can make as many as nine cuts a shift. But mining hardly ever runs smoothly; if one of the machines malfunctions, if a cable is run over and shorts out, a waterhose springs a leak, or the section runs into water, bad top, or an uneven seam, the whole coordinated process quickly comes to a halt. When equipment malfunctions the twelfth member of the crew, the electrician/ mechanic, who has been doing general maintenance, springs into action, while the foreman orders the crew to do "dead work," such as cleaning up fallen rock and coal or setting timbers. Miners tend to have a negative attitude toward dead work since it is both unskilled and involves more physical exertion than operating the machines.

The second mining system also uses the room-and-pillar configuration of cross-hatched tunnels but mines coal with a 30-ton machine called a "continuous miner" that performs four of the steps in the conventional system. Continuous miners are constructed much like machine loaders but have an additional maneuverable eight-foot-wide cutting drum with steel bits to claw out the coal at the average rate of six tons a minute. With the drum rotating just under the roof, the operator moves the machine forward into the face and brings the drum down to tear out a swath of coal; it falls onto the "dust pan," is gathered onto a conveyor belt, and is deposited onto a shuttle car. Since safety regulations forbid the operator to run out from under the roof bolts, the depth the miner can cut is governed by the distance from the drum to the cockpit. But a careless mine operator with a pushy foreman may go out from under the roof support to get just a few more tons of coal. When the bits strike rock they create a shower of sparks that can set off an explosion in a gassy or dusty entry. In a section with crumbly top and little gas an operator can take off some rock with the coal, but this sort of decision requires considerable knowledge.

The continuous miner creates 107 decibels and quantities of dust that can completely block visibility (MESA Workbook 11 1976:25). Since the passage of the 1969 Federal Mine Safety Act continuous miners have been required to spray water on the coal to keep down the dust, but the fine dust that causes black lung is still clearly visible dancing in the beams of light. When the nozzles become clogged, as they do continually, the dust gets thicker.

After the continuous miner finishes a cut, general laborers set temporary timbers and the roof bolter comes to bolt the top. Twice as many bolts are needed as in the conventional system since the continuous miner cuts approximately twice as deep. The continuous mining system has two or three steps and usually works two or three entries on one side of a five-entry section for a day or two, then drives up the other entries. Continuous miner sections tend to outproduce conventional sections by 20 to 40 percent, with crews of eight miners rather than the twelve required for a conventional section.*

The name "continuous miner" is misleading, for the machine is continually stopped to wait for a shuttle car, to maneuver for

---

* The UMW won the requirement of helpers for the roof bolter and continuous miner as a safety measure in the 1974 contract. These miners provide an extra pair of eyes for the most dangerous jobs but are not fully employed in the production process; thus this provision has an adverse affect on productivity (Walton and Kauffman 1977:V36–40).

another cut, to check the roof, to tram another face, or to wait for the repair of frequent breakdowns. Time and motion studies estimate that in a five-foot seam, continuous miners could produce 1600 tons a shift but in practice 350 or 400 tons is considered good (Suboleski 1977:4). This means continuous miners actually mine and load coal for an average of a little over an hour in an eight-hour shift. What do the miners do during all this time? They wait an average of 70 minutes for shuttle cars and an average of 90 minutes for delays during cuts for such tasks as checking gas levels and fixing nozzles. The time between when a miner stops cutting in one entry and starts in the next adds up to 90 minutes in a shift. Breakdowns, inspections, bit changes, start-up time, and unexpected delays claim another 80 minutes. Perhaps a more appropriate name for the process would be "fitful mining," but it does have the advantage for the miners that the work pace is varied with frequent and often prolonged breaks.

The continuous miner operator is the lead worker on the shift. He often sets the pace and tone for the section. As the time and motion studies indicate, there are ample opportunities for the operator to slow down or speed up coal production by creating delays or avoiding them. He often coordinates the rest of the crew to ensure a smoothly running section. Foremen cognizant of the operators' crucial role treat them gingerly.

One unique aspect of underground mining is that the miners, and particularly the continuous miner operator and the roof bolter, create the work space which they and many other people must inhabit and later pass through as the section drives forward. They must know a great deal not only about equipment but also about the conditions of the coal and the top. Shoddy workmanship is not exported in the form of a product but retained as a source of danger in the workplace. Therefore, although miners may sabotage equipment to delay the work process, they value careful work and use strong sanctions against reckless workers.

The third major underground mining system is the mechanized longwall. This system is more automated than the other two. A shearing machine with rotating heads is drawn along a face of coal up to 800 feet long making a 30-inch-deep cut. The coal falls into a metal trough and is moved along the face by a chain conveyor. At the end of the face it is deposited on a belt which carries it to the main belt or waiting coal cars. The roof is held up by huge ten-ton hydraulic jacks (chocks) with two to six legs. As the shearer advances, the chocks are moved forward, leaving the roof to cave in behind. The rectangular block of coal to be mined may be a mile long and as wide as the longwall equipment. To prepare a longwall section two or more entries must be driven up on both sides of the block, which can take between four months and a year. The entries are used as air ducts and for the conveyor belt. At one end of the longwall is a sophisticated electronic consol that monitors the machine's hydraulic and electrical systems for malfunctions. The longwall work force consists of a shear operator who rides with the shear, two to three chock setters who lower the chocks one at a time and advance them, a tail entry man who advances temporary roof supports (hand jacks or wooden cribs) as the face advances and may carefully blast the end of the coal face to make room for the shear, a head entry man at the other end of the face who advances the roof supports and the haulage belt, a switch attendant stationed at the consol who watches the dials and attends the telephone and switches, and a mechanic. This crew is roughly the size of a continuous-miner crew and can potentially run an incredible amount of coal: the record for three shifts is 12,395 tons, but even the more typical 700 to 800 tons a shift is twice a miner section (Chironis 1977:39).

Longwalls, however, are costly ($4 million) and temperamental. They require a seam with less than 5° rolls along the face and a roof with specific characteristics. There is a lot of down time. For instance, if the roof sets down on the chocks, they may be wedged so tightly that they cannot be moved forward, requiring the roof above them to be drilled and blasted. If a chock malfunctions and cannot be fixed, it must be left behind and the other chocks moved over to fill the gap. The production may overload the haulage system and have to stop to wait for belts and coal cars to catch up. If a miner has to stop the haulage belt to get on or over it or to haul supplies, the longwall automatically stops (Arble 1976).

The nonface jobs underground tend to involve individuals or small groups of miners performing tasks with very little direct supervision or push for speed. A number of miners I interviewed were glad to get jobs away from the face, not only because they were safer but because they were free to set their own work pace and style. One bratticeman said he did not see a foreman in days, and if he caught up on his work he could turn out his light and go to sleep. Another man, a belt examiner, walks the two and one-half miles of belt up and back every night; he checks in with the general foreman at the beginning of the shift, but usually tells the foreman what needs to be done because he knows more about the condition of the belts. Since his job takes only five hours, he has ample time to stop and chat with the miners stationed along the belts and on the sections. Some tasks which must be completed quickly and require a fairly large crew may be assigned to a foreman to provide constant supervision but most nonface miners will see a foreman only a few times a shift.

Surface Mining

In 1976 surface mining produced 56 percent of coal tonnage with 29 percent of mining employment. Operators have been attracted to surface mining because of its smaller initial capital investment and its much higher productivity. The labor process in surface mining is similar to that in road construction. Instead of going in under the earth and rock to extract the coal seam, the "overburden" is removed, exposing the coal for easy loading into trucks using front-end loaders. If the overburden contains rock strata, it must be drilled and blasted. It is then scooped up by huge power shovels, cranes, and front-end loaders, and loaded into dump trucks which take it to the spill pile. If a pile is close to the trench or bench being mined, a large drag-line crane or bucket-wheel excavator can remove the overburden without the use of dump trucks, increasing productivity substantially.

The Struggle for Control of the Labor Process

What can be learned from this description of the labor process about the struggle for control in coal mining? The outcome of the struggle is determined by the relative effectiveness of the power resources available to capital and to labor, and by the relative ability of the combatants to mobilize those resources. Although certain resources can be used by individuals—bosses or workers—to gain control over an aspect of the process, significant control of the entire process requires coordination and unity. This section will explore the power resources that have been important in this context and the factors that have affected the ability of miners to unite around that struggle.

Power Resources

Since the 1920s the coal operators have shifted their focus from controlling the miner to controlling the work process. In the handloading era, the operator did not supervise the labor process closely but had potent resources for controlling the miner: he could fire summarily, he paid the worker in script, and he housed the worker in a company town patrolled by company guards. All these resources have been gradually eliminated.

The change from pay in ton to pay by the hour, the result of the rationalization and mechanization process, has had the contradictory effect of facilitating further rationalization while reducing the operators' leverage over the workers. Under the tonnage system, the employer bought the miner's intention to produce coal, for the miner was paid for the product of his labor. With hourly rates, the operator "rents" the miner's capacity to work for a specified period but the amount or quality of work is unspecified. Operators try to get as much as they can from their employees during the rental period, but because of the new terms of the labor exchange they have lost the employee's economic advantage as a source of motivation. They must develop other ways to cajole or coerce him to apply himself to the employer's purpose.

One way the operators have attempted to increase their control of the labor process is by hiring an increased number of supervisors, who have an arsenal of techniques to get work out of the rented worker, including the threat of reassignment to a disagreeable or dangerous job. Most of the coercive ones depend ultimately on the right to fire, but the UMW is at present sufficiently strong to make it difficult for an operator to fire a union miner for working too slowly. In response, in the 1978 contract the operators insisted on the inclusion of an Arbitration Review Board decision that allowed them to fire wildcat strikers, and of an incentive plan for buying back the miners' motivation. The incentive plan is sugar-coated with the provision that miners in each mine may vote on it and that it must not compromise safety.

Job fragmentation, work process specification, and mechanization are other power resources management has attempted to use. The more complicated face tasks, once performed by one pick miner, are now divided among at least seven job classifications. This specialization tends to narrow the decision-making scope of each job and to make some jobs more monotonous.*

Along with the technological developments and governmental safety regulations have come increasing stipulations by engineers and line supervisors of how the coal is to be mined. Work stipulation is nevertheless much less detailed than in most industrial settings, not only because of the variable and unpredictable conditions in a coal mine but because management's ability to enforce its procedures by maintaining surveillance of the workers is limited. In addition, government safety regulations stipulate many procedures that cut productivity, and ordering miners to violate them can lead to grievances and legal action; foreman who try to encourage short cuts must do so covertly while overtly warning against them. Given these problems in stipulating the labor process in detail, miners can effectively resist by working to rule, which quickly slows and tangles the production process.

Mechanization of coal mining, at least until the development of the longwall, involves machines whose speed and direction is controlled by the workers. They would thus fit into Bright's fourth level of mechanization and would be expected to require more skill than hand tools (Braverman 1974:221). The expectation seems justified in this case, for operating a number of large, high-speed machines safely in a cramped, dimly lit space requires dexterity, judgment, responsibility, and the mastery of a new body of knowledge about the mechanized technology. Still, the specialized functions of the machines limit the operators' ability to make decisions about the production process: a continuous miner operator cannot decide to use his machine to undercut and call in a shooter to blast the coal; a roof bolter is expected to follow a roof-support plan that is approved by government inspectors and stipulates the length and pattern of the bolts.

The collective strength of the miners enlarges their ability to exercise discretion in the labor process. It enables them to decide

* Specialization cannot develop to the point of assigning a few routine motions to each worker because as mining conditions change and emergencies arise, tasks must change. Circulation between jobs, particularly by younger unskilled miners, prevents job fragmentation from fragmenting the miners' skills.

how fast to work, how many shortcuts to take, when to take breaks, when to insist on a change in the production plan because of conditions they have run across, and whether to go ahead running a malfunctioning machine or to insist that it be fixed. The 1974 UMW contract gave the miners the right to refuse to work if they believed themselves to be in "imminent danger." Even union miners, however, are reluctant to exercise this right without the backing of their "buddies" for fear of management disciplinary action, and nonunion miners have much less discretionary power overall. Their choice is often whether to run an unsafe piece of equipment or be fired (Woolley and Reid 1975). In this sense the power the miners have won through collective struggle makes their work more skilled since they must decide when to obey the boss. This is the side of the knowledge-power dialectic that Braverman did not explore: not only is skill a crucial resource for gaining power over the work process, but worker power over the work process increases the skill content of their jobs by allowing them to make more decisions.

Until the introduction of the longwall method, the rationalization and mechanization of coal mining had contradictory effects on skill levels. Increased management stipulation of how jobs are to be done and job fragmentation have tended to lower skill levels; mechanization, on the other hand, has necessitated new dexterities and technical knowledge. Despite all the changes, deep mines remain peculiar and dangerous work environments requiring a large body of esoteric knowledge and dexterity—even getting around in a low coal mine involves learning to "walk" again. Coal operators and presidents cannot send in untrained scabs or troops to dig coal with bayonets, and the miners gain power from the scarcity of their skills. The coal operators' dependence on their employees is not only a product of miners' esoteric knowledge but also of miners' monopoly on information about their immediate unpredictable work conditions.

Another source of miners' power is their control of the speed of their machines. Slowdowns are a readily available tactic. Miners have been able to use slowdowns to discipline their bosses. One miner I interviewed told of a foreman who tried to take away the section's traditional but noncontractual sandwich break at the beginning of the shift. The crew cut production from 90 buggies a shift to 20. Since the foremen are typically evaluated in terms of production, such slowdowns usually force them to apologize and plead for coal. Knowledge of the production process and of government safety regulations enable a "slowed down" miner to parry his boss's orders, but the crucial factor is collective strength—the union, the contract, and the unity of the crew. The hourly wage rate makes uniting a crew for a slowdown easier because their paychecks are not jeopardized. These collective actions require coordination and sophistication about contractual safeguards and slowdown tactics. One miner explained the slowdown as follows:

> You can stop production just like that. But you got to know what you are doing. I mean everybody knows what's going on usually. You can stop it legally. You can pull safety on them. You can stop and check your water sprays after every third buggy: "There is not enough water on this miner!" It's a federal law. You can stop and set all of your timbers just right, you know. If you work to rule you can really hurt them, and then you can deliberately sabotage the stuff. You can run over cable. You can just drive your buggy real slow: "Can't you go any faster?" "No, sir!" Nothing in the contract that says how fast you have to work. (Interview June 23, 1978, Southwest Virginia)

Through these disciplining efforts miners on unified sections have taken back control of the labor process from the foreman, to the extent that savvy foremen let the miners get the coal and spend their time checking that safety regulations are met. Many miners even see the job of coordinating the work force as the responsibility of the continuous miner operator, not the foreman.

Reinforcing the effectiveness of the miners' power resources is the wildcat strike. It has been used to prevent dismissals, disciplinary actions, and the removal of worker-elected mine and safety committees. It has been used to force changes in the labor process directly, by demanding that a foreman be fired, a hazardous condition be eliminated, or work rules be changed, and it has been frequently used to resist management attempts to divide the work force through favoritism in promotions, layoffs, and awarding overtime (Dix et al. 1977). The success of wildcats in protecting the membership has increased the miners' willingness to risk using other power resources in the struggle for control of the labor process.

A number of factors have contributed to the increasing use of wildcats in the past decade—the institutionalization of the picket line, complete with moral and coercive sanctions, the absence of a strong no-strike clause in UMW contracts, weak union leadership, and a strong demand for mine labor. The use of the wildcat strike is not without contradictions. Many miners become impatient when frequent strikes threaten their standard of living, and the threat of an unruly work force has led the operators to redouble their efforts to avoid, bust, or redomesticate the miners' union.

The Ability to Use the Power Resources

This analysis underscores the importance of unity to the miner's ability to bring potential resources to bear. Coal operators have recognized the importance of this unity and attempted to destroy it. The relative lack of success of the coal operators' "labor of division" is not because of lack of effort. They fought unionization with some of the most ruthless tactics in U. S. labor history, and when it came anyway they domesticated the union leadership and promoted division in the ranks. Racial and ethnic prejudices have been manipulated by discrimination in hiring and promotion to divide miners. Seniority rights, although backed by the union to blunt the bosses' ability to use favoritism in promotion, produced a group of older workers with more to lose in militant actions. However, awarding special privileges on the basis of skill and seniority, creating two strata of workers with different interests, has been resisted during the rank-and-file mobilization of the past decade. (Differentials between the highest- and lowest-paid regular employees will be reduced to 12 percent by 1980.) Designing the work process to isolate workers and block communication, a successful tactic in other industries, has not proceeded very far in mining. However, in the 1977/1978 contract negotiations the operators won numerous divisive provisions including incentive bonuses, the right to fire wildcat leaders, maintenance of the great disparity between pension payments for old timers and recent retirees, and switching from the union health plan to each company getting insurance with a private carrier.

Miners have been able to overcome these labors of division and the individualism of the dominant ideology partly because characteristics of the labor process promote unity such as the many opportunities for unmonitored communication among miners.* The increasing division of labor and mechanization in mining have at the same time necessitated closer coordination of the labor process. Where a hand loader often worked alone in his own "room," now teams of eight to twelve miners must cooperate to complete a number of operations in sequence in two to five entry working areas or one longwall face. Although divisions of skill, status, and pay may divide these teams, the need to cooperate closely to accomplish production and minimize danger promotes unity. The careless hand loader endangered only himself; the modern miner can endanger his whole crew and potentially everyone in the mine. There is therefore strong group pressure on the miners to keep their "buddies" safety in mind. In addition, "running good coal" is a collective accomplishment from which many miners get satisfaction; it is not the result of management dictation but of initiative and cooperation. This cements the solidarity of the section, even though it may involve competition with other sections. For a hand loader the competition was between individuals, it had a direct effect on his pay check, and it often involved divisive maneuvering for good rooms and scarce coal cars. That strong solidarity existed in spite of this is at least partially due to the clarity of the rate of exploitation with tonnage pay and its attendant abuses (such as no pay for dead work and shortweighting), as well as to the shared oppression outside the mines in the coal camps.†

Although major improvements in safety have been made, coal mining is still the most dangerous industry in America, with one of every twelve miners having a lost-time injury each year and all being able to expect gradual suffocation from black lung. However, this common danger can result in counterphobic denial and fatalism rather than militant unity. It is only when miners believe that the operators are negligent, that something can be done to improve these conditions, and that they have the power to force improvements that mine dangers will be a potent force

---

* The importance of the labor process in promoting militant solidarity among miners is underscored by striking similarities between coal miners in this study and gypsum miners in Gouldner's (1954) study in a conservative Great Lakes farming community in the late 1940s.

† Rick Simon notes the singular juxtaposition in the handloading era of relative freedom on the job and repression in the coal camp (1978:192). This reversal of the usual urban industrial setting may foster militant solidarity.

for militant solidarity among miners. Two developments in the late 1960s provoked miners to struggle to improve safety. The publicizing of the dangers of black lung in the late 1960s led to a successful three-week wildcat for improved compensation in West Virginia. Prodded into action by public outrage over the 1968 Mannington mine disaster, Congress passed a new mine safety act. Since federal enforcement has been less than zealous, determined rank-and-file insistence backed by wildcats has been necessary to get compliance. The result has been no major disasters in union mines since Boyle was ousted in 1972, while disasters have continued at non-union mines.

The labors of unification of miners as well as favorable conditions are important to the achievement of solidarity. Miners take care to socialize neophytes to being responsible to their "brothers" and to insisting on being "done right" by the bosses. Widespread practical joking also unifies a crew. Most important are the self-conscious collective struggles to resist management's devisive tactics.

Thus, while unity is clearly enhanced by forces beyond the mine, certain characteristics of the work process and efforts of miners appear to be necessary if not sufficient conditions. The future of miners' power in the labor process would appear to hinge on whether new production systems can be imposed that will eliminate miners' power resources and weaken their unity.

There are many differences between the labor process in surface and underground mining. Some strongly affect management's ability to control and the miners' ability to unite. For one thing, danger may not be as unifying a force because the danger is not shared to the extent that it is underground.* Except for the mechanic and the powderman, every surface miner is a heavy equipment operator, controlling the speed and direction of his machine, which requires considerable knowledge of both the machine and the overburden being moved. In recent years the fatality rate has been as high for surface miners as for deep miners (although the rate for nonfatal injuries has been much lower). The highwall continually threatens to cave in and the equipment may roll on the loose, steep terrain. But while large vehicle operators must be constantly alert to protect

---

* See Gouldner (1954) for an interesting elaboration of this point in a different context.

themselves and others, a reckless operator will endanger himself and perhaps one or two others, not a whole crew.

Although the basic principles of surface mining remain the same, the size of the equipment used, and the size and dispersion of the work force vary with the terrain. In mountainous Appalachia, contour strip mines follow the shallow portion of a seam along a slope, using smaller cranes and bulldozers to remove the overburden. They typically run to shifts with up to fifteen miners per shift. In the relatively flat eastern and western Great Plains, trench mines use drag-line cranes large enough to fill a football stadium to scoop up 200 tons of earth and rock in a bucketful. Trench mines tend to be more extensive with bigger crews.

Surface miners are also considerably more isolated than face crews in deep mines. They sit in enclosed cabs or cockpits enveloped in noise. Communication necessitates stopping their machines and disembarking, and although this occurs periodically—when a piece of machinery is down and backs up the whole process or during the half hour lunch break—opportunities to communicate are less frequent than in underground mining. In addition, the crew is dispersed over a quarter mile area: some members may never see each other during working hours. There is no bathhouse or long ride from portal to work site to provide an opportunity for community building.

As in underground mining, the foreman begins the shift with a five-minute briefing; the crew then proceeds with a minimum of further directions. Many miners are jealous of their prerogatives and react hostilely to "know-it-all" bosses. Thus although the foreman can maintain visual surveillance over the whole job, he does not automatically have more control of the labor process than an underground foreman. A united crew can use the greater visibility to coordinate resistance to a foreman's abuses. As one surface miner observed, "You can tell if a foreman has come around and harrassed somebody. It is just like putting the brakes on a runaway car. You can just see everything gradually slow down."

Another difference between underground and surface mining operations affecting the balance of power between the workers and bosses is the number of employees at each site. The work force in surface mining is on the average one-quarter the size of that in deep mines (*Coal Data* 1976:II-19). Workplaces with few employees are difficult to organize in any industry, and coal is no exception—small deep mines are also difficult to organize. The resistance is undoubtedly related to the closer contact between bosses and workers on small jobs, but also to the fact that a "critical mass" of workers seems to be needed to get a sense of class identity. The development of miner solidarity in strip mining is further hindered because of the short lives of the mines: when the seam or lease runs out, the site is closed and the crew reassigned or laid off. Deep mines, on the other hand, often last for decades, working seams one below another.

The Future of the Labor Process in Coal Mining

The trend during the move from pick-and-shovel mining to the "conventional" mechanized system to the continuous miner system has been for fewer miners to produce more coal on less working space with more foremen. Despite the contradictions, management's capacity for close supervision has increased. The automated longwall appears to extend management's control in a number of ways. The crew is more closely coordinated, even though it is dispersed over a larger area, and is working on one rather disjointed machine. Although the foreman cannot see the whole crew and movement along the face is impeded by the conveyor and a tangle of hydraulic hoses, it is obvious if anyone falls behind and the foreman can quickly investigate the source of the problem.

The longwall also appears to reduce skill level. The direction of each element of the machine is fixed. The shear operator controls the speed of the shear and the height and depth of the cut, but cannot change the shear's fixed path along the face. The shear operator and the consol attendant, who coordinates longwall production with the haulage system, set the pace of the system. The chock operator follows after the shear performing five simple operations in a fixed sequence to advance each chock. The head and tail entry men do a number of manual jobs approximating those of the facemen and helpers on other mechanized sections. In comparison with the continuous miner system, longwall reduces the sphere of decision making of all but the manual laborers and mechanics. On the other hand, since the longwall operation is sensitive, requiring closer coordination not only among the section crew but also with the haulage work force, workers must not only know what to do but precisely when to do it. Because of this, longwall is susceptible to sabotage. However, the system attacks the miners' power in numbers by producing twice as much coal as a continuous miner section with the same size crew. Thus the longwall system weakens a number of miners' power resources but may have contradictory effects on their unity. While increased coordination may promote unity, the miner's role in achieving that coordination has decreased. Whether the miners can develop ways of maintaining their power in the labor process with this new technology remains to be seen.

New mining systems are being developed rapidly, including: continuous miners with their own roof-support system, trailing conveyors and remote controls for especially dangerous situations, hydraulic mining in which soft coal is blasted loose with water and pumped out of the mine in slurry pipes, and the collection of the gasses produced by burning the remaining coal in a mined-out section *in situ*. Each of these innovations, and others on the drawing boards, could have a profound impact on the labor process in coal mining, and most would probably reduce the power of the miners. But *Coal Age*, the industry's organ, sees longwall as the major innovation in underground mining in the foreseeable future (Chironis 1977:3).

In coal mining, the capitalist project of appropriating the labor process by rationalization and mechanization has so far been limited: mechanization has been held back by technical and geological factors, while rationalization has been stunted by strong miner resistance and by other contradictions endemic to coal mining.* Although there has been a fragmentation of the work, closer supervision, and more detailed stipulation as to how the work is to be done, the miners have developed collective tactics for retaining their power. Knowledge of the production process is an important resource in the struggle, but both coal operators and miners employ other resources as well. Ultimately, the effectiveness of the miners' power resources rests on their ability to unite, and thus miner unity is a crucial locus of the struggle for control.

---

* Resistance has often focused on safety issues. Miners have been able to mobilize public and governmental support for their safety claims even though productivity is adversely affected.

Origins of the Assembly Line and Capitalist Control of Work at Ford

David Gartman

> Please, Mr. Foreman, slow down your assembly line.
> Please, Mr. Foreman, slow down your assembly line.
> No, I don't mind workin', but I do mind dyin'.*

Since its orgin, the assembly line has been killing auto workers in a number of ways. Death might come in the literal form of a fatal industrial accident on the relentless, driving line, as it did recently at a GM assembly plant in California.† Or it might be the "spiritual" death brought on by a lifetime of boring, monotonous, and meaningless work. The assembly line has also meant the death of an important aspect of working-class power, for it has been a crucial factor in the demise of a tradition of skilled, intelligent labor, which is an important resource in the struggle against capitalist exploitation. This essay will trace the origins of the assembly line in the firm usually credited with its invention, the Ford Motor Company, and place this technological innovation in the context of the class struggle from which it emerged.

Marx viewed the development of the forces of production not as an autonomous, self-directing phenomenon but as a *social* process, driven by the conflict of social classes. Thus he wrote in *The Poverty of Philosophy:*

> The very moment civilization begins, production begins to be founded on the antagonism of orders, estates, classes, and finally on the antagonism of accumulated labor and actual labor. No antagonism, no progress. This is the law that civilization has followed up to our days. *Till now the productive forces have been developed by virtue of this system of class antagonisms.* (1955:53)

Within the context of class societies, technology becomes another means of controlling and exploiting the class of direct producers. Thus Marx showed in the first volume of *Capital*

---

* Lyrics by former production-line worker, Joe L. Carter. Reprinted in Georgakas and Surkin (1975:130).
† "Auto worker killed," *Los Angeles Times,* October 21, 1977.

how the machinery of modern industry degrades workers and renders them more powerless to resist exploitation. Harry Braverman's brilliant analysis of the degradation of work in the twentieth century, *Labor and Monopoly Capital,* confirms Marx's theory in every respect.

Yet Marx and Braverman are not Luddites, seeking to destroy the technological wonders that capitalism has built. Both see machinery in general as a crucial factor in freeing humans from the "realm of necessity." They assert that the liberating potentiality of technology is often suppressed and perverted by capitalism, resulting in particular uses of technology that ensure the control and exploitation of workers by capital. One of the most important examples of the perverted use of technology in the twentieth century is the automobile assembly line.

Actually, the assembly line does not stand as an independent technological innovation. Rather, it stands as the culmination of a series of steps which wrested skills from workers' hands and thereby laid the foundation for this latest degradation. Taken together, these measures constituted a system of mass production. The basic principles of mass production are the division of labor, accuracy, and continuity. The product is divided into a number of parts produced by different workers with such accuracy as to be interchangeable. These parts are then assembled. All production flows continuously from one stage to the next. Most of these principles are not new to twentieth-century capitalism, but their integration into a new system of production took place largely in the late nineteenth and early twentieth centuries in the United States. Here there were markets large enough to absorb the output of mass production and make its expensive technology pay off. Here there were labor shortages and consequent high wages which placed a premium on labor-saving production methods. The industry largely responsible for this integration of mass production principles was the automobile industry, and, more specifically, the Ford Motor Company. So closely are mass production and Ford associated that this system of production is often known internationally as "Fordism." The examination of the history of the Ford Motor Company can therefore provide crucial insights into the emergence of this new system of capitalist production.

The Ford Motor Company began as most other auto firms did—on a very small and uncertain basis. Shortages of capital and an uncertain market made more than miniscule operations impossible. Founded by Henry Ford in 1903, the Detroit firm consisted of eight people (including Ford): a shop assistant, three skilled mechanics, a patternmaker, a draftsman, and a blacksmith. These workers worked in a very rudimentary shop with a few basic tools solely in assembly operations. This was typical of all early auto firms. Parts were purchased on credit from machine shops—in Ford's case, largely from the Dodge brothers—and assembled by a small crew of trained and skilled mechanics who operated as a team. Labor was necessarily skilled because the imperfect and unstandardized parts had to be drilled, milled, ground, planed, and bored before they would fit together satisfactorily. The team planned production, solved design problems, and constructed the entire car as a unit. The final assembly procedure at the Ford shop, following contemporary practice, was stationary. The frame was placed on wooden horses on the shop floor. Then the two-to-five-man work team proceeded to install the motor, transmission, springs, axles, etc. Much time was spent carrying tools back and forth to the toolroom and transporting the various parts from the stockroom.

As production at Ford grew, this labor process was simply multiplied until the whole shop floor was filled with long lines of stationary positions, a few workers at each. Work on subassemblies—motors, transmissions, axles—took place on workbenches and was similarly stationary and skilled. When Ford began to produce many of his own parts in 1906, skilled mechanics were again crucial. Parts were turned out on universal machine tools and for each separate work process, a worker had to set up the machine, determine the depth, speed, and feed of the cut, regrind cutters, and inspect the finished work (Nevins and Hill 1954; Avery 1929; Maltese 1975; Chinoy 1964).

It is clear that in the early years of the Ford Company, the labor process was thus largely in the control of skilled workers who generally determined the intensity and productiveness of work. Their power over the labor process was a result not only of the indispensability of their skills, but also of the general shortage of skilled labor in the Detroit area at the time. This labor shortage greatly debilitated capital's main sanction with which to assert control, the threat of firing.

This simple, undivided, skilled labor process did not last long at Ford, however. Ford and his managers undertook a constant revision of methods aimed primarily at taking control over the labor process from the workers' hands and centralizing it in the hands of capital. The purpose of this centralization was not merely control for its own sake: control gave capital the ability to increase exploitation and hence surplus value. The end result was mass production. The first step along this road was a progressive process of dividing labor. In assembly, the first division seems to have been one between parts carriers and mechanics. Instead of allowing skilled mechanics to waste their expensive labor power wandering around the shop in search of parts and tools, in about 1908 unskilled workers were hired to handle such tasks. Although this division was probably motivated partly by what Braverman has called the Babbage principle—dividing high-priced, skilled labor from lower-paid, unskilled labor so that the total wage bill can be cut—an attempt to control the pace of labor was also at work. Skilled assemblers became tied to one spot, and their discretionary time—their wandering about—was cut down. They had to remain busy at their assembly work or suffer the harassment of Ford foremen. The pores of the working day were beginning to fill up, thus intensifying labor. In a further development, stock handlers, who transported the parts for an entire car on a truck, became specialized in handling one part only. Work within assembly gangs was also becoming progressively more divided. There seems to have been a division within the work gang first, one worker doing only a particular part of the whole assembly job. Then there emerged a specialization between gangs. One group of two to five men handled the attachment of the motor to the frame; other groups specialized in axles, springs, transmissions, etc. The gangs moved from one stationary chassis to the next as they completed their particular jobs. Thus, in the assembly department, the "all-round" mechanic slowly gave way to the specialized worker (Avery 1929:1638; Sward 1948:32; Russell 1978:33).

This division of labor and elimination of skilled workers was largely made possible by the emergence of precisely machined and thus interchangeable parts. As long as parts were imprecisely machined, much skilled hand labor was required to fit them together into a properly functioning piece of machinery. The first decade of the twentieth century, however, saw the development of more rigid and heavier tools, carbon alloy tool steels, and, most importantly, of the universal grinding machine, all of which ensured the production of parts with such precision that one was exactly like the other (Woodbury 1972; Rosenberg

1972; *American Machinist,* January 23, 1913). Skilled mechanics were no longer required to assemble them, and as assembly work became more standardized, skill and uncertainty—the bases of workers' power in the shop—were eliminated. Labor could be further divided among numerous unskilled workers. Ford was not the first to introduce the production of interchangeable parts. It had been achieved much earlier in the manufacture of farm equipment, fire arms, and sewing machines. Henry Leland of the Cadillac Motor Company first applied the idea to automobile production around 1908. But the innovative Ford shops were right on his heels and soon far surpassed other firms in the rigor of their methods.

The next step taken by Ford and his assistants to centralize the control of work was to ensure its continuity. This was initially achieved by the progressive arrangement or layout of the shop. Machine shop practice had been to arrange work in departments in which similar work processes were performed. Thus all grinding machines and operations were grouped in one department, as were milling, boring, lathe operations, etc. This, of course, created a maze of transportation problems. Parts crossed and recrossed the shop several times before their completion. But as soon as the volume of production became sufficient to make the devotion of a machine to a single work task feasible, auto manufacturers sought to solve these problems by what was called progressive work layout. Shops were arranged in the line of work-finishing travel rather than in groups of similar machines. As one Ford manager, William Knudsen, states: "All noses must be pointed in the same direction."

The assembly line was by no means an original conception of Henry Ford. There seems to have been some sort of assembly line in the famous Venice Arsenal as early as 1438. In more recent times, Cyrus McCormick was using the principle of automatic conveyance of work in the production of reapers in 1847, while the slaughterhouses of Chicago used mechanical conveyors in the "disassembly" of livestock long before Ford came onto the scene (Burlingame 1949:57–58, 170, 282–84). In automobiles, Ransom Olds, whose auto shops had achieved the requisite volume of production much earlier, seems to have been the pioneer, adopting progressive layout around 1903. But when Ford moved to its new Bellevue factory in 1906, the new production manager, Max Wollering, took the opportunity to arrange the work progressively (Nevins and Hill 1954:364–72;

Sward 1948:33–35). But it does appear that only with Ford's innovation did the principle of the mechanical conveyance of a product past successive assembly stations gain critical importance for American industry as a whole.

While efficiency was undoubtedly a concern here, the attempt to control the labor process and hence the workers was also a factor. Work became more regimented. With successive work operations crowded next to one another, parts moved faster and there were fewer delays. The intensity of work was increased. In 1915, two production experts who studied the Ford shops wrote that because the arrangement of successive operations in the closest proximity helps "to minimize transportation and to maximize the pressure of flow work, it succeeds in maintaining speed without obtrusive foremanship" (Arnold and Faurote 1972:6–8). Workers were tied to one spot, having no excuse to wander around; supervision was consequently easier and tighter. Further, such progressive work arrangement necessarily meant an increased division of labor and loss of skill. Instead of being required to set up and perform all the work sent to a general department, the typical Ford worker was confined to one highly specialized task. For example, instead of performing a large variety of drilling operations sent to the drilling department, one worker drilled only the hole in the left stub axle as this part progressed in the axle department.

These earlier methods of degrading and speeding-up work were a phenomenal success. In April 1905, before their inception, Ford had produced an average of 25 cars a day with 300 workers. In July 1908, Ford was maintaining a 100-car-a-day level with around 500 workers (Nevins and Hill 1954:272, 321). All of these innovations were possible because of the expanding market for automobiles in the United States. Without strong expectations that the resulting product would be snatched up by an eager market, Ford and other auto capitalists would never have taken the financial risks involved in these production methods.

The embryonic beginnings of the assembly line at Ford were marked by the introduction of several new production methods specifically and consciously designed to give capital control over the pace or intensity of work. The first of these was the work slide, introduced in the Ford shops around 1908. This was an inclined trough of sheet metal placed between work stations along a workbench. As one worker completed his operation on a particular part, it slid down to the next worker. At the same time, such processes as the assembly of the piston and the connecting rod, previously performed by one worker, were divided between several workers connected by work slides. The piston and connecting rod assembly job was divided between three workers; whereas previously this job required 3 minutes 5 seconds to complete, it could now be completed in 1 minute 24 seconds. Similar devices called roll-ways linked the work on large parts and resulted in similar savings of labor time (Arnold and Faurote 1972:103–08).

How were such substantial savings possible? Ford and his production engineers claimed that the slides and the division of labor eliminated the time a solitary assembler spent walking back and forth at the workbench and made workers more proficient in their minute operations. This may have been partially true, but something more was also involved here. The work slides and the division of labor enabled Ford and his agents to better control the pace of work. The two production experts from *Engineering Magazine* cited earlier stated that before these work slides and roll-ways were installed,

> The straw boss could never nail, with certainty, the man who was shirking, because of the many work-piles and general confusion due to the shop floor transportation. As soon as the roll-ways were placed the truckers were called off, the floor was cleared, and all the straw boss had to do to locate the shirk or operation tools in fault, was to glance along the line and see where the roll-way was filled up. As more than once before said in these chapters, mechanical transit of work in progress evens up the job, and forces everybody to adopt the pace of the fastest worker in the gang. (Ibid:279–80)

In order to ensure the pace of this fastest worker was very fast indeed, Ford management used "pacesetters"—particularly fast and loyal workers were rewarded with extra compensation—at strategic places on the line.

This division of labor and control of pace also drastically reduced the skill and discretion of workers in the labor process. Workers could easily be replaced from the large industrial reserve army of unskilled immigrants, and capital's threat to fire began to carry real weight, forcing workers to knuckle under to speeded-up work. The reaction of the workers was not surprising. William Klan, head motor-assembly foreman, stated: "The men didn't like it, because they had to work harder. The pieces were there and they didn't have time to walk back and take a rest in between" (Russell 1978:39). Furthermore, the centralization of the conception and skill of work eliminated the worker's discretion over work. As long as workers made important decisions about how work was done, as long as the work depended on the *willing* cooperation of workers for its proper completion, Ford and his managers could not exploit them ruthlessly, no matter what the condition of the labor market. However, when a substantial portion of the skills and discretion of workers in the labor process were eliminated, willing cooperation was no longer necessary. Ford and his men could drive workers mercilessly, for their power to resist was greatly diminished. As Arnold and Faurote wrote in 1915, Ford's production methods created "ideal factory conditions—conditions under which there is absolute freedom [that is, freedom of *capital*!] . . . from any restraint of individual effort toward labor-cost reduction." (1972:159) In other words, Ford's mass production methods rendered workers largely powerless and hence gave capital a free hand to step up exploitation.

These nonmechanical assembly-line methods were used primarily in subassembly operations. Similar nonmechanical labor-saving (i.e., labor-speeding) devices were introduced in the final assembly in 1913. Work was divided between a number of work stations laid out in a line across the shop floor. The wheels were attached to the chassis and placed in two-channel iron tracks that stretched past the work stations across the shop floor. At given intervals the foreman would blow a whistle, signaling the workers to push their chassis forward to the next station on the line. Auto bodies were also assembled this way, except that the bodies had to be placed on four-wheel trucks and rolled along by hand. The whistle blasts of the Ford foremen bring to mind the military regimentation of a drill team (Arnold and Faurote 1972:153; Avery 1929; Nevins and Hill 1954:473–74).

From Ford's point of view, these nonmechanical methods still left much to be desired. The pace of work was enforced by capital, but it still depended on the workers to push the cars and parts along. The mechanical assembly line, whereby an autonomous mechanism ultimately controlled by capital moved the work, was preferable. The first such "moving assembly line" was installed in the fly-wheel magneto (a type of electric generator) assembly process at Highland Park. A single worker at a bench had performed the magneto assembly in about 20 minutes. A chain-driven moving line was introduced on March 1, 1914, and the operation split into twenty-nine separate operations. The labor time immediately dropped to 13 minutes 10 seconds of one man's time, a 34 percent saving. After the work force was improved by substitution and experience, assembly time was reduced to *5 minutes of one man's time, a 75 percent saving!* The number of workers in this section of the shop was promptly cut from twenty-nine to fourteen (Arnold and Faurote 1972:112–14).

Similar mechanical assembly lines were introduced into the final assembly process. The careful recording of data by Ford managers helps us to sort out the real factors behind the large labor savings. In 1913, the stationary assembly of a chassis had required 12 hours 28 minutes of the labor of one worker. At least 17 percent of this was the labor of component carriers. (We know this because about 100 of the 600 men working on the assembly floor at Ford at this time were employed exclusively as component carriers.) Experiments began with an independently moving assembly line—independent of workers, that is—in August 1913. Some Ford production managers tied one end of a rope to the front of a Ford chassis, which was already on wheels and the other end to a windlass operated by the managers. Parts were placed upon the shop floor in the order of their usual assembly on the chassis. The managers turned the windlass, pulling the chassis across the floor past the successive piles of parts. Six assemblers traveled along with the chassis, picking up the parts and assembling them. In these first experiments, assembly time was reduced to 5 hours 50 minutes of one man's time, a 53 percent savings (ibid.:135–36; Sward 1948:36–37; Nevins and Hill 1954:473–74).

How was the large saving in labor time achieved? Ford and his managers usually made one or both of two claims. First, they claimed that this moving assembly line eliminated the time-consuming task of bringing parts to the car. Instead, the cars were brought to the workers and the parts, which were stationary on the shop floor. Second, following Adam Smith, they claimed that the increased division of labor allowed workers to increase their productivity by repeating one small task time and time again (Ford 1923:80,88; Arnold and Faurote 1972:105–06, 245).

Both of these arguments fall under the weight of the evidence of these first experiments. First, since the work of component carrying made up only 17 percent of total assembly time, eliminating it does not explain a saving of 53 percent. Second, there was no division of labor in these experiments with the moving line—the same six assemblers followed the car throughout the assembly process—and savings due to increased efficiency through specialization were therefore impossible. The *only* possible explanation of this reduction in labor time is that capital sped up the assembly process. Ford managers, not the workers, controlled the pace of work by turning the windlass. In one of his rare honest moments, Ford himself admitted that by using the assembly line, "We regulated the speed of men by the speed of the conveyor . . ." (Ford 1931:39).

A regular assembly line using the rope and windlass was set in operation on October 7, 1913. After careful motion study, work was divided between 140 assemblers, who were spread out along a line 150 feet long. The workers on this line completed 435 chassis assemblies in one 9-hour day, or 2 hours 57 minutes of worker time for each chassis. The first chain-driven lines were introduced in the final assembly at Ford on January 14, 1914. By April 30, mechanical conveyors had reduced final assembly time to 1 hour 30 minutes of worker time, a labor-time savings of 88 percent over the old stationary assembly method! (Arnold and Faurote 1972:136–38; Nevins and Hill 1954:471–76) With these impressive successes, the moving line quickly spread to every applicable operation in the Ford shops.

Apart from giving capital control over the pace of labor, the mechanical assembly line furthered capitalist control over the labor process by further elimination of skill. Previously skilled mechanics were assigned minute tasks, and countless unskilled immigrant workers filled many of these newly degraded jobs. Ford admitted that there existed in his shops "the pressing to take away the necessity for skill in any job done by anyone" (Ford 1923:102). The two production experts from *Engineering Magazine* noted:

> As to machinists, old-time, all-round men, perish the thought! The Ford Company has no use for experience, in the working ranks, anyway. It desires and prefers machine-tool operators who have nothing to unlearn, who have no theories of correct surface speeds for metal finishing, and will simply do what they are told to do, over and over again, from bell-time to bell-time. (Arnold and Faurote 1972:41–42)

Ford and other capitalists claimed that deskilling of work was necessary because of the shortage of skilled workers in Detroit.

But this is only part of the explanation. The shortage of skilled labor not only made expansion difficult, but it also made workers difficult to control on the shop floor. Skilled workers resisted exploitation and often did largely as they pleased, because they knew that Ford would not fire them for want of replacements. And even if they were fired, they knew that they could easily get a job elsewhere. Thus two historians of the Ford Motor Company stated that in the early days "many of the men neglected their work, malingered, put imperfect parts into cars, and cheated the timekeeper" (Nevins and Hill 1954:382). Hence one motive of deskilling work was undoubtedly to put teeth into the threat of firing and give capital more power to enforce its will on the shop floor. With the simplification of work, Ford created an instant labor surplus by opening jobs to unskilled immigrant workers. With the possibility that workers could easily be replaced by countless other workers clamoring at the Ford gates for jobs, the threat of firing became real, and workers were forced to submit to the discipline of capital. Thus, the *Engineering Magazine* writers Arnold and Faurote reported that:

> New regulations, important or trivial, are made almost daily; workmen are studied individually and changed from place to place with no cause assigned, as the bosses see fit, and not one word of protest is ever spoken, because every man knows the door to the street stands open for any man who objects in any way, shape or manner to instant and unquestioning obedience to any directions whatever. (1972:328)

How far the degradation of work and workers had gone by 1916 can be surmised from the following story told to a member of the Federal Trade Commission by the superintendent of an automobile factory in Geneva, Switzerland:

> There applied for work at this factory one day a man who represented himself to be a skilled erector of automobiles. The plant needed such a man, hired the applicant, and assigned to him the assembly of an automobile. It soon became apparent that this employee did not even know where or how to commence the assembly. The superintendent said to him:
> "We thought you were a skilled erector of automobiles."
> "I thought I was," replied the new employee.
> "Where did you work?"
> "At the plant of Ford Motor Co."
> "What did you do?"
> "I screwed on nut No. 58."
> (Federal Trade Commission 1939:669n)

Although the assembly line contains certain nonexploitative features, purely technical advantages that would be desirable in any system of production, regardless of the social relations of production—e.g., the mechanical conveyance of heavy and bulky parts relieves workers of much backbreaking work and mechanical coordination ensures that work flows smoothly—entangled with its basically neutral, technical advantages are more exploitative features that motivated its introduction by capital: deskilling of work, control of work intensity, and general capitalist domination of the labor process. In order to maximize surplus value against the opposition of an exploited, dispossessed class of direct producers, it is necessary for capital to completely control the labor process. Without taking full account of these class-based motivations, specific to capitalist social relations, it is impossible to fully understand the introduction and use of specific technological forms.

The introduction of the assembly line at Ford was not, however, the end of the struggle between auto workers and capitalists. Auto workers were down, but not out for the count. They struggled against Ford's degrading measures in a number of ways. First, as long as other auto firms had not fully adopted Ford's methods, they could simply quit and get a less rationalized, capitalist-dominated job elsewhere. And indeed, in the beginning, they left Ford in droves. A foreman on the chassis assembly line stated: "We all would get new men every day. They kept coming and going. . . . There were a lot of people who wouldn't even try. They thought they couldn't do it" (Russell 1978:39). As a result, annual labor turnover rates approached 400 percent in the years around 1914. Second, workers simply stayed away from work and absentee rates climbed to about 10 percent a day (Ford 1926:160–61; Sward 1948:47–51, 56). Finally, the Industrial Workers of the World (IWW) made halting attempts to unionize Ford workers in 1913. These forms of resistance brought on new attempts by Ford to control the workers, including the infamous five-dollar day and the inquisitional sociological department.

The struggle between labor and capital in the auto industry has continued in various forms up to the present. Ironically, the assembly line, originally so instrumental in winning capitalist control of the labor process, at the same time weakened capital by adding a resource to the workers' side in struggle. Because of the intricate coordination and interdependency resulting from mechanized lines, they are highly susceptible to disruption by a mere handful of workers. To their chagrin, auto capitalists discovered this in 1936–1937, when a small number of courageous unionists shut down practically the entire industry by simply putting down their tools and their backsides. Auto workers have continued to use sitdown strikes, wildcats, slowdowns, and skippies (skipping, for example, every fifth part to come down the line). In this respect the auto assembly line has confirmed Marx's prognosis for capitalist technology: it contradicts the repressive social system of production it was invented to serve.

Roots of Power: Employers and Workers in the Electrical Products Industry

Jeremy Brecher

Introduction

Over the past few years, great strides have been made in establishing the extent to which the labor process within capitalism has been shaped, not simply by technical imperatives, but by the need of employers to control and exploit workers. Unfortunately, this realization has sometimes been joined to a tendency to examine the labor process in isolation from the more general context of conflict among social groups and classes. An inexorable capitalist impulse toward "job degradation" or "rationalization" has in some analyses tended to replace the once-tauted technological compulsion toward "greater efficiency." A valid understanding of the capitalist workplace requires, on the contrary, that the evolution of the work process be understood in the context of the development of relations between workers and employers, and of various groupings within each class. The labor process itself is only one aspect, albeit a crucial one, of this overall development. The intentions and actions of workers need to be examined along with those of management, and many dimensions of workplace and community life besides the labor process itself must be taken into account.

The interdependence of the labor process and other aspects of class relations can be seen particularly clearly in the electrical machinery industry. Indeed, the development of the labor pro-

---

This article is based on an Institute for Labor Education and Research pamphlet drafted by Jeremy Brecher, with editorial assistance from staff members of the Institute. The pamphlet itself will be puslished by the ILER for use by unions and rank-and-file electrical workers in the near future. The author would like to acknowledge the help of Ronald Schatz, who served as consultant on the paper, and the members of the Work Relations Group, whose discussions have contributed much to the ideas presented here.

cess itself cannot be understood except in the broader context of worker struggle on the one hand, and nonlabor process aspects of management strategy on the other.

The electrical machinery industry began in the 1880s with the production of lamps, turbines, generators, transformers, and related materials. Control of patents and financial resources were used to combine many competing companies into two monopolies, General Electric and Westinghouse. As the uses of electricity grew, their dominant position allowed them to expand into a wide variety of other fields. As factories turned from steam to electricity, for example, electrical motors and other industrial applications of electricity became important. As consumer appliances, radios, and finally televisions became mass market products, the electrical manufacturers moved into these fields. With the rise of electronics after World War II, military, industrial, and consumer applications expanded greatly. Meanwhile, the electrical corporations developed into multinational operations, able to move their facilities, technology, and other resources around the globe. Today, the U. S. electrical products industry employs approximately 1.75 million workers (U. S. Bureau of Census 1976:9; this is based on Census Standard Industrial Category 36, "Electric, Electronic Equipment").

Their powerful position has allowed the electrical manufacturers to apply a series of tactics to divide and control the workers, including the deskilling of work, automation, payment plans, job ladders, paternalistic welfare programs, relocation of plants and other facilities, diversification, union splitting and union busting, and playing different groups of workers—blue- and white-collar, black and white, male and female, foreign and United States—off against each other. These tactics, and the ways workers have responded to them, are the subject of this article.

The Breakdown of Jobs

When Thomas Edison opened his first factory for the production of lamps at Menlo Park in 1880, the workers he hired were skilled craftsmen. Not only did they possess a wide range of manual skills for the manipulation of glass and wire, but they also knew the basic theory on which lamps were constructed. Their skill and knowledge were central to the early production of electrical equipment. But over the next thirty years, electrical employers transformed the work of making lamps. The jobs were simplified and divided into minute segments, with the former skills built into specialized machines. This allowed the companies to cut costs, increase production, and eliminate skilled workers. The craftsmen, who had used their own skill and knowledge to produce the lamps, were replaced by workers —predominantly women—who performed only one special operation and required little training to do the job (Baker 1964:195). Such a pattern has been repeated over and over again in the electrical industry, down to the present day. Where jobs involve special engineering and one-of-a-kind production, they remain the province of skilled craftsmen. But wherever possible, the companies have tried to break down jobs requiring skill, knowledge, and judgment on the part of workers into jobs that are simple and repetitive.

Skilled work still predominates in the "heavy current" part of the industry. Such electrical apparatus as turbines, generators, and transformers generally involve months of slow, careful work, and are usually made to order and specially engineered (Backman 1962:5; Twentieth Century Fund 1945:758). The emphasis is on quality over speed. For some jobs, more than a decade of experience may be necessary. But in other parts of the industry, employers have replaced skilled labor with machines and with less skilled workers whenever the market for a product becomes large enough to make this pay. The assembly of the 600-odd parts of a TV set, for example, has been broken down into 1,600 separate operations. The work is so highly subdivided that most operations take less than 30 seconds (Hall 1975:269).

The principal production occupations in the industry are assembly, capacitor and coil winding, inspecting, machining, fabrication, processing, and maintenance (U. S. Bureau of Labor Statistics 1976:630–34). Most of these have been subject in one way or another to the "breakdown of jobs." Management generally attempts to break down work into the most repetitive, least skilled form possible. Just how far this can go was made clear by three assembly workers in a Chicago area consumer appliance plant, who described their jobs:

"The job doesn't take much training. You can learn it in—oh, gee whiz—a matter of seconds. You're not doing anything complicated that would take maybe a day or two to train you in. Maybe you might have to put on a nut here and tighten it up, which I do. Maybe run a wire through a hole and tighten it up, and put a fitting on it."

"It's just a job, because there's really nothing to it. Place the motor. Put the housing on, tighten it. A twelve-year-old could do it."

"You just grab a chassis and drop it." (Purcell and Cavanaugh 1972:72–73)

Such simplification of jobs allows management to structure the work in such a way that every second of a worker's time is used to the full. The extremes to which this can go are indicated by a government-sponsored study of electronics, which recommended the following "principles of motion" for hand assembly operatives:

(1) Both hands should begin movements simultaneously.
(2) Both hands should complete their movements at the same instant.
(3) Both hands should not be idle at the same time except during rest periods.
(4) Motion of the arms should be in opposite and symmetrical directions and should be made simultaneously.
(5) Hesitation should be studied and its cause eliminated whenever possible.
(6) Hand motions should be as simple as possible to provide the fastest motions. The fewer the body motions, the faster the motion. The classification of motions in order of economy are:
   a. Finger motions only.
   b. Finger and wrist motions.
   c. Finger, wrist, and forearm motions.
   d. Finger, wrist, forearm, upper arm motions.
   e. Finger, wrist, forearm, upper arm, and body motions.
(7) Material and equipment should be located as nearly as possible within the normal grasp area.
(8) Sliding, rather than carrying, is usually quicker to transport small objects.
(9) Straight line motions requiring sudden changes in direction are not as desirable as continuous curved motions.
(10) The sequence of motions should be arranged so that they increase the possibility for rhythm.
(11) Equipment and materials should be put in place before work

begins and their positions should be known by the worker so as to reduce searching, finding, and selecting (Bureau of Business and Economic Research 1962:343).

Job Enrichment

In response to the workers' hostility to boring, repetitive jobs, some electrical industry employers have started experimenting with "job enrichment." In some cases such programs may ease some of the more brutal effects of job subdivision. A young woman who worked in assembly at an electronics plant in Portland, Oregon, reported:

> They have this job enrichment. You assemble a whole unit; each person does a number of different operations. Bad as it is, I know when I'm working it would be worse if I had to do just one operation. (Brecher and Costello 1976:49)

Such reorganization, however, can simply be a management excuse for speed-up. In another case, for instance,

> each woman on the final assembly line had an operation to perform that took only hundredths of a minute. . . . The same pattern of movement [was] repeated over and over again by seventy-five women. . . . 836 electric irons got assembled every 60 minutes on this particular line. The women were doing a mechanical job which became second nature to their fingers and hands. . . . They found some relief from boredom by engaging in constant conversation. . . . Came the day the company had a new speedup idea: the module assembly system, as it was called. . . . Under the new system, one worker would assemble half of the iron, a second worker the other half—with each worker now performing not just one monotonous operation but a number of them. Instead of 75 workers the new system cut the number of workers down to 64, to turn out the same eight hundred thirty irons every 60 minutes. . . . The increased speedup, together with the additional operations required from each woman, now demanded steady mental concentration as well as harder physical work. Little chance, any more, for kidding around, for chitchat, for grievance discussion, for helping each other and for switching jobs on the line. Faced with a choice between two evils—the old continuous assembly line or the new modular system—the workers determined to stick with the lesser evil. The old line was bad

enough but the new one was intolerable. (Matles and Higgins 1974:284-90)

Automation

The electrical industry is marked by a striking paradox. While it is based upon the most advanced modern technology, much of it uses forms of hand assembly that are hundreds of years old. While it turns out equipment of great value, the machinery used is relatively cheap: the electrical products industry is substantially below the average for manufacturing as a whole in the capital invested per production worker (Backman 1962:192). Nonetheless, in recent years employers have begun to introduce automated equipment. In some cases this has reduced the skill level of highly skilled jobs. A process tester at Western Electric described the effect of automation on her job:

> We have to adjust different parts so they read right on the test sets, and if they don't read right, we have to make them read right. You have to find out what is wrong and fix it. It's a real challenge. . . . It's like solving a puzzle, and I loved that. That's why I don't like these new computers they have. Right now they break down a lot. I suppose once they get the bugs out of them they'll be very good because they can put low-grade people on them because there's not much to do but watch them. You put the program in and that's it. . . . Just sit there and push something all day long, that would be terrible. (Balzer 1976:224)

Automation can also be used to make a repetitive job more mentally and physically demanding for the worker who does it. A worker at Westinghouse told a union official how, with more advanced technology,

> "Making small parts can be monotonous, very monotonous; but there is also more effort. . . . When the machine does the first piece, the operator unlocks the piece from the jig, blows it out with an air hose, puts another piece in and locks it. By that time the machine has come out of the second piece in the row; she moves to the next one, she unlocks it . . . ."
> Q: "In other words she is following the machine down the row of jigs?"
> "Loading it and unloading it; when she goes home at night she's shaking." (United Electrical, Radio, and Machine Workers 1963:24)

Thus machines, far from being used to make life easier and more pleasant for human beings, are instead often applied by management in order to drive them harder.

Further technological change is currently under way. Miniaturization of electric components and circuits, in which chemical and metallurgical processes replace manufacturing and assembly, has become increasingly widespread. Microcircuits have replaced a great many traditional electronic components. Numerically controlled machine tools have been used more and more widely.* Assembly operations are being partially automated by the introduction of new soldering, welding, fastening, indexing, and component feeding equipment. Computers are being used to control the production process, such as in the assembly of circuits and the production of resistors (Bureau of Labor Statistics 1966:91–97).

Payment Plans

Throughout its history, the electrical industry has seen a continuous struggle between workers and employers over the rate of production. A major goal of worker action has been to control the pace of work; management has in turn struggled to destroy what it considers workers' "restriction of output."

Thus from the early days of U. S. industry, it was traditional for craftworkers to set production quotas or "stints"—their own rules about how much work a worker should do in a day. With the development of unionism in the electrical industry, such rules were enforced by the unions. On the other hand, a major employer weapon for making the workers work faster was piece rate and incentive pay which, in effect, bribed the workers to break their own output ceilings. During and after World War I, workers at both Westinghouse and General Electric conducted a series of strikes in which company "premium pay" plans were a major issue (Montgomery 1976a:19). With the defeat of this early unionism, however, incentive plans became extremely widespread in the electrical industry, worker regulation of out-

---

* For more on numerically controlled machine tools, see Noble, in this volume, and Braverman 1974:197–206.

put became weak, and wages were repeatedly cut while competition for bonuses became common (Twentieth Century Fund 1945:748).

One of the key objectives of electrical workers in building a union in the 1930s was to reestablish a degree of control over the pace of production. In general, the unions did not demand the complete abolition of incentive systems; they demanded that they be simplified, that inequalities be eliminated, and that time studies be subject to checking by the union. Beyond this, the workers established a considerable amount of direct control over the work process through the grievance procedure, steward system, and their own ability to stop production when they disapproved of company-set rates. In many cases, workers established their own work standards, and "rate busters" who exceeded them could be disciplined by the union (ibid.:789).

Employers repeatedly attacked this ability of the workers to affect production rates. For example, Philco Radio, the first company in the industry to recognize a union in the 1930s, subsequently provoked a four-month strike in the settlement of which it won "a free hand in production problems, subject only to union complaint," so that "restrictions" on production could be eliminated (ibid.: 789).

Another tack has been the company demand for the right to re-time jobs, even when the jobs have not changed. In 1946, for example, GE complained that productivity had declined 25 percent since the war and demanded that the contract permit reevaluation of piece rates and production standards (Meyerowitz 1969:75). The power of the electrical workers was then sufficient to prevent this—and the speed-up that would have resulted—but in later years weak and divided workers were often unable to prevent such rate cutting (Matles and Higgins 1974:212).

Whether or not workers have been able to establish some formal control over incentive systems, they have usually developed techniques for manipulating such systems to their own advantage. These constitute a worker tradition of informal resistance on the shop floor, a tradition in which new workers are rapidly instructed. A number of these techniques were described by a young man who went to work at Western Electric in 1973. The starting point was a general worker policy of working slowly when jobs were being timed. Here is what happened when the time study people came around to reevaluate the rates:

> One day they watched Claire as she worked on a board. After they left she told me, "You see, I work steady, but I'm not going to kill myself, because once they set the rate you have to live with it." That's what everyone said: don't work too hard when the time study people come, don't kill yourself, don't show them any short cuts, just work steady. (Balzer 1976:127–28)

Once rates are set, workers are able to use the shortcuts that they have developed to get a little time for themselves. The same young man reported:

> No matter how rates are made, workers seem to find more efficient ways to do things. Most workers are willing to share these short cuts with fellow workers, but are reluctant to let the company know about them. This is because there is a general belief that sharing such information with the company will result in pushing up the rates and will not lead to monetary rewards for the workers. (Ibid.:131)

Workers establish their own definition of a normal rate, and try to enforce it among themselves. A new worker is taught to ignore management pressure to achieve higher bonuses by increasing output:

> I told Linda how much trouble I was having even coming close to the rate. She said, "Don't even come close to it, not until you've been here a long time. If you're doing the rate after being here for six months," she said, "then they'll think you can really do twice the rate once you've been here for a couple of years. I never made the rate when I started working here. I didn't care. Now I've been here a couple of years, and I can make the rates on most of the boards. But I know if I began going over the rate too much they'd just pick the rate up on me." (Ibid.:124)

Because workers have so often been able to turn incentive plans to their own advantage, the electrical companies have increasingly tried to replace them with a system of "measured day work." Here, workers are still faced with production quotas set by time study, but instead of receiving a bonus for making the rate, they are paid a standard day wage and face discipline if they fail to make the rate. The stick replaces the carrot. For example, Westinghouse introduced day work in all new plants after 1945, and it tried to introduce measured day work to its turbine plant in Philadelphia in 1955, only to be prevented from doing so by a 299-day strike. In East Pittsburgh, wage increases have not been applied to incentive rates, so that the significance of incentives has diminished. GE introduced measured day work, backed by closed-circuit TV surveillance of workers, at Schenectedy in 1965 (Aronowitz 1965:46). While most workers are still covered by incentive plans, management hopes that measured day work will be the wave of the future.

Internal Labor Markets

Another management technique for manipulating the workers is the supposed opportunity for advancement. Employers generally maintain a "job ladder" which serves as a carrot to encourage workers to exhibit "good behavior" in hopes of advancement to a higher grade or to a supervisory position. As a layout man at Western Electric put it:

> They run this place just like Hitler's Germany. They play on your fear, one against the other. They keep telling you keep your nose clean. Then they dangle the carrot, and they keep you on the string as long as possible. Jeez, I can give you all kinds of examples of that. When they're thinking of promoting a layout to supervisor, they call several of you and tell you individually you got a real good chance. Well, you find out they told that same stuff to a half-dozen other guys, and they think you'll kill yourself to look better than the other guy.
>
> I'm telling you all kinds of stuff like that happens in here. Everybody is watching to get ahead and not step on anybody's toes. Well, once they know that, they've got you. (Balzer 1976:97–98)

In most cases, of course, the opportunity for advancement is very limited. A twenty-four-year-old assembly worker in Chicago said:

> First of all in the shop, there is no question, there are no chances for promotion. I am at the limit for the seniority that I have. . . . I know that I'd have to be here a good twenty years to get the next labor grade, which is just an increase of four or five dollars a week. (Purcell and Cavanaugh 1972:155–56)

In the early years of unionism, during the Great Depression, a major union goal was to substitute seniority for "straw boss favoritism" (Twentieth Century Fund 1945:762). While promotion by seniority led to division between different groups of workers, it at least reduced this kind of direct employer manipulation. In many plants, however, seniority provisions are weak. In small plants, promotion is often completely at the discretion of management (Bureau of Business and Economic Research 1962:160, 242), and even in large, unionized plants, employer favoritism is often allowed by contract. An assembler in a Cleveland lightbulb factory reported:

> People working here are still taking home $130 a week after fifteen years, the same as I make after two. There really is no advancement. One opening came up for a good job; six people bid for it, but were turned down as "theoretically unqualified." The boss's nephew, right out of high school, got the job. The second guy ever to go from assembly to the tool and die department was the son of the president of the union. People were outraged. People in general just don't advance. (Brecher and Costello 1976:52–53)

Company Welfare

The electrical industry has long used company welfare programs and various paternalistic benefits to win the workers' loyalty, tie them to their employers, and prevent vigorous worker organization. A report to a union convention from a Schenectedy GE local in 1936, for example, noted: "Because of the nature of paternalistic plans that tie all workers to the company, it is difficult to get men with long service to join the union" (Matles and Higgins 1974:64). Nearly forty years later, a Western Electric worker said: "I can't walk out, I have too much invested. They've got me by the balls. I got time in here. I got security in here. I've got all kinds of benefits. That's how they entice you in here, with social welfare" (Balzer 1976:99). Under such conditions, taking an action that risks your job means losing these accumulated benefits as well as the paycheck itself.

Runaway Plants

From their earliest days, the transfer of work and plants from one location to another has been one of the basic antilabor tactics of the electrical companies. According to one historian, Thomas

Edison took his company from New York City to Schenectady in part because he was "disgusted by the labor troubles" of the metropolis (quoted in Northrop 1964:11).

Many electrical products go through a standard cycle. When they are new and experimental, they are developed in or near a large metropolitan center, drawing on an available pool of engineers and skilled workers, university research centers, specialized suppliers, and temporary facilities requiring little permanent investment. As the technology becomes more stable, markets grow, and large-scale production becomes possible, the plants are moved to other areas, particularly economically backward ones where low-skill labor is available at low wages. This cycle has been repeated by Edison's original electrical machinery plants, by the radio industry in the late 1920s, by television in the 1940s and 1950s, and by the modern electronics industry (R. H. Hall 1975:313). It is a counterpart of the breaking down of skilled jobs into repetitive, low-skill ones discussed above.

Before World War II, about 87 percent of electrical manufacturing was in the nine states east of the Mississippi and north of the Mason-Dixon line, mostly in small cities (Twentieth Century Fund 1945:745; Purcell and Cavanaugh 1972:14). Following the war, the electrical companies began a deliberate program of relocation and "decentralization." The great expansion of the industry was into the rural areas of the North and West, the small towns and suburbs in the South, and the suburban areas outside large cities—the opposite of the small northeastern cities in which they had previously been concentrated (Purcell and Cavanaugh 1972:24, 35). This relocation was a deliberate attack on the power, wages, and conditions won by the workers in the preceding decade. In 1944, describing GE's plan to decentralize, Charles E. Wilson noted that labor costs were lower and ties between labor and management closer in the smaller communities (Meyerowitz 1969:50). A former member of GE's "employee relations staff" was somewhat more outspoken about GE's "growth and diversification policy":

> From the labor relations point of view, this diversification is highly significant. It is clearly impossible to shut down this company by striking a key plant. . . . Moreover, in planning its general program of expansion during the last decade, GE has kept in view the employee relations aspect of plant operations and has built second or satellite plants in many cases where operations of a group of

plants might be jeopardized by a strike in a sole supplying plant. (Northrop, quoted in Backman 1962:215)

Besides the attempt to make themselves "strike-proof," management has had several other motives for this migration:

- To reduce wages. Wage rates are generally lower in industrially underdeveloped rural and small-town areas. A confidential study in 1957, for example, found that average wages for TV set production in the New York metropolitan region averaged about $1.80 an hour, with Philadelphia and Chicago about the same, but that nonmetropolitan areas in Illinois and Indiana averaged $1.50-$1.62 for the same work (R. H. Hall 1975:270).
- To escape unions and union conditions. As a study of electronics noted, the industry

> is characterized by a variety of competing unions and by disparities not only of wage rates but also of fringe benefits, seniority rules, and occupational differentials. . . . In small localities . . . an employer might well expect to find labor unorganized, or organized by a union of his preference. Many an employer in a large metropolitan center, contemplating his high wage levels, the narrowing of the wage gaps between unskilled and skilled workers, and an aging work force protected by seniority rules, has welcomed an opportunity to start over with a new work force and a revised wage structure. (Ibid.:271)

The more militant industrial unions tend to be concentrated in the older plants.

- To escape work rules and work standards. Electrical workers have fought tenaciously against company attempts to speed up work by raising production standards. As the same study points out, "By moving to new areas where the labor force is unfamiliar with the traditional standards, manufacturers can often attain higher levels of output per man-hour along with lower wage scales" (ibid.:288).
- To find areas where there is a lack of competition for workers. For all their touting of competition, the electrical employers prefer not to compete with others for labor. In small towns and rural areas they frequently become the chief local employer. Often their wages and conditions are better than others available locally, even when low by national standards.

The threat to move jobs and plants can also be used as a club over both workers and local communities. GE, for example, has frequently warned local officials a few days before an expected strike that if the GE plant was not kept open for strikebreakers, the company would move (Meyerowitz 1969:89–90).

Offshore Plants

Around 1960 there began a new migration of jobs, this time out of the United States and to less developed foreign countries. U. S. companies began leasing their patents and selling licenses for their technologies to foreign companies, especially Japanese, to produce consumer electronic products and components abroad. Over the past ten years, U. S. firms have received more than $200 million for licensing and technical assistance agreements from Japanese consumer electronics companies now selling their products in the United States (*Wall Street Journal* December 16, 1976). Much of this technology resulted from research financed by the U. S. government.

As the 1960s progressed, U. S. multinational corporations began opening their own plants in low-wage countries in Latin America and Asia, transferring their production there. Both foreign and U. S. firms could sell in the U. S. market as a result of tax and other loopholes and reduced tariffs—tariffs for TV's, for example, fell from around 30 percent in 1960 to 5 percent in 1973 (Bywater 1973:20).

The Japanese and runaway American companies have concentrated on goods, such as consumer products and components, that have mass markets and relatively stable technologies. Since the mid-1950s, Japanese companies have taken over much of the U. S. market for radios, phonographs, TV sets, tape recorders, and CB radios. Between 1966 and 1970, average employment in U. S. TV plants dropped nearly a third, while hours worked fell by 42 percent (Walsh 1977:1177). From 1971 to 1977, the number of TV assembly workers declined further, from 43,000 to 29,000 (*New York Times,* May 28, 1977). In 1975–1976, the Japanese share of the U. S. color TV market increased from 15 percent to 40 percent in 18 months (Walsh 1977:1175). This trend is likely to continue in the future, particularly in the areas of videotape equipment for home use and computer production. Almost any mass-produced electrical product is vulnerable to such "migration," and even more sophisticated products, such as nuclear power equipment and machine-tool numerical control systems, are also threatened by it.

There is one overwhelming reason why so much production is moving to "offshore" locations: lower labor costs. Most jobs that have "run away" are precisely the kind of low-skill assembly jobs that have been created by the breakdown of work into minute tasks. This process—what the Electronic Industries Association's 1976 *Electronic Market Data Book* calls "deskilling of the operator" (cited in NACLA 1977:13)—allows the assembly jobs to be separated from the more sophisticated research and engineering tasks and shipped to wherever workers can be hired most cheaply. These are primarily economically underdeveloped countries in Latin America and, above all, in Asia. Here are the average hourly wages for unskilled workers in Asian countries to which U. S. plants have moved:

Country	Hourly wage*	Country	Hourly wage*
Indonesia	17¢	Malaysia	41¢
Thailand	26¢	South Korea	52¢
Philippines	32¢	Hong Kong	55¢
India	37¢	Singapore	62¢
Taiwan	37¢		

* Unskilled workers, U. S. dollars, 1976, calculated as an average of monthly high- and low-wage rates for a standard forty-six-hour week.
Source: Business Asia, April 30, 1976 (cited in NACLA 1977:15).

Most of the countries to which American factories have run away have one thing in common: almost all are ruled by dictatorial governments, backed by the U. S. government, which suppress political opposition and working-class movements. This is the social and political underpinning for their extremely low wage rate.

Industry Diversification

A substantial part of the strength of the electrical employers has lain in their ability to play off different groups of workers against each other. The comments of a former GE employee relations staffer about the divisions among workers in that company suggest how eager employers are to exploit these divisions:

> There has been a diversification of employee types and interests. Some plants have mainly men; others are as high as 85% female. The population of some plants is old, of others very young. By expanding into new locations and population centers during the last decade, GE has added to this diversity of labor force composition. . . . Where once the great bulk of GE employees were hourly workers, today a clear majority are salaried. . . . A combination of this trend toward salaried personnel and plant dispersal has reduced union organization in GE to a representation of about 40% of the total work force, as against a high of nearly 70% twenty years ago. . . . The unions who represent GE workers are probably more divided in character and number than unions in any other segment of industry. (Northrop 1964:5–6)

The electrical machinery industry comprises extremely different types of production, including:

—Heavy electrical apparatus such as turbines, generators, and transformers, and large electric motors, often involving individually engineered products and heavy, skilled work.

—Consumer electronics products, such as radios, TV's, hi-fi's, and electronic components, involving light, repetitive assembly work.

—Consumer appliances, involving traditional assembly-line production.

—Military and industrial electronics, requiring custom engineering and light assembly.

These differences are accentuated by the geographic pattern of the industry. Heavy apparatus tends to be concentrated in the older plants in northeastern cities. Light electronic assembly for consumer and other goods is concentrated in the South and in offshore plants; aerospace electronics, with its heavy proportion of research and development, is concentrated on the West Coast.

Hundreds of thousands of electrical workers are employed by the two giant companies, GE and Westinghouse. Yet at the other end of the scale there has been a tremendous growth of companies employing from a handful to one or two hundred workers. These small companies are concentrated in such fields as military electronics, which require little investment per worker. This diversity is complemented by a great deal of division among different groups of electrical workers. Among the significant divisions are those of race and ethnicity, those between white-

and blue-collar workers, those between highly skilled and less-skilled workers, those between members of different unions, and those between men and women. Because of limited space, we will deal here with only the latter two divisions.

Balkanized Unions

In contrast to such major American industries as automobile, steel, trucking, or coal mining, there is no dominant union in the electrical industry. Rather, workers are divided into five major and many lesser unions: GE alone boasts that it negotiates with over one hundred different labor organizations. The history of this division is important for an understanding of the current situation of the electrical workers.

In the years before and during World War I, craft unionism spread through much of GE, and most of the 14,000 GE workers at Schenectady were union members by 1911. At Westinghouse, major strikes occurred in 1914 and 1916. In many cases the workers were able to establish not only shorter hours and higher wages, but also substantial control over work processes and rules. After World War I, however, these early unions were broken. The heads of GE and Westinghouse were hostile to craft unionism. According to Ronald Schatz, a labor historian whose research has focused on the electrical industry:

> The essence of craft unionism in metal-working industries was control of the work process by skilled workers. Corporations which were continuously introducing new methods of production could not tolerate the possession of such power by workers. (Schatz 1975:190)

This did not mean that the big electrical companies opposed all unionism under all circumstances. Both GE and Westinghouse supported employee representation plans—"company unions"—as an alternative to craft unionism. Gerald Swope, president of GE, went to the head of the American Federation of Labor in 1926 and asked him to organize the industry on industrial lines. Such a union, Swope hoped, would raise the wages of GE's smaller competitors to GE's level, and thereby strengthen GE's competitive position (ibid.:191). As long as a union didn't interfere with management's control of production, it could be tolerated. Swope's offer was not accepted at the time, but a decade later, when industrial unionism began to spread through the electrical industry, it was generally allowed by the large manufacturers—in contrast to such industries as steel and auto, where bloody strikes were required to establish collective bargaining.

The United Electrical Workers (UE), formed from the unification of more than a dozen local union movements, spread rapidly through the industry in the early 1930s. In some cases the union took over employee representation plans; in others, workers conducted sporadic guerrilla warfare, disrupting production through sitdowns, slowdowns, and work stoppages; in a few cases, the union was established only through major strikes. By 1940, 154,000 electrical workers were represented by UE. With the great expansion of the industry during World War II, UE at its peak was bargaining for 600,000 workers (ibid.:194–95).

The high point of union strength came in the strike of 1946, the first nationwide strike in the industry's history. Workers' mobilization was so effective that the president of GE charged his plants and offices were "picketed in such a manner and such numbers as to amount to seizure" (Meyerowitz 1969:74). The companies sought injunctions against mass picketing in many cities, only to see them defied by the strikers; violent confrontations with police often followed. White-collar and blue-collar workers for the first time walked picket lines together. Community support for the strikes was strong. The settlement of the strike was a clear union victory. As a GE official later recalled:

> The effectiveness of the strike; the violence in some locations, notably Philadelphia; the strike truce to which GE acquiesced; and the spectacle of GE's president going hat in hand to the UE to accept the union's terms—all confirmed the extent of the union triumph. (Northrop 1964:20–21)

This union power was soon undermined by a combination of civil war within the union movement and employer offensive. With the rise of the cold war, open conflict broke out between UE's left-wing leadership and its anti-Communist opposition. Other CIO unions began raiding UE, whereupon UE ceased paying CIO dues. The CIO established a new electrical workers union, the International Union of Electrical Workers (IUE), headed by a former UE president. Meanwhile, GE and Westinghouse had developed a new labor policy aimed at reducing union power. They renounced all their existing union contracts and called for NLRB elections. In the resulting free-for-all—heavily colored by congressional hearings designed to portray UE as a Communist threat to U. S. security—the electrical workers were parceled out among UE, IUE, Teamsters, Machinists, Auto Workers, and numerous other unions. This division allowed the major corporations to reestablish the upper hand, largely through a labor policy known as Boulwarism, after GE's top labor official, Lemuel Boulwar. The basic tactic was for company negotiators to listen to the demands of union officials and then, practically without prior notice, to present their contract proposals in a vast public relations campaign targeted for the communities their workers lived in. The company refused to change its offer significantly, eliminating the give-and-take of normal collective bargaining. The goal was to persuade the employees to withdraw their support from the union by showing that the union was unable to win them anything. Given the disunity of workers, this policy had the effect of playing the unions off against each other. Boulwarism was eventually declared an unfair labor practice by the NLRB.

The electrical workers remained divided throughout the 1950s and 1960s. Working conditions won before 1946 deteriorated in many places, and wages fell further and further behind that of comparable workers, such as those in auto and steel (Schatz 1975:202). Well-organized groups of workers could still win some concessions locally, but at the national level the corporations had close to a free hand. The few attempts at national strikes were handily defeated. Under increasing rank-and-file pressure, the unions were finally forced to cooperate in coordinated bargaining. In 1969–1970, 14 unions waged a 101-day strike against GE, the first since 1946. According to *Time* magazine:

> In the minds of the strikers, the primary issue was not even economic. Their aim was to force GE to abandon its bargaining strategy of "Boulwarism." . . . Union loyalists have long regarded this strategy as an attempt to fix wages unilaterally, but the many unions representing GE workers were too divided to challenge the tactic effectively. (Cited in Matles and Higgins 1974:283)

In subsequent negotiations, the unions have continued coordinated bargaining, and the electrical companies have not resorted to "Boulwarist" tactics.

Nonetheless, divisions among workers in the industry remain deep. Any real power over the problems affecting electrical workers will require a kind of unity not seen since 1946.

Women and Men

Work throughout the electrical industry has traditionally been divided into "men's jobs" and "women's jobs." Wherever the work requires a high degree of skill, such as making one-of-a-kind equipment, or wherever it involves work on heavy apparatus, it has been defined as "men's work." Wherever it has been possible to break the work down into repetitive jobs that require limited skill and strength, it has been defined as "women's work." These jobs are largely concentrated in the lamp, communications, electronic component, and electronic assembly sectors of the industry (Backman 1962:205–06). A government study described typical "women's work" in the industry thus:

> Large numbers of women perform processing operations of a routine nature which require very little knowledge but a great deal of finger dexterity, close work, and patience, since parts are often minute. (Quoted in ibid.:205)

Discrimination against women is not new to the industry. For example, in 1937 Westinghouse had separate job classifications and seniority lists for men and women, and a minimum wage of 63¢ for men but only 44¢ for women (Twentieth Century Fund 1945:762, 768, 777). Such a pattern was typical.

The number of women in the industry increased greatly during World War II. The union pressed to bring wages closer to equality, culminating in a 1945 War Labor Board order that GE and Westinghouse establish equal pay for equal work (Matles and Higgins 1974:138). In 1946, GE president Charles Wilson sought to reestablish a lower wage rate for women workers, whom he insisted on referring to as "bobby-soxers" (ibid.:147). As recently as 1970, workers had to demand that GE stop classifying certain jobs, performed mainly by women, at lower rates than those received by sweepers and other unskilled men (ibid.:263). And a worker at the Merrimack Valley works of Western Electric found that in 1973:

> Relatively few women have moved up the graded system and into supervisory positions. As one goes up the graded skill ladder, the

number of women dramatically decreases. Although women represent nearly 90% of the 32 grade workers, they represent only slightly more than 50% of the 34 grade workers, 28% of the 36 grade workers, and only 20% of the 37 grade workers. Until 1970 there wasn't a single woman supervisor. . . . The best paying jobs in the shops and all levels of supervisory positions were, and still are, dominated by men. In the skilled crafts where there are 600 workers there are only two women, one of whom is a trainee. There are 378 section chiefs (first line supervisors) and only fifteen are women, and of the 137 department chiefs, only one is a woman. (Balzer 1976:292–94, 297)

The degradation of jobs has been intimately connected with the allocation of male and female labor. Where possible, employers have been eager to break down jobs into lower paid "women's work." This first happened in the production of lamps between 1880 and 1910, and again in production of smaller electrical apparatus during World War II. Electronic tube manufacturing, which started as the realm of skilled male workers, was transformed into the realm of women performing limited, repetitive tasks after mass production was introduced in 1923 (Baker 1964:198; R. H. Hall 1975:280). In 1945, the union was engaged in strenuous conflict with the electrical manufacturers over their attempt to break down skilled "men's jobs" into lower paid "women's jobs" (Meyerowitz 1969:55). Indeed, this issue has been at the core of many of the struggles for control of the production process.

Conclusion

The labor process in the electrical industry has been shaped by many factors—economic, technical, and social. But at the core of each development have lain the intentions of employers and workers, and their power to put these intentions into effect.

- The early job structures of the industry and their remnants today were determined by the power of the skilled craftsmen and their tradition of craft control.
- Management's policies—not only in deskilling and restructuring the labor process but in relocating workplaces, in changing from a male to a female labor force, and in a myriad of other details—have in large part been directed toward reducing the

power of the workers over their conditions both within and outside of the labor process.

- Management's ability to "degrade," "rationalize," and otherwise shape the labor process has depended upon its ability to divide, demoralize, or co-opt workers' movements.
- Conversely, to the extent that workers have been militant and united, they have succeeded in restraining management's juggernaut and molding the labor process closer to their own intentions.

Person and Machine in a New England Factory

Susan DiGiacomo Mulcahy and Robert R. Faulkner

This paper examines work individuation among semiskilled female operatives in a New England factory. The description and analysis are based on participant observation in "the mill" during the summer of 1973. The senior author was employed as a machine operator for three months, and detailed field notes were kept of factory activities.

Some investigators of task structure and social organization have decried the adverse effects of "asocial," "individualistic," and "depersonalized" work arrangements (Bell 1956:9; Blauner 1960, 1964:24–26; Caplow 1954; Wilensky 1964; Young 1972); but little ethnographic work has been directed toward establishing how such relationships are produced and perpetuated as a result of the labor process. Technological, aural, spatial, and interactional features combine to produce a particular organization of work and an orientation toward co-workers. "Individuation" is an appropriate name for these processes. It denotes a work process in which people are separated from one another and there is an absence of structured interpersonal relations on the job, save those of a most superficial sort. Implied in this definition of individuation is a conception of the asocial character of both the task structure and the relations among operatives at the production level. Workers are physically isolated from each other; the noise of the machines precludes the development of regular and periodic communication. Machine operations require constant attention, virtually eliminating oppor-

---

An earlier version of this paper, entitled "Work Individuation Among Women Machine Operators," appeared in *Sociology of Work and Occupations* 4, no. 3 (August 1977), pp. 303–26. Similar material is used in this article by permission of Sage Publications, Inc. The authors would like to thank Andy Zimbalist, Oriol Pi-Sunyer, Nancy Munn, Harriet Lyons, and David Mulcahy, who provided useful comments and gave needed encouragement for this project. We would also like to thank the personnel manager of ABC, and the operators of ABC for their time, patience, and cooperation.

tunities for interaction away from ongoing operations. And the factory culture is permeated with a set of assumptions and values which discourage socialization. Singly and in combination these factors combine to strain the conditions that facilitate cohesive relations among laborers. Considerations of production and machine operation have unqualified priority as maxims of conduct.

Setting

The factory, ABC Brush Company (all names are fictitious), is located in a small, semirural town in New England. It is one of the largest brush companies in the world and employs some 1,000 workers. Approximately 65 percent of ABC's business is in personal brushes of various descriptions, especially toothbrushes and hairbrushes. The remaining 35 percent is in a variety of molded plastic products such as dinnerware, light fixtures, and television parts. ABC was a privately owned company until 1963, when a major national corporation absorbed it. It is now a division of that corporation, although it retains its original name.

The plant is made up of several large buildings of mixed architectural styles, ranging from solid, turn-of-the-century brick to late 1960s prefabricated, with a river running through the center of the complex. Each building is known as a "mill." The fieldwork for this paper was conducted in the newest of the mills, a single-story concrete and metal building about five minutes' walk from the main office. Outwardly, this mill looks pleasant enough. The exterior is painted in coordinated shades of tan; there is a paved, fenced parking lot for employees, and an impeccably groomed expanse of lawn, complete with neat little shrubs in beds of peat moss.

The tranquility of the exterior belies the harshness of the interior. Inside there is a single large working area, known as "the floor," arranged in a grid pattern, like city streets, with broad aisles marked with bright yellow tape, and rows of machines and storage areas. The walls and floor are a nondescript cement gray; the machines are a uniform pea green. Glaring lights hang at regular intervals from the ceiling. Here and there, there is a skylight through which a patch of blue may be glimpsed. High up in the eaves at either end of the room are two fans; they make a great deal of noise and are supposed to circulate the air, but to no avail. There are no windows. On either end there are also two triangular panels of semitranslucent siding through which one may watch the changing light as afternoon fades into early evening and then into night.

There are several roller belts running lengthwise from the back to the front of the mill, and an overhead roller belt system that carries finished products to the loading platform. These make a clicking, slightly grinding noise not unlike that made by children's roller skates on a paved street, but much louder and all-pervasive. Against this background, each machine adds its own sound to the din as it is set into motion by the operator at the beginning of the shift. The noise level is ear-shattering. At the time of the senior author's employment, it was in excess of the limits set by federal regulations (90 decibels over a period of eight hours).

The mill is divided in half, one side being devoted to the production of toothbrushes, the other to hairbrushes. Fieldwork was conducted mostly on the "hairbrush" side, and it will be with this side that we will be primarily concerned. There are major differences between the machines on the two sides, but only minor variations between machines on the same side, so that a hairbrush or toothbrush operator, having learned to run one machine, can learn to run all the others on her side with a minimum of instruction and help, and an increasingly shorter adjustment period.

The machines each require one operator and stand about six feet high and four feet wide. On the hairbrush side, they are arranged in four rows running the width of the mill. All the machines in a row are facing the same direction, so that operators are face-to-back. To each operator's left is a roller belt with a metal shelf about fourteen inches wide in front of it, on which the operator keeps her scratch paper, pencil, computer cards, and the box in which she puts finished brushes. When filled, this box may be simply pushed onto the roller belt, which carries it to the front of the mill, where its contents will be inspected for defects.

To each operator's right, there is a wooden frame built to hold boxes of "backs," brushes without bristles, which are molded in another mill. Directly in front of each machine is a rubber mat to cushion the operator's feet, for she must remain standing in most cases, and the floor is solid concrete.

Most of the machines in the mill are over fifty years old. There is no preventive maintenance and the machines are never completely overhauled. When a part fails it is repaired, often with little more than a bit of wire and a tap from a repairman's hammer. This process is repeated until the part is no longer salvageable, when it is replaced. The result of such maintenance procedures is a machine full of parts in various stages of disintegration, and frequent mechanical breakdowns (the range is one to three breakdowns per machine per shift).

Work in the mill is more or less equally divided between men and women. The work force is composed of five major work groups: management, stockboys, adjusters, operators, and inspectors. The first two groups (with the exception of secretaries) are composed entirely of men; operators are women. Until recently, only men held the position of adjuster, but shortly after the period of study ABC began to encourage women (including operators) to apply for work as adjusters, and there are now women adjusters in all of the mills.

Management includes secretaries and men in positions of authority, from the foremen to the top executives and including time-study men. The representative of management with whom the operators deal most frequently is the foreman, although secretaries, junior executives, and time-study men make occasional appearances on the floor. The relationship between management and workers ranges from mutual tolerance to mutual contempt.

Adjusters repair the machines when they break down, and their job involves a variety of movement and some degree of judgment and creativity: they must first diagnose the machine's problem and then set about correcting it. A new adjuster must come to ABC with some mechanical knowledge, such as experience repairing industrial sewing machines or other high-speed machinery. Adjusters are also paid more than operators, and a top-level adjuster earns about 25 percent more than a top-level operator. For these reasons, adjusters are perceived by operators to "work less" than they do. Observations of this sort are common among operators, and indicate certain ideas about the nature of work.

Stockboys are responsible for bringing the plastic brush backs to each machine, and for making sure that the trays in which the finished brushes are stacked are available to the operators. The inspectors' task involves weeding out unsatisfactory brushes.

Task Structure and the "RE"

The technology is large- and medium-batch unit production, and involves a set of routine machine operations (Woodward 1965). Management seeks to standardize the raw material and operations in order to minimize exceptions, but the machines still break down, thus introducing some variability into the work, some excitement onto the mill floor, and in some cases an occasion for interworker conflict. When there are nonroutine exceptions, such as a temperamental machine, they are usually handled by the adjusters, but in some cases the operators devise ways of meeting their production quotas (the "reasonable expectancy" or "RE") by patching up the machines themselves. Overall, however, the production process is planned, allowing little discretion concerning the materials and their scheduling. Interdependence between operators and technical supervisors is kept at a minimum, and the relationship is directive.

"Making the RE" is the goal of the operator. This quota is not "reasonable" in the sense of "moderate" or "average"; it is close to Frederick Taylor's physiological maximum (Braverman 1974). It is a singular method for determining wages. The percentage of the RE that an operator is able to turn in affects her paycheck not directly, as piece rate does, but indirectly, over time. There are three pay grades, which to a certain degree represent "skill"; these are C, B, and A, in ascending order. After a week in training, the neophyte starts as a C operator, and it is expected that she will eventually be able to produce about 80 percent of the RE. In order to become a B operator, she must raise her percentage to 93 percent and keep it there for about three months; to become an A operator she must produce 98 to 99 percent, again for a three-month period. If an operator works at it steadily, the entire progression may take as little as a year, but more often it requires two or three.

All the machines run at different speeds, since they handle different types of brushes, and have different REs. The RE, like the machine number and the number of the brush for which the machine is currently "set up," is supposed to be posted visibly and legibly on the front of the machine, but this is often not the case, especially on machines that have recently been re-set up. For the new operator the numerical system is confusing, and the absence of needed information only adds to the confusion.

An operator is required to stand at her machine and run it for eight hours, with two ten-minute breaks and a half hour at lunch. The machines handle from four ("single set up"—slower running, since they automatically stop for each changeover) to eight ("double header"—faster, continuous motion) brushes at a time. The right side of the machine drills holes in the brush backs, and the left inserts knots of bristles in the holes, "stapling" them with bits of wire. Operators are also called "staplers." An operator keeps her machine supplied with backs and "nylon" (brush bristles), and clears debris from the moving parts with an air hose. She also trims and cursorily inspects finished brushes. She keeps careful track of how many brushes she has produced, for she must turn in a "batch ticket" every two hours. At the end of the shift, she turns in a complete tally of everything she has done, and a computer card for each type of brush she has made, with her operator number and the number of brushes she made written on it.

Out of a total of 101 different brush types produced during the senior author's employment, 8 were assigned REs below 100 brushes per hour; 29 were assigned REs of 100 to 200 brushes per hour; 42 were assigned REs of 200 to 300 brushes per hour; and 22 were assigned REs of 300 to 600 brushes per hour. Thus an operator running a machine for which the RE is 253 brushes per hour would have to make a changeover (insertion and removal of brushes) approximately every fifteen seconds. To the unskilled newcomer, the task at first seems impossible. The fast pace, the noise, the heat, the glaring lights, the multiplicity of things that must be done in fractions of seconds are overwhelming. Yet eventually a systematic work process emerges. The operator gains progressively greater routine control over her movements and over the machine.

Becoming a competent operator carries with it two principal rewards. First, there is the satisfaction of having achieved some degree of control over one's own movements and one's tools. The operators display a certain amount of pride in their ability to do their jobs well, indicated by the resentment they express when shifted by the foreman from their machines to less prestigious "finishing" operations. Second, escape from on-the-job fatigue is associated with the attainment of some technical control. Falling into a rapid, rhythmic pace or "pull" is adaptive; indeed, it is the only reasonable way of coping with this type of stress. To the uninformed observer, this looks boring and possibly even a little alarming. The operators wear no expression on their faces as their hands move rapidly, keeping pace with the machinery; they become "narcotized" by the combination of noise and fast rhythmic motion—the effect is very much like being wrapped in layers of cotton wool. There is a decrease in awareness of the environment and of the physical stress involved in operating a machine, so that one often does not realize that one is tired until the eight-hour shift is over.

Operators are restrained from communicating with each other by physical barriers of various types. First of all, there are the machines themselves. Even if an operator turns a full 180° to speak to the operator behind her, she comes face to face with only a machine that completely hides the other operator from view. She has difficulty leaning around either side of her machine, for to her left is a metal shelf and roller belt, followed by another shelf for operators on the other side of the row. To her right is the frame that holds the boxes of "backs" and the cardboard boxes or wooden trays in which the finished brushes are sent down the roller belt for inspection. The operators on each side of the roller belt face each other, but the shelves and roller belt constitute a waist-high barrier about four feet wide—too wide for them to lean across and talk.

When the employees are organized into groups of two to five for work on small assembly lines or such "finishing" operations as boxing, the foremen try to manipulate the space to produce structural noninteraction. One evening the senior author and another operator were set to the task of inserting spools of dental floss into plastic cases molded by ABC. The "natural" arrangement would have been to place them sitting at a table across from each other, with dental floss and plastic cases at one end and boxes for accumulating finished products at the other. This would maximize comfort, place the materials within easy reach, and permit conversation. Instead, they were placed at separate tables at right angles, not semifacing but semi-back-to-back, standing (although the tables were so low that one had to stoop from the shoulders, a painful position if continued for long), and with the materials inconveniently just out of reach.

The high noise level also facilitates individuation. Communication is discouraged and limited to a few brief job-related remarks. It requires too much physical effort and time away from the machine for two operators to carry on a sustained conversation. If one operator shouts, she runs the risk of distracting another operator, and operators rely in part on the different sounds their machines make at various points in the cycle as signals for making the changeover.

People Out of Place: Down Time and Conflict

Social structural features exacerbate these "natural" tensions of the pressure to make RE, the noise, and the spatial separation. Mechanical failure—a constant feature of work in the mill—throws these aspects of social structure into relief.

The proper procedure for an operator in the event of a breakdown is to stop the machine immediately to prevent further damage, and shut off the power so that the adjuster will not be accidentally injured should he start the machine inadvertantly. There is a supply of "down-time slips" at each machine on which the operator writes the date, her name, number, shift, and the time at which she shut off her machine. There is a list of thirty-eight possible reasons for mechanical failure on the down-time slip, and the operator circles those that apply; she then puts the slip on the adjusters' table. The first idle adjuster who comes back to the table will pick up the slip and go to investigate the problem. When he finishes, he will record on the down-time slip his name, the time at which he began to work on the machine, the time he stopped, and the total time spent working on it. The down-time slip is then turned in to the office for processing. ABC keeps work records on all its employees.

While an adjuster is fixing the machine, the operator is supposed to find herself a "spare" machine and work on it until her assigned machine is again in working order. In theory, there are half a dozen spares in working condition and supplied with materials; in reality, there are perhaps half that number. Some are "down," and others have no backs or nylon. The result is that if there are more operators with "down" machines than there are "spares" on the floor, some operators will have nothing to do between the time their machines break down and the time the adjusters finish repairing them. The ideal operator/adjuster ratio is 4:1, but in actual practice it is more often 6:1. On a troublesome night all of the adjusters may work constantly, and the operators may be forced to waste as much as half an hour waiting for their machines to be repaired. This situation gives rise to a number of interpersonal "hassles" and possibilities for conflict.

(1) *Conflict between operator and adjuster.* In terms of conditions of work as well as pay, adjusters are perceived by operators to have things much better than they do, and this generates a certain amount of resentment. Adjusters "work less" than operators: that is, they are not *constantly* working. If all the machines run smoothly for a while, as sometimes happens, they get a rest. They are not forced to stand in the same place and repeat the same movements for eight hours. From the operator's point of view, if a worker enjoys a variety of movement and physical comfort (such as being able to sit down), he or she cannot be said to be "working." An example from our field notes illustrates this:

> Took a break with Edith and Karen at 9:20, and they mentioned one of the adjusters. He was probably having a soda in the cafeteria, Karen observed. "He's got a racket," she said a little enviously. Adjusters only have to work when a machine goes down. At the beginning of the night, Jacques came over to change a drill, and stayed to talk a bit. Karen teased, "Why don't you go do some work?"

The general feeling among operators is that most adjusters hardly know what they're doing, even when they *do* work. There is some humorous and even sarcastic crossing of swords between the two groups. Adjusters return like for like, and accuse the operators of causing the machines to break down:

> Annie says that every time she sees Jacques coming to fix her machine, she feels like writing "Jacques trouble" on her batch ticket to explain why she didn't make the RE.
>
> My machine broke down, and when I went to the adjusters' table to fill out a down-time slip, Jacques was there. He grinned and said, "Operator trouble, as usual."

The joking relationship evidenced in the above quotations serves to ease an inherently strained situation. It is also a mark of acceptance; no one jokes with a newcomer until he or she becomes a known quantity. The joke is also a form of communication well suited to the noisy environment. Jokes may be shouted across short distances, and content is standardized and limited, usually to job-specific themes, so that if the noise obliterates part of an utterance it is not hard to guess what was missed.

At times, however, attempts on both sides to lessen conflict via joking fail, and sharp words are exchanged. Adjusters may give operators a hard time about fixing their machines for a number of reasons: it may be close to the end of the shift and the adjuster does not wish to get involved in a project that will last past quitting time; he may already be occupied with someone else's machine; he may not believe the operator (especially if she is still a novice) when she informs him that something is wrong; he may become impatient when the same operator repeatedly calls for the same machine to be fixed for the same malfunction, since her insistence implies incompetence on his part. Quoting again from field notes:

> I severely damaged my credibility one night by making a mistake, one induced by fatigue, boredom, and consequent absentmindedness—putting the wrong brush into the wrong holder, thus causing the machine to jam. I got a patronizing lecture from the adjuster whom I called to "fix" the machine. Later that same night, my machine went down again, the problem this time being with the machine and not with the operator. However, the only available adjuster—the same one I had called before—was considerably less sure of that than I was. It took some effort on my part to persuade him to at least come over and look at the machine.
>
> One night I observed a brief, angry exchange between a harried adjuster and a nervous operator whose machine was down and who had been walking around for some time looking for a spare. None of them seemed to have backs. In a more rational frame of mind, Edith blames the people in Molding for being so slow about sending backs over, but since these people are unavailable, she vents her frustration on the adjusters. Tom was at work with another adjuster on a machine (not Edith's), and she remarked sharply to him that "there are half a dozen slips at the desk"—implying that he was lazy and was not doing his job properly.

(2) *Conflict between operator and management.* When her machine breaks down, the operator finds herself wandering around the floor, looking for a spare. The less time she spends producing, the worse are her chances of making the RE, and, in the long run, of making the next pay grade. Pressure also comes from management, in the person of the foreman. Strolling up and down the aisles, he notices an operator walking about or standing around, apparently doing nothing. He approaches her and asks suspiciously, "What's your problem?" In order to avoid this kind of encounter, an operator will sometimes retreat to the

ladies' room to enjoy a cigarette. She must be careful not to get caught, since these unofficial breaks are not permitted. Operators also take such breaks to shorten the long stretch between the end of supper and the beginning of the last period. Also, if an operator finds that she is having an extremely "good night" and has made the RE before the period is over, she will have a cigarette in the ladies' room. No operator will produce more than the RE even if she is capable of it. If an operator demonstrates an ability to surpass the RE, the foreman will consider raising it, forcing all the other, less able operators to work harder.

Thus, the relationship between workers and management is fraught with difficulties. Operators regard management, from the foremen all the way up to the executives, as deficient in common sense and experience in doing what the operators define as "work" (i.e., running a machine). The time and motion experts are especially despised. Their air of self-assurance and superiority (totally unfounded, in the eyes of the operators), plus the fact that they trespass on the operator's personal territory, the nine square feet of floor space behind her machine, make them enormously irritating to the operators, many of whom spend years developing their own patterns of movement and have an intimate knowledge of the peculiarities of each machine.

(3) *Conflict between two operators.* Here there are two possibilities. The first concerns the operator who exceeds the RE and is subject to criticism by the others, whom she has obliged to work harder. The second is the uncomfortable situation which arises when there are more unoccupied operators than there are spare machines, and the operators find themselves competing for the spares. Here the conflict is less overt and rarely verbalized, although it occurs with much higher frequency. The shop-floor ethos, with its emphasis on the individual, dictates primary concern for one's own best interests—making the RE and avoiding the inquiries of the foreman.

(4) *Conflict between operator and inspector.* The inspector has final jurisdiction over which brushes measure up to ABC's standards and which do not. If an operator sends down a box of brushes with more than a few obvious defects, the inspector will come down the line and tell her that her machine is not working properly and must be fixed. This is objectionable to the operator, not only because it implies a failure to take responsible

action but also because if she takes the inspector's advice she exposes herself to the several possibilities for conflict between herself and adjusters, foremen, and other operators.

In sum, conflict situations in the mill arise when contact between an operator and her machine is temporarily severed, usually by a mechanical breakdown. The operator is thus forced into contact with other people, and her troubles begin. Given that interpersonal contact on the floor is thus charged with the possibility for conflict, it follows that the most easily maintained relationship is that between an operator and her machine. The work space behind her machine is a socially "safe" space for the operator, and when she is obliged to leave it she is "out of place." Any intrusion into this "safe" space, especially by management, is unwelcome, since it constitutes an invasion of the operator's territory and of the operator/machine dyad. This state of affairs tends to encourage the operator to develop to the fullest possible extent her technical skill on the machine. Some of the more experienced operators have even learned to make minor adjustments and repairs themselves, thus expanding and refining their relationship with their machines at the expense of contact with other people. The benefits of learning to adjust one's machine are twofold. First, by developing a smoother, more complete relationship with the machine the operator extends the amount of control she has over her own work situation, loses less time in repairs, and increases her chance of making the RE and ultimately of making more money. Second, as her requests for help from the adjusters decrease in frequency, she exposes herself to fewer and fewer possible situations of interpersonal conflict.

The thrust of ABC's shop-floor ethos is thus individual independence. The absence of pressures toward interworker cooperation exerted by the technical requirements of machine operation, as well as the lessened effectiveness of verbal communication as a result of the noise and the distance between operators severely weaken the social supports of interdependence. This is true not only in terms of the organization of production, but also in an emotional sense, for the operators we worked with and listened to do not characteristically form strong personal attachments to others. That exceptions can be found goes without saying, but the essential independence of the individual woman operator is impressive.

If work individuation is to perform a function, it must be

realistically related to the private, though situationally induced, desires of the operator and the structural requirements of the factory. This, we believe, is what individuation is designed to accomplish. A sort of counterpoint between technology and fundamental work reality is formulated. Declaring extensive personal relations to be useless or trivial is but one, perhaps rather uncommon, solution to the problem; more often, the reality of the work situation is accepted and characterized positively for what it is. And an attitude toward it—active pursuit of self-interest, technical competence, and the accent on "working hard"—is enjoined as reasonable and proper.

Beside suggesting some of the factors that enhance individuation, we have attempted to document the important fact that individuation can be and often is accepted as a matter-of-fact aspect of the work experience. Individuation does not mean chaos and resignation; it means acceptance of one's work as appropriate. The irony is that it will most likely be seen as appropriate when consensus is developed between a worker and her associates. Thus, we speak of the social organization of work individuation.

Afterword

In 1977, ABC began acquiring new stapling machines, called Boucheries. Made in Belgium, they represent the latest technological improvements in this type of machinery. ABC now has six, and eventually hopes to convert entirely to these. The new machines change some of the specifics of machine operation, but the net effect is to further encourage the trends described above.

The new machines are much larger than the old ones—approximately seven feet high and eight feet wide. They are spaced about six feet apart and arranged side by side in a line parallel with the other rows of stapling machines. Some of the operator's tasks have been incorporated into the functioning of the machine: changeovers are automatic and the machine itself trims finished brushes. A number of other "fine adjustments" the operator makes in order to fit the backs more easily into the old machines have also become unnecessary. The operator feeds backs into the machine through a chute, inspects finished brushes, and keeps track of production.

When in use, the new machines run twenty-four hours a day without stopping. When an operator goes on break, someone else relieves her. The machines can be set to automatically produce a given number of brushes, so that it is really the machine and not the operator that makes the RE. Each operator runs two of these machines, instead of one. Although there is less physical work involved, there is greater pressure to keep accurate count of the larger number of brushes coming out of the machine(s) per hour and greater responsibility for quality control than in the past.

The introduction of the Boucherie into the mill has had several effects:

(1) Management moves firmly into the driver's seat. Increased amounts of discretion in controlling the work process shift toward the information brokers—the time and motion experts—the managerial organizers of labor, those concerned with profits, and those whose decisions shape the future of the company.

(2) Workers move firmly toward their individualistic goals. The tendency to individuation is pushed even further as the Boucherie allows the operative to get into the rhythm of the machine for longer periods of work time than was formerly possible, demands that she carefully focus on the quantity and overall quality of her output, and keeps her out of potential conflict with other workers and foremen. There is now less opportunity to quarrel with anybody over anything on the shop floor because fewer people are out of place for longer periods of time.

(3) The new machines run faster than the old ones, but they do not require the same manual skills. Certain rather delicate maneuvers, such as bristle loading, are eliminated, and the vast technical differences between the Boucherie and the old machines prevent even experienced operators from attempting to make occasional repairs. The transformation of machine operator into machine tender is nearly complete.

Insurance: A Clerical Work Factory

Maarten de Kadt

It's 9:05 A.M. Winding my way to my desk, my supervisor's supervisor grabs me gently by the neck and suggests that I get a hair cut. It is also his very subtle way of telling me that he noticed that I came in after the appointed time of 9:00 A.M. There are no time clocks or bells at this insurance company office; unlike some insurance companies, this one prides itself on not having that form of regimentation. My paternalistic boss does just fine without it.

This kind of incident occurred more than once in the four years that I worked in the company's Newark office. And although the management style was different in the other company offices I worked in, the watchfulness was the same. In my eight years with the company I "rose" from underwriter trainee (read: mail boy) to senior underwriter. My job was to review information about people or corporations (the insured) that wanted insurance, decide whether or not to issue a policy, and figure out the appropriate amount of money to charge (the premium). According to the Department of Labor, I had to use "considerable judgment in making decisions" Bureau of Labor Statistics 1978: 128). I was therefore categorized as a "professional" worker.

An underwriter used to be responsible for the main decision-making function in the insurance business. I remember being told countless times that we as underwriters were the heart of the insurance operation. In recent years much of underwriting has become a clerical operation. While many of the work procedures which were common more than two decades ago are still in use, a large part of the work has become standardized and can in many cases be done simply by referring to various tables and charts; much has even been computerized. For more complicated kinds of insurance risk, the traditional methods of

---

Thanks to Sherry Gorelick, Andrew Zimbalist, and Beverly Elkan for their careful reading of, and comments on, earlier drafts.

rating are still used. Thus the history of clerical work in the insurance industry is the history of a process in which new techniques have been developed and implemented alongside the old.

The importance of underwriting judgments to the survival of an insurance company has diminished. The business has shifted to the recording and retrieving of information. The clerical work necessary to keep track of a large insurance corporation's investments (an important source of profit) can be performed by a small centralized group of workers. Insurance itself generates the overwhelming bulk of record keeping which requires a large clerical staff. It is this large clerical staff that the management attempts to control.

The Organization of Clerical Work

The insurance and banking industries employ about 30 percent of all U. S. clerical workers (Tepperman 1976:91). Approximately 50 percent of insurance company employees are classified by the Department of Labor as clerical workers (Bureau of Labor Statistics 1978:756). These are the people who type, file, code, rate, correspond; who do routine underwriting, routine claims adjusting, routine field coordination; and who are even routinely categorized as "supervisor underwriting clerk." Professional workers who supposedly use "considerable judgment in making decisions," in reality often perform no more than the routine clerical tasks of categorizing risks. Given the increasingly clerical nature of the jobs of "professional" workers (underwriters, claims adjustors, and the like) and of "sales" workers (those who sometimes leave the company office to call on company agents), the number of workers actually doing clerical work is understated by the Bureau of Labor Statistics.

The company for which I worked was organized in 1792. The founders employed only three people, one of whom was a clerk. The insurance in those first years was listed each time a policy was issued. Those simple lists, which showed the date of issue, the purpose of the insurance, the premium collected, and any losses were the extent of the record keeping at that time. Furthermore, an individual member of the office staff could handle all the business that came in. Today the same company employs 30,000 people, with offices in over 100 countries.

The Newark office in which I worked was a typical medium-sized insurance company office. My desk was in the middle of a large open floor of an office building. By 9:05 A.M. the steady click, click of many typewriters could be heard. The telephones had started to ring. Most of the windows to the outside world were in the offices of the managers. Those offices were arranged around the outside of the floor. Not only could these managers look outward, but they could look inward as well: each of these offices had windows overlooking the open floor. The desks on the open floor were arranged in columns and rows. On one side of my desk there were five more desks, on the other there were four. Behind me there were three rows of desks and in front there were eleven more. This part of the office was laid out in a matrix of about ten by fifteen desks. Here 150 employees did their daily work.

Around this matrix was a series of desks turned sideways to the matrix. These were either the desks of supervisors or of the secretaries to the managers in the windowed offices. A stranger could easily get lost among this sea of desks. Those of us who worked there, however, saw our own desk as a form of personal territory—as easy to find as our own homes. Each desk had some of the personal touches of the incumbent—a photograph, pen and pencil set, a name plate, some unique arrangement of the work to be done, and the like. Some of the desks had chairs next to them and telephones on them. Most did not. Only those of us who had to make outside calls as part of our function had phones.

Employees are overseen by supervisors; supervisors are in turn overseen by an office manager in his glasswalled office. Supervisors of typists, underwriter assistants, file clerks, etc., are most often women; I have never heard of a woman office manager.

The physical arrangement of the workplace is a primary means of control. Managers can, simply by raising their heads, oversee the activities of workers on the floor. In a different context, *Business Week* put it as follows:

> Visibility may be a key factor [in management's decision to apply the open floor office]. Mervin G. Morris, president of Mervyn's, a department store chain based in Hayward, Calif., theorizes that boosts in productivity result from "the hidden feature about open

planning." As he explains: "The mere fact that you are out there, that all eyes are on you, causes you to spend less time lighting cigarettes and visiting." (March 21, 1974:30)

All of us on the insurance company "floor" were continuously aware of the constant surveillance—so aware that we had developed ways of appearing busy when we were actually socializing with our fellow workers. Those of us who had telephones found this easy: we simply used the old call-your-neighbor-on-the-phone trick. Thus both of us looked busy.

Management surveillance, while the most effective form of control, was not the only one. Control was also exercised through an informal set of relations that did not go along each section's chain of command. Workers in one section often oversaw those in other sections. Policy typists often had to answer to raters for errors found in issued policies; raters answered to underwriters; and underwriters often had to account to field representatives. This informal network set up a series of checks over the amount and the quality of work each employee performed.

Management also used the division of labor to control the work. The office contained two kinds of division of labor. While an outsider would not notice the functional subdivisions within the matrix of desks, they were very obvious to those of us who worked there. In one area of the office were people involved with writing insurance; near them was a group of rating clerks; in a third area were those who coordinated field activities; in a fourth, those involved with claim settlements (more claims people worked on another floor as well); and finally, behind a row of filing cabinets was an additional group of typists, policy writers, file clerks, and letter writers. These were a general pool of clerical workers who supported the activities of other office personnel.

Each section had its own hierarchy of supervision and surveillance, and the division of functions was carried much further. In the underwriting areas, for example, work was divided between "personal" and "commercial" (individual consumers as opposed to entrepreneurial insureds). Personal lines activities were further divided between homeowner policy underwriting, personal automobile underwriting, and so forth, while commercial lines were divided between commercial fire underwriting, package policy underwriting, workers' compensation underwriting, commercial automobile underwriting, and so on.

This division of labor has taken many years to evolve. Management frequently changes the division when the previous arrangement no longer seems to work. For instance, it used to be that different lines of insurance were processed by different insurance companies, or at least by different subsidiaries of a single company. Insurance workers who have been working in the industry for close to twenty years remember offices divided by wrought-iron railings. On one side of the railing were the fire insurance workers, while on the other were the liability insurance workers. Then came a new division of labor into personal lines and commercial lines. This division has proven to be less costly for the insurance industry. By combining fire and casualty insurance into single departments, thus requiring the maintenance of fewer underwriting files and fewer physical inspections of insured premises, the work of two employees has been combined. With the re-division of labor, the work of insurance has been speeded up.

Many less complex variations of the division of labor based on clerical function have been tried, all in an attempt at speed-up, but they have not all worked. There was a short period of time during which this company, in an attempt to speed up clerical work by reducing information gathering, combined several additional lines of insurance in the job of single underwriters. But the work was not performed quickly enough because skilled workers were attempting to underwrite in areas for which they were not trained while at the same time letting the work they could do quickly sit. As a result, company expenses rose and the program was discontinued within a few years.

The second category of division of labor within the insurance company office is just as important as the first. Within each functional division is a division according to the complexity of the task to be done. This is a division of labor according to the Babbage principle (see Braverman 1974:79–82). For instance, all mail not marked personal or confidential is opened by low-paid workers, often retired men trying to supplement low pension payments. The opened mail is then categorized according to insurance function. Simple rating jobs or simple underwriting jobs are given to workers who are paid less than those who presumably have had more training and can do the more complex procedures. Filing is not done by those trained to do jobs for which more money is paid. Underwriters, paid more than typists, do not have typewriters near their desks. Underwriters fill in forms for others to type.

Each underwriter is given his or her own authorization: junior underwriters (now often categorized as clerical workers because it is clear to everyone that they are no longer given the opportunity to exercise judgment in making decisions) do their underwriting according to standardized criteria and have some of their work second-guessed by "more experienced" workers. More experienced underwriters (categorized as professional workers) may not be permitted to write insurance policies in excess of, say, a limit of liability of $1 million without management approval. These more highly paid workers make decisions according to "company policy," a form of less well defined but nevertheless standardized criteria. It is for their supposed exercise of "considerable judgment" that they receive the higher wage.

Let us follow an application for insurance submitted by a machine-shop owner. This would be a commercial risk. It is given to someone responsible for that function in that territory. Credit information about the insured, including a history of the operation's losses (the fewer the better), can be ordered by an "underwriter assistant"—a worker whose position in the insurance company hierarchy is between a policy typist (usually a woman) and an underwriter (still usually a man). With some exceptions, the underwriter assistants are women. When the description of the machine-shop owner's operations is complete, a decision whether or not to issue the policy is made. This decision is made according to cut-and-dried criteria. After categorizing the operation of the applicant—for instance, if the potential insured only wants liability insurance—the category (machine shop) can be looked up in a manual. The decision maker is practically told by the content of the manual whether or not to have the policy issued. The easier it is to categorize the risk, the lower down in terms of pay grades is the decision maker.

After the policy issuance is approved, the policy needs to be rated—that is, a premium must be established. On very large risks, this procedure may be performed by a more senior employee, but mostly a junior underwriter or an underwriter assistant does the rating. In many cases, procedures to determine insurance premiums have become standardized. This on-going tendency began in personal lines insurance, since there are only a few variables that determine the premium to be charged for such policies as automobile insurance (location, liability limits, age and make of car, and age, sex, and experience of the driver); the same is true for homeowners' policies (value of the house, limits of liability, location of the house, and the building's construction).

Underwriting assistants used to be called rating clerks. In the company I worked in the previously subdivided task of rating has been combined with several other tasks in an attempt to "humanize" the work of these relatively low-paid workers—worker's daily activities are deemed to be humanized when they become responsible for several routine tasks.* A double process is thus taking place within the insurance industry. First the underwriter's tasks are becoming more like those of the rating clerk, in that the underwriter is required to refer to various manuals to make insurance decisions. (Experienced underwriters often refused to submit to this reduction of their independent decision-making responsibilities by issuing policies without the requisite manual check; younger underwriters no longer get trained to do their work as independent decision makers. Fifteen years ago I went through a seventeen-week classroom training course. Today training for underwriters is either carried out on-the-job or in two-week classroom courses.) At the same time, already degraded tasks—those of the rating clerk, the letter writer, the general information gatherer, and the performers of several other tasks—are being combined by management into the responsibilities of a single employee according to recent management theories that combining tasks reduces worker boredom and increases worker productivity. There is therefore a contradictory process at work, one that disguises the general tendency of the degradation of clerical work by combining several degraded tasks to make the overall job appear "enriched"—without giving the worker any additional discretion over his or her own work.

When the insurance policy we have been following has been rated and the premium and conditions have been accepted by the insured, the policy is ready for final typing. For relatively simple insurance contracts, the underwriter assistant will have

* For a discussion of work humanization that goes well beyond its relation to the division and re-division of labor, see de Kadt 1977 and Zimbalist 1975.

written out a sample policy that will be typed by a policy typist. Many simple commercial insurance policies have not yet been, or do not readily lend themselves, to being computerized. Nevertheless, they are on printed forms that have blanks to be typed in. Changes in the printed forms are made by endorsements, which need to be specially prepared. They too are written out by the underwriter or underwriter assistant.

Policies for larger and more complex risks cannot be issued on already printed forms; too many changes in wording would be required. Exceptions to standard restrictive policy wording are noted on company forms by more highly paid underwriters. These changes in policy wording, which in effect give additional insurance coverage, sometimes need management approval. Auditing teams randomly check to see that the appropriate approvals have been received. When approved, these "tailored" policies are typed by magnetic card or tape machines with the appropriate special wording typed in manually as required. Today the cost of issuing tailored policies such as these has been sharply reduced because the work is performed by machine operators who receive less pay for each policy prepared than the typists who used to do the work. The revolution in clerical office work has done much to reduce the number of insurance policies that are actually typed by clerical employees. Policy-writing and letter writing is increasingly done on data- or word-processing machines.

The company used to hire a separate worker to check each typed form. It no longer does this, as mistakes are often caught by the insured. An errant typist can be identified because she has put her initials on each form she typed, and any typist who makes too many mistakes may not keep her dull job very long. Here quality control is both a control over clerical work and an attempt to keep costs down.

A copy of the finished policy gets sent to the insurance seller (in this and in many other insurance companies the insurance seller is not a company employee), who is responsible for finding policy errors. Other copies are distributed within the company to the billing clerk (the premium must be billed), to the local office files, and to the overseeing office files. The latter two are ostensibly used when policy changes are required or when losses occur, but each copy is also used to keep a check on the employees in the policy writing chain described above. Policies are often reviewed by managers before they are filed.

With the development of new office technology and the elimination of some tasks, each employee now handles a greater volume of work. This is the case even for those employees who use traditional methods to issue more complex policies. The company I worked for has had computer systems since 1959, but it is only in the last decade that these have been developed to the extent that much of the work of policy typing and rating has been eliminated. Today policies that have been sufficiently standardized (most personal lines, but only some commercial lines) are produced directly by computer. No longer are a rating clerk, a policy typist, a billing clerk, and a filing clerk required in the issuance of every policy. If a potential insured meets standardized criteria, he or she is approved for insurance by an employee still called an underwriter. Laird Cummings captures the elimination of decision making when he quotes four insurance company employees:

> "We have rules, memos, bulletins, and we follow that. We don't make our own decisions or rules."
>
> "Our decisions are knowing the rules."
>
> "There's not that much decision work because you have set rules you have to go by. The company makes your decisions."
>
> "There's really no decisions. We have pretty pat methods."
>
> (Cummings 1977:85)

After the company employee, using the standardized criteria, approves the issuance of the policy, the appropriate information is sent to a data-entry clerk. This employee enters the information into a computer terminal. The computer handles the rest, often including the mailing of the policy directly to the insured and to the insurance seller. Thereafter policy information is readily available from the nearest computer terminal in every company office. The speed of clerical work has again increased.

Standardization of work has not only permitted greater speed, but it has given management another point of control over the work performed. The greater the standardization of each task, the easier it is for management to count the work the employees do. The number of policies a data-entry clerk enters onto the computer can be compared to the number other clerks enter. The numbers of policies a file clerk files can be compared to that of other file clerks. Mail volume is often counted. The number of different kinds of insurance policies rated are tabulated. Even if a single employee performs several tasks, many of these are standardized, routine, and counted by management. Often work counts have been so heavily emphasized by management as a method of control that the workers have figured out ways to systematically overstate the amount of work performed. If, for example, the number of phone calls is being counted, the call-your-neighbor trick would count as two calls—one for each employee. Who is to say how many files a file clerk returns to the drawers? The different thicknesses of files, their different uses, their frequent misfiling (whether this is accidental or on purpose does not matter for the point being made) all render the file clerk's count a product of her own judgment. Thus the control of the work process is itself a contradictory process because the work (the newly standardized side-by-side with the more traditional) is done by people who react to its organization.

The Social Relations of Insurance Work

The contradictory process that characterizes the control of clerical work must be considered in conjunction with the control of the clerical workers themselves. A large corporation such as the one I worked for uses all sorts of informal control methods. Some are paternalistic, such as employee access to a company country club and a company-sponsored employee organization. Others have financial trappings, such as low-cost lunches in some of the company offices. All attempt to pull the employee into the company "family." Jean Tepperman explains it well:

> Enlightened companies are also advised by personnel experts to establish written policies to make employees feel they are being dealt with fairly—"according to the rules"—so they won't feel the need for the protection of an organized employee group. The company should make employees think that they are being listened to by establishing an employee-complaint "hotline" or suggestion system. One management text said that in the DuPont company "a special effort is made to encourage every person to come through with one suggestion that can be accepted. They feel that this will make a 'believer' out of him [sic] for life."
>
> Management training today stresses *motivating* employees, rather than just ordering them around. Giving the worker a sense of involvement. Some even set up student-council-type employee organizations, which get to decide weighty matters like what kind

of food to have for the Christmas party. Also imitating high school, one anti-union expert urged managers to turn the official company newspaper over to employees, so they wouldn't be as likely to start a protest newsletter.

The catch is the unilateral judgment. After all of the formal procedures and communications, it's still the boss who decided. And all the participation may just end up like the individually controlled thermostats rumored to be in Boston's old John Hancock building. You could adjust your own thermostat, all right—but it wasn't hooked up to anything. (Tepperman 1976:135)

Most of these management techniques are used by the company I worked for. In addition, this company promotes "participatory management." This is a program in which managers are supposed to consult employees about new programs they are about to initiate. Employee suggestions are supposed to be considered and integrated into the company's changing operations, to give employees a sense of participation. Management, however, only uses those employee suggestions that meet its goals, and most participatory management becomes a program in which managers call meetings to announce new methods of operation to employees and then, without regard to input received, change the operation as originally intended.

The social relations between the workers and the senior managers within the office I have been describing, and within most company offices, were rarely overtly antagonistic. Most of the employees were cooperative, and in fact were even eager to cooperate. Whenever an employee was hired who did not "fit in," he or she was soon fired—the ultimate form of control. This did not happen often because new employees were carefully screened. Most of my fellow workers all the way up and down the hierarchy were interested in having the satisfaction of doing their jobs well. This is not to say that no conflict existed. As long as workers have no direct interest in the tasks they perform, as long as they simply execute the conceptions of others, as long as the task or tasks they perform are repetitive, as long as the worker's interest is primarily in receiving some remuneration for time put in, as long as employers attempt to keep wages relatively low (long a characteristic of the insurance industry's clerical production line), then in spite of an individual's desire to do the work well, subtle reactions to production and profit pressures will set in. This certainly was the case in the offices in which I worked.

One of these reactions is to quit with the hope of finding something better. Corporations (and this insurance company is no exception) rely on the pink collar version of the revolving door—on what Louise Kapp Howe calls

> A&P [attrition and pregnancy] to keep . . . clerical salary levels down. Except for a select proportion—the cream—who were to be groomed . . . for somewhat higher roles, [the companies count] on the exit of many noncollege employees after several years and the entrance of new high school graduates to take their places at beginners' wages. (Howe 1977:152)

As long as there are a large number of young women applying for clerical work within these companies, management is not compelled to offer a living wage.

The revolving door is applied to males as well as females, to the college educated as well as the noncollege educated. It is applied in whatever manner seems appropriate for each category of worker. Low wages speed the revolving door: "You may think our salaries are low, but if you'll check you'll find they are at least competitive with those of other insurance companies in this city and usually they're higher. We keep in close touch, you know" (quoted in Howe 1977:167). That the average male clerical worker's wage is higher than the average female clerical worker's wage is clear. Sex discrimination in U. S. business is rampant, and is used by the company to keep wages down. But with the possible exception of the few who are groomed for somewhat higher roles—and there is room for only a very few—the male insurance clerical work force is also increasingly oppressed.

While I have not been able to get exact figures, the turnover of the underwriting staff during the eight years I worked for the company was high. Of the twenty-five or so men who went through the classroom training course with me, I was almost the last to leave; most had left within two years. Lateness and absenteeism are also rampant. Programs are often changed in an attempt to achieve better effect, but there never was an end to employee complaints. As long as wages stay low, the revolving door continues to turn.

But the revolving door does more than just keep wages down. As soon as one worker leaves a corporation, he or she is quickly replaced by someone who will be receiving a lower wage and who, because of increased job standardization and the use of electronic data processing, will require little training. Thus job deskilling makes turnover less costly to management. Furthermore, a lot is often lost by jumping employers—pension interests, vacation time, seniority, and the like. This often encourages employees to stay put, and is an additional control on those who do.

For those who choose to stick with one employer, it gets harder and harder to leave as time goes on. It soon becomes impossible to receive a higher wage by switching employers. I know many who have tried and who have resigned themselves to staying put, taking whatever annual increase "their" company will give them—an increase that is getting proportionally smaller all the time. These women and men become stopped in dead-end jobs in which they have no choice but to continue to work.

Control over clerical workers is reinforced by the stratification of job and wage categories according to alleged differences in the capacities of the employees. Only in such a highly articulated system of apparent skill differences carefully placed on a corporate hierarchy can so many employees be overseeing so many others. As we have already seen, the supervision of employees by employees in this company crosses rigid departmental and hierarchical lines. The supervision of each employee thus becomes multidimensional. That supervision includes, but is not limited to, the eyes of the manager behind glass, the prodding of the clock watcher in front of it, the corrections of fellow workers nowhere near glass, the observations of workers in other departments of the quality of work, and the review of work by local and distant reviewing authorities. The insurance company office is at once a highly integrated system of work in which the ability of one employee to function well depends on the willing cooperation of many others, and a system in which the workers are carefully and consciously separated from each other because their work is organized in such a way that they remain separated, each worker doing his or her part of the whole.

Men and women clerical workers in the insurance industry have a lot in common, yet they are kept apart from each other as groups and from each other as individuals. What this contradiction will mean over a long period is unclear. Until now there has been very little unionization in the world of insurance clerical work, although clerical workers as a whole have been organizing (Lublin 1978; Tepperman 1976:94–115), but most of that organization has been by and among women. With more and more clerical workers crowded into large corporations, the social relations among workers and between workers and management are bound to change.

Increased Productivity: A General Management Goal

Management's attempts to control the clerical work process and clerical workers in the insurance industry, while particular to that industry also have relevance to clerical workers in other industries. The meaning of the words processed by workers in different industries may change but the methods of processing words and the workers' reactions to those methods are similar. A study by the Department of Health, Education, and Welfare, discussing "white collar woes," says the following:

> The office today, where work is segmented and authoritarian, is often a factory. For a growing number of jobs, there is little to distinguish them but the color of the worker's collar: computer keypunch operations and typing pools share much in common with the automobile assembly-line.
>
> Secretaries, clerks, and bureaucrats were once grateful for having been spared the dehumanization of the factory. White-collar jobs were rare; they had higher status than blue-collar jobs. But today the clerk, and not the operative on the assembly-line, is the typical American worker, and such positions offer little in the way of prestige. Furthermore, the size of the organizations that employ the bulk of office workers has grown, imparting to the clerical worker the same impersonality that the blue-collar worker experiences in the factory. The organization acknowledges the presence of the worker only when he [sic] makes a mistake or fails to follow a rule, whether in a factory or bureaucracy, whether under public or private control. (HEW 1973:38–39)

The insurance workplace is only one office to which this description applies.

Control over clerical work is a general management concern. The factory-like atmosphere of bank check clearance operations and of the back office in stock brokerage firms is well known. Telephone supervisors are known to eavesdrop on employees' phone calls, a form of control ostensibly "solely for the purposes of business service improvement" (J. Montgomery 1974). The open floor of the insurance company renders eavesdropping by senior managers unnecessary, but it is just as effective.

The control over the clerical labor process and over clerical workers in the insurance factory, although increasingly aided by the introduction of new machinery and new divisions of labor, remains one of control by humans over other humans. Historical changes in the forms and technology of management control over clerical work show that work systems themselves can be changed. There is no one way to process information. The clerical work factory has been designed to keep down the cost of record keeping while maintaining control over the workers who keep records.

Fighting the Piece-Rate System: New Dimensions of an Old Struggle in the Apparel Industry

Louise Lamphere

The apparel industry, or the "needle trades," provides an example *par excellence* of a labor-intensive, low-wage industry where women make up a large proportion of the labor force. Most of the women are employed in production, which is 80 percent female, and are paid on an incentive or "piece-rate" basis. The impact of technology has been, and will probably continue to be, low, especially as it affects women workers. Instead, workers have had to deal with two other issues: the tendency of this and other labor-intensive industries to "run away" to areas of cheaper labor, and the continuation of the piece-rate system within the context of increasing centralization of production and new strategies to "improve management techniques" (U. S. Bureau of Labor Statistics (BLS) 1977a:4). The reactions and counterstrategies of women workers and union locals to these recent trends will provide the focus for this paper. Much of my analysis will concentrate on data gathered on the shop floor of a New England apparel plant. However, to set the stage for this analysis I will first examine long-term characteristics and recent changes in the industry as a whole.

Long-Term Characteristics of the Apparel Industry

The major technological innovation that made mass production of clothing possible and that still structures production was the invention of the sewing machine by Elias Howe in 1846 and its improvement by Issak Singer a few years later (Seidman 1942:15). This facilitated the transfer of tailoring from the

---

This paper is based on research funded by the NIMH Center for the Study of Metropolitan Studies, Grant No. 1 RO1 MH27363, "Women, Work, and Ethnicity in an Urban Setting."

home to the factory, increased the use of semiskilled workers who sewed by machine, and replaced the hand-tailoring of more skilled workers.

With the inexpensive and portable sewing machine at the center of the industry, it takes relatively little capital to set up an apparel shop—only $50,000 in 1974 (NACLA 1977:6). The key to success is not continual investment in new plant and equipment, but style creativity and merchandizing (Helfgott 1959:25). As a result, the industry has since its early days been characterized by a division between "inside shops" or manufacturers (who perform all the steps of the process, including designing, purchasing fabric, cutting, sewing, and selling) and "outside shops" or contractors who sew already-cut garments received from a jobber and return the finished garments to the jobber to be sold (see Levine 1924: Ch. 2 for an early history of this division).

In the late nineteenth and early twentieth centuries, these outside shops were called "sweat shops" because they were located in tenements on the Lower East Side of New York City where unsanitary conditions, long hours, and extremely low wages prevailed (see Levine 1924: Ch. 4; Seidman 1942: 56–60; Zaretz 1934: Ch. 2 for a description of conditions). Unionization and government regulation have reduced a number of the evils of the "sweat shop," but small production units, the contracting system, and lower wages with poorer conditions in smaller shops have persisted. As late as 1972, 50 percent of the firms employed less than twenty workers and only 14.3 percent employed over 100 (U. S. Department of Commerce 1976: vol. 1, p. 23, Table 5).

Easy entry has created a highly competitive industry: there were 24,428 apparel establishments in 1972. Competitiveness is exacerbated by the importance of style change and seasonality. In branches producing more standardized products (such as bras and underwear), employment fluctuates by 27.8 percent between the peak and off seasons, while in establishments producing women's suits, coats, and dresses, employment may fluctuate as much as 132 percent (Helfgott 1959:41).

Seasonality is seen by some authors as a product of the "buying habits of the public" or the "whims of fashion-conscious American women" (ibid.:41, 57). However, it is clear that the apparel industry has expanded its market through seasonal and yearly changes in fashion; the need to be "fashionably dressed" is a major factor in the "planned obsolescence" of clothing in a capitalist economy. In some socialist economies (e.g., China), clothing has become more standardized and is worn until it is outgrown or worn out, not until it has "gone out of style." Hence the capitalist mode of production itself may provide the prerequisites for keeping the industry attuned to changes in fashion; this in turn creates small production units, short production runs, and fierce competition.

The industry is currently organized into several branches. More than 35 percent of the workers are engaged in making clothing for men and boys, about 30 percent produce women's outerwear, and 22 percent make women's and children's undergarments, children's outerwear, hats, caps, and millinery and fur goods. Another 12 percent turn out curtains and housefurnishings (BLS 1969:14). There is a strict sexual division of labor in all branches. Women were employed in cutting operations until the cutting knife replaced shears during the 1870s, and men have dominated this skilled work ever since. Men are employed as sewing machine operators, but primarily in men's clothing and suits. Women are mainly sewing machine operators (sewers and stitchers), occupying 90 percent of these jobs (BLS 1977a:8). Recent wage surveys of subdivisions of the industry show that men are cutters, spreaders, machine repairmen, and janitors, while women are machine operators, baggers and boxers, garment folders, thread trimmers, basting pullers, final inspectors, and under pressers (BLS 1971:3; BLS 1974:3).

There are substantial wage differences between the sexes. Between 1971 and 1976 women in three branches of the industry earned between $.36 and $1.02 an hour less than men (BLS 1971:2; BLS 1974:3; BLS 1977b:4). Wages for women are based on a piece-rate system and tend to hover around the minimum wage, especially in the less unionized branches of the industry. For example, in 1974, when the minimum wage was $2.00 per hour, women sewing machine operators averaged $2.59 an hour in the trousers industry while male cutters and markers averaged over $3.00 an hour and sewing machine adjusters earned $3.80 an hour (BLS 1974:3). In the more heavily unionized suit-and-coat branch of the industry, women sewers earned an average of $3.74-$3.88 an hour in 1976 while male cutters earned $5.64 an hour (BLS 1977b:5, 10).

The History of the Piece-Rate System

Given the low-profit, labor-intensive, and highly competitive nature of the industry, the apparel manufacturer has always sought to get as much work out of the workers as possible. The piece-rate system has been the main method of keeping production high. The piece-rate system had its beginning in the "task-system" of the 1870s (Zaretz 1934:34). A team made up of a machine sewer, a baster, and a finisher was paid by the "task," that is, a specific number of garments. Weekly wages were cut and hours lengthened by sweat-shop employers by increasing the number of garments in a "task," until it became difficult to complete even four or five tasks a week (Seidman 1941:4) Early strikes attempted to abolish the task and contracting systems, and to substitute a weekly wage. In 1919–1920 the three major unions were able to establish weekly wages in their major contracts.* Some contracts retained piecework, however, and a "log" or schedule system replaced the old task system. Each type of garment was divided into working parts with rates fixed on each part. During the 1920s the unions lost the battle to eliminate piecework, since an expanding number of small, nonunion shops paid piece rates and severely threated the unionized sectors of the industry (Carpenter 1972:103). The unions were willing to accept responsibility for establishing "standards of production" for those workers paid on a weekly basis, but they were never able to convince management that the workers would produce a "commensurate" amount of work under weekly pay. By the mid-1930s the return to piecework was virtually total.

Unions, especially the Amalgamated Clothing Workers of America (ACWA) under the leadership of Sidney Hillman, came to believe that they should control the piece-rate system rather than abolish it. This was a natural outgrowth of the policy of "union-management" cooperation which saw unionized workers allied with "responsible" manufacturers against nonunionized

* The three major unions are the craft-oriented United Garment Workers, the Amalgamated Clothing Workers of America (ACWA), which split off from the UGW and organized the men's clothing branch of the industry, and the International Ladies Garment Workers Union (ILGWU), which organized the women's garment industry. In June 1976 the ACWA merged with the Textile Workers Union of America (TWUA) to form the Amalgamated Clothing and Textile Workers Union (ACTWU).

segments of the industry (ibid.:43–45). Hillman argued that the union should support the "efficiency" of union shops since "inefficiency" (lower production and higher wages) would eliminate the employer altogether. As an AWCA publication suggested, "If the firm makes a good profit, the workers are in a better position to ask for a raise. When the employer goes out of business, the workers lose their jobs. The success of the business is something which both the employer and the union consider of first importance" (ACWA 1941:25).

Retention of the piece rate and endorsement of "scientific management" became the policy of both the ILGWU and the ACWA. Both unions hired outside efficiency experts and proposed industrywide piece rate schemes. For example, the ILGWU adopted a "unit system" of piece rates whereby each operation was rated according to the style and difficulty of the operation, in turn determined by timing individual operators.

Although the piece rate is now a fixture of every garment shop, worker suspicion of management's use of piece rates has persisted. Women sewers, like their predecessors in the early period of unionization, feel that the system can be used against them. They realize that it induces individuals to "speed up," which causes fatigue, promotes individualism rather than collectivism among the workers, can be used to shorten the season since it encourages workers to get the work out faster and earlier, and by setting times by the faster workers can be used to cut rates, hence lowering the wage. I will discuss the way women workers struggle against these management tactics below.

Recent Changes in the Industry

There has been a tendency for the apparel industry to move out of high-wage areas, as well as to introduce techniques for simplifying production and for further separating the design and sales functions from production. The first phase of this trend was the move out of New York City to Long Island and the surrounding states of Pennsylvania, New Jersey, and Connecticut, which began with the standardization of women's clothing in the 1920s and continued with the post-World War II shift to more informal dress. These changes made it possible to mass-produce garments through "section work," splitting production into smaller operations (e.g., sewing shoulder seams, setting sleeves, hemming), each done by a different machine operator. Skilled tailors and hand sewers were eliminated and contractors were able to move to the cheap female labor force (Helfgott 1959:76, 82). Jobbers and manufacturers remained in New York City, where proximity to design centers and markets was crucial.

A more recent movement has been to the southern states (NACLA 1977), the U. S.-Mexican border area (NACLA 1975), and low-wage Asian countries. Between 1950 and 1973 the proportion of the apparel industry located in the Northeast declined from 62.3 percent to 35.7 percent, while in the South it increased from 16.7 percent to 44.2 percent (NACLA 1977:11). By 1973, there were 103 garment shops operating along the Mexican border, although both the entry and failure rate of firms is very high (NACLA 1975:15).*

This second wave of migration has also been accompanied by changes in the organization of production. Southern shops tend to be larger, often over 250 employees (BLS 1971:2), and the "progressive bundle" system is used more frequently. Under this system, bundles of garments flow in a logical order from one operator to another, which is much more efficient than the older "line system" (treating garments separately) and "bundle system" (where there is no logical spatial organization of the operators) (ibid.:2).

The Role of Technology

Although apparel is the least mechanized of all manufacturing industries, there have been significant technological innovations

* Lower wages were clearly the major reason for the move. In 1974, workers in New York State earned an average of $3.69 per hour while workers in the South earned between $2.53 and $2.68. In the men's coat and suit industry, workers in the mid-Atlantic region, including New York City, earned $4.26 an hour while in the Southeast (Kentucky and Georgia) they earned an average of $3.20 an hour (BLS 1977b:8). Workers in the Northeast generally receive eight or more paid holidays, while workers in the Southeast receive six or less (NACLA 1977:13). Rates of unionization are low in the South, due to "right to work" laws. In the Northeast, the industry is 80–90 percent organized, but it is only 25–30 percent organized in the Southeast (ibid.:16; BLS 1971:2). Even within the South there are $.32 to $.35 wage differentials between unionized and nonunionized plants.

Fighting the Piece-Rate System 263

in the last few years in the areas of cutting, sewing, and sales/distribution.

In cutting, new computer-guided laser systems rapidly and precisely cut fifty layers of cloth at a time. Laser systems and numerically controlled cutting devices have been implemented only in larger shops, primarily in the men's suit industry where material is costly and accuracy is important. Nevertheless, they represent a clear assault on the more highly paid men's jobs, a strategy for reducing the wage bill of larger firms (BLS 1977a: 2–3).

Most sewing innovations have centered around eliminating the most skilled part of the work: guiding the material through the machine at an extremely fast pace. Sewers only spend 20 percent of their time actually sewing; the rest is spent handling the garment (ibid.:4). A few devices (like thread cutters, parts stackers, needle positioners, and button feeders) have been added to the machines to eliminate some of this work.

More substantial changes take place with the introduction of numerically controlled sewing machines. Here the machine is computer-programmed to sew a particular operation, the stitcher becomes a machine loader and fabric positioner able to tend more than one machine at a time. Training takes less time on these machines, a clear indication that the job is "deskilled." Machines already installed have eliminated jobs as well. For example, an automated button sewing system has increased production from 190 dozen pieces to 330 dozen pieces a day and a tape-controlled machine that sews shirt collars can attain the same level of output with 64 percent fewer workers (ibid.:4).

In the apparel plant where I worked, tape-controlled machines were used in the embroidery department. The operator's job was to load and set a device controlling a whole row of machines that embroidered a design on ten to twelve garments simultaneously. In the sewing department, a device was in the planning stages that would eliminate the most tricky and skilled operation performed in attaching collars. It would guide the collar and neck opening through the sewing machine, leaving the stitcher to load and unload the machine.

A final innovation is "sonic sewing" where a wheel or "horn" vibrates the fabrics at such high speeds that they are fused together (ibid.:4). The cloth used must have a high percentage of synthetic content in order to be fusable, but the technique is already being used on labels, linings, and short seams.

The Bureau of Labor Statistics predicts that these innovations will be limited to larger plants and/or clothes made of a high synthetic content. But with the use of PROMs (Programmable Read Only Memory Units)—computer-controlled mini-memory units that can be attached to individual machines—some of the machine-guided systems may become more widespread (ibid.:4).

More important is the use of computers in sales and distribution. By 1974, 297 computers had been installed for sales analysis, processing inventory, and work flow management (ibid.:4). There was a reduction of the apparel labor force of 200,000 workers in 1974–1975, bringing the industry total to 1.2 million, down from 1.4 million in 1969. The BLS predicts a rise in the work force to previous levels, but increased numbers of jobs will be in sales, management, and professional categories, not among operatives and craft workers (ibid.:9).

The BLS also suggests that the companies are centralizing production and assembly—for example, by doing the cutting in one plant and sewing the garments in another. It also notes a trend toward shipping cut parts to low-wage areas in foreign countries where they are assembled and sent back to the United States for marketing. As part of this centralization, "increased emphasis has been placed on raising productivity through improved management techniques. Work flow studies for determining plant layout, and time and motion studies to optimize the arrangement of machines and operators, are being applied more widely in apparel plants" (ibid.:4–5). Despite these developments, the piece-rate system is likely to be a fixture in the industry for at least the next decade.

Scientific Management and the Piece Rate: A Case Study

The center of the struggle between workers and management in the garment industry revolves around the way work is organized and how the piece-rate system is implemented—old issues that have persisted in modernized form. The dialectical relationship between new management policies and worker response is best seen through an examination of the work situation itself. During 1977 I worked for five months as a trainee sewer for a children's outerwear manufacturer in New England, and I also spent several weeks in the firm's computerized distribution center, filling orders and pinning garments preparatory to boxing. My experiences provide data as to how recent changes in the garment industry have affected the attitudes and behavior of women workers.

The plant was established in a New England industrial town in the 1930s, although the main offices remained in New York, creating the territorial division between production and design/sales noted earlier. The company had a reputation for being a sweatshop, especially in the 1930s when sewers were paid $3.50 a week until the NRA mandated weekly salaries of $13. As one Polish worker reported,

> "Oh yes, that was a sweat shop. I was underpaid. You had to put out a lot of garments to make your rate—that was on piecework, you know. They make money like that—the company—they make millions. They could've paid us better. I worked there so long; you think they'd give me something for workin' there so long—nothin', not even a good watch." (After her retirement in 1978 and 29 years of work for the company.)*

The plant was organized in 1951 by the Amalgamated Clothing Workers. The union contract negotiates piece rates, protects jobs (since laid-off union members are the first to be recalled), guarantees seniority, and provides small pensions and a medical-care program. Workers get three weeks' vacation (paid as a percentage of wages earned), in addition to eight paid vacation days and a paid birthday.

In the past ten years there have been two important changes in the company. First, as the paternalistic owner reached retirement age, he sold out to a large conglomerate. The company was already in the process of expanding, having added a plant in Virginia and a distribution center (warehouse) in New England, but the conglomerate increased the productive capacity of the company by 50 percent, starting a sewing plant in Alabama, a knitting mill in New England, and a sewing operation in Puerto Rico.

Second, as increasing numbers of older workers retired from this particular plant, management hired recent Portuguese and Latin American immigrants to New England to replace them.

* Oral interview with Mrs. S. conducted on July 22, 1978, by Eva Houser of Johns Hopkins University as part of her dissertation research.

The sewing departments were characterized by the personnel manager as "predominantly Portuguese." "They are the backbone of our sewing operation," he commented.

The Organization of Production

The plant is located in a three-story brick mill building and has a number of conveniences that make it one of the better workplaces in the town in which it is located. Cutting is done on the third floor and the offices are on the first floor. The heart of the sewing operation takes place on the second floor, where there are seven departments; three additional departments are on the third floor and two at the back of first floor.

At first sight the room seems chaotic—filled with sewing machines all rapidly whirring away, chutes of cut and partially sewn garments, and between 200 and 300 women. However, there is order in the chaos. Each department stretches across the large room with a central aisle bifurcating it. Work comes down from the cutting room in large wooden trolleys and is placed at the "back" of a department, near one set of windows. Sewing machines are set up in rows of three or four from back to front, though some rows run crossways. The work is cut in "lots" of 80–120 dozen garments, and the lots are further divided into bundles of 2½ or 5 dozen garments. The "progressive bundle" system is used. All the parts of a garment are tied in the same bundle, with a "ticket" that specifies the "operations" that have to be done to complete the garment. Each operation has a number and each style of garment has a rate for each operation. For example, I was trained to do Operation 37, "set sleeves," and the piece rates varied depending on the size of the garment in the bundle and whether it was a dress or polo shirt.

At the row of machines close to the "back" of the department, women perform the first operations in the process (shoulder seams, neck bindings, collars). As the work progresses toward the "front," labels are attached, and the tops and bottoms of girls' dresses are joined. Next the sleeves are set and the sides are seamed. Finally, across the center aisle, the garments are hemmed, pressed, folded, and pinned. They are then taken off the floor to be boxed and sent to the distribution center, where shirts and pants are assembled into outfits and orders from across the country are filled.

The Piece-Rate System

The piece-rate system used in this plant is a variation of the "unit system," but is based on a complex decimal system that is both easy to computerize and baffling to the workers since it is not clearly related to the garments bundled in dozens or to minutes that show on the wall clocks. The hour is divided into 100 parts and the rates calculated accordingly. For example, 10 minutes is really .167 of an hour, and a piece rate of .073 means that an operation must be performed on a dozen garments in 4.38 minutes if a sewer is to earn the *base rate* of $3.31 per hour on which the piece rates are figured. Workers are guaranteed the minimum wage ($2.30 an hour, or $92 a week, in 1977), but they can earn above that if the dozens of garments finished throughout the week average more. This is called a worker's "piece-work average." For example, the rate on "set sleeves" ranges from .068 for sleeves on small boys' polo shirts to .089 on little girls' dresses, with some very difficult shirred sleeves having a rate of .106. If the rate is .073, a sewer must complete a dozen garments (setting two sleeves in each) every 6.3 minutes and 76 dozen garments a day in order to earn the minimum wage. To earn $3.30 an hour ($132 a week), a sewer had to complete 110 dozen garments a day.

The Training Program

The firm's training program is an excellent example of the recent industry trend toward centralizing production and improving management techniques. The program was initiated in January 1976 as part of conglomerate policy and has apparently standardized training in northern as well as southern plants.

Each of the "operations" has been categorized into "A," "B," and "C" jobs. A sewer can be trained for an "A" job (neck binding, collars, sleeve bindings) in six weeks, for a "B" job (labeling) in twelve weeks, and for a "C" job (set sleeves, seam sides, hemming) in eighteen weeks. An efficiency curve for each type of job indicates the percent efficiency a sewer must attain each week in order to become 100 percent efficient at the end of the training period. For setting sleeves this meant producing 110 dozen pairs of set sleeves a day after four and a half months.

A training department is directed by a second-generation Portuguese woman who has had years of experience as a "floor lady" or department supervisor.* Under her are three young bilingual first-generation Portuguese women who do the actual instruction, in either Portuguese or English. The supervisor has worked out a "method" for each task, a series of steps that the instructor shows the trainee, including where to place the pieces of the garment, how to pick them up, how to sew them, and how to stack them in a pile afterward. On the first day, one of the instructors shows the girls how to "control," thread, and sew simple seams on an industrial machine. She gives each trainee a series of timed tests that involve sewing circles and zigzags (without thread in the machine); she gives dexterity and shape perception tests as well. On the basis of these tests and the needs of the departments, she assigns a girl to an "A," "B," or "C" job.

On the second day, girls are assigned to their operation and have met their future floor ladies. Since I was learning to set sleeves, I was trained on a "merrow machine"—a three-needle machine that sews a "bound seam" as it cuts off excess material. Both the preliminary instructor and a second instructor showed me how to set sleeves, first on "dummies" (garments not used in production) and then on "real work" brought from my future department. Despite the elaborate paper work of the training program, teaching is by demonstration, not by verbal or written instruction. There is a tremendous amount of hand/eye coordination in sewing, and these techniques seem best communicated by watching a skilled sewer.

By the end of the first week, a girl is usually put into her

---

* The training program uses the "scientific management" terminology of "supervisor," "training center instructor," and "production manager." These terms have not supplanted those used in the workplace itself, such as calling the workers "girls" ("old girls" and "new girls," or recent employees). Supervisors are "floor ladies" and the managers are "bosses." I have used the word "girl" instead of woman since it is the term used by the women on the shop floor.

department, depending on how well she is doing and whether there is a machine ready for her. The training supervisor told me I now knew how to do the job, and it would be good to get out in the department and "feel the pressure" of everyone working under the piece-rate system. The mechanic who adjusted my machine as I moved into my new department said, "Now you are in the zoo. Back there [in the training room] it's nice and quiet, but out here there's all the noise and talk—a real zoo."*

A girl's work is monitored each day by an instructor. If errors are found by other workers or by quality-control checkers, the instructor is called in to help with repairs and supervise the trainee more closely. The dozens completed per day are noted before quitting time, and the next morning the instructor marks the girl's progress on an efficiency chart tied to her machine. If her improvement falls below the efficiency line on the chart, the instructor suggests techniques for improvement. When the trainee seems to be making the minimum wage (about 70 percent efficiency), and *if* she is still on the job, she is given a certificate for completing the program and is transferred to the supervision of the department floor lady. If she has worked for ninety days, she is enrolled in the union.

The training program streamlines production and brings work under the supervision of management in the following ways.

(1) By using the skill of trained sewers (like the head of the training program), the motions of the sewers are rationalized. Since 80 percent of a sewer's time goes into nonsewing motions, this is a direct attempt on management's part to raise production by reducing this portion of the work. Each trainee is supposed to learn an operation the same way. There is some resistance to this on the part of sewers, since they incorporate their own "tricks" into their routines and so speed up their work, and there is often a struggle between an instructor and an "old girl" when an instructor is assigned to teach an experienced employee how to

---

* Marx, in the first volume of *Capital* (1967:326), notes that merely bringing workers together creates greater production since "mere social contact begets in most industries an emulation and a stimulation of the animal spirits that heighten the efficiency of each individual workman." Marx also provides an interesting and insightful analysis of the English apparel industry in the mid-nineteenth century (ibid.:447–59).

do "correctly" an operation she has been performing for several years.

(2) The close supervision of trainees (e.g., the use of time clocks and efficiency charts) pushes the new employee to work faster until she is able to pace herself solely through the operation of the piece-rate system and the incentive of "making money" (factory vocabulary for making over the minimum wage).

(3) The training program uses bilingual instructors and is thus an extremely effective way of integrating Portuguese workers into the production system, especially since most floor ladies do not speak Portuguese. Once a girl has learned the job, there is less need to communicate to her, and when the need arises a nearby bilingual worker can interpret.

(4) The program cuts down on worker conflict by slowly integrating the new worker into production and by providing a neutral person outside the department authority system—the instructor—to act as mediator if the trainee makes mistakes that affect the work of others (and cause their day's wages to decline). It also takes the burden of close supervision off the floor lady, who has a great deal else to do.

(5) Finally, and most importantly, the training program controls the turnover rate in a nondisruptive way. There is a high turnover rate in the apparel industry (BLS 1969:16), and workers are often hired at peak seasons and let go a few weeks later. Trainees may even be used for pinning and boxing when orders must be completed, an indication that these women are an accessible surplus labor force. The testing and close supervision reveal those girls who are willing to "stick with" the job. A large number of trainees quit after a few weeks: some rebel against the supervision, others find it difficult to attain any speed, others feel they can find better jobs, and still others have difficulty with family responsibilities (such as arranging babysitters). Trainees are the first to be laid off in a slack period, and many do not return when production picks up again.

Thus the training program is a major attempt by the firm to regulate a fluctuating labor force and to control the work process more directly. That an informal method of teaching and that learning individualized "tricks" and skills persist indicates how difficult it is for management to totally rationalize and deskill important aspects of sewing.

On the Shop Floor: Fighting the Piece-Rate System

Within a particular department, especially among experienced workers, there are other signs of resistance to management control of production and attempts to protect their collective interests. The work force is divided along age and ethnic lines; language and cultural differences have created barriers to communication between Portuguese and non-Portuguese workers. Though some women are relatively isolated, most get together in informal groups of two to five co-workers at breaks and lunch hour, but there is relatively little crossing of Portuguese/non-Portuguese lines in these groups.

All workers, however, face the same conditions. Despite the "deskilling" of sewing, the women are conscious that their work is skilled, involving a great deal of hand/eye coordination, dexterity, attention, and, above all, speed. As my sewing instructor said on my first day, "Not anybody can do this work—sewing. You have to have patience. It's almost as if the machine can tell if you are too nervous or too impatient."

The women are also aware that they are being paid low wages. I explained to two of the older workers that I had been told that the base rate was $3.31 per hour, which I would be making in three or four months. An Italian woman snapped back, "I've been here ten years, and I don't make that!" A French Canadian woman said, "You tell them that if an old girl who's been here twenty-two years can't make it, then you can't do it."

On the one hand, the piece-rate system forces the sewer to work as rapidly as possible without making a mistake. On the other hand, because of the way in which management enforces the system, the women are under constant threat of being further underpaid (if the rates drop) or even eliminated (if styles are simplified or operations eliminated).

Women deal with the piece-rate system in several ways. First, they keep careful track of how many dozen pieces they have sewn each day and keep a sharp eye out for rates that are too low for the difficulty of the style. Second, they watch that cutting-room mistakes are not blamed on individuals and that individuals are treated fairly by the floor lady or the training instructor. In some instances, women cover over for mistakes of others or "just let the work go through," so that a woman will not lose wages by having to do the work over.

Both Portuguese and non-Portuguese women expressed their awareness of the skilled nature of their work and complained of low pay and of policies that had the effect of lowering wages. Although few Portuguese women are active in the union leadership, both Portuguese and non-Portuguese women seem equally supportive of the union. But there are tensions between the two groups. The attitudes and behavior of Portuguese immigrants are slightly different from those of their co-workers who come from groups with a longer history in New England. The Portuguese women's response to work is a product of contradictory forces that are an outcome of their rural, small-holder backgrounds (in the Azores and on the Continent) and the socializing pressures of the workplace itself. On the one hand, management hires Portuguese workers because of their reputation as hard workers, and the Portuguese fulfill the expectation. This leads some of the other workers to see the Portuguese women as working too hard, sometimes cutting corners to keep their wages up or engaging in "rate busting." "She never misses a penny," one woman commented about an Azorean woman in my department. A co-worker commented that the same woman "ruined that job for everyone" by working so fast that the piece rate on the job was lowered and the workers had to increase their output to make the same pay. "And she makes more than anyone on the floor" was the final comment. On the other hand, the Portuguese women often feel discriminated against and say that the Americans do not work hard enough. Non-Portuguese, who have their own prejudices, may accept preferential treatment by mangement or act in other ways to segregate themselves from Portuguese workers.

There are, however, informal institutions that cut across ethnic lines and bring the workers together. These include wedding and baby showers and retirement parties, which are organized along department lines and which express solidarity and good feeling among workers. Equally important is an informal set of work rules that makes sure the work is equally shared and that "rate busting" is kept at a minimum. While the economic situation and background of long, hard work pushes the Portuguese women to be "rate busters," there are important socializing pressures to act in a less individualistic manner. Newcomers to a shop floor, including new immigrants, are socialized to these rules, and they are enforced by both Portuguese and non-Portuguese workers.

One of the clearest examples occurred among those of us in my department who were setting sleeves on little girls' dresses. There was an informal rule that everyone should "work by sizes": each sewer should work on a bundle of small-sized sleeves (size 4) and then the largest size (6X), and finally sizes 6 and 5. In this way, no one ends up doing all of the larger sizes, while another girl makes more money by working faster on the smaller sizes. A newly arrived continental Portuguese girl was the center of conflict for several days because she was observed leaving the large sizes. Her instructor and the head of the training department (both Portugmese) were brought in to explain the "rules" to her, and her co-workers also spoke to her. Even women who had jobs adjacent to us (including a Brazilian and an Azorean) were interested in seeing that the work was fairly distributed and explained the situation, urging her to change her behavior. When another continental Portuguese woman, fairly new to the department, returned from vacation and pulled over a chute of dresses to her machine without looking to see if she had taken a disproportionate number of small-sized bundles, she too was told to "work by sizes" (by the Brazilian woman and a third Portuguese-speaking woman, an Azorean). In both instances, because the women knew little English, Portuguese-speaking women communicated and enforced the rules; in cases involving English speakers (like myself), other non-Portuguese women participated more directly. In the course of time, the Portuguese women learn to defer less to the bosses and to be wary of management decisions.

New Management Policies and the Role of the Union

While workers on the shop floor are conscious of recent management tactics, important issues may not emerge as part of an overall pattern until they reach the attention of the union through individual grievance procedures or at monthly meetings. Both workers and the union business agent are clear about the difference between dealing with the old paternalistic management and the new conglomerate. For example, while the business agent felt that the old company "owed us something," he characterized the new management as a "cold-blooded corporation" that lacked compassion for workers and "was concerned only with the dollar sign."

In 1977, management attempts to erode the position of the workers focused on three areas. First, the company wanted to set piece rates without calculating in a 20 percent allowance to make up for fatigue and the need for a rest. It maintained that this was already built into the piece rates in use. The union insisted that the company had timed a girl and then multiplied the hour's production by an eight-hour day, without making the 20 percent reduction. The company admitted that it felt that wages of over $4.00 an hour indicated "inflated rates" and so justified its attempt to re-time and lower the rates. The union hired an engineer and was able to raise the rates on set sleeves by about 10 percent, a temporary victory for the union in an area of constant conflict.

A second set of issues has remained unresolved and focuses on the operation of the new distribution center. The workers complained that the number of stockmen had been cut back and that they were being pressed to work harder with closer supervision. In addition, the company policy of hiring temporary workers through employment agencies was reducing the possibility that sewers could transfer to the more highly paid "order picking" jobs at the warehouse and was at the same time keeping a segment of the labor force out of the union.

A third and crucial set of issues centered on "full employment" for the sewers at the main plant. As part of an agreement with the union, workers at the main New England sewing facility are to get full employment during slack seasons while workers from newer plants in the South are to be laid off first. At the end of spring season production in March 1977, a number of sewers were laid off. It was not until later that the union discovered that other shops in Maine had work, while in Georgia workers were employed, though not full time. The production manager admitted that 5000 dresses had been cut at the New England plant, sent to Georgia, and then sent out to a contractor (presumably at lower wage rates). In the meantime, New England pieceworkers had been out five, six, or seven weeks. The union took this to arbitration. The company argued that it tried to spread the work evenly, and that the "full employment agreement" had been negotiated with the original management twenty-five years ago and did not hold for today's situation.

All of these examples indicate ways in which an expanding

apparel company can move to cut its labor costs while at the same time centralizing production and distribution. As the case study shows, the firm is following trends in the industry as a whole, often doing so through day-to-day shifts in policy that slowly erode the power of the union and require careful watchfulness on the part of the workers if their position within the production process is not to be threatened. Lowering the piece rates on particular operations and resisting union attempts to raise them, cutting the permanent labor force at the distribution center in favor of hiring temporary help through an agency, and slowly sending work to the South are all part of the same management strategy to cut labor costs and increase profits.

Conclusions

I have argued here that although there have been important technological innovations in the apparel industry, their application to large sectors of the industry has been retarded by its highly competitive, seasonal nature under a capitalist economy. Thus the industry has remained labor-intensive, utilizing a large pool of low-paid female workers mainly as sewing machine operators. It is just this quality of labor intensiveness that has led to the phenomenon of the runaway shop, as employers have sought cheaper labor in the South, in the Carribean and Mexican border areas, and in Asia.

For those workers who remain, their struggle has not centered around the threat of technological innovations, but around an old struggle in this industry—the administration of the piece-rate system which employers have always used to increase productivity (by making workers work faster) and to increase competition for higher wages. This struggle has taken on new forms through more efficient techniques of scientific management. Historically, production was first split into smaller and smaller units through the advent of "section work" and the elimination of the task system where several workers completed a whole garment. More recently, operations continue to be divided; for example, setting sleeves and sewing sides become separate tasks done by two groups of workers. At the same time other operations are eliminated and garments are simplified. In addition, piece rates are now calculated through complicated, yet easily computerized, systems, and training programs are used to rationalize a sewer's movements and train her to monitor herself in increasing her production.

Workers have evolved a number of strategies to deal with the piece-rate system, ranging from keeping close track of their own work, protesting against rates which seem unfair, and constructing a set of informal work rules which reduce "rate busting" and spread work evenly. Apparel unions are in a weakened position, since movement to southern "right to work" states has reduced union membership and leverage against individual companies. However, union locals try to fight management tactics, and workers continue to struggle against scientific management, working out formal and informal ways of protecting their jobs, their pay, and their skills.

The Piece Rate:
Class Struggle on the Shop Floor.
Evidence from the Costume Jewelry Industry in Providence, Rhode Island

Nina Shapiro-Perl

Introduction

When standing alongside such industrial giants as automobiles, rubber, steel, electronics, or mining, the costume jewelry industry is dwarfed in comparison. In 1972 it employed 21,400 workers across the country, with 43 percent of the industry's shipments coming from Rhode Island (Seltzer 1976: Appendix). While costume jewelry is Rhode Island's leading industrial employer, it is not exactly part of the nation's economic backbone.

Costume jewelry does, however, provide an excellent illustration of the historical and dialectical processes determining the condition of work in twentieth-century America—revealed to us by Harry Braverman in *Labor and Monopoly Capital*. We note in the following pages the destruction of jewelry craftsmanship, the deskilling and erosion of the wages of the jewelry work force, and the application of scientific management techniques to certain stages of the jewelry-making process. We consider, for example, how in labor-intensive operations jewelry manufacturers make use of time and motion studies in establishing piece rates to increase worker productivity in place of widescale technological innovation.

In terms of its present-day characteristics, the costume jewelry industry conforms to James O'Connor's typology of manufacturing concerns in the competitive sector (O'Connor 1978:159–60). The unstable seasonal nature of costume jewelry gives rise to a workforce that sometimes of choice, but most often of necessity, is unable to find work in the monopoly or state sector. This in part explains the high concentrations of women, immigrants,

---

I wish to thank Susan Porter Benson, Kate Dunnigan, Peter Perl, and Dave Snapp for their invaluable editorial and substantive criticism and personal support. My further thanks extend to jewelry workers, both on and off the shop floor, who provided me with insight and inspiration in the course of my work.

and minorities in the industry. These traditionally powerless groups often exhibit a low level of militance in the workplace that further determines an underdeveloped labor movement long characteristic of the jewelry industry. The absence of unions and formal signs of militance might be mistaken for the absence of class struggle in jewelry shops. But politically conscious forces in the industry note a high level of submerged anger and frustration as well as individual and collective strategies of resistance to management's prerogatives. In most cases, these acts of resistance remain to be summed up as forms of class struggle.

It is with this in mind that my focus here will be on the struggle around the piece rate, one of many forms of class struggle in the industry. I will examine management's manipulations of the piece-rate system and the way the jewelry workers fight these manipulations, based on their knowledge and control, however fragmented, of the labor process. Finally, I will explore the limits of a fightback that targets the labor process per se, and consider the significance of the struggle itself.

In building upon the brilliant work of Braverman, this study is offered as a modest contribution to extending the discussion of class formation and social transformation "into class situations, into the subjective experiences of class, and into the experience and forms of class struggle" (Dale Johnson 1978:42).

Early History of the Jewelry Industry

In 1794, Nehemiah Dodge, a goldsmith in Providence, R. I., invented a process of plating gold and silver onto base metals, an achievement that marked the birth of the costume jewelry industry because it enabled craftsmen to produce jewelry more quickly and cheaply. "Job lots" replaced the production of single custom items and jewelry came to enjoy a wider market (Douglas Johnson 1976:2).

Jewelry manufacturing in the 1800s was marked by the advent of simple power machinery and the phasing out of the master craftsmen (Frankovich 1971:83–88) who had crafted a piece from initial design to final polishing; they were replaced by growing numbers of artisans and workers at different levels of skill who "specialized" in certain stages of jewelry making. By

1856 there were fifty-six jewelry-making firms in Providence, employing 1400 people (Frost 1897:2513). Between 1875 and 1899 the jewelry/silverware industry had 10,000 workers (Douglas Johnson 1976:6), and by 1880 Rhode Island was producing one-quarter of all jewelry and silverware in the United States (by value) and probably one-half the amount in quantity (Frost 1897:2513). The division of labor that had taken place by 1899 is reflected in that year's census, which lists jewelry workers engaged in producing jewelry findings (raw, unassembled jewelry parts), electroplating, enameling, engraving, chasing (a form of polishing), die skinking, and lapidary work (Frankovich 1971:83–88).

Skill and Wages

Mechanization created some new skills in the industry, as such previously unknown processes as electroplating, toolmaking, and die cutting became central to the industry. But the overwhelming result of the division of labor and of mechanization was the burgeoning number of new jobs (e.g., assembling, linking) that from the start involved far less skill than had the master craftsman. This transformation ultimately led to the modern costume jewelry industry, whose jobs today involve repeated detail operations, shorter training periods, and significantly lower wages.

Whereas one hundred years ago jewelry craftsmen enjoyed some of the highest wages in industry,* the price of the jewelry worker's labor steadily eroded. Accompanying this trend was the influx of large numbers of women workers into semiskilled and unskilled jobs. Women's "superior sense of delicacy and refinement" (Gorham 1893) suited them to the job, according to one large manufacturer. Such an assessment also suited their employers, who could then "justifiably" pay women entering these jobs less than men who refused such low pay. By 1930, the once male-dominated work force in jewelry was 54 percent female (Providence Community Center 1939:15).

* Providence Community Center, *Preliminary Report on Jewelry Manufacturing & Silverware Industries in Rhode Island*, under the sponsorship of the U. S. Employment Service 1939:33.

The wages of the jewelry workers were further depressed by the region's large pool of unemployed labor. The labor supply swelled with the waves of immigrants to New England between 1880 and 1920. By 1930, approximately 46 percent of the jewelry work force was foreign-born (ibid.:21). The movement of the textile industry to the South in the 1920s began creating additional massive unemployment for immigrants, who were now forced to seek jobs in jewelry.

Compounding these problems, jewelry workers were plagued by weak or nonexistent unions. The widening gap between the skilled and unskilled made organizing increasingly difficult, especially since the mass of jewelry labor was drawn from such traditionally powerless groups as immigrants, minorities, and women.

The Persisting Structure and Character of the Jewelry Industry

The division of labor and specialization that created new types of jobs affected the structure of the industry as a whole. Firms unable to produce all of the components for the finished product "in-house" purchased findings from "finding houses" and subcontracted work to job shops ("jobbers") that specialized in soldering, assembling, plating, etc. Jobbers in turn farmed out work to home workers (Douglas Johnson 1976:26, 28–29). While there was fierce competition between the growing number of firms involved in the same kind of work, an industry-wide cooperative division of labor took hold and exists today.

A 1935 study of the jewelry and silverware industries in Rhode Island sponsored by the U. S. Employment Service notes that the jewelry industry

> has maintained the same relative standing since 1899 [due to] specialization of R. I. jewelry in products requiring less skilled workers, a high proportion of semi-skilled female workers in R. I. and the absence of strong union organization. (Providence Community Center 1939:15)

The main change in the jewelry industry in the first quarter of the twentieth century was simply an increase in size, reaching a peak of 288 firms in 1929, before the depression took its toll.

The 1930 census records nearly 12,000 workers in all phases of jewelry manufacturing (ibid.:17–18).

While the years 1935–1975 saw the jewelry/silverware industries more than double in size—from 177 to 419 firms in Providence alone—what is remarkable is how little its character and structure have changed. It is still comprised of numerous highly competitive small- to medium-sized firms, none of which controls a major sector of the market. For example, in 1935, 88.1 percent of all firms employed between 2–100 workers and in 1974, 88.6 percent of all firms still employed less than 99 people (Douglas Johnson 1976:25, 27). The work force remains largely unorganized* and according to the 1976 estimates of George Frankovich, executive director of the Manufacturing Jewelers and Silversmiths of America, 75 percent of the work force is unskilled and over 65 percent is female (quoted in ibid.:15–16). Statistics for 1977 indicate that manufacturing wages in Rhode Island rank third lowest in the United States, with most of the state's manufacturing work force in costume jewelry (personal communication with R. I. Department of Labor and Department of Economic Development).

Perhaps the most notable feature in the history of jewelry manufacturing and the key to understanding its relatively unchanging character over the last one hundred years is the low level of technological innovation and the high degree of labor intensiveness.

Labor Intensiveness, Technology, and Rationalization

Jewelry manufacturers today continue to emphasize the delicate handwork and manual dexterity required in jewelry making and they note how "the production process for precious, as well as low- and medium-priced [costume] jewelry is not conducive to automation" (George Frankovich quoted by Douglas Johnson in Johnson 1976:16). But informed sources in the industry say the

---

* The Jewelry Workers Organizing Committee was formed in 1977 and is made up of jewelry workers, community activists, and students. Its aim is to coordinate the efforts of projects that will empower jewelry workers to overcome unemployment, health and safety problems, poor wages and benefits, and turn them into a long-term strategy for organizing jewelry workers.

real reason the manufacturers have not automated further is that cheap labor represents a dramatic savings when compared with the cost of re-tooling production. In labor-intensive industries like jewelry, if labor, the main variable in the cost of production, can be kept cheap, market prices can be lower, high profits can continue (Bookman 1977:68), and mechanization can be minimized. It is cheaper to lay off workers during traditionally "slow" seasons than to have expensive machinery sit idle. As Braverman notes, at some points

> the worker is cheaper than the machinery which replaces him or her. [This] is determined by more than a mere technical relationship: it depends as well upon the level of wages, which in turn is affected by the supply of labor as measured against the demand. And the supply of labor [itself] depends in part on the mechanization of the industry. (Braverman 1974:237)

Jewelry manufacturers have employed several strategies in their effort to increase productivity, cut costs, and assert control over the labor process. Some "job out" certain stages in the process and avoid the problems and expense that come with a large "in-house" work force. Others expand their operations by adding shifts, particularly "mothers' shifts," that attract thousands of women during the hours their children are in school. Still others have acquired small- or medium-sized firms, often those in financial straits. And a key management strategy—used alone or in combination with the above methods—is to increase the existing work force's productivity. Traditional management practices of close supervision of workers, rule enforcement, production minimums, and paternalism have been combined with the "improved," "motivational" methods. These involve such incentive schemes as bonuses, piecework, and profit-sharing.

The technological innovations that have occurred in these labor-intensive operations have tended to preserve their labor-intensive character while increasing the workers' productivity and maximizing control over the work force. For example, one current method of jewelry making, "set-up and charge," "improved" upon the traditional method of hand-held torch soldering wherein the semiskilled solderer produced fewer pieces and had some say in how a jewelry piece could best be soldered. Set-up and chargers are now confronted with a precise plan of how a job is to be assembled (set-up) and soldered (charged).

Workers are instructed to set-up jewelry according to a prethought-out process on precut, heat-resistant boards, stamped with the design impressions of the jewelry style. Chargers no longer make decisions; this is done for them by a coterie of designers, engineers, and foremen who "intellectually disassemble the work process and return it, as it were, to the working class in a piecemeal fashion" (Sattel 1978:37). Set-up and charge marks a midway point in jewelry rationalization: the worker produces more and makes fewer decisions in the course of the work than the torch solderer but still retains some control over the labor process. She can, for instance, alter job instructions and regulate the pace of work. The "solderer" has not as yet become simply a monitor of a machine that automatically solders mechanically assembled findings. There is an automatic solderer on the market, however.

At the other end of the spectrum in jewelry-making operations are those processes that have been highly mechanized and rationalized, and where the workers' skills and control over decision making have been all but eliminated. A good illustration of such a development came with the invention of the ominously named "Cyclomaster" in 1959, which transformed the work of electroplating, one of the few remaining skilled jobs in the industry. Where six or more electroplaters had once dipped racks of unplated jewelry into baths by hand and regulated the amount of plating material to maintain consistency in the strength of the solutions, the Cyclomaster dips racks into solutions in twenty-one automatic stages, traveling along a monorail for forty feet or more. This machine replaced the jobs of skilled electroplaters with one operator who loads and unloads the racks from the Cyclomaster (Reseigh 1959). Electronic controls, embodying the know-how and judgment of electroplaters, now regulate the amount of electric current and materials for plating jewelry lots. The Cyclomaster's dramatically increased capacity to handle more racks has led to an expansion in the work force, but in one of the lowest-paying occupations, "racking and stringing." In this woman-dominated domain, workers string jewelry pieces onto racks in preparation for cleaning and plating.

The level of technological development and rationalization is unevenly distributed throughout jewelry manufacturing. Like Braverman's characterization of the apparel industry, jewelry today is made up of many shops, most of them relatively small, a great many [of which] are still in the stage of traditional "rationalization," breaking down operations into a large number of smaller and simpler steps. At the same time, these steps are being speeded up by the introduction of a variety of devices. (Braverman 1974:211)

On the other hand, some operations are rationalized to the extent that the workers' grip on the labor process has all but been broken. But as Braverman points out:

Taylorism cannot become generalized in any industry or applicable in particular situations until the scale of production is adequate to support efforts and costs in "rationalizing" it. It is for this reason above all that Taylorism coincides with the growth of production and its concentration in ever larger corporate units. (Ibid.:101 n)

The last decade has witnessed some important changes in the jewelry industry in Rhode Island. Small- and medium-sized firms have gone under, unable to compete with the infusion of cheaper imports into the market, chiefly from Hong Kong, South Korea, and Taiwan (Goldberg 1977:116). The rising cost of raw materials and of capital expenditure on antipollution equipment have cut into company profits. Increases in the federal minimum wage and the resurgence of union activity have threatened the comfortable cheap labor supply that manufacturers so heavily rely on and diligently maintain. Simultaneously, a few jewelry conglomerates have emerged, buying up the smaller firms and threatening others with their command of wider market distribution systems. While in 1977 the majority of the 30,000 workers engaged in jewelry manufacture and jewelry-related industries still worked in shops that averaged between 20 and 25 people (Harrington 1977), jewelry manufacturing in the late 1970s may be showing the early signs of a classically competitive industry in decline.

H&B Creations: A Brief Ethnography

Having sketched the transformation of the costume jewelry industry over time and the state of the industry today, let me now examine the labor process and social relations governing production in one phase of jewelry manufacture, the "set-up and charge" department of H&B Creations, a large jewelry company in Providence, R. I.*

H&B Creations employs 500 people, many of them first-generation Portuguese immigrants, in a sprawling one-story factory in an industrial section of Providence. H&B typifies the larger costume jewelry firm of today, housing separate departents for different operations and methods of jewelry production (electroplating, toolmaking, polishing, casting, lost wax, footpress, set-up and charge, etc.) under its one roof. The majority of its work force is employed in jobs classified and paid as "unskilled" or "semiskilled," though these labels often bear little relation to the actual skills required of workers on the job (Bookman 1977:124). Over 60 percent of the workers are women, the majority of whom are steered into jobs said to require the "feminine" traits of nimbleness, dexterity, and patience. The women's wages generally start at $2.70 per hour, while men, directed into "heavier" jobs, start at $3.00. Most workers train for less than a week on the job. toolmakers, a local of the International Association of Machinists, are the only organized group of workers in the plant.

H&B promotes itself as a progressive employer offering a variety of fringe benefits, including piecework. The company's cheery paternalism—"It's teamwork that got us this far!"†—wears thin when workers daily confront an employer that pays meager wages, provides no sick leave, no job security, no functional job descriptions, and no system of awarding raises. Workers express resentment at such management practices as eroding piecework earnings, handbag/lunchbucket searches on leaving work, and serious violations of health and safety standards.

---

* The data for this section are based on anthropological fieldwork carried out by the author for six months in 1978 in a large costume jewelry factory in Providence. As an ordinary production worker with no prior factory experience, I was arbitrarily assigned to the set-up and charge department when hired on by the company. The identity of the company, the identifiable characteristics of the workplace, and the names of the people mentioned herein have been changed to preserve their anonymity.

† One of the owners of H&B Creations introducing a profit-sharing plan to an assembly of workers.

The Set-up and Charge Department

Set-up and charge (hence to be known as SUC) is one of several methods of jewelry making at H&B Creations. As described above, a set-up and charger assembles jewelry findings with a hand-held tweezer in a manner prescribed by supervisors and "built into" heat-resistant graphite boards. According to the supervisor's instructions, the worker "charges" or applies solder to the findings. The charger holds a soldering gun—a plastic syringe filled with soft lead-based solder—and applies the needlepoint to the spot where the findings are eventually to melt together in the oven. Solder jets out of the syringe needle by air pressure, powered through a plastic tube. The charger's quick pressure on a foot pedal triggers the electric current to activate the syringe in her hand.

At full capacity the SUC department at H&B Creations has forty production workers who sit on high-backed stools at four-foot-wide, waist-high benches, arranged in two parallel rows; each row holds ten facing benches. At the end of the two double rows are three anhydrous ammonia gas ovens with their own iron-mesh conveyor belts. Women working the ovens continuously pick up completed boards from the benches and feed them into the ovens, where they are carried by belt through high heat for several minutes. The furnace solders the findings together and "jewelry" emerges from the other end of the oven. The jewelry pieces are dumped into boxes for inspection within the department before being routed to the polishing or electroplating department. The cooled boards are recycled to the workers.

Atop the pyramid of the all-female work force of thirty-odd production workers and three supervisory personnel is the only male in the SUC department, the foreman, Fred. Second in command is the "floor lady,"* Bea, who carries Fred's directives about job instructions, piece rates, rules, and "company policy" to the "girls." Bea also manages the record keeping of each

---

* The power regulations between management and workers are built into the language of the shop, capturing the differentiation even within management ranks: foreman, floor lady, floor girls, girls. The term "girls," which workers and management use to refer to female production workers, is common parlance in work situations where women are concentrated into low-status jobs. Such parlance may reflect the unquestioned acknowledgment of women workers' low social status. Because the author assumed the role and labels of the people around her, parts of this article reflect the colloquialisms of the shop.

worker's output and payment. Assisting Bea are two first-generation Portuguese "floor girls," both fluent in Portuguese and English. Bilingual floor girls are crucial to a department that is over one-third Portuguese, the rest being a mixture of Afro-Americans, first- and third-generation Italian-Americans, and third-generation Irish and Anglo-Saxon Americans. The floor girls have the moment-to-moment responsibility of assigning and supervising work, training new girls, and supplying work materials. They also take the brunt of the workers' frustration with management, and mediate disputes among the workers themselves. Both floor girls were recently promoted from bench-work, and in their new nerve-racking job earned $.30 per hour more than they had as benchworkers.

The floor lady or floor girl trains the workers to set-up and charge in about fifteen minutes. It takes from one to two weeks for a worker to "get the hang of it" and anywhere from three to six months to come to perform most jobs with peak speed and accuracy. Chargers start at a base rate of $2.70 per hour, but are paid either this hourly rate or a piece rate (a rate of pay for a given number of pieces), depending on the type of job to which they are assigned. Jobs that involve inspecting or repairing pieces that fellow workers have set-up and charged are paid by the hour, but all work that involves setting-up and charging new findings is considered "piecework."

The Piecework "Bait and Switch" Routine

In an industry like jewelry, noted for its extremely low wages, piecework incentives are an important management tool for luring workers into the industry and keeping them there, through the glittering possibilities of "extra" money for higher productivity. As one worker put it: "I came to H&B Creations 'cause you can 'make money' here." "Making money" is the apt shorthand that workers use for the money earned over the hourly rate of pay at which the worker is hired. The worker is guaranteed her hourly rate of pay whether or not she makes the piece rate. But before she can earn a penny "extra" in piecework, she must produce the equivalent of her hourly rate in piecework values. On a job like "snake-rings," for example, with a piece rate of $1.35 per 100, a worker must produce *over*

200 pieces an hour in order to earn more than the $2.70 she is guaranteed.

It is possible under certain circumstances for pieceworkers in the SUC department at H&B to earn from $1.00–$3.00 beyond their hourly rates, boosting weekly earning by almost 100 percent. But such higher earnings are contingent on other uncertain factors, factors that rest completely in the hands of management. Directly through rate-setting and payment schemes, and indirectly through control of the labor process, management controls the purse-strings at all times. Thus the "promise" management makes to pieceworkers—that one can earn as much as one produces—is often broken. Once workers have been baited by the lure of higher earnings, management "switches" to another game plan. Through the following methods, management extracts high productivity from pieceworkers while cutting back on its payments:

—From the very outset, the piece rates are set by management in accordance with the already low wages in the industry.
—Payment schemes, such as the "makeup" system, assure management higher output while actually subtracting earnings from pieceworkers by averaging their highest and lowest productivity rates.
—Management can lengthen production time but simultaneously reduce workers' pay by creating shortages of materials or changing job instructions.
—Management can enforce a speed-up by re-timing piece rates so that the worker is paid less than before for the same quantity of work put out.

Piecework provides the illusion that one's payment is related to one's productivity. As Braverman points out: "The pay of labor is a socially determined figure, relatively independent of productivity . . . ." (Braverman 1974:98). It depends on social and historical factors like those we have noted above. Piecework appears to "unite" productivity and payment, and workers respond to this appearance, thinking that their hard work and high output will be met in handsome piecework payments. They become outraged when management ruptures this "unity." Thus on the shop floor, piecework becomes a battlefront between workers and management. Everyday, workers challenge management's manipulations of the piecework system and develop their own strategies of resistance, though they may not fully realize the significance of their actions.

Time and Motion Studies and Rate-Setting

In order to establish a piece rate for a new job, management personnel perform a time and motion study on one or more workers who have been "practicing" the new style or "sample" for a few days. The time-study person will appear on the floor with a stop watch and time sheet in hand and tell the worker to "work as if I weren't here." The time-studier will concentrate on noting down every *motion* the worker makes, from picking up an earring post to charging a finding. After noting the *times* for certain operations, the time-studier will retire to the office with this data and, along with other management personnel, will figure out a system of predetermined work time, or a "piece rate," for the given job.

Raw data from this time study are only one of several factors in the calculation of a rate. Others include output on samples before the timed test, costs of production, standardized time and motion data, and the hourly rate of pay in the industry as a whole. Workers have little control over these last three factors, but they have considerable leverage in regulating output during the time study and in sample work before the study. Since most workers recognize that their pace on the time study determines to some extent the price that will eventually "come down" from the office, they will "go slow" on the test and tell co-workers to do the same. Shortly after my friend Rose was timed on the "snake ring," she told me; "They time you to get the price of the piece. I tried to go slow to get a higher price." A few days after Rose was timed, a "good" price came down from the office. Rose was delighted: "See how slow I went. We got a good price!"— implying that her performance on the test had determined the piece rate or "price" of the "snake ring." Other workers were more conscious that management had intervened in this apparently "pure scientific process" of timing and rate-setting. As Francis put it, "Not all the price is decided on the test results in the office. They watch our output good . . . even on the samples that don't have prices yet." Francis would therefore tell the other girls to "go slow" on the samples too. Practice had shown her that piece rates are set squarely in management's interests.

But how exactly is the piece rate arrived at? Through analysis of the time and study data and other inputs noted above, management determines that 200 snake rings, for example, can be produced per hour. By lining up this hourly production rate with the hourly rate of pay, i.e., 200 rings for $2.70, management determines a piece rate: $1.35 per 100. Through this method management has effectively *predetermined* that the company will have to "pay out" little extra piecework money.

This strategy is never explicitly verbalized, but the evidence that reveals its existence is clear:

> —Practice has shown that different piecework jobs with time and motion variations peculiar to each nonetheless end up paying out at approximately the same price. Different jobs usually require a good part of an hour's production just to "earn" the equivalent of $2.70 in piecework values.
>
> —It is apparent that H&B Creations cut back its piecework payments, i.e., it became harder to "make the rate," when federal minimums increased. One worker said: "Two years ago [January 1976, when federal minimum wages increased from $2.10 to $2.30], the piece rates began to change. It got harder to 'make money.'" Jewelry manufacturers forestalled significant increases in their wage bills by manipulating the piece rates.
>
> —It becomes more difficult to "make money" on piecework as one's base rate of pay increases through seniority or merit increments. The higher her hourly wage, the more a worker must put out in piecework values before she can start earning extra money.

Re-timing and rate busting, like the original setting of rates, are anything but "scientifically" determined by the gadgetry of the stop watch, time study, and computer calculations, as management would have us believe. Scientific management "investigates not labor in general, but the adaptation of labor to the needs of capital. It enters the workplace not as a representative of science, but as a representative of management masquerading in the trappings of science" (Braverman 1974:86). In such an atmosphere, it is no wonder that it appears that a rate gets slashed when a "certain point" has been passed, a "scientifically determined point" that transcends human deliberation and manipulation. And it is no wonder that a co-worker gets blamed for hitting that mysterious point.

Erosion of Real Earnings on Piecework

Once management has set the piece rates, further manipulation of payment schemes is put into motion on the shop floor by management's representatives, the foreman, floor lady, and floor girls. Floor girls "mix" piecework and hourly rate work for a worker so that weekly wages will be lower than if the worker made piecework all week. A more objectionable scheme, known as the "makeup" system, involves applying piecework money a worker earned (*above* the hourly scale on one job) to "makeup" for the money the company paid her in hourly wages for a job on which she was *under* the piecework quota. In other words, if a worker is able to earn an extra $10 above base pay through fast work on "snake rings" but was later in the week assigned to the slower "golden touch" job, where she fell the equivalent of $10 below rate, she could lose her earlier $10 bonus through the makeup.*

The floor lady and floor girls implement the makeup system by assigning "good" and "bad" piecework jobs to the same worker in a given week. One worker expressed her disgust at the makeup system as follows: "They get all that production out of us for the time we're 'making money' and then they put us on a job where we can't make the rate—and they get the money *we* already made."

Indirectly management can also control piecework earnings by controlling "production time" on the shop floor. Making the rate depends on the constant supply of materials, the good working order of equipment, flexibility around job instructions, as well as on the worker's steady stream of energy. A shortage of boards for setting-up and charging or a bad soldering gun will directly affect production time, and one's chance to "make money." In the process of production, problems do of course come up around job instructions, quality of pieces, shortages of materials, etc. We are not speaking of that here: rather, management will slow down production to control "runaway" piecework by *creating* shortages of boards, selectively enforcing job instructions, and intentionally neglecting equipment that has all but broken down. One worker remarked: "They put a lot of girls on the same job so there's not enough boards to go 'round, and then they don't have to pay out."

---

* The company proceeds on the assumption that it is only "fair" that a worker "fully earns" her hourly rate in piecework values. Let us correct this mystification: even when workers have failed to "make the rate," itself a creation of management, in fact they have created value appropriated by the company that far exceeds the hourly wages they are paid.

Rate Busting

The ultimate authority management wields is the ability to have a job re-timed and the piece rate lowered. This usually amounts to what is commonly known as "rate busting." As one veteran pieceworker lamented: "I never knew a rate to be *raised* after a time-study" (Mathewson 1969:68). Managers in jewelry usually reorder a time study when a few fast workers have mastered a job and are really "making money."*

At one time workers in my department were earning from $5.00 to $6.00 per hour on the "love necklace" that was priced at $1.16 per 100 pieces. On the basis of workers' output, management was forced to act in its own interest and reset the rate to cut back its wage bill. The test was performed and a few days later the "new price" came down from the office. The rate had been slashed from $1.16 per 100 pieces to $.82 per 100. The girls who had been "making money" on the love necklace were furious. They would now have to produce over 40 percent more necklaces to make the equivalent of $1.16 per 100. But a curious and significant thing happened: the workers' hostility only momentarily focused on the foreman, management's representative on the shop floor. The girls then jumped on one worker, Fatima, who was blamed for going too fast and breaking the rate. Fatima had been making $6.00 an hour on the necklaces. The other workers didn't begrudge her the money—everybody wants to make money—but her "crime" had been to break the informal code among pieceworkers—controlling one's output to preserve a good rate.† She had put "her money" above everyone else's, since her conspicuously high output had precipitated a rate bust by management. Workers such as Angela, "the fastest we have," would forsake a few dollars on the love necklace to "save" the rate. Fatima had not simply made a mistake: she was a well-seasoned worker who knew the ropes. She was, however, basically individualistic, a trait reinforced by the piecework system, and it was this that had caused the problem. Significantly,

---

* Occasionally a foreman may order a re-test if the original piece rate was so difficult to make that workers "turned off" production, and as a result output on that job was low.

† Historically, pieceworkers have had informal codes to prevent management from rate busting. See, for example, Braverman 1974:97–102; Baritz 1960:97–100; and Mathewson 1969:1931.

The Piece Rate: Class Struggle on the Shop Floor   293

though, workers dubbed this "rate busting." And although Fatima had not busted the rate—management had—an attack on management was conspicuously absent. This sort of reaction is understandable in an environment where management's prerogatives go largely unquestioned, shrouded in a cloak of "science." Conflicts between management and workers are reconstituted in the workers' minds as conflicts among themselves.

Workers on piecework quickly learn that while they can sometimes earn extra money, the golden possibilities the piecework incentive first seemed to offer ("the more you produce, the more you earn") grow dim. The various management techniques that "rob" workers of piecework earnings trample many workers' sense of "fair play." Some quit almost immediately in frustration. Others resign themselves to the hard reality of the rules, having long accepted the legitimacy and prerogatives of management, however "unfair" they may be. One black worker, Francis, who had worked in and out of jewelry shops for twenty years, put it this way: "Poor people always lose. You get used to it." Yet this same woman was one of the most creative and vigorous fighters against management's manipulations of the piecework system. In one instance, she learned from another worker that the "big boss" was eager for stepped-up production on a particular job and therefore was not having the pieces inspected very carefully. She alerted the others so that they could turn out the pieces faster, without fear of "quality" interfering with production time. "If he says they're good, then that means we can go faster." Thus while piecework appears to, and actually does, encourage individualism and competition, a collectivism underlies the system too. Workers may stack or hoard boards, or "steal" them from each other, to shorten their production time. Like Fatima, they may take the "get it while you can" approach, but they may also act collectively, as when Angela took forced breaks and Rose slowed down on the time study. Workers often share boards and other resources with each other; they help each other on jobs even if it cuts into their own piecework time. Even with the individualistic "pulls" on them, in the final analysis many realize they are up against the same problems, the same rules, and the same system of piecework that must be "beaten." One Portuguese worker made this explicit: "I can't understand all this fighting over boards. We all work for the same company." Significantly, she used a phrase one often hears from management, but changed its message. And while Francis and others felt "beaten back" by the "way things are run around here," they fought back vigorously as individuals and as part of a group. Both in systematic and unsystematic ways, they developed ways to manipulate the piecework system in their own interests.

Workers Fight Back

"Everything changes when the girls are on piecework," said one floor girl, recently promoted from benchwork. "No jokes, no nothing—they don't wanna hear their work is bad. They're your friends when they're on piecework. Not when they're off."

There is truth in this. Piecework offers workers the chance to make more money than the meager hourly wage, management's manipulations notwithstanding. And since the contest over the weekly paycheck is waged anew every day, the real commodity relation between labor and capital asserts itself daily. Such amenities as joking, smoking, and friendships take a back seat until breaks and lunch. Workers compete for "good" jobs and resources. Floor girls, floor lady, and foreman use piecework as a lever to "cool out" angry workers, and sometimes use it to exact sexual favors. Piecework becomes "everything," and sometimes the pressure becomes too great for management and workers alike. Some workers quit, saying they can't take the pressure. Others cry, or ask for transfers. Others, like Rose, say they feel better on piecework because they are making money and "that's what I am here for." But management and workers alike are well aware that piecework always involves a conflict—and both sides brace for the struggle. This struggle usually focuses on the workers' slowdowns, on the makeup system, and on job instructions.

In labor-intensive industries such as jewelry, the work itself is physically exhausting. Seasoned veterans work hard *selectively*, when it is in their interests as workers. In a sense, they are continuously making a study of their own "time and motion" as they work—*not* in the manner of management, where human beings are treated as machines with movable parts, but in the way that workers, as subjects of the work process, investigate, sum up, and apply their knowledge of the process to control it in their own interests. Workers can, for the moment anyway, determine the standard for a "fair day's work," determine the price of their labor—within given limits—and, in some cases, even determine how a job is done. This control is fragile and fleeting, as we have seen, for management can come in at any moment and slash a rate, shattering worker strategies of output regulation.

The makeup system generates some of the sharpest struggle between workers and management. When management subtracts piecework earnings through the penalty system of the makeup, the company creates new problems for itself, because workers will consciously restrict output in retaliation. Hilda, for instance, had been working on "silver bars" for a week, a job so difficult that even the fastest workers fell behind rate. When Hilda was switched to snake rings, an easier job, her reaction was, "Why should I break my neck on snake rings?" She realized that any extra money she made on the rings would be subtracted to "make up" for slow work on the silver bars: "I know I can 'make money' on the snake ring, but why should I give them all that production when I won't get the money?" Given the logic of the makeup system, Hilda held back production; others did the same thing. Eventually this general slowdown, though unarticulated and unsystematic, *generated a re-test of the silver bars.* Workers effectively used the makeup system against itself by holding back *all* production until the rate was changed. They could then earn piecework money that they had a chance of keeping.

One working mother, Elaine, carefully manipulated her "time" at work to fight the makeup system. She had been earning about $4.00 per hour on the rose-petal earrings on Monday and Tuesday. Wednesday morning she was taken off the rose petal after three hours and put onto the low-paying silver bars. She was furious: she'd lose her piecework money on the rose petal. She couldn't refuse the job because that was grounds for dismissal; she could leave for the day, telling Bea, the floor lady, she was sick. She reasoned: "I won't make any money at home, but at least I won't lose any, which I would if I stayed here." By leaving work, or even taking a whole day out, she'd be "standing still." On this particular day, however, Elaine took a more brazen step: she proceeded to "lose" her time card for the silver-bar job—a serious violation of company policy. These time cards account for every moment of a worker's day: they note not only one's presence at work, but also record the job worked, the production time on it, and the quantity produced in that time; they serve as a paper reflection of production for every worker in the department and for the department as a whole. Near the day's end, Bea discovered the "lapse" in Elaine's day. Elaine was questioned closely. We all looked about for the missing card. Bea was frazzled and suspicious. The intense scrutiny intimidated Elaine so much that she ended up approximating her *actual* production on the silver bars, which resulted in her losing some of her rose-petal earnings. Nonetheless, Elaine had struggled to preserve the rose-petal money she had worked so hard to gain.

Workers share know-how and teach each other shortcuts that cut production time on piecework jobs. By changing the original motion function that was time-studied, the workers throw off the calculation that management used to set the piece rate. A veteran worker, Trudie, showed me how to work faster by doing a job with two hands at once, rather than having one hand repeat a motion twice as many times. In another instance, Bea was teaching me a new job and I noticed that she was operating the foot pedal differently than she had first instructed me. She admitted this was indeed a faster way to "charge," but told me not to tell the other girls about it: "You know what would happen then." Bea's fears of "runaway" piecework were beside the point. She was letting me in on a trade secret since I had discovered it anyway, while she was also dividing me from the other workers.

The most clear-cut case of changing original job instructions to shorten production time involved the "paradise ring." The left side of the chart gives the original instructions, the right side the changed procedure developed by the workers.

Original Instructions*	*Changed Procedure*
(1) Pick up U-shaped finding.	(1) Pick up U-shaped finding.
(2) Pick up bar and insert bar into groove.	(2) Pick up bar and insert bar into groove.
(3) Pick up soldering gun and charge four joints where bar meets U-shaped ring.	(3) Place ring to side of bench.
(4) Put down soldering gun.	(4) Repeat operations 1–3 until you "build a pile" of rings.
(5) Place ring in square on cardboard grid of 100 or 144 squares.	(5) One at a time, charge ring in four places with soldering gun and place ring in square on cardboard grid.

* This is a reconstruction of the verbal instructions given by the floor lady to the girls on the paradise ring. The "Changed Procedure" is a reconstruction of worker-generated changes in job instructions. Instructions in the set-up and

(6) Begin process again until all squares on grid are filled.

(7) Repeat process for new grid.

(6) Repeat operation #5 for each ring until the pile is gone or the grid is filled up.

(7) Start process again.

The original procedure was neither delicate nor difficult, but it was dull and the rate of $1.50 per 100 pieces was hard to make. To make $3.00, or about $.30 over the hourly rate, a worker would have had to produce more than 200 pieces an hour, and even fast workers couldn't make this rate. So they began "piling." When Fred, the foreman, found Jo-Ann and Emelia piling, he ordered them to stop, saying that piling bent the rings. But he also appealed to their sense of fair play: "After all, this was the way the job was timed." Jo-Ann and Emelia weren't impressed. Only by piling would they be able to make the rate, though not by much.

It is difficult to understand why management doesn't allow piling, since they got more production and paid out very little in piecework money. Quality may have been the reason, but in other cases quality matters little. The same contradiction—between management's desire for productivity and its reluctance to pay for it—was played out time and again. Management's desire simply to maintain control over the work force may in itself provide the real explanation for this behavior.

Concluding Remarks

We have examined some of the strategies, both collective and individual, that workers use to fight management's manipulations of the piecework system. These particular forms of struggle have been made possible by the grip that jewelry workers still retain on the labor process. They can use their knowledge to control their production time and they can manipulate their working conditions. But we have also noted how these small victories are easily smashed by the immense power management

---

charge department of H&B Creations were never written out for the workers, though management consulted a book that listed all the piecework jobs, their lot number, the specific operations for each job, and the piece rate for each job, among other things.

wields over the production process. Even workers' slowdowns on the time study are well known to management and may even be figured in when the piece rate is computed. Thus, important as these worker strategies are, their effectiveness must be questioned in that they target the labor process per se rather than the larger social relations that govern production.

The greatest importance of the fightback over piece rates probably lies in the summing up of the struggle itself that has yet to be done. Right now, it is a struggle largely unconscious of itself. The fightback that workers wage daily over piecework is not recognized as the struggle against management that it is. With the virtual absence of unions or union drives in the jewelry shops, management's prerogatives go largely unquestioned, no matter how unfair most workers may say they are. The fightback appears as an individual war to earn a fair wage or as an unsystematic group strategy that rarely gets off the ground. Summing up the struggle can educate the less conscious participants to their *existing* power as workers, not to mention their *potential* power. In addition, it fortifies and propels the more advanced jewelry workers in their fight for a better quality of life that, for the moment anyway, takes the form of the struggle for a higher wage.

Bibliography

Acker, Joan, and Van Houten, Donald. 1974. "Differential Recruitment and Control: The Sex Structuring of Organizations." *Administrative Science Quarterly* 19:152–62.

Allen, Arthur, and Schneider, Betty. 1956. *Industrial Relations in the California Aircraft Industry*. Berkeley: Institute of Industrial Relations, University of California.

Amalgamated Clothing Workers of America. 1941. "Clothing Unionism." Cited in Kurt Brown, *Union-Management Co-operation: Experience in the Clothing Industry*. Washington, D. C.: The Brookings Institution.

American Machinist. January 23, 1913. "The Automobile and Machine Tools."

Arble, Meade. 1976. *The Long Tunnel: A Coal Miner's Journal*. New York: Atheneum.

Archibald, Hugh. 1922. *The Four Hour Day in Coal*. New York: H. W. Wilson Co.

Arnold, Horace, and Faurote, Fay. 1972, originally 1915. *Ford Methods and Ford Shops*. New York: Arno Press.

Aronowitz, Stanley. 1965. "Against the Mainstream: Interview with James Matles of the U. E." *Studies on the Left* 5, no. 1.

———. 1973. *False Promises*. New York: McGraw-Hill.

Avery, C. V. 1929. "How Mass Production Came Into Being." *Iron Age*, June 13, 1929.

Backman, Jules. 1962. *The Economics of the Electrical Manufacturing Industry*. New York: New York University Press.

Baker, Elizabeth Faulkner. 1933. *Displacement of Men By Machines: Effects of Technological Change in Commercial Printing*. New York: Columbia University Press.

———. 1957. *Printers and Technology: A History of the International Pressmen and Assistants' Union*. New York: Columbia University Press.

———. 1964. *Technology and Women's Work*. New York: Columbia University Press.

Balzer, Richard. 1976. *Clockwork*. Garden City: Doubleday.

Baratz, Morton S. 1955. *The Union and the Coal Industry*. Port Washington, N. Y.: Kennikat Press.

Baritz, Loren. 1960. *The Servants of Power*. Middletown, Conn.: Wesleyan University Press.

Barnett, George. 1909. *The Printers: A Study in American Trade Unionism*. Cambridge, Mass.: American Economics Association.

Bell, Daniel. 1956. *Work and Its Discontents*. Boston: Beacon Press.

Bendix, Richard. 1956. *Work and Authority in Industry*. Berkeley: University of California Press.

Benet, Mary K. 1972. *The Secretarial Ghetto*. New York: McGraw-Hill.

Bituminous Coal Operators' Association (BCOA). October 6, 1977. Statement presented at the first session of the National Bituminous Coal Wage Agreement Negotiations, Washington, D. C.

Blauner, Robert. 1960. "Work Satisfactions and Industrial Trends in Modern Society." In *Labor and Trade Unionism*, edited by S. M. Lipset and W. Galenson. New York: John Wiley.

———. 1964. *Alienation and Freedom*. Chicago: University of Chicago Press.

Bobick, Thomas, and Giardino, Dennis. 1976. "The Noise Environment of the Underground Coal Mine." Information Report 1034, Mining Enforcement and Safety Administration, printed in *Noise Control*, MESA Work Book, no. 11.

Bookman, Ann. 1977. "The Process of Political Socialization among Women and Immigrant Workers: A Case Study of Unionization in the Electronics Industry." Ph.D. dissertation, Harvard University.

Boorstin, Daniel J. 1965. *The Americans: The National Experience*. New York: Random House.

Braverman, Harry. 1974. *Labor and Monopoly Capital: The Degradation of Work in the Twentieth Century*. New York: Monthly Review Press.

Brecher, Jeremy. April 1978. "Beyond Technological Determinism: Some Comments." Talk presented at the Organization of American Historians Convention.

Brecher, Jeremy, and Costello, Tim. 1976. *Common Sense for Hard Times*. New York: Two Continents/Institute for Policy Studies.

Brecher, Jeremy, and the Work Relations Group. 1979. "Uncovering the Hidden History of the American Workplace." *Review of Radical Political Economics* 10, no. 4.

Bright, James R. 1958. *Automation and Management*. Boston: Harvard Business School.

Brophy, John. 1964. *A Miner's Life*. Madison: University of Wisconsin Press.

Brown, Geoff. 1977. *Sabotage: A Study in Industrial Conflict*. Nottingham, Great Britain: Spokesman Books.

Brown, Murray, and Rosenberg, Nathan. 1961. "Patents, Research and Technology in the Machine Tool Industry." *The Patent, Trademark and Copyright Journal of Research and Education* 5 (Spring).

Burawoy, Michael. 1976. "The Organization of Consent: Changing Patterns of Conflict on the Shop Floor, 1945–1975." Unpublished doctoral dissertation, University of Chicago.

Bureau of Business and Economic Research. 1962. *A Study of the Problems of Small Electronics Manufacturing Companies in Southern California*. San Diego: California State College.

Bureau of Vocational Information. 1929. Collection deposited in Schlesinger Library, Radcliffe College, Cambridge, Mass.

Burlingame, Roger. 1949. *Backgrounds of Power: The Human Story of Mass Production*. New York: Scribner's.

Burns, J. C. 1977. "The Evolution of Office Information Systems." *Datamation* (April): 60–64.

Bywater, William. 1973. "Imports and Unemployment." In Proceedings of the New York University Twenty-fifth Annual Conference on Labor, New York University.

Cannon, James. 1974. *Leased and Lost: A Study of Public and Indian Coal Leasing in the West*. New York: Council on Economic Priorities.

Caplow, Theodore. 1954. *The Sociology of Work*. Minneapolis: University of Minnesota Press.

Carpenter, Jesse T. 1972. *Competition and Collective in the Needle Trades, 1910–1967*. Ithaca, N. Y.: New York State School of Industrial and Labor Relations.

Chinoy, Ely. 1955. *Automobile Workers and the American Dream*. Garden City: Doubleday.

———. 1964. "Manning the Machines: The Assembly-Line Worker." In *The Human Shape of Work*, edited by Peter Berger. New York: Macmillan.

Chironis, Nicholas P., ed. 1977. *Coal Age Operating Handbook of Underground Mining*, vol. I. New York: McGraw-Hill.

Christiansen, Erik. 1968. *Automation and the Workers*. London: Labour Research Development Publications, Ltd.

Christie, Robert. 1956. *Empire in Wood: A History of the Carpenter's Union*. Ithaca, N. Y.: The New York State School of Industrial and Labor Relations.

Coal Data 1976. National Coal Association.

Commons, John R. 1918. *History of Labor in the United States*. New York: Macmillan.

Commons, John R., et al. 1910. *A Documentary History of American Industrial Society*. Cleveland: Arthur H. Clark Co.

Condit, Carl W. 1960. *American Building Art: The Nineteenth Century*. New York: Oxford University Press.

Conference on Office Technology. 1978. Massachusetts Institute of Technology, Cambridge, Mass.

Coyle, Grace. 1928. *Present Trends in the Clerical Occupations*. New York: The Woman's Press.

———. 1929. "Women in the Clerical Occupations." *The Annals, American Academy of Political and Social Sciences* 143:180–87.

Crozier, Michel. 1964. *The Bureaucratic Phenomenon*. Chicago: University of Chicago Press.

———. 1973. *The World of the Office Worker*. New York: Schocken.

Cummings, Laird. 1977. "The Rationalization and Automation of Clerical Work." M. A. thesis, Brooklyn College.
Davies, Margery. 1974. "Woman's Place Is at the Typewriter: The Feminization of the Clerical Labor Force." *Radical America* 8 (July–August):1–28.
Davis, Mike. 1975. "The Stop-Watch and the Wooden Shoe: Scientific Management and the Industrial Workers of the World." *Radical America* (January–February).
de Kadt, Maarten. 1976. "The Development of Management Structures: The Problem of the Control of Workers in Large Corporations." Ph.D. dissertation, New School for Social Research.
———. 1977. "Working Conditions: Subsidy in Blood." In *U. S. Capitalism in Crisis*. New York: Union for Radical Political Economics.
De Vinne, Theodore L. 1871. *The Printers' Price List: A Manual for the Use of Clerks and Bookkeepers in Job Printing Offices*. New York: Francis Hart and Co.
Diebold, John. 1952. *Automation*. New York: Van Nostrand.
Dix, Keith, et al. 1977. *Work Stoppages and the Grievance Procedure in the Appalachian Bituminous Coal Industry*. Morgantown: Institute for Labor Studies, West Virginia University.
Dodd, George. 1975, originally 1843. *Days at the Factories: Manufacturing in the Nineteenth Century*. Yorkshire, England: E. P. Publishing Ltd.
Doring, Martin and Salling, Raymond. 1971. "A Case for Wage Incentives in the N. C. Age." *Manufacturing, Engineering and Management* 66, no. 6.
Drucker, Peter F. 1967. "Technology and Society in the Twentieth Century." In *Technology in Western Civilization*, edited by Kranzberg and Pursell. New York: Oxford University Press.
Dugan, James. May 18, 1976. Speech before the Twentieth North American Newspaper Web Conference in Pheonix, Arizona. Reprinted as Harvard Business School Case on *The Washington Post C*, Part III. Cambridge, Mass.
Eavenson, Howard N. 1915. "Safety Methods and Organization of the United States Coal and Coke Company." *Transactions*, American Institute of Mining Engineers 15:319–64.
"Effects of Mechanization and Automation in Offices." 1960. Parts I, II, III. *International Labor Review* 81 (February-March-April).
Emspak, Frank. "Crisis and Authority in the Seventies." Unpublished manuscript.
Espinosa, Juan, and Zimbalist, Andrew. 1978. *Economic Democracy: Workers' Participation in Chilean Industry, 1970–1973*. New York: Academic Press.
Executive Council of the International Typographical Workers Union. 1964. *A Study of the History of the ITU*. Colorado Springs: ITU.

Federal Trade Commission. 1939. *Report on Motor Vehicle Industry*. 76th Congress, 1st Session, House Document No. 458. Washington: U. S. Government Printing Office.

Feldberg, Roslyn, and Glenn, Evelyn. 1977. "Category or Collectivity: the Consciousness of Clerical Workers." Paper presented at the meetings of the Society for the Study of Social Problems, Chicago.

Field, Walker. 1942. "A Re-examination into the Invention of the Balloon Frame." *Journal of the Society of Architectural Historians* 2 (October):3 29.

Fischer, Britta, and Lesser, Mary. 1973. "Engineers." *Science for the People* 5, no. 3:16–21.

Ford, Henry (in collaboration with Samuel Crowther). 1923. *My Life and My Work*. London: Heinemann.

———. 1926. *Today and Tomorrow*. London: Heinemann.

———. 1931. *Moving Forward*. London: Heinemann.

Forrester, J., et al. 1955. "Strengthening Management for the New Technology." *American Management Association*.

Frankovich, George R. 1971. "History of Rhode Island Jewelry and Silverware Industry." In *Rhode Island Yearbook*. Providence: Rhode Island Foundation.

Freedman, Henry B. 1978. "Computer Assisted Makeup and Imaging Systems (CAMIS)." Program of Policy Studies in Science and Technology, The George Washington University, Washington, D.C.

Friedan, Karl. 1978. "The Effect of Workers' Ownership and Workers' Participation on Productivity." National Center for Economic Alternatives, Washington, D. C.

Friedman, Andrew L. 1977. *Industry and Labor: Class Struggle at Work and Monopoly Capitalism*. London: Macmillan.

Friedmann, Georges. 1961. *The Anatomy of Work*. New York: Free Press.

Frost, Walter B. 1897. "Jewelry Manufacture." In *New England States* 4:2512–14.

Garson, Barbara. 1973. "Women's Work." *Working Papers* 1(Fall): 5–14.

———. 1975. *All the Livelong Day: The Meaning and Demeaning of Routine Work*. New York: Doubleday.

GE Company, Management Consulting Services Division. 1953. "Next Step in Management—An Appraisal of Cybernetics."

Georgakas, Dan, and Surkin, Marvin. 1975. *Detroit: I Do Mind Dying*. New York: St. Martin's Press.

Gerth, H. H. and Mills, C. Wright, eds. 1958. *From Max Weber: Essays in Sociology*. New York: Oxford University Press.

Giddens, Anthony. 1975. *The Class Structure of the Advanced Societies*. New York: Harper & Row.

Giedion, Sigfried. 1941. *Space, Time and Architecture*. Cambridge: Harvard University Press.

Gilchrist, Bruce, and Weber, Bruce. 1972a. "Sources of Trained Computer Personnel—a Quantitative Survey." *Proceedings 1972 Spring Joint Computer Conference.* Montvale, N. J.: AFIPS.

———. 1972b. "Employment of Trained Computer Personnel—a Quantitative Survey." *Proceedings 1972 Spring Joint Computer Conference.* Montvale, N. J.: AFIPS.

Glenn, Evelyn, and Feldberg, Roslyn. 1978. "Clerical Work: The Female Occupation." In *Women: A Feminist Perspective,* edited by Jo Freeman. Palo Alto: Mayfield Publishing Co.

Goldberg, J. 1977. *The Jewelry Industry: An Economic, Financial and Marketing Investigation.* Merrick, N. Y.: Morton Research Corporation.

Goldner, Fred, and Ritti, Richard. 1962. "Professionalization as Career Immobility." *American Sociological Review* 27, no. 4:489–502.

Goldstine, Herman. 1972. *The Computer: From Pascal to Von Neumann.* Princeton: Princeton University Press.

Goodrich, Carter. 1925. *The Miner's Freedom.* Boston: Marshall Jones Co.

Gorham Manufacturing Company. 1893. *Women's Work at the Gorham Manufactory.* Providence: Gorham Mfg. Co.

Gorz, Andre. 1973. "Technical Intelligence and the Capitalist Division of Labor." *Science for the People* 5 (May).

Gottschall, ed. 1977a. "Vision '77." Part I. *The International Journal of Typographics (U&lc)* 4, no. 3.

———. 1977b. "Vision '77." Part II. *The International Journal of Typographics (U&lc)* 4, no. 4.

Gouldner, Alvin W. 1964, originally 1954. *Patterns of Industrial Bureaucracy.* New York: Free Press.

Greenbaum, Joan. 1976. "Division of Labor in the Computer Field." *Monthly Review* (July/August):40–55.

———. 1977. "In the Name of Efficiency: A Study of Change in Data Processing Work." Ph.D. dissertation, Union Graduate School.

Gyllenhammer, Pehr. 1977. "How Volvo Adapts Work to People." *Harvard Business Review* (July/August):101–13.

Hall, Max, ed. 1959. *Made in New York: Case Studies in Metropolitan Manufacturing.* Cambridge: Harvard University Press.

Hall, Richard H. 1975. *Occupations and the Social Structure.* 2nd ed. Englewood Cliffs, N.J.: Prentice-Hall.

Hamblen, John W. 1972. "Production and Utilization of Computer Manpower in the United States." *Proceedings 1972 Spring Joint Computer Conference.* Montvale, N. J.: AFIPS.

Harrington, Clyde. October 23, 1977. "Legislators Hear About Jewelry Firm's Problems." *Providence Journal.*

Harvard Business School. 1976. *The Washington Post A,* Part I. Boston: Intercollegiate Case Clearing House.

Helfgott, Roy B. 1959. "Women's and Children's Apparel." In *Made in*

New York, edited by Max Hall. Cambridge: Harvard University Press.
Hilaael, Timothy M. 1975. "Job Design in Word Processing? Administrative Support Systems: A Research Report on Secretarial Support in the Bell System." (May).
Hoos, Ida. 1962. "When the Computer Takes Over the Office." In *Man, Work and Society*, edited by S. Nosow and W. Form. New York: Basic Books.
Howe, Louise Kapp. 1977. *Pink Collar Workers*. New York: G. P. Putnam's Sons.
Hughes, Everett C. 1959. *Men and Their Work*. Chicago: University of Chicago Press.
Hume, Brit. 1971. *Death and the Mines: Rebellion and Murder in the United Mine Workers*. New York: Grossman Publishers.
International Press Institute. 1978. "U. S. Newspapers in the Eighties." *IPI Report*, Monthly Bulletin of the International Press Institute, vol. 27, no. 8 (September):5–10.
Johnson, Dale L. 1978. "Strategic Implications of Recent Social Class Theory." *The Insurgent Sociologist* 8, no. 1 (winter):40–44.
Johnson, Douglas. 1976. "The Rhode Island Industry: Perspectives on Development and Reform." Ph.D. dissertation, MIT.
Kanter, Rosabeth. 1974. "Women and the Structure of Organizations." In *Another Voice*, edited by M. Millman and R. Kanter. New York: Anchor.
Kelber, Harry, and Schlesinger, Carl. 1967. *Union Printers and Controlled Automation*. New York: Free Press.
Kelly, J. Frederick. 1924. *Early Domestic Architecture of Connecticut*. New Haven: Yale University Press.
Kornhauser, Arthur. 1965. *Mental Health of the Industrial Worker*. New York: Wiley.
Kornhauser, William. 1963. *Scientists in Industry: Conflict and Accomodation*. Berkeley and Los Angeles: University of California Press.
Kouwenhoven, John A. 1948. *Made in America*. Garden City: Doubleday.
Kraft, Phil. 1977. *Programmers and Managers. The Routinization of Computer Programming in the United States*. New York: Springer-Verlag.
Krebs, D. E. 1911. "Standard Panel System of Longwall Mining, Worked Advancing." In *Proceedings*, West Virginia Coal Mining Institute.
Krohn, Roger. 1971. *The Social Shaping of Science: Institutions, Ideology and Careers in Science*. Connecticut: Greenwood Publishing Corporation.
Kusterer, Ken. 1976. "Knowledge on the Job: Workers' Know-How and Everyday Survival in the Workplace." Ph.D. dissertation, Washington University, St. Louis.
Langer, Elinor. 1972. "Inside the New York Telephone Company." In

Women at Work, edited by William O'Neill. New York: Quadrangle Press.
Layton, Edwin T. 1973. "Engineers in Revolt." In *Technology and Social Change in America,* edited by E. Layton. New York: Harper & Row.
Lazonick, William. 1979. "Industrial Relations and Technical Change." *Cambridge Journal of Economics* (Fall).
Leaver, E. W. and Brown, J. J. 1946. "Machines Without Men." *Fortune* (November).
Lefkoe, M. R. 1970. *The Crisis in Construction.* Washington, D. C.: Bureau of National Affairs.
Levine, Louis. 1924. *The Women's Garment Workers.* New York: B. W. Huebsch.
Lipset, S. M.; Trow, M.; and Coleman, J. 1956. *Union Democracy: The Inside Politics of the International Typographical Union.* Glencoe, Ill.: Free Press.
Lockwood, David. 1958. *Black-Coated Workers.* London: Allen and Unwin.
Loft, Jacob. 1944. *The Printing Trades.* New York: Farrar and Rinehart.
Lubin, Isadore. 1924. *Miners' Wages and the Cost of Coal.* New York: McGraw-Hill.
Lublin, Joann S. February 24, 1978. "Secretaries' Revolt." *Wall Street Journal,* p. 1.
Lundgren, Earl. 1969. "Effects of N/C on Organizational Structure." *Automation* 16 (January).
Lynd, Staughton. 1976. "Workers' Control in a Time of Diminished Workers' Rights." *Radical America* 10, no. 5 (September-October):5–19.
———. 1978. *Labor Law for the Rank and Filer.* San Pedro California: Singlejack Books.
Lynn, F.; Roseberry, T.; and Babich, V. 1966. "A History of Recent Technological Innovations." In National Commission on Technology, Automation and Economic Progress, *The Employment Impact of Technological Change,* Appendix, vol. II. *Technology and the American Economy.* Washington, D. C.: Government Printing Office.
Maltese, Francesca. 1975. "Notes for a Study of the Automobile Industry." In *Labor Market Segmentation,* edited by R. C. Edwards et al. Lexington, Mass.: D. C. Heath.
Manpower Report of the President. 1975. Washington, D. C.: Government Printing Office.
Marglin, Stephen. 1974. "What Do Bosses Do? The Origins and Functions of Hierarchy in Capitalist Production." *Review of Radical Political Economics* 6 (Summer):60–112.
Marx, Karl. 1955. *The Poverty of Philosophy.* Moscow: Progress Publishers.
———. 1967. *Capital: A Critique of Political Economy.* New York: Modern Library Edition.

Mathewson, Stanley B. 1969, originally 1931. *Restriction of Output Among Unorganized Workers.* Carbondale, Ill.: Southern Illinois University Press.
Matles, James, and Higgins, James. 1974. *Them and Us.* Boston: Beacon Press.
McColloch, Mark D. 1975. "White Collar Electrical Machinery, Banking and Public Welfare Workers, 1940–1970." Ph.D. dissertation, University of Pittsburgh.
McDonald, F. James, et al. 1977. *GM Executive Conference on the Quality of Work Life.* Detroit: General Motors Corporation.
Meier, R. L. 1951. "The Origins of the Scientific Species." *Bulletin of the Atomic Scientist* 8:169–71.
Meissner, M. 1969. *Technology and the Worker.* San Francisco: Chandler.
Melman, Seymour. 1951. "The Rise of Administrative Overhead in the Manufacturing Industries of the United States." *Oxford Economic Papers* (N. S.) 3 (February).
———. 1959. "Report on the Productivity of Operations in the Machine Tool Industry in Western Europe." European Productivity Agency Project No. 420.
MESA Work Book No. 11. 1976. *Noise Control.* Mining Enforcement and Safety Administration.
Meyerowitz, Ruth S. 1969. "The Development of General Electric's Labor Policies, 1922–1950." M. A. thesis, Columbia University.
Mills, C. Wright. 1956. *White Collar.* New York: Oxford University Press.
Mills, Ted. 1975. "Human Resources—Why the New Concern?" *Harvard Business Review* 53 (March-April):120–34.
Montgomery, David. 1974. "The New Unionism and the Transformation of Workers' Consciousness in America, 1909–1922." *Journal of Social History* (Summer).
———. 1976a. "Whose Standards? Workers and Reorganization of Production in the United States, 1900-1920." Unpublished manuscript, University of Pittsburgh.
———. 1976b. "Workers' Control of Machine Production in the Nineteenth Century." *Labor History* 17 (Fall):486–509.
———. 1979. *Workers' Control in America.* New York: Cambridge University Press.
———. Forthcoming. *The Fall of the House of Labor.* Unpublished manuscript.
Montgomery, Jim. March 21, 1974. "Listening In." *Wall St. Journal.*
Moore, Wilbert E. 1951. *Industrial Relations and the Social Order.* New York: Macmillan.
Morris, Homer. 1934. *The Plight of the Bituminous Coal Miner.* Philadelphia: University of Pennsylvania Press.
Mumford, Lewis. 1924. *Sticks and Stones: A Study of American Architecture and Civilization.* New York: W. W. Norton.
National Center for Productivity and Quality of Working Life. 1977.

"The Attrition Clause at *The New York Times*." In *Productivity and Job Security: Attrition–Benefits and Problems*. Washington, D. C.: Government Printing Office.
National Science Foundation. 1977. *Women and Minorities in Science and Engineering*. NSF: 77–304.
Nelson, Daniel. 1975. *Managers and Workers: Origins of the New Factory System, 1880–1920*. Madison: University of Wisconsin Press.
Nevins, Allan, and Hill, Frank. 1954. *Ford: The Times, the Man, the Company*. New York: Scribner's.
Nichols, Theo, and Beynon, Huw. 1977. *Living with Capitalism: Class Relations and the Modern Factory*. London: Routledge and Kegan Paul.
Noble, David F. 1977. *America By Design: Science, Technology and the Rise of Corporate Capitalism*. New York: Alfred A. Knopf.
North American Congress on Latin America. 1975. "Hit and Run." *Latin America and Empire Report* 9, no. 5 (July–August).
―――. 1977. "Capital's Flight: The Apparel Industry Moves South." *Latin America and Empire Report* 11, no. 3 (March).
―――. 1977. "Electronics: The Global Industry." *Latin America and Empire Report* 11, no. 4.
Northrop, Herbert R. 1964. *Boulwarism*. Ann Arbor: University of Michigan, Graduate School of Business Administration, Bureau of Industrial Relations.
Northrup, Herbert, and Foster, Howard, 1975. *Open Shop Construction*. Philadelphia: University of Pennsylvania Press.
Nyden, Paul John. 1974. "Miners for Democracy: Struggle in the Coal Fields." Ph.D. dissertation, Columbia University.
Nygaard, Kristen. 1977. "Management Information Systems." Paper presented at the North Staffordshire Polytechnic Institute, Stafford, England.
O'Connor, James. 1978. "Competitive Capital and Monopoly Capital." In *The Capitalist System*. 2nd ed., edited by R. Edwards et al. Englewood Cliffs, N.J.: Prentice-Hall.
Ollman, Bertell. 1971. *Alienation*. London and New York: Cambridge University Press.
Page, William N. 1894. "The Economics of Coal Mining." *The Mining Industry*, vol. 3. New York: Scientific Publishing Co.
Palmer, Brian. 1975. "Class, Conception and Conflict: The Thrust for Efficiency." *Review of Radical Political Economics* 7 (Summer).
Parker, Edward W. 1900. "Coal-Cutting Machines." *Transactions*, American Institute for Mining Engineers 29:405–59.
―――. 1910. "Recent Developments in the Undercutting of Coal by Machinery." *Transactions*, American Institute for Hiring Engineers, 41.
Perlman, Selig, and Taft, Philip. 1935. *History of Labor in the United States, 1896–1932*, vol. 4. New York: Macmillan.

Perrucci, Carolyn. 1969. "Engineering and the Class Structure." In *The Engineers and the Social System,* edited by C. Perrucci and Gerst. New York: John Wiley and Sons.

Piore, Michael. 1968. "The Impact of the Labor Market Upon the Design and Selection of Productive Techniques Within the Manufacturing Plant." *Quarterly Journal of Economics* 82.

Porter, Arthur R., Jr. 1954. *Job Property Rights: A Study of the Job Controls of the International Typographical Workers.* Oxford: King's Crown Press.

Providence Community Center. 1939. *Preliminary Report on Jewelry Manufacturing and Silverware Industries in Rhode Island.* Under the sponsorship of the U. S. Employment Service, Providence.

Purcell, Theodore, and Cavanaugh, Gerald. 1972. *Blacks in the Industrial World.* New York: Free Press.

Raskin, A. H. July 29, 1974. "City Papers on Threshold of Future As Result of 11-Year Automation Pact." *New York Times,* pp. 12, 13.

———. 1978. "The Big Squeeze on Labor Unions." *The Atlantic Monthly* (October):41–48.

Reidelbach, J. A. 1970. *Modular Housing in the Real: A Study of the Industry and the Product.* Annandale, Va.: Modco.

Reseigh, Arthur. March 29, 1959. "Machine's Use to Create Jobs." *Providence Journal.*

Richards, John A. 1872. *A Treatise on the Construction and Operation of Wood Working Machines.* London and New York: E. & F. N. Spon.

Richardson, Dorothy. 1972. "The Long Day." In *Women at Work,* edited by William O'Neill. New York: Quadrangle Press.

Rico, Leonard. 1967. *The Advance Against Paperwork.* Ann Arbor: Graduate School of Business Administration, University of Michigan.

Rinehart, James. 1978. "Job Enrichment and the Labor Process." Paper presented to *New Directions in the Labor Process,* a conference sponsored by the Department of Sociology, SUNY, Binghamton, N.Y., May 5–7, 1978.

Rosenberg, Nathan. 1963. "Technical Change in the Machine Tool Industry, 1840–1910." *Journal of Economic History* 23:414–43.

———. 1972. *Technology and American Economic Growth.* New York: Harper & Row.

———. 1975. "America's Rise to Woodworking Leadership." In *America's Wooden Age,* edited by Brook Hindle. Tarrytown, New York: Sleepy Hollow Restorations.

Ross, Douglas. 1959. "The APT Joint Effort." *Mechanical Engineering* (May).

———. 1978. "Origins of APT Language for Automatically Programmed Tools." Softech, Inc.

Rotella, Elyce. 1974. "Occupational Segregation and the Supply of Women to the American Clerical Labor Force, 1870–1930." Paper

presented at the Berkshire Conference on the History of Women, Radcliffe College, Cambridge, Mass.
Roy, Donald F. 1951–1952. "Quota Restriction and Goldbricking in a Machine Shop." *American Journal of Sociology* 57.
———. 1953. "Work Satisfaction and Social Reward in Quota Achievement: An Analysis of Piecework Incentive." *American Sociological Review* 18.
———. 1954–1955. "Efficiency and 'The Fix': Informal Intergroup Relations in a Piecework Machine Shop." *American Journal of Sociology* 60.
Rothstein, William G. 1969. "Engineers and the Functionalist Model of Professions." In *The Engineers and the Social System*, edited by Perucci and Gerst. New York: John Wiley and Sons.
Rushing, William A. 1967. "The Effects of Industry Size and Division of Labor on Administration." *Administrative Science Quarterly* 12:273–95.
Russell, Jack. 1978. "The Coming of the Line." *Radical America* 12 (May-June).
Sattel, Jack. 1978. "The Degradation of Labor in the 20th Century: Harry Braverman's Sociology of Work." *The Insurgent Sociologist* 8, no. 1 (Winter):35–39.
Schatz, Ronald. 1975. "The End of Corporate Liberalism: Class Struggle in the Electrical Manufacturing Industry." *Radical America* 9, nos. 4–5.
———. 1977. "American Electrical Workers: Work, Struggles, Aspirations, 1930–1950." Ph.D. dissertation, University of Pittsburgh.
Schrank, Robert. 1978. *Ten Thousand Working Days*. Cambridge, Mass.: MIT Press.
Seidman, Joel. 1942. *The Needle Trades*. New York: Farrar and Rinehart.
Seltzer, Curtis. 1977. "The United Mine Workers of America and the Coal Operators: The Political Economy of Coal in Appalachia, 1950–1973." Ph.D. dissertation, Columbia University.
Seltzer, J. 1976. *The Costume Jewelry Industry: An Economic, Marketing and Financial Report*. Merrick, N. Y.: Morton Research Corporation.
Shepard, Jon M. 1972. *Automation and Alienation: A Study of Office and Factory Workers*. Cambridge: MIT Press.
Simon, Rick. 1978. "The Development of Underdevelopment: The Coal Industry and Its Effects on the West Virginia Economy, 1880–1930." Ph.D. dissertation, University of Pittsburgh.
Smith, Merritt Roe. 1976. *Harpers Ferry Armory and the New Technology*. Ithaca, N.Y.: Cornell University Press.
Spencer, Charles. 1977. *Blue Collar: An Internal Examination of the Workplace*. Chicago: Lakeside Charter Books.
Stephanz, Kenneth. 1971. "Statement of Kenneth Stephanz." In *Introduction to Numerical Control and Its Impact on Small Business*. Hearing

before the Subcommittee on Science and Technology of the Select Committee on Small Business, U. S. Senate, 92nd Congress, 1st session (June 24, 1971).

Stetson, Damon. November 6, 1978. "*The Times* and *News* Resume Publication." *The New York Times,* pp. 1, 86.

Stickell, Grayson. 1960. "How Can New Machines Cut Costs?" *Tooling and Production* (August).

Stinchcome, Arthur. 1965. "Social Structure and Organizations." In *Handbook of Organizations,* edited by James March. Chicago: Rand-McNally.

Stone, Katherine. 1975. "The Origins of Job Structures in the Steel Industry." In *Labor Market Segmentation,* edited by R. C. Edwards et al. Lexington, Mass.: D. C. Heath.

Straton, John W. "Improving Coal Mine Productivity." *Mining Congress Journal* (July 1977):20–24.

Stroup, Thomas A. 1923. "Cause and Growth of Unionism Among Coal Miners." *Mining and Metallurgy* (September).

Suboleski, Stanley. 1977. "Boost Your Productivity by Adding Continuous Miners." *Coal Age Operating Handbook of Underground Mining,* vol. 1, edited by N. Chironis. New York: McGraw-Hill.

Suffern, Arthur E. 1926. *The Coal Miners' Struggle for Industrial Status.* New York: Macmillan.

Swados, Harvey. 1957. *On the Line.* Boston: Little Brown.

———. 1962. *A Radical's America.* Boston: Little Brown.

Sward, Keith. 1948. *The Legend of Henry Ford.* New York: Rinehart.

Taft, Philip. 1978. "The Limits of Labor Unity: The Chicago Newspaper Strike of 1912." *Labor History* 19, no. 1 (Winter):100–29.

Tams, W. P. 1963. *The Smokeless Coal Fields of West Virginia.* Morgantown: West Virginia University Library.

Taylor, Frederick Winslow. 1947. *Scientific Management.* New York: Harper & Row.

Taylor, J. C. 1978. "Fragmented Office Jobs and the Computer." Mimeo.

Tepperman, Jean. 1976. *Not Servants, Not Machines.* Boston: Beacon Press.

The Carpenter. Official Monthly Publication of the United Brotherhood of Carpenters and Joiners.

The Times of London. 1929. *Printing in the Twentieth Century: A Survey.* London: The Times Publishing Co.

Tulin, Roger. April 2, 1978. "Machine Tools." *New York Times,* p. 16.

Twentieth Century Fund. 1945. *How Collective Bargaining Works.* New York.

United Brotherhood of Carpenters and Joiners of America. 1901. *By-Laws of the Manhattan Borough District Council and Rules for Local Unions.* New York.

United Electrical, Radio, and Machine Workers of America. 1963. *U. E.*

Guide to Automation and the New Technology. New York: United Electrical Workers.

United States Coal Commission. 1923. *Comparative Efficiency of Labor in the Bituminous Coal Industry Under Union and Non-Union Operation.* Washington, D. C.: Government Printing Office.

———. 1925. *Report, Part III; Bituminous Coal–Detailed Labor and Engineering Studies.* Washington, D. C.: Government Printing Office.

United States Commissioner of Labor. 1905. *Regulation and Restriction of Output.* Washington, D. C.: Government Printing Office.

United States Department of Commerce. Bureau of the Census. 1972. *Census of Construction Industries.* Washington, D. C.: Government Printing Office.

———. 1974. *Annual Survey of Manufacturers, 1974.* Washington, D. C.: Government Printing Office.

———. 1976. *1972 Census of Manufacturers.* Washington, D. C.: Government Printing Office.

———. 1977. *1977 Statistical Abstract of the United States.* Washington, D. C.: Government Printing Office.

———. 1977. *Residential Alterations and Repairs.* Washington, D. C.: Government Printing Office.

United States Department of Health, Education and Welfare. 1973. *Work in America.* Cambridge, Mass.: MIT Press.

United States Department of Housing and Urban Development. 1976. *HUD Statistical Yearbook.* Washington, D. C.: Government Printing Office.

United States Department of the Interior. 1888. *Report on Power and Machinery Employed in Manufacturing,* 10th Census Series, vol. 22. Washington, D.C.: Government Printing Office.

United States Bureau of Labor Statistics (Department of Labor).1966. *Technology and Manpower Trends,* bulletin no. 1474. Washington, D. C.: Government Printing Office.

———. 1969. *Labor in the Textile and Apparel Industries,* bulletin no. 1635. Washington, D. C.: Government Printing Office.

———. 1971. *Industry Wage Survey: Men's and Boys' Shirts and Nightwear,* bulletin no. 1694. Washington, D. C.: Government Printing Office.

———. 1972. *Labor and Materials Requirements of Private, Single Family Homes,* bulletin no. 1755. Washington, D. C.: Government Printing Office.

———. 1973. *Outlook for Technology and Manpower in Printing and Publishing,* bulletin no. 1774. Washington, D. C.: Government Printing Office.

———. 1974. *Industry Wage Survey: Men's and Boys' Separate Trousers,* bulletin no. 1906. Washington, D. C.: Government Printing Office.

———. 1977a. *Technological Change and its Labor Impact in Five Industries,* bulletin no. 1961. Washington, D. C.: Government Printing Office.

———. 1977b. *Industry Wage Survey: Men's and Boys' Suits and Coats*, bulletin no. 1962. Washington, D. C.: Government Printing Office.
———. 1976. *Occupational Outlook Handbook, 1976–1977 Edition*. Washington, D. C.: Government Printing Office.
———. 1978. *Occupational Outlook Handbook, 1978–1979 Edition*. Washington, D. C.: Government Printing Office.
United States Industrial Commission. 1902. *Foreign Born in the Coal Mines*, vol. 15. Washington, D. C.: Government Printing Office.
Vonnegut, Kurt. 1952. *Player Piano*. New York: Delacorte Press.
Wagoner, Harless. 1968. *The United States Machine Tool Industry from 1900 to 1950*. Cambridge: MIT Press.
Walker, Charles R. 1957. *Toward the Automatic Factory: A Case Study of Men and Machines*. New Haven: Yale University Press.
Walker, Charles, and Guest, Robert. 1952. *The Man on the Assembly Line*. Cambridge: Harvard University Press.
Wallin, Chad. 1966. *The Builder's Story: An Interpretive Record of the Builders Association of Chicago*. Chicago: Builders Association of Chicago.
Walsh, John. 1977. "International Trade in Electronics: U. S.-Japan Competition." *Science* 195, no. 4283 (March).
Walton, Daniel R., and Kauffman, Peter W. 1977. *Preliminary Analysis of the Probable Causes of Decreased Coal Mining Productivity (1969–1976)*. Contract Report for U. S. Department of Energy, Division of Solid Fuels, Mining, and Preparation, Reston, Va., Management Engineers Incorporated.
Watson, Bill. 1972. "Counterplanning on the Shop Floor." Boston: New England Free Press.
West Virginia Coal Mining Institute. November 28–29, 1931. *Proceedings*. Morgantown.
Whyte, William F. 1955. *Money and Motivation*. New York: Harper & Row.
Wilensky, H. 1964. "Varieties of Work Experience." In *Man in a World of Work*, edited by H. Borrow. New York: Houghton-Mifflin.
Winfrey, Carey. July 3, 1978. *"The Times* enters a New Era of Electronic Printing: How It Was, How It Is." *New York Times*, pp. 21, 38.
Woodbury, Robert S. 1972. *Studies in the History of Machine Tools*. Cambridge: MIT Press.
Woodward, Joan. 1965. *Industrial Organization: Theory and Practice*. London: Oxford University Press.
Woolley, Bryan, and Reid, Ford. 1975. *We Be Here When the Morning Comes*. Lexington, Ky.: University Press of Kentucky.
Word Processing. 1976. A bi-monthly publication of the Office Products Division, IBM.
Young, Esther. 1972. "Individuality in a Factory." *American Behavioral Scientist* 16 (September):65–74.

Zaretz, Elbert. 1934. *The Amalgamated Clothing Workers of America: A Study of Progressive Trade Unionism.* New York: Ancon Publishing Co.

Zimbalist, Andrew. 1975. "The Limits of Work Humanization." *Review of Radical Political Economics* 7, no. 2 (Summer).

Zisman, Michael D. 1978. "Office Automation: Revolution or Evolution?" *Sloan Management Review* (Spring):1–16.